GIVE YOURSELF THE EDGE IN WINNING GOVERNMENT CONTRACTS.

If you're ready to compete for lucrative government business, then give yourself a clear advantage. The practical, proven information you'll need is in these new Global publications.

Strategies and Tactics for Winning Government Contracts (WGC)...

gives you essential information on how to sell to the federal government. It discusses different types of government contract methods, solicitations and contracts. Plus, it provides insight on how the government evaluates your offer.

In a straightforward, easy-to-read format, Strategies and Tactics for Winning Government Contracts helps you:

- Avoid procedural stumbling blocks by detailing procurement regulations
- Choose from a variety of contract method alternatives
- Follow step-by-step the six phases of contract operations, from identifying your product to post-contract management.

$79⁹⁵

Selling to the Federal Government through Schedule Contracts (GSC)...

an insider's look at the schedule contract system. Find out how to get on GSA schedule, how the schedule operates, and what the various types of schedules are — along with their characteristics.

With GSC you'll learn:

- Valuable definitions and explanations of schedule components
- How to manage schedule contracts
- How to formulate pricing
- The protest process
- Potential problem areas and how to avoid them

$59⁹⁵

Open the door to government contracts. Call (800) 854-7179 now.

Global Engineering Documents

A Division of Information Handling Services

2805 McGaw Ave., P.O.Box 19539
Irvine, CA 92714
Phones: (714)261-1455, (800)854-7179
Telex: 692-373

15 Inverness Way East
Englewood, CO 80150
Phones: (314)726-0444
(800)854-7179

7710 Carondelet Ave., Suite 413
Clayton, MO 63105
Phones: (314)726-0444
(800)854-7179

1990 M Street N.W., Suite 400
Washington, D.C. 20036
Phones: (202)429-2860
(800)854-7179

COPYRIGHT © 1987
GLOBAL ENGINEERING DOCUMENTS
ALL RIGHTS RESERVED

Every effort is made to make this publication as accurate as possible. The company, however, assumes no liability for damages arising from error or omissions in the making up or the printing of its publications.

THE SCIENCE OF NEGOTIATION

The Practical Approach to Negotiating Government Contracts and Other Complex Agreements

BY

DAVID K. EARY

PRESIDENT

GOVERNMENT CONTRACT SERVICES COMPANY

P.O. BOX 9957

BERKELEY, CALIFORNIA 94709

ISBN 0-912702-37-0

KF
849
.E18
1987

Preface

In 1984 Congress passed Public Law 95-654, commonly referred to as the *Competition in Contracting Act.* This law was enacted with the primary purpose of increasing the amount of competition received by the government when contracting for goods and services. One of the major provisions of this law eliminated a long-standing policy previously stated in the Federal Procurement Regulations that the sealed bid method of contracting—referred to as "the formally advertised method"—was the preferred method of government contracting. This Act, for the first time, recognized that negotiated contracting can be just as competitive as the sealed bid method, and that there are some inherent benefits which were not being taken advantage of because of the stated preference for the sealed bid approach. The Congress, by implementing this Act, elevated the acceptability of negotiated contracting as a method of government procurement to a level where it is now considered equal to the sealed bid method.

This is a change of major importance. In Fiscal Year 1985, the first full year after implementation of the Act, the federal government spent approximately $200 billion acquiring supplies and services for its own use. Of the $200 billion, over 80% of these goods and services were reported as having been acquired using government negotiation procedures and techniques. Private industry also establishes the majority of its contracts and purchase orders for goods and services using the negotiated method of contracting. Given the enormous amount of money exchanging hands using this contracting method, it is surprising so little emphasis has been placed on the importance of learning proper negotiation skills.

The problem is that negotiation is an elusive discipline because it is both an art and a science. In the federal government, the emphasis on contract negotiations has historically been on the scientific or objective approach to negotiations. Guidance and training provided to government personnel has concentrated on this approach to the process. In private industry, the practice of negotiating has historically been considered a function of the sales department. Influenced by classic selling techniques, the concept of negotiations in industry has traditionally centered on the human behavioral or subjective approach to negotiations. This has frequently been referred to as the "art of negotiating."

Although the federal government has recently begun to acknowledge the importance of the subjective aspect and has begun stressing to its contracting personnel that the two approaches must be combined, industry is still principally relying on the subjective approach. This book attempts to bridge this information gap by addressing the practical, or *"scientific,"* aspects of negotiating, which should be combined with the behavioral or artistic approach to the process. Negotiating theory is discussed, the differences between the subjective and objective approaches examined, the federal government's approach to negotiating contracts reviewed, and specific recommendations on how to implement a scientific approach are provided.

The federal government's contract negotiating system is used as a model for studying proper negotiating procedures and techniques for three reasons. First is the considerable amount of experience the government has had with this contracting method and upon which the government's system was based. Second is the amount of information made available describing the process. The federal government is truly unique in the amount of information it makes available describing its negotiating procedures and the amount of information made available regarding individual contracts. Lastly, the procedures and techniques applicable to government contracting can be used in any complex negotiation situation.

As evidenced by the dedication to this manual, my experiences have convinced me that the federal procurement system creates an environment in which complex agreements can be successfully negotiated and contracts established which represent a fair and reasonable outcome for the contractor, the government, and ultimately, the taxpayer. Implementing the scientific approach to contract negotiations will help create a similar environment in any negotiating situation. All parties involved, either directly or indirectly, can win in the end. In successful negotiations, there are no losers. This is the theory upon which this book is based.

Dedication

This book is dedicated to past and present U.S. Government contracting officers and specialists in all agencies of the federal government. Also, it is dedicated to the unheralded contractors who satisfy legitimate government needs by providing quality products and services at fair and reasonable prices. Despite often inaccurate media coverage, self-serving political rhetoric, and those contractors who intentionally abuse the system, these individuals, agencies and companies have managed to make the federal procurement system work against all odds. They have made it the most effective and fair procurement system existing anywhere in the world today.

Table of Contents

PREFACE i
DEDICATION iii

CHAPTER 1: INTRODUCTION TO CONTRACT NEGOTIATIONS

Defining Negotiation 1-1
Successful Negotiations 1-2
The Science of Negotiations 1-3
The Importance of Negotiations 1-4
Negotiating Government Contracts 1-4
Tri-Win Negotiations 1-5
Contract Negotiators 1-6
Reference Sources 1-7
Organization and Content of This Book 1-8

CHAPTER 2: NEGOTIATION THEORY

Competitive vs. Collaborative 2-2
Give and Take 2-2
Trade-Offs 2-2
Domination 2-3
Compromise and Concession 2-3
Agreement vs. Mutually Acceptable Understanding 2-4
The Sliding Scale Theory of Negotiation 2-4
Stalemates and the Sliding Scale Theory 2-6

CHAPTER 3: THE 25% SOLUTION TO CONTRACT NEGOTIATIONS

The Negotiation System 3-1
The *25% Solution* Concept 3-2
The Company's Position 3-8
The Other Party's Position 3-8
The Objective Position 3-9
The Uncontrollable Parameters 3-9
The Subjective Approach Fallacy 3-12

CHAPTER 4: GOVERNMENT NEGOTIATIONS

Negotiated vs. Sealed Bid Contracts 4-1
Impact of the *Competition in Contracting Act* 4-2
Choosing To Negotiate 4-2
Noncompetitive Contracting 4-3
Negotiated Government Solicitations and Contracts 4-4
Unsolicited Proposals 4-5

CHAPTER 5: GOVERNMENT NEGOTIATING PRINCIPLES

The Government Procurement System 5-1
Practical Consideration 5-5
The Principle of Competition 5-5
Federal Acquisition Regulations 5-6
Armed Services Pricing Manual 5-7
Multiple Award Schedule Policy 5-7
Truth in Negotiations Act 5-7
Government Contracting Officers 5-8

CHAPTER 6: GOVERNMENT NEGOTIATING PROCEDURES

Pre-negotiation Procedures 6-1
Acceptable vs. Unacceptable Proposals 6-1
Competitive Range 6-3
Responsible Contractors 6-3
Notification of Unacceptability 6-5
Award Without Negotiations 6-5
Cost and Pricing Data 6-6
Cost and Pricing Data Exemptions 6-7
Certified Cost and Pricing Data 6-7
Defective Cost and Pricing Data 6-8
Cost and Price Analysis 6-8
Pre-award Audits and Inspections 6-8
Source Selection 6-9
Cost Accounting Standards 6-9
Establishing Negotiation Objectives 6-10
Price Negotiation Memorandum and Approvals 6-10
Documentation and Review Process 6-11
Contracting Officer Prohibitions 6-12
Best and Final Offers 6-12
Changing Your Offer 6-12
Reopening Negotiations 6-13
Contract Award 6-13

CHAPTER 7: PRE-NEGOTIATION PLANNING

Determining the Purpose of the Negotiations 7-2
Selecting the Negotiating Team 7-3
Negotiation Objectives 7-3
Fact-finding 7-3
Establishing Pre-negotiation Objectives 7-4
Objective Range 7-6
Documenting Objectives 7-7
Negotiation Conference Agenda 7-7
Identifying Concessions 7-7
Summarizing Position 7-8

CHAPTER 8: CONDUCTING NEGOTIATIONS

Controlling Negotiations 8-2
Place 8-2
Agenda 8-3
Time 8-3
Attendance 8-4
Method of Communication 8-4
Understanding the Stages in the Process 8-5
The Phases of a Negotiation Conference 8-5
Introduction Phase 8-6
Ice-Breaking Phase 8-6
Opening Posturing 8-7
Establishing Mutual Understandings 8-7
Negotiating Minor Points of Contention 8-8
Sequential Elimination of Most Issues 8-9
Final Posturing 8-9
Final Resolution 8-10
Review and Summary 8-10
The Parting 8-10

CHAPTER 9: POST-NEGOTIATION ACTIONS

Final Information Gathering 9-1
Documentation and Review 9-1
Review and Approval 9-2
Confirmation 9-3
Contract Administration 9-4

CHAPTER 10: NEGOTIATION SKILLS AND TECHNIQUES

Negotiating Skills 10-1
Negotiation Strategies 10-1
The Reasonable Approach 10-2
Understanding Human Behavior 10-2
Ethics and Legality 10-2
Preparation 10-3
Negotiation Tactics 10-3
Proposing Alternatives 10-5
Audit Mentality 10-5
Assume the Best, Anticipate the Worst 10-5
Multi-year Contracting 10-5
Personality Clashes 10-6
The Truth above All 10-6
Additional References 10-6
Potential for Successful Negotiations 10-6

APPENDICES:

Appendix I: *CFR*, Title 48, Chapter 1, *Federal Acquisition Regulations*, Subchapter C, Part 15, Contracting by Negotiation. A-1

Appendix II: *CFR*, Title 48, Chapter 2, *Department of Defense Federal Acquisition Regulations Supplement*, Subchapter C, Part 215, Contracting by Negotiation. A-55

Appendix III: *CFR*, Title 48, Chapter 5, *General Services Administration Federal Acquisition Regulations Supplement*, Part 515, Contracting by Negotiation. A-91

Appendix IV: *CFR*, Title 41, Chapter 5, *General Services Administration Multiple Award Schedule Procurement Acquisition Policy.* A-103

Appendix V: *Armed Services Pricing Manual,* Department of Defense, Chapter 8, How To Negotiate and Justify a Price. A-115

Chapter 1

Introduction to Contract Negotiations

Defining Negotiations:

Learning the formal definition of negotiating is easy. All you need do is find the word in any nearby dictionary. The *American Heritage Dictionary of the English Language,* for example defines the word "negotiate" to mean:

> "... to confer with another or others in order to come to terms, to arrange by conferring, i.e., negotiate a contract."

This is a relatively simple definition, easy to read and easy to understand. Learning the full meaning behind the concept of successful negotiations, however, is not as easy. The difference is that the concept of successful negotiations includes reaching an agreement on terms which are acceptable to you and those whom you represent. One definition of successful negotiations is:

> "conferring with another or others in an effort to successfully convince the other party to accept the terms and conditions you desire to have included in any subsequent agreement."

This definition includes the terms "successfully" and "desire." The dictionary definition of the word does not. It is these two terms which distinguish successful negotiations from the formal definition. The government adopted this approach to negotiations in the recently rewritten *Department of Defense Armed Services Pricing Manual (ASPM).* In this manual, negotiations are defined as:

> "... the process of bargaining among buyers and sellers—negotiation—is the way to prove to the contractor the reasonableness of your findings and conclusions."

The government implies the "successful" and "desired" nature of successful contract negotiations by including in the definition that government contracting officers must "prove to the contractor" the "reasonableness" of their point of view. There is no mention made of considering the reasonableness of the prospective contractor's findings and conclusions. This one-sided approach to negotiations, as taken by the Department of Defense, is indicative of the competitive nature of the negotiation process. The General Services Administration (GSA), the largest non-DoD procurement agency of the federal government, defines the negotiation process somewhat differently, defining it as:

> "... a process of communication by which two or more parties attempt to reach a mutually advantageous relationship on a matter of mutual concern.... it is a process of both parties working to maximize their gains while attempting to satisfy some of the needs of both parties."

This is a more balanced and noble definition of the negotiation process. It is not, however, a good definition of the concept of successful negotiations. Although GSA goes on to state that the negotiation process is not simply a process of making concessions and mutual sacrifice for the sake of agreement, this balanced approach to the definition of the negotiating process fails to recognize the competitive nature of the process.

Baseball players do not approach a game attempting to satisfy some of the needs of the opposing team. Listening from outside of the locker room, you will *not* hear them say to each other before a game, "Let's win this game and make sure we let the other team satisfy some of their needs. Let's allow them to get on base as often as possible as long as they don't score." After all, the ultimate goal in baseball is the perfect game: no runs, no hits, no errors, and no men allowed on base. Despite this being the goal, if the strategic situation dictates, the manager of a baseball team may choose to intentionally walk a batter. The manager purposely allows the man on base.

The distinction between these two approaches to the baseball game is that, in the latter case, the manager is not putting the man on base because he would be satisfying one of the opposing team's needs. Rather, the manager puts the man on base in an attempt to increase the chances of his team reaching its major goal: winning the game.

The approach illustrated by this example is the same approach taken by DoD and described in the definition of successful negotiations. It is the approach which must be taken to maximize the potential for conducting successful negotiations in any situation.

Successful Negotiations:

The goal of successful negotiations is not simply to reach an agreement with the other party. Rather, the negotiation process should be viewed as a means of attempting to control an agreement between yourself and another party. If you do not control the end agreement, deciding whether to give due consideration to the other party's needs and point of view, the other party will. If you let the other party take control, they may or may not give due consideration to *your* needs and point of view. This does not mean you should not consider the other party's needs and point of view if you are in control. It is always in your best interest to consider the other party's position. Like the baseball manager, you should not let the other party's needs be an obstacle to your success. Use the other party's needs to your advantage. Sometimes, even though you satisfy the other party's needs and not your own in the short term, taking a specific action or agreeing to a specific request by the other party may be in your best overall interest in the long term. Satisfying the other party's needs while fostering your own interests increases your potential to control the negotiations. Being in control of the negotiations, giving due consideration to the other party's position, places you in a position to ensure that any resulting agreement, although possibly containing terms and conditions not preferred by you, will not contain terms and conditions which are unacceptable to you. There is a substantial difference between an agreement containing terms and conditions not desired, and those containing terms and conditions considered unacceptable. It is this difference and the resulting acceptability of the negotiation outcome which is the true test of a successful negotiation—it is also the challenge.

This book is designed to help you successfully meet this challenge by taking control, to the maximum extent possible, of complex negotiation situations. The focus of this book is negotiating government contracts and other complex agreements. The amount of preparation required is usually not justified in simple contracts or other minor matters. However, the principles and concepts involved in negotiating complex contracts are just as applicable to conducting negotiations with a street vendor over the price of a piece of costume jewelry.

The Science of Negotiations:

When Gloria Gamble and Stephen Austin of Information Handling Services and I were writing Global Engineering's *Strategies & Tactics for Winning Government Contracts,* we chose to introduce the chapter on contract negotiations simply by asking the question:

"Negotiating—is it an art or a science?"

In answering this question, we came to what we believed to be the only logical conclusion: it is truly a combination of both. The concept of negotiation as an art and a science is the principle upon which this book is based. Unfortunately, too many companies, organizations and individuals approach negotiations from only one point of view, ignoring the essential nature of the other. Recently the trend has been to place the emphasis on the artistic aspects of the negotiation process. GSA, for example, states:

"Negotiation is an art utilizing scientific principles and methods".

This statement relegates the scientific aspect of negotiations, altogether, too minor a role. This is certainly true within the government where, historically, the formal contract negotiation process has emphasized the scientific or objective approach to negotiations—almost to the total exclusion of the artistic aspects. Private industry, on the other hand, largely due to the study of contract negotiations generally being considered a function of sales, has historically tended to concentrate on the artistic or the subjective side of the process. It is primarily dominated by the human element present in all negotiation situations. Another way to describe the artistic approach is to consider it as being the *personal* approach to contract negotiations. The scientific side to the negotiation process is the methodological or systematic approach. The artistic approach is a *subjective* approach—the scientific approach is *objective* in nature.

Although in this book contract negotiations will be addressed from both points of view, the artistic approach to the process is not the focus. There are a number of books already on the market which address the subject of negotiations from the human behavioral point of view. Rather, as evidenced by the title, it is the intent of this book to present and expand on the scientific approach to the contract negotiation process. Also, to discuss how this scientific, or objective, approach can be combined with the subjective to maximize the potential for successful contract negotiations.

The Importance of Negotiations:

It is important to develop adequate negotiating skills because we live in a world of negotiation. Some refer to it as a world full of compromise. The term "compromise," however, is too narrow a term. We negotiate between husband and wife, mother and child, and between countries. The end result of the negotiations can be an agreement to go to a specific restaurant for dinner, a specific time your teenage daughter must return home from a date, a contract, or an international treaty or agreement concerning nuclear disarmament. Considering the amount of negotiating taking place on a daily basis, it is surprising relatively so little has been written on the subject and that the concept of successful negotiations is so infrequently discussed. Consider the lack of college courses provided on the subject of negotiation. When the subject is discussed, it usually is from the standpoint of getting another party to do what you want through manipulation and coercion. Rarely does the advice concentrate on defining what it is you want and how to get the other party to willingly agree.

The bottom line to succeeding in any negotiation situation is to do whatever is legal, ethical, and works. This includes combining subjective and objective approaches to the negotiation process. The specific approach or combination of approaches most appropriate to a specific situation depends on the specifics of the situation, including the subject, the personnel and the circumstances involved. There is no one universal right way to successfully negotiate an agreement.

Although the focus is on the scientific approach to negotiating complex contracts and more specifically, complex government contracts, the principles, techniques and recommended procedures can be applied to any negotiation situation.

Negotiating Government Contracts:

In business, people negotiate internally within the organization as well as externally—internally with employees, superiors and peers, and externally with customers, suppliers, contractors, banks, etc. Negotiations are being conducted at all levels, at all times. The negotiating environment within the federal government is basically the same. However, when commercial business organizations negotiate directly with the government, there are two characteristics of the government negotiating process which must be considered. It is these characteristics which make federal government contract negotiations unique.

First, is the potential dollar value of the contracts involved. The federal government is the single largest consumer of goods and services in the United States. Not only does the government purchase almost every legitimate commodity and service known to mankind, it does so in extremely large quantities. Often, this results in relatively large dollar value contracts compared to a company's typical commercial contracts. Try and think of any other customer spending $200 billion per year, each and every year.

The second unique characteristic of government contract negotiations are the procedures the government follows when negotiating contracts. The government has a very formalized and highly detailed set of procedures for negotiations.

These procedures are published, are applicable to all government contracting and contractor personnel, and are available for review by the general public. No other customer will tell you as much about its internal organization, policies or procedures, as will the U. S. Government. There is no question that the most successful government contractors usually know what the government is going to do before the government does. The reason is simple—the government must negotiate in accordance with the *Federal Acquisition Regulations* and the Agency supplements to these regulations.

Perhaps the best way to illustrate the significance of this aspect of government contracting is to refer to the movie *Patton,* starring George C. Scott. At one point in the movie, as Patton is defeating Rommel in a desert battle, Patton, as portrayed by Scott, is shown standing on a hilltop overlooking the battlefield as the German forces under Rommel begin to retreat. Patton exclaims, "Rommel, you S.O.B., I read your book!" Patton knew that the old adage, "know your enemy," is one of the best strategies to follow in any military operation. He had read Rommel's book on tank warfare tactics and had used the knowledge he gained to defeat Rommel in an actual battle.

The same principle applies to negotiating complex agreements. If you are negotiating with the government, read the government's book and you will be in a much better position to succeed in controlling the negotiations. If you are negotiating with another commercial firm, obtain as much information as you legitimately can about the company and its policies regarding negotiating contracts.

A poor negotiator on the part of the government can cost the taxpayer a lot of money.

A poor negotiator on the part of a contractor can destroy the company. It is not at all unusual, given the size of many government contracts, for one poorly negotiated contract to be the cause of the company going out of business. Although it is neither the intent, nor the policy, of the government to award contracts which end up this way, contractors cannot afford to rely on government personnel to protect their interests in this regard. Only a company's own negotiator can ensure that the proposed outcome is in the company's best interests.

There is no end to the number of horror stories concerning contractors awarded government contracts which they can never hope to perform and who subsequently either lose money on the contract, or lose their entire business. Invariably, this occurs because someone representing the contractor agreed to do some thing they either could not do at all, or could not do for the price agreed upon. They simply negotiated a bad deal. You cannot afford to let this happen to your company or your organization.

Tri-Win Negotiations:

This book has been written to help you in your efforts to negotiate the best deal possible, to allow you, like Patton, to understand where your enemy is likely to be coming from. It is my firm belief, and my experience over the last sixteen years has shown this to be true, that there always exists in government contracting not only the potential for a win-win outcome, but that the possibility of a win-win-win or tri-win outcome is ever present as well. This tri-win outcome consists of an agreement which represents:

- *A win for the contractor*—a good contract at a fair price, ensuring a fair and reasonable profit;

- *A win for the government*—quality products at fair and reasonable prices; and

- *A win for the taxpayer*—a legitimate government need satisfied at a fair and reasonable price to the taxpayer.

This is the official policy of the government as specified in *FAR* Subpart 15.802, as well as a common sense objective for all parties involved.

Experience has shown that whenever the balance of the tri-win equation leans too heavily toward one side, eventually it will be corrected. If a contractor is earning too high a profit, in the long term he is going to lose that business to a competitor willing to accept a lower profit, or the government will change its contracting approach. If the government is too demanding, potential contractors will no longer be interested in the government contract and the requirement will go unfulfilled. If the taxpayer demands that too low a price be paid, in the long run the government is going to suffer with poor products or services and will eventually be forced to pay a higher price in order to obtain products and services of adequate quality.

If all of the parties involved follow the established rules, the tri-win outcome will result. The good news regarding government contracting is that you can force not only the government, but also your competitors, to play in accordance with the rules. Always keep in mind that the government and your competitors are also in a position to make sure you play by the rules, if necessary. This is what makes the government contract negotiation process such an excellent process to study. The principles and concepts behind the government contract negotiation process are applicable to all difficult negotiation situations, including negotiations involving government grants, major commercial contracts, and other complex agreements.

The tri-win objective is also the same in all negotiations. In the commercial business sector there will also be unrepresented third parties affected by the outcome of the negotiations. If negotiations are being conducted between you and your subcontractor, the unrepresented third party is your customer. If the negotiations are between you and your customer, your subcontractors will be impacted by the outcome. It is important to always remember that negotiations are not isolated events. They do not take place in a vacuum. The complete impact of the negotiated agreement, including the effect on parties outside of the negotiation process, must be considered in successful negotiations.

Contract Negotiators:

You will encounter good and bad contract negotiators, both within and outside of the government. Successful contract negotiators are prepared to deal with either type on an as-needed basis. The best way to be prepared is to understand the rules the other party's negotiators are supposed to follow and to thoroughly understand your rights and obligations relative to the specific negotiations.

No other customer will let you inside of its head to the degree the U.S. Government will. The government not only tells you exactly what its objective is going into the negotiations, it tells you how it is going to establish its negotiation position. Nor will any other customer demand as much information from you going into negotiations. The government recognizes that its rules are available for your review. To create parity in the negotiation process, the government attempts to gain as much information as possible from you. No matter how much information the government obtains, contractors should always have at least two advantages when it comes to negotiating government contracts.

First, contractor personnel can learn the government's rules to the same extent as government personnel. There is no way government personnel can learn as much about a contractor's company policy, as the contractor can about the government. The government, however, comes close as a result of the *Truth in Negotiations Act* and other laws and regulations providing government personnel with the the authority to:

- obtain cost and pricing data from potential contractors and subcontractors;
- conduct on-site audits;
- obtain company financial information and reports; and
- conduct other pre-award fact-gathering activities.

The second advantage contractors have is that government personnel will usually not be able to become thoroughly knowledgeable regarding their specific products or services. Government personnel, both contracting and technical, are usually responsible for buying or managing so many different items, they are rarely given the opportunity to become truly expert in any one commodity or product. A contractor, on the other hand, should be an expert regarding the product or service being provided. To compound the contracting officer's problem in this regard, within the government there exists a school of thought which holds that government contracting officers and specialists do not need to know very much about what they are buying. Rather, they only need to know the rules under which they must accomplish the buying. As long as government personnel remain overburdened from a commodity standpoint, and as long as this obsolete school of thought continues to exist in some areas, contractors have this second advantage over government contracting officers: a thorough knowledge of the product or service being negotiated.

Reference Sources:

The material presented in this book is derived from a number of sources. Since much of the negotiation process depends on the characteristics of the individuals involved, much of what is presented herein is based on over seventeen years of personal experience with the federal supply and procurement system. My personal observations and opinions were formed from this experience, which involved all sides of the government procurement process as a government engineer, military officer, civilian contracting officer, government procurement manager, and as a consultant working with all types and sizes of government contractors.

Secondly, government regulations, policies and publications concerning contract negotiations have been extensively used in preparing this work. These documents include:

- The *Federal Acquisition Regulations (FAR);*
- Agency Supplements to the *FAR;*
- *The Armed Services Pricing Manual (ASPM),* 1986 Edition;
- Federal Procurement Data System reports;
- Government Negotiation Training publications;
- Actual Contract Negotiation Case Studies; and
- Interviews with Government and Contractor Personnel.

Selected excerpts from these references are included as appendices in this book.

The net result is a comprehensive overview of the government contract negotiation process, including recommendations on how to use this process as a guide for negotiating any complex contract or agreement.

Organization and Content of This Book:

This chapter serves as an introduction to the definition of negotiations and the concept of successful negotiations. Also, the government contract negotiation process was introduced; and it was explained how this process can serve as a doorway to a better understanding of sound negotiation principles and techniques. Also discussed have been the two basic approaches to the negotiation process—the artistic approach and the scientific approach.

Chapter 2 further discusses general negotiation theory including a discussion of the principles behind the artistic approach to contract negotiations. The goals and objectives of successful contract negotiations, and other approaches which can be taken when negotiating complex agreements, are also discussed in this chapter.

Chapter 3 introduces the recommended scientific approach to the contract negotiation process: the *"25% Solution to Contract Negotiations."*

Chapter 4 discusses the unique aspects of federal government contract negotiations, including the legal and regulatory background behind the system.

Chapter 5 covers the principles and policies of government contract negotiations.

Chapter 6 describes the actual procedures which are to be followed by all government contracting personnel when negotiating contracts.

Chapters 7 through 9 go into detail on how to prepare for complex negotiations, how to conduct the negotiation conference, and the post negotiation actions which should be taken after negotiations have been completed.

Lastly, Chapter 10 explains various recommended strategies and tactics for negotiating complex agreements, as well some tactics which are not recommended.

Throughout this book, any reference to government contracting officers shall mean contracting officers, contract specialists or buyers, as appropriate. The term "government" refers to the federal government. Also, when discussing contracting officer actions, the discussion is based on what contracting officers are supposed to do according to the regulations. If a government contracting officer acts contrary to the regulations, the federal procurement system provides specific procedures for contractors to follow to enforce the appropriate rules.

After reading this manual, you should be familiar with government negotiating procedures and how to participate successfully in this process. Also, you should be able to use the techniques and procedures described herein and apply them to negotiating complex agreements in almost any negotiating setting.

Chapter 2

Negotiation Theory

There is a widely-held belief that skilled negotiators are born, not trained. This perhaps explains why the subject of negotiations is so frequently overlooked as a discipline or only receives cursory treatment in many management publications. It also may explain the proclivity toward the artistic approach to the process.

The difficulty in explaining negotiation theory is that there is no universal axiom applicable to all negotiation situations. Even the highly regimented Department of Defense recognizes this in stating:

> "How the Government's representatives plan and conduct their negotiations is their own choice. There is no one way to do it."

DoD recognizes that a successful negotiation must be situational. The proper approach not only depends on the known situation, the subject of the negotiations, and the people involved, but the dominating influence could be *other* circumstances which, on the surface, appear to be totally unrelated to the particular contract being negotiated. In government contracting this is often the case. On several occasions, as a government contracting officer, I found myself in an uncomfortable negotiating position because of a seemingly unrelated event. For example, a contracting officer located in an office in San Francisco could be attempting to purchase an emergency supply of wiping rags in order to resupply a Navy ship departing an East Coast port earlier than anticipated because of a flare-up in the Middle East. Certainly, the contract negotiations would be different than if the purchase were a routinely-scheduled replenishment acquisition, without the pressure generated by the need for immediate delivery. The driving force behind the government's negotiation position in this situation is a seemingly totally unrelated event, unless the prospective contractor had done a thorough job in preparing for the negotiations and learned what was going on. This knowledge could certainly affect the contractor's approach to the negotiations as well.

Successful negotiators recognize that the best approach to take regarding a specific negotiation depends on the specifics of the situation. Successful contract negotiators also recognize that the ultimate goal of negotiation is to achieve a result which maximizes the benefits to their organization while minimizing the costs. The benefits and costs can be financial, but are certainly not limited to financial considerations.

As mentioned in Chapter 1, most of the popular theories regarding the negotiation process are based on the artistic approach to the process and are derived from the study of human behavior and group dynamics. These theories include:

- Conflict resolution theories,
- Transactional analysis,
- Leadership theories,

- Interpersonal relationship theories,
- Hierarchy of needs theory, etc. Each of these theories of human behavior is an area of study in itself. While a basic understanding of human behavior theory is necessary to successful negotiations, it is only a part of understanding the entire process. Also, understanding human behavior is a never-ending process. As GSA points out in its negotiation training materials:

> "Effective negotiators are life-long students of human behavior."

One of the goals in the negotiation process is to be in control of the negotiations. One of the benefits of controlling the negotiations is that you can determine the type of negotiating environment established. There are several climates which can be created, including those which follow.

Competitive vs. Collaborative:

A competitive climate is one in which there is usually one winner and one loser—it is an adversarial environment. A poker game or a boxing match are examples. A collaborative environment, as defined by the government, is one in which:

> ". . . it is possible for all participants to achieve their goals, and goal achievement by one person involves or leads to goal achievement by another . . ."

An army squad involved in a combat situation is a clear example where a collaborative climate should be established. It is clearly in the best interest of everyone in the squad to do so. Is the collaborative environment the best to create in a contract negotiation situation? It all depends on the situation. Certainly, in most cases, a collaborative climate is the most appealing and it will probably be in your best interest to foster such an environment. This is not always the case. You must never lose sight of the fact that negotiations are basically competitive in nature. As a minimum, each party is competing for control of the negotiations if not for the complete agreement.

You can maximize your potential to control negotiations by being adequately prepared to establish or respond to either of these climates as the situation demands.

Give-and-Take:

This concept of negotiations involves a willingness to give something of value, in return for receiving something of value. Approaching negotiations in this way assumes that some interests must be sacrificed, that something of value must be given away in order to reach a mutually acceptable outcome. This is not always true and in many negotiating situations mutual sacrifice may not be required. There may be a common point where neither party is forced to make a sacrifice. To be successful, any approach to contract negotiations must be capable of capitalizing on these opportunities when they arise. The give-and-take approach to negotiations fails in this regard.

Trade-Offs:

Trade-offs are similar to the give-and-take approach. Again, it assumes that for every concession you receive, a like concession must be given in return. This again severely and artificially imposes a limitation on the negotiations which may or may not be necessary.

Domination:

Domination is the type of negotiation where one party dominates the negotiation process and the final agreement, regardless of the needs of the other party. When this approach is taken, one party will enter the negotiation process expecting all movement to be on the part of the other party. The government recognizes the short-term nature of any benefits gained using this approach to contract negotiations and advises its contracting officers not to exercise this technique. This advice applies even if the government is the only buyer and is in a dominant position as a result. Rather, the government recognizes that domination demands that the other party agree to sacrifices to the extent that the negotiations will not produce a fair and reasonable agreement. Such agreements, in the long run, are not in the best interest of either party.

It is essential that you do not confuse domination with controlling the negotiation process. The government, for example, recommends against dominating negotiations. Concurrently, government policy directs contracting officers to control the negotiations at all times. The difference is that controlling means directing the negotiations and includes the necessity of considering the other party's position in the process. To maximize your potential for control, you should do so in a way in which the other party not only perceives that a win-win agreement is reached, but you should exercise control in a way which leaves the other party with the impression that they were in control of the negotiations all along.

Unlike domination, controlling the negotiation process does not necessarily mean being able to get everything you want incorporated into a final agreement. It is controlling the outcome of the negotiations based on a reasonable evaluation of the situation and the needs of both parties.

Compromise and Concession:

For some reason the term "compromise" has been given a bad reputation in modern society. It has become synonymous with "giving in". The government makes a clear distinction between compromise and concession, stating that:

> "Compromise as a device for moving toward agreement is questionable because it is usually offered on the basis of arbitrary position changes purely for shortcutting negotiation procedures. This leads to agreements which may not be satisfactory to either side. Splitting differences is too arbitrary. . . . Making concessions is a more orderly process, because it demands that every change in position has a reason to substantiate it. . . . The concession route is the preferred approach for moving toward agreement for Government contracting."

Here the government has fallen into the classic trap of falsely labeling compromise as a bad negotiating approach. The problem lies in the basic definitions the government is applying to these two words. Once more, referring back to the *American Heritage Dictionary,* "compromise" is defined as:

> "A settlement of differences by mutual concessions."

There is no mention of the qualifier "arbitrary," nor does it require that equal concessions be made on both sides. *Funk & Wagnall's Standard Handbook of Synonyms & Prepositions* includes "concession" as a synonym for "compromise" with the qualifier that;

"Compromise is mutual concession by those of opposing views and interests, each yielding something to the other or others;
Concession is a yielding to another of that which one would like to retain..."

Using these definitions, the government's statements might be revised. Certainly the government's preferred method is not one of giving away something it would like to retain. In the final analysis, compromise is not an inherently bad approach, and neither is the concession approach. Both have their place in the negotiation process. It points out, however, that labels have a way of being misconstrued and you should be careful how they are used. For example, based on the government's definitions, you should not suggest a "compromise" to a government contracting officer; rather, suggest a "concession."

Agreement vs. Mutually Acceptable Understanding:

The word "agreement" was not included in the dictionary definition of negotiation referenced in Chapter 1. This is because the purpose of negotiations is not necessarily to reach an agreement, but to reach a *mutually satisfactory* arrangement. This is an important and critical distinction. Many negotiating hours are wasted attempting to get the other party to agree when all that is needed is acquiescence.

In successful contract negotiations, the negotiating parties do not have to "agree" in the classic sense; they must be willing to accept an agreement which represents a mutually satisfactory outcome. Keeping this in mind may save you time and avoid creating an adversarial negotiating environment.

The Sliding Scale Theory of Negotiation:

This distinction between acceptance and agreement can be illustrated by viewing negotiations as the movement of the point of acceptance along a sliding scale. Negotiating price with the government is one way to illustrate this concept.

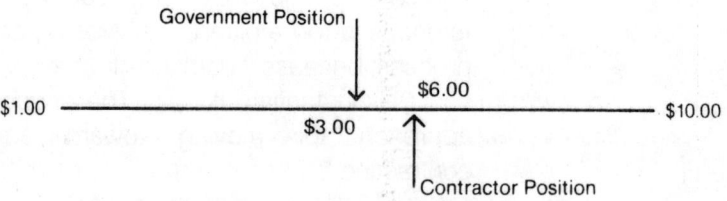

The price range scale used in this example is $1.00 to $10.00. It could just as easily be $5.00 to $10.00 or $.01 to $1,000,000. The relative position of the government and the contractor would remain the same. If there was no room for flexibility on either side, there would be never be an end agreement since the price goals are not the same. Rarely are the objectives of both parties exactly the same. There are too many variables affecting the price. Fortunately, just as rare are the occasions where these positions are so firm that there is no room to negotiate.

The contractor will usually have an idea of what it wants in the way of price for supplying a particular product or service to the government at a particular point in time. However, in most situations, the contractor will be willing to receive a little less, as long as the end price is not too far from their predetermined desired price. Along the price scale, there exists a range of prices, each of which would be acceptable to the contractor.

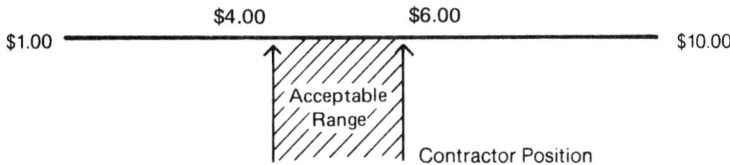

The government contracting officer must also, by regulation, establish an acceptable price range and have the range approved prior to conducting negotiations. They are required to establish a target price, that which the contracting officer wants to pay the contractor, along with a minimum and a maximum price objective. The minimum objective is the lowest amount considered fair and reasonable, beyond which if the contractor received the contract, it would be unlikely that the contract would be performed in accordance with the requirements of the contract. The maximum amount is the highest amount the contracting officer can justify as fair and reasonable. Any amount above this price would be considered unreasonable. Either the contractor would be making too much money, the contractor would not be performing the contract efficiently and reasonably, or there is another alternative available to satisfy the government's requirement at a price which would be lower. Once again, along the price scale there exists a range of prices, each of of which would be acceptable to the government as being fair and reasonable.

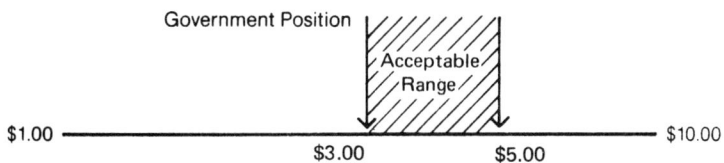

The basis of the sliding scale approach to negotiations is a recognition that at some point along the scale these two price ranges will overlap. This approach recognizes that there is a potential agreement regarding price which can be reached and that the resulting price will be acceptable and satisfactory to both parties. In this example, the range of mutually acceptable prices can be clearly seen by showing the acceptable price range for both parties on the same scale.

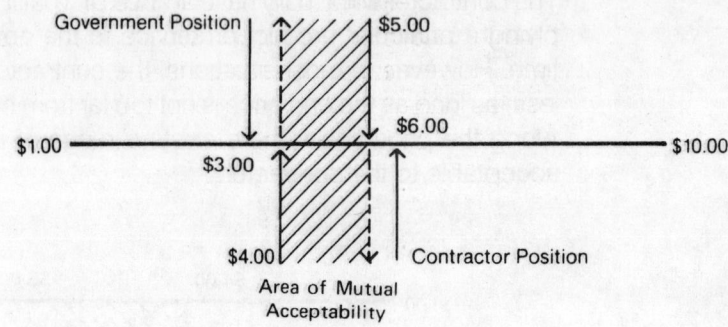

Usually, as in this example, there will generally be more than one point along the scale which overlaps the two acceptable price ranges. The goal of successful negotiations is to recognize that ranges such as these exist and then establish a price at the far end of the other party's range which is in your best interest. In the example, a successful negotiation from the contractor's point of view is a price at the far right side of the government's acceptable range of $6.00. The goal of the government is to reach an agreement on price which is at the left end of the contractor's acceptable price range—or $4.00. A price anywhere between $4.00 to $6.00 would be satisfactory to both parties. However there is considerable difference between the end outcomes. The better you are able to determine the other party's acceptable range, the better the chance of controlling the agreement and meeting your objectives at the highest possible level.

Stalemates and the Sliding Scale Theory:

Stalemates occur when there is no overlap of the acceptable ranges and there is no common acceptable point along the scale. This can be shown by the following illustration.

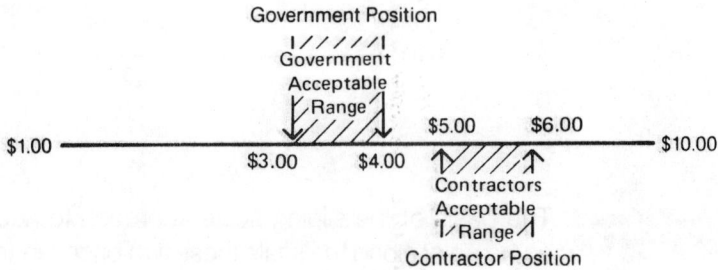

At no point is there a mutually acceptable price based on the objective ranges established by both parties. The government's maximum acceptable price is $4.00, the contractor's lowest acceptable price is $5.00. If this situation actually occurs, either there will be no end agreement resulting from the negotiations, or one or both parties will not be satisfied with the end outcome. As mentioned previously, such agreements are in neither party's best interest in the long run.

What should you do if you find yourself in this position? First, you must be certain that this stalemate situation actually exists. Generally, if you have reached the point of serious negotiations, this should not be the case. Although it might appear to be the situation, it could simply be tough negotiating by the other party. Usually, if you have reached the point of conducting serious negotiations, there is some common point which can be found.

If not, and you find yourself truly at an impasse, you must re-evaluate your position given the situation, considering any new information obtained during the negotiations. If your position remains the same, you must be prepared to walk away from the negotiations. There will always be a point at which it is not in your best interest to enter into a agreement with the other party. It is the possibility of reaching this point in the negotiation process which demands that you identify in advance the point at which you will walk away.

In this chapter we have discussed the basic concepts of negotiations and some of the different approaches and theories to contract negotiations. Regardless of the theory followed, or approach taken, the practical guidelines contained herein should prove useful in any negotiation situation. The information presented in following chapters will help you to draw upon the government's experience and expertise in contract negotiations. In any contract negotiation process, it is important that you "know your enemy." Knowledge is synonymous with power when negotiating contracts, and power can be converted into money. Money in contract negotiations frequently, but not always, is the measure of success.

Chapter 3

The 25% Solution to Contract Negotiations

After observing hundreds of contract negotiations in a variety of settings over the last sixteen years, I have come to believe that there is only one sound approach to contract negotiations in order to maximize the potential for controlling the contract negotiation outcome. It is by implementing some form of what is referred to in this book as the *25% Solution to Contract Negotiations*. This *25% Solution* is simply a scientific approach to contract negotiations whereby the negotiation process is viewed as a distinct system, comprising specific components or subsystems common to all negotiation situations.

The Negotiation System:

The negotiation system is composed of four separate and distinct subsystems or components, each equally and inherently possessing a 25% probability for influencing the whole system. The four components are: the company's position, the other party's position, the objective position, and the uncontrollable parameters related to the specific negotiation situation.

All negotiations consist of these four elements. Each component possesses the same potential for influencing the outcome of a specific contract negotiation. However, it is only the inherent potential which is equal. The actual influence exerted by each component on the final outcome will vary from situation to situation, depending upon the circumstances and the capabilities of the individuals and organizations involved. The following illustrates the components inherent in the negotiating process.

THE CONTRACT NEGOTIATION PROCESS
MAJOR COMPONENTS

- The Company's Position
- The Other Party's Position
- The Objective Position
- The Uncontrollable Parameters

Contract negotiations must be approached from the beginning, recognizing the potential for each component to equally influence the final agreement, as well as the possibility that any one element could dominate the final agreement. You will be in a much better position to maximize your organization's potential to control the negotiation process and establish a final agreement meeting your objectives by keeping this in mind.

The 25% Solution Concept:

To illustrate this *25% Solution* concept, all negotiations can be viewed as is shown in the following figure 1. Notice that each element has an equal potential to influence the negotiation outcome. Figures 2 and 3 illustrate that the actual influence exerted on the outcome by any one element will vary depending upon the circumstances involved and the skill of the negotiators. The objective of successful negotiations is to maximize your potential to influence the outcome given the uncontrollable circumstances surrounding the negotiations.

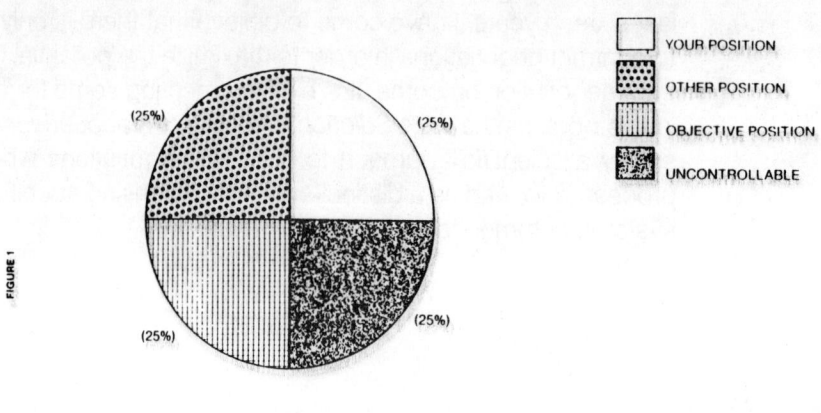

NEGOTIATION POTENTIAL

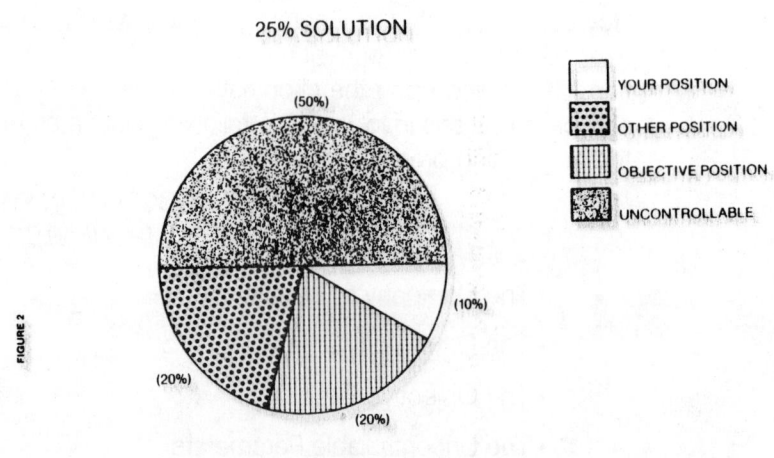

NEGOTIATION INFLUENCE

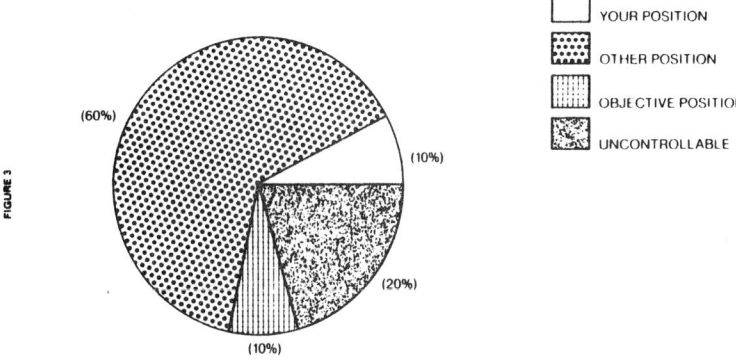

FIGURE 3

NEGOTIATION INFLUENCE

Another way to view this approach to contract negotiations is by viewing the process as a formula:

THE 25% SOLUTION TO NEGOTIATIONS
FORMULA

A+B+C+D=E

A—Your Position
B—Their Position
C—The Objective Position
D—Intangibles Parameters
E—The Negotiation Outcome

The 25% Solution will help you to consider all of the factors applicable to a particular negotiation by providing a systematic method for establishing your negotiation objectives. Every factor which must be considered in contract negotiations can be classified into one of the four negotiation system components or subsystems. This approach to contract negotiations will also help during the actual negotiation conference, in evaluating the success of the negotiations, and in evaluating the adequacy of the final agreement. Each component of the negotiation process needs to be analyzed relative to the following possible "Areas For Negotiation":

THE CONTRACT NEGOTIATION PROCESS
AREAS FOR NEGOTIATION

- Technical Requirements
- Cost and Price Analysis
- Quality Requirements
- Quantity Requirements
- Delivery Terms and Conditions
- Administrative Terms and Conditions
- Other Contract Requirements

There will potentially be negotiable issues under each of these categories in any contract negotiation. Each category needs to be evaluated in relation to the four components prior to establishing your overall negotiation position. The following are sample worksheets which can be used to assist you in performing these analyses.

25% SOLUTION TO CONTRACT NEGOTIATIONS
NEGOTIATION PREPARATION ANALYSIS
COMPANY POSITION SUMMARY

REFERENCE NUMBER:_____

1. Technical Requirements

2. Cost and Price Analysis:

3. Quality Requirements Analysis and Comments:

4. Quantity Analysis and Comments:

5. Delivery Terms and Conditions:

6. Administrative Terms and Conditions:

7. Other:

THE 25% SOLUTION TO CONTRACT NEGOTIATIONS
NEGOTIATION PREPARATION ANALYSIS
OTHER PARTY'S POSITION SUMMARY

REFERENCE NUMBER:_____

1. Technical Comments:

2. Cost and Price Analysis:

3. Quality Requirements Analysis and Comments:

4. Quantity Analysis and Comments:

5. Delivery Terms and Conditions:

6. Administrative Terms and Conditions:

7. Other:

25% SOLUTION TO NEGOTIATIONS
NEGOTIATION PREPARATION ANALYSIS
THE OBJECTIVE POSITION SUMMARY

REFERENCE NUMBER:_____

1. Technical Comments:

2. Cost and Price Analysis:

3. Quality Requirements Analysis and Comments:

4. Quantity Analysis and Comments:

5. Delivery Terms and Conditions:

6. Administrative Terms and Conditions:

7. Other:

25% SOLUTION TO NEGOTIATIONS
NEGOTIATION PREPARATION ANALYSIS
INTANGIBLE PARAMETERS SUMMARY

REFERENCE NUMBER:_____

1. Technical Comments:

2. Cost and Price Analysis:

3. Quality Requirements Analysis and Comments:

4. Quantity Analysis and Comments:

5. Delivery Terms and Conditions:

6. Administrative Terms and Conditions:

7. Other:

Each of the four potential influences on the negotiation process holds equal potential for controlling the contract. Notice that these elements can be further grouped into two *subjective* positions and two *objective* positions. The subjective components are your position and the other party's position. These parochial components are dominated by self-interest. The other two components are unbiased components where the dominant factors are objective in nature. These are the objective position and the uncontrollable parameters. Parochial interests are irrelevant in these last two categories.

In the first group, the determination of the negotiating position is based on implementing internal policies and regulations, personal objectives and organizational goals. All of these are controllable to some degree. In the latter group, the determinations are made based on evaluating the impact of unalterable facts affecting the negotiation. Viewing each different area of negotiation from the four different perspectives and analyzing the potential end contract in the same way will provide a comprehensive base upon which to establish your overall negotiation position.

The Company's Position:

This is not your position going into the negotiations. Rather, it is your totally biased, best-case scenario or wish list for the negotiations. This position will normally be the basis for establishing your maximum objectives. In developing this position you should ask yourself:

"If all goes well, what would we like to see in the final agreement?"

The only restrictions placed on you when developing this position are the limitations of legality, ethics, and reasonability. These limitations should apply in all of your negotiations. To do otherwise would be a short-term approach to the process, doomed to failure in the long run. This is especially true when dealing with the government. These restrictions will be discussed in further detail in Chapter 10.

The Other Party's Position:

This consists of your best analysis and estimate of the other party's position relative to the negotiations. Questions which should be asked include:

- What are the other party's needs?
- What is your estimate of their budget for the contract?
- What type of organization are you dealing with?
- What alternatives do they have other than establishing a contract with you?
- Has the other party conducted negotiations with your organization previously?
- Have they purchased the same or similar products or services previously? If so,

—When?
—How much was paid?
—What type of competition did they receive?
—Who was the competition and who received the award?
—How did the successful awardee perform, etc?

- What is the other party's previous experience with your organization?
- How much flexibility do their negotiators have?

These are all sample questions you can ask when developing your assessment of the other party's position. In negotiations with the government, you have an advantage due to the vast amount of information which can be obtained pertaining to the government's acquisition procedures and its prior procurement history relative to the products or services you wish to supply. To maximize your potential to control the negotiations in the government setting, you must take advantage of the information available.

The Objective Position:

This will be the hardest assessment for you to make. Despite the level of difficulty, in order to conduct successful negotiations, you must be able to step back and analyze the entire situation from an unbiased point of view. If you cannot, you must arrange to have someone who can take a look at the matter. In larger organizations, teams are established to perform exactly this function.

One way to accomplish this task, if you are unable to bring in outside help, is to view the situation as if you were an auditor reviewing the end contract after award.

- Is your position reasonable from a purely objective point of view?
- Is the other party's position as you estimate it to be, reasonable from an objective point of view?

As you go through this process, you will be able to identify areas of non-reasonability as well as additional information which will be valuable in establishing your minimum and your target objectives. Remember that your company's subjective position will be the dominant factor in establishing your maximum objectives.

The Uncontrollable Parameters:

In every negotiation situation there are going to be circumstances which will influence the final agreement, but which cannot be directly controlled by either party. Many negotiations break down over these types of issues when, in fact, neither party had any control over the matter. Rather than fighting over the issue, the parties should be working together to reach a suitable agreement within the limitations imposed by these uncontrollable conditions.

Usually, but not always, there are long-term problems or situations which create an environment under which the negotiations take place.

- The status of the economy
- Legal restrictions
- Budgetary restrictions
- Emergency situations
- Third-party actions

These are just a few of the elusive or uncontrollable factors which can significantly influence the outcome of a particular negotiation. It is imperative to identify these factors and determine their effect on each of the positions previously described. In evaluating these factors, many will be determined capable of being influenced but not totally controllable. Such factors, the type and amount of effort needed to influence their impact on the negotiations, and the potential benefits of doing so, need to be addressed when discussing each party's position in the negotiations. Those factors which are truly uncontrollable should be identified as such. After identifying the uncontrollable parameters, stop spending time trying to change or influence them. Rather, spend your time developing the best possible position given the fact that these circumstances are unchangeable. Major impasses often occur over issues such as these. Much time is wasted and animosity built up over simply getting to the point of realizing that some elements are uncontrollable. Identifying these factors during the preparation stage will help to minimize the potential for wasting time and creating an unfavorable negotiating climate. The information will also strengthen your starting position.

It is important that only those factors which are uncontrollable by either party fall under this category. If the factor or element is controllable in any way, it should fall under one of the biased position categories.

After the preceding worksheets have been completed and reviewed, the negotiation objectives can be established and the summary negotiation worksheet prepared.

25% SOLUTION TO NEGOTIATIONS
NEGOTIATION PREPARATION ANALYSIS
NEGOTIATION POSITION SUMMARY

REFERENCE NUMBER:_____

1. Technical Comments:

2. Cost and Price Analysis:

3. Quality Requirements Analysis and Comments:

4. Quantity Analysis and Comments:

5. Delivery Terms and Conditions:

6. Administrative Terms and Conditions:

7. Other:

These documents will prove extremely useful throughout the negotiation process and you will find they will continually be used as a reference during the process. These worksheets can also be used for briefing non-team members within your organization, as well as providing supporting documentation for any review process established within the organization.

The Subjective Approach Fallacy:

This model of negotiating points out the danger of only approaching the negotiation process from the human behaviorial point of view. The subjective approach to the negotiation process relies on a knowledge of one's own personal strengths and weaknesses, combined with the personal needs hierarchy of the other party. It concentrates on the human element of the process. As shown by the *25% Solution* approach, concentrating on only the human behavioral elements of the negotiating process is the same as concentrating on only 50% of the factors which might possibly affect the process— *Your Company's Position* and *The Other Party's Position*. This approach ignores the importance of the *Objective Position* and the *Uncontrollable Parameters* which, when combined, are just as important as the two subjective elements. This illustrates the necessity of adopting some form of scientific approach to the contract negotiation process in order to maximize the potential for a successful outcome given the circumstances of the specific negotiation situation.

As mentioned earlier in this chapter, one of the benefits of negotiating with the government is the amount of information available to you. One of the drawbacks is the amount of information you must make available to them. Certainly, of all the negotiation systems in place, the government negotiating system is the one which operates in the most open environment with the maximum amount of information available to both parties. This is why the government negotiation system is such an excellent system to study.

When negotiating with parties other than the government, the same amount of information may not be available. However, the type of information you can and should obtain from the government is the same as that which you should try and obtain regarding any party with whom you are going to be negotiating. A study of the government contract negotiating system, as it is designed to work, can serve as a standard in preparing for any contract negotiation.

The next three chapters provide an overview of the government negotiation process. Chapter 7 begins the discussion of applying the principles and techniques of government contract negotiations to the negotiation of any complex contract or agreement.

Chapter 4

Government Negotiations

Negotiated Versus Sealed Bid Contracts:

There are two contracting methods employed by the federal government when establishing contracts for all of the goods and services it acquires: the sealed bid method and the negotiated method. Reviewing the definitions in the *Federal Acquisition Regulations* proves this to be true. The definition for sealed bid is actually a set of specific procedures which must be followed in order for a particular acquisition action to be considered a sealed bid procurement. *FAR* Subpart 14.101 states that:

> "Sealed bidding is a method of contracting that employs competitive bids, public bid openings, and awards."

The following steps are involved in sealed bid procurements:

1. Invitations for bids must describe the requirements of the government clearly, accurately and completely. Unnecessarily restrictive specifications or requirements that might unduly limit the number of bidders are prohibited.

2. Invitations for bids must be publicized through distribution to prospective bidders, posting in public places and other appropriate means.

3. Bidders must submit sealed bids to be opened at the time and place specified in the solicitation for the public opening of bids.

4. After bids are publicly opened, an award is made to that responsible bidder whose bid, conforming to the invitation for bids, is most advantageous to the government considering only price and price-related factors included in the invitation.

The definition for negotiation is much simpler. *FAR* Subpart 15.101 states:

> "Negotiation means contracting through the use of either competitive or other than competitive proposals and discussions. Any contract awarded without using sealed bidding procedures is a negotiated contract."

The *FAR* describes negotiation as a procedure that includes the receipt of proposals from offerors, permits bargaining, and usually affords offerors an opportunity to revise their offers before award of a contract. These definitions clearly point out that there are only two contracting methods within the federal government. The very definition of the term negotiation makes these two contracting methods mutually exclusive. Any contract established by a means other than the sealed bid method of contracting is a negotiated contract.

Impact of the *Competition in Contracting Act:*

Prior to 1984, government regulations specifically stated that the official government policy was that there was a "preference" for sealed bid contracting. Contracting officers could only negotiate a contract if they were able to cite one of seventeen exceptions to the requirement that the sealed bid contracting method be used for all acquisitions. Often, Congress and the press believed that the only competitive government procurements were those accomplished using the sealed bid process. In 1984, Congress passed the *Competition in Contracting Act.* The Act was passed in response to what congress perceived as a failure of the federal procuring agencies to eliminate suspect pricing practices and continuing contractor abuses within the federal procurement system. This was coupled with concern over the general lack of competition being experienced in the federal procurement system.

In Fiscal Year 1985, prior to implementation of the *Competition in Contracting Act,* contracts covering 50% of the total dollar value of all contracts over $25,000 were awarded noncompetitively. During the same fiscal year, after implementation of the act, noncompetitive contracts only represented 34.6% of the total dollars. This downward trend has continued into Fiscal Year 1986. In the fourth quarter of FY 1986, those noncompetitive contracts for which the contracting process started after implementation of the act represented 30.3% of the total dollars awarded. Those contracts for which the process started prior to the act again represented approximately 50% of the total dollar value for all such contracts. Based on these statistics reported by the Federal Procurement Data Center, the *Competition in Contracting Act* has moved the system in the direction of the desired effect: increasing the value of government contracts being awarded under competitive procedures.

One of the additional major changes brought about as a result of the passage of this act was the recognition that negotiated contracts could be just as competitive as those established using the sealed bid contracting method. For the first time, negotiated contracting was unquestionably classified as an alternative competitive procurement means. The act not only eliminated the formal preference for the sealed bid method, it eliminated the seventeen Negotiation Authorities which were the exceptions to contracting under the sealed bid method. Rather, the act implemented a set of strict circumstances which must exist in order to allow non-competitive negotiations to be conducted—not simply all negotiations. This opened the door for more and more competitive negotiations to be used for acquisitions which previously may have been considered sealed bid contracting candidates.

In Fiscal Year 1985, approximately 9% of all contracts were awarded by the sealed bid method of contracting. In FY 1986, this was reduced to less than 4. The increase in the number of contracts being negotiated versus those being awarded via the sealed bid method makes it all the more important that government contractors fully understand federal contract negotiation procedures.

Choosing To Negotiate:

Under current federal procurement regulations (post-*Competition in Contracting Act*), contracting officers are advised under *FAR* Subpart 6.401 that sealed bidding and competitive proposals are both acceptable procedures for promoting and providing for full and open competition. Contracting officers are directed to exercise good judgment in selecting the method for contracting which best meets the needs of the government if the sealed bid method is not appropriate. They are directed to use the sealed bidding process if:

- Time permits the solicitation, submission, and evaluation of sealed bids.
- The award will be made on the basis of price and other price related factors.
- It is not necessary to conduct discussions with the responding offerors about their bids; and
- There is reasonable expectation of receiving more than one sealed bid.

Contracting officers are allowed to request competitive proposals if, in their judgment, sealed bids are not appropriate.

This is in significant contrast with the previous *FAR* 15.104 which stated:

"No contract shall be entered into as a result of negotiation unless—

(a) The contemplated contract action comes under the one of the statutory authorizations permitting negotiation;

(b) All required determinations and findings have been made; and

(c) All required clearances and approvals have been obtained."

Previously, Subpart 15.200 identified the statutory authorities for using negotiation as a contracting method. These authorities were considered "exceptions to the general requirement for formal advertising."

This change in government policy has been discussed in depth due to its critical and significant impact on government contracting. As is evident from the discussion of this change, much more latitude has been granted contracting officers to using the negotiating method, instead of being forced to follow the sealed bid method. Considering that for many years the word "negotiated" had a negative connotation within Congress and the media, it is amazing that this policy was enacted. Compared to sealed bidding, negotiation is a much more flexible contracting method. The negotiation method permits corrections of minor errors as well as bargaining in the sense of discussion, persuasion, alteration of initial assumptions, and give-and-take. Price, schedule, technical requirements, type of contract, or other terms of a pending contract can be discussed and negotiated when this method is used. Under the sealed bid method, there is very little room for error and almost no flexibility. This method consists of a set of step-by-step procedures which must be strictly followed.

The recognition by Congress that negotiation, in itself, is neither wrong nor noncompetitive, was long overdue. Rather than forcing contracting officers to use the sealed bid method as much as possible, even when a negotiated contract may clearly have been a better approach, they now have a choice. As a result of the *Competition in Contracting Act,* the emphasis is finally being placed on forcing contracting officers to justify using noncompetitive contracting procedures, and not simply the negotiation method.

Noncompetitive Contracting:

The *Competition in Contracting Act (CICA)* significantly changed the government's policy concerning sealed bid versus negotiated contracting by eliminating the formal preference for the sealed bid method. It also substantially changed the procedures which a contracting officer must follow when justifying a noncompetitive procurement.

After *CICA*, the official policy is that contracting officers shall promote full and open competition in soliciting offers and awarding government contracts using the competitive procedures described in the *FAR*. Sealed bid, competitive proposals, or a combination of these procedures are considered competitive methods of procurement. GSA's Multiple Award Schedule Contracting program is also recognized as a competitive procedure. Prior to *CICA* here were seventeen contracting authorities which existed authorizing negotiated contracting including noncompetitive negotiations. After *CICA*, the contracting officer no longer has to justify using the competitive negotiated procurement method. However, they now must provide even more justification than before when awarding noncompetitive contracts. The *FAR* currently lists seven exceptions to the general requirement that contracting officers promote full and open competition. Procurements under the following categories may be noncompetitively negotiated if adequately justified in accordance with the detailed requirements of one of these exceptions:

- Only one responsible source.
- Unusual and compelling urgency.
- Industrial mobilization; or experimental, developmental, or research work.
- International agreement.
- Authorized or required by statute.
- National security.
- Public interest.

Formal justifications must be prepared defending the contracting officer's decision to use other than full and open competition procedures for any specific procurement. This justification is processed for review and approval prior to the noncompetitive solicitation issuance.

Negotiated Government Solicitations and Contracts:

With the advent of the *FAR*, the government established—in theory—a single uniform solicitation and contract format for use by all federal agencies. Since the *FAR* was implemented, however, the agencies in their usual fashion have tailored these standard formats to meet their individual needs. It has reached the point where it is difficult to remember that a uniform format exists. Still, the basic requirements of the uniform format must be provided somewhere in the solicitation, although not always in the same place. If the solicitation does not address the major issues required by the *FAR*, the solicitation is considered to be deficient and should be amended or canceled.

Each solicitation should consist of the following major components:

- **Part I—The Schedule.** This part is the meat of the solicitation or contract. It contains a description of the products or services being sought and the contract terms and conditions specific to the acquisition.

- **Part II—Contract Clauses.** This section contains the standard government contracting clauses common to most government contracts. The clauses contained in this section are often referred to as "boiler plate" clauses. This section will frequently simply consist of a complete list of clauses indicating those applicable to the specific solicitation or contract.

- **Part III—Documents, exhibits and other attachments.** This part contains a list of references or other attachments forming part of the solicitation or contract. Any documents referenced in this section are incorporated with the same force and effect as if they were included in their entirety in the solicitation or contract, unless specifically stated otherwise. It is essential that any referenced documents be obtained and reviewed prior to establishing your negotiation objectives.

- **Part IV—Representations and instructions.** In this section, prospective contractors must certify as to the nature of their business, the size of the company and other information concerning the status of their company i.e., small or large, women-owned, operating in a labor surplus area, etc. Contractors must also acknowledge their commitment to comply with all of the terms and conditions of the solicitation or contract.

The schedule is the most important part in a solicitation. This is supported by the *Order of Precedence* clause referenced in all government contracts stating that the terms and conditions of the Schedule take precedence over all other references when there is a conflict between any of the contract terms and conditions. The Schedule is comprised of the following sections:

- Solicitation/Contract Form (SF 33).
- Supplies Services and Prices/Costs.
- Descriptions/Specifications/Work Statement.
- Packaging and Marking.
- Inspection and Acceptance.
- Deliveries and Performance.
- Contract Administration Data.
- Special Contract Requirements.

As can be seen by these headings, the schedule is the section which provides the specifics for the individual procurement.

Unsolicited Proposals:

An unsolicited proposal is a proposal submitted to the government which was developed and submitted on the initiative of a contractor. Unsolicited proposals cannot be submitted in response to a formal or informal request for proposals. Government agencies will evaluate unsolicited proposals and determine if a contract should be established. There are a couple of points to keep in mind regarding submitting unsolicited proposals to the federal government:

- There are a specific set of procedures which must be followed when submitting the unsolicited proposal.
- Certain specific information must be included in the unsolicited proposal.

The fact that an unsolicited proposal was submitted and a contract determined appropriate, is not in itself adequate justification for the government to conduct a noncompetitive negotiation with the contractor who submitted the proposal. Additional noncompetitive justification is required. It is not uncommon for unsolicited proposals to be the most difficult to negotiate.

Chapter 5

Government Negotiating Principles

The Government Procurement System:

No other customer will let you know as much about their internal policies and procedures as will the U. S. Government. This is one of the principal benefits available to contractors when doing business with the government. Representatives of IBM, General Electric, General Motors and others will not tell you very much about their thought processes during contract negotiations. The government will, either directly or indirectly.

One of the reasons so much information is available is simply due to the very nature and size of the government as a bureaucracy. Because of this, the government attempts to standardize almost everything—including the way its representatives purchase goods and services. As a result, the rules and procedures government contracting personnel are to follow are published and available for public review. It is impossible to play any game well without knowing the rules. The government not only publishes the rules, it publishes its game plan for all to see. Given the amount of information available, it is not surprising that some contractors play the game extremely well.

In addition to the information available regarding the process, the government has also endeavored to create a procurement system which is open to all who wish to participate. This is because one of the principles of the government procurement system is that free and open competition will automatically lead to fair and reasonable prices. This is simply the law of supply and demand. The more demand, the more supply there will be until the point is reached where an adequate supply is available to consumers at fair and reasonable prices. Neither sellers nor buyers set the price. The marketplace automatically establishes a fair and reasonable price. The entire regulatory body of government procurement procedures is based on this principle. As a result, the system is designed to encourage as much participation from suppliers as is possible given the nature of the government's requirements.

The significance of this is that the system is designed to be open to new competition. From a contractor's point of view, this is both good and bad. On the good side, it means there will always be a way to compete for the government business related to your product or service area. Despite this opportunity, many prospective contractors decide not to do business with the government for a variety of reasons—some true, most false. The number of excuses seem almost endless:

- the government will only buy the product or service from the one company the agency likes;
- the bids are all rigged;
- the prices the government pays are too low;
- the government only awards contracts to the low bidder who usually is incompetent;
- contractors are able to bid so cheap because they provide poor quality products and my company makes a quality product;
- a good contractor simply cannot compete;
- there is too much red tape;
- the government will not allow you to earn a reasonable profit;
- the government is too slow to pay; and so forth.

If you ask anyone familiar with the federal procurement system, from either the contractor or government side, they will tell you that in the vast majority of acquisitions these excuses are not valid. Sometimes, however, due to the nature of the government's requirements or the nature of the competitors, government business related to a particular product or service may not be desirable. This, however, is the exception. All one need do to verify the potential desirability of government business is to look at the list of the top 100 government contractors. The names of the largest and most respected corporations in the country will be found on the list. Table 1 is the list for FY 1986. Companies do not do business with the government because it is undesirable business.

The reason the government market is so appealing to these corporations, besides the obvious fact that there is a considerable amount of money involved, is that the foundation of the government procurement system itself is sound. The government does not award contracts simply to the lowest bidder. Certainly contracting officers cannot legally rig a bid in favor of one company. Only when you or your competition allow this, can it occur. If you are awarded a contract, the government should be one of your better-paying customers—as long as you perform in accordance with the contract terms and conditions. Reports from most contractors indicate that the *Prompt Payment Act* works in ensuring proper payment and that they are paid on time. If the prices the government pays are too low, why are so many companies so eager to win government contract awards?

Don't let the myths of doing business with the government deter you from the potential benefits of participating in the system. Remember that the system is designed to generate competition. Taking advantage of the rules and procedures of the system will minimally provide you the opportunity to compete on a fair and equitable basis for any government business in which you are interested. The rest is up to you. The system has done its job at that point.

FEDERAL PROCUREMENT DATA SYSTEM

TOP 100 FEDERAL CONTRACTORS

ACTIONS REPORTED INDIVIDUALLY ON SF279

Fourth Quarter Fiscal Year 1986 Year To Date

AS OF 03/25/86

	NUMBER OF ACTIONS OVER $10,000	PERCENT OF TOTAL	$(000)	PERCENT OF TOTAL
TOTAL FEDERAL	414,767	100.00	182,558,799	100.00
TOP 100 SUBTOTAL	88,810	21.41	115,176,372	63.09
1 GENERAL DYNAMICS CORPORATION	2,426	.58	8,387,594	4.59
2 ROCKWELL INTERNATIONAL CORP	2,540	.61	7,698,142	4.22
3 MC DONNELL DOUGLAS CORPORATION	2,634	.64	6,626,747	3.63
4 GENERAL ELECTRIC COMPANY	4,480	1.08	6,078,134	3.33
5 LOCKHEED CORPORATION	2,227	.54	5,705,362	3.13
6 GENERAL MOTORS CORPORATION	5,963	1.44	5,144,469	2.82
7 MARTIN MARIETTA CORPORATION	1,095	.26	4,190,393	2.30
8 RAYTHEON COMPANY	2,261	.55	4,107,916	2.25
9 UNITED TECHNOLOGIES CORP	3,729	.90	3,809,135	2.09
10 BOEING COMPANY THE	2,800	.68	3,783,484	2.07
11 GRUMMAN CORPORATION	1,960	.47	2,992,323	1.64
12 WESTINGHOUSE ELECTRIC CORP	1,842	.44	2,438,068	1.34
13 AMERICAN TELEPHONE & TELG CO	1,230	.30	2,366,343	1.30
14 UNIVERSITY OF CALIFORNIA	550	.13	2,139,369	1.17
15 HONEYWELL INC	2,693	.65	1,904,027	1.04
16 ALLIED-SIGNAL INC	3,418	.82	1,902,424	1.04
17 LITTON INDUSTRIES INC	1,521	.37	1,674,947	.92
18 SPERRY CORPORATION	3,719	.90	1,672,214	.92
19 INTERNATIONAL BUSINESS MCHS	3,103	.75	1,660,993	.91
20 TEXTRON INC	1,639	.40	1,647,267	.90
21 LTV CORPORATION THE	780	.19	1,483,269	.81
22 RCA CORPORATION	1,215	.29	1,441,438	.79
23 TEXAS INSTRUMENTS INCORPORATED	745	.18	1,440,748	.79
24 DU PONT E I DE NEMOURS AND CO	351	.08	1,145,179	.63
25 TRW INC	1,214	.29	1,143,033	.63
26 EG&G INC	390	.09	1,130,792	.62
27 EATON CORPORATION	644	.16	1,075,171	.59
28 GTE CORPORATION	910	.22	1,041,940	.57
29 FORD MOTOR COMPANY	624	.15	979,000	.54
30 SINGER COMPANY THE	989	.24	962,030	.53
31 CALIFORNIA INST TECHNOLOGY	677	.16	905,748	.50
32 ITT CORPORATION	1,041	.25	859,153	.47
33 CHEVRON CORPORATION	206	.05	849,960	.47
34 ROYAL DUTCH SHELL	87	.02	836,622	.46
35 NORTHROP CORPORATION	849	.20	807,550	.44
36 GREEN RIVER COAL CO INC	1	.00	768,647	.42
37 HARSCO CORPORATION	120	.03	707,557	.39
38 GENCORP INC	360	.09	656,897	.36
39 ATLANTIC RICHFIELD COMPANY	18	.00	654,824	.36
40 GOODYEAR TIRE & RUBBER CO	770	.19	597,929	.33
41 TELEDYNE INC	1,111	.27	563,788	.31
42 MOTOROLA INC	1,279	.31	550,263	.30
43 PAN AM CORPORATION	315	.08	515,402	.28
44 CFM INTERNATIONAL INC	213	.05	512,272	.28
45 HARRIS CORPORATION	897	.22	499,038	.27
46 COMPUTER SCIENCES CORPORATION	1,481	.36	486,402	.27
47 MORTON THIOKOL INC	197	.05	485,728	.27
48 EXXON CORPORATION	91	.02	485,721	.27
49 HERCULES INCORPORATED	393	.09	481,759	.26
50 TENNECO INC	672	.16	480,030	.26

5-3

AS OF 03/25/86

FEDERAL PROCUREMENT DATA SYSTEM

TOP 100 FEDERAL CONTRACTORS-Continued

ACTIONS REPORTED INDIVIDUALLY ON SF279

Fourth Quarter Fiscal Year 1986 Year To Date

		NUMBER OF ACTIONS OVER $10,000	PERCENT OF TOTAL	$(000)	PERCENT OF TOTAL
51	UNITED STATES PHILIPS TRUST	704	.17	477,688	.26
52	CONGOLEUM CORPORATION	321	.08	465,089	.25
53	MASSACHUSETTS INST TECHNOLOGY	318	.08	426,852	.23
54	FEDERAL REP OF GERMANY	912	.22	417,331	.23
55	ADDINGTON INC	7	.00	412,030	.23
56	FMC CORPORATION	356	.09	403,777	.22
57	OGDEN	154	.04	402,772	.22
58	BURROUGHS CORPORATION	819	.20	384,841	.21
59	MOTOR OIL HELLAS-CORINTH REFIN	8	.00	380,628	.21
60	UNC RESOURCES INC	96	.02	367,841	.20
61	LORAL CORPORATION	328	.08	361,216	.20
62	MITRE CORPORATION THE	143	.03	359,442	.20
63	BATTELLE MEMORIAL INSTITUTE	567	.14	352,311	.19
64	MORRISON KNUDSEN CORPORATION	188	.05	337,958	.19
65	JOHNS HOPKINS UNIVERSITY	86	.02	329,254	.18
66	CHRYSLER CORPORATION	66	.02	324,029	.18
67	HUDSON WATERWAYS CORP	13	.00	319,826	.18
68	OLIN CORPORATION	242	.06	315,520	.17
69	ASHLAND OIL INC	189	.05	314,308	.17
70	AEROSPACE CORPORATION THE	51	.01	306,088	.17
71	MOBIL CORPORATION	66	.02	303,986	.17
72	GOULD INC	561	.14	300,579	.16
73	PENN CENTRAL CORPORATION THE	709	.17	295,584	.16
74	EMERSON ELECTRIC CO	474	.11	293,553	.16
75	CONTROL DATA CORPORATION	616	.15	293,166	.16
76	SCIENCE APPLICATIONS INTL	1,000	.24	283,855	.16
77	DRAPER CHARLES STARK LAB	108	.03	278,108	.15
78	ASSOCIATED UNIVERSITIES INC	23	.01	263,917	.14
79	MC DERMOTT INTERNATIONAL INC	171	.04	262,336	.14
80	UNIVERSITY OF CHICAGO THE	56	.01	255,601	.14
81	SUN COMPANY INC	21	.01	254,088	.14
82	HEWLETT-PACKARD COMPANY	1,933	.47	250,122	.14
83	DYNALECTRON CORPORATION	409	.10	243,029	.13
84	OSHKOSH TRUCK CORPORATION	73	.02	242,113	.13
85	AMOCO CORPORATION	113	.03	241,868	.13
86	COASTAL CORPORATION THE	70	.02	238,357	.13
87	MASON HANGER-SILAS MASN INC WV	104	.03	237,795	.13
88	GATES CORPORATION THE	53	.01	232,803	.13
89	FIGGIE INTERNATIONAL HOLDINGS	237	.06	232,666	.13
90	OHIO VALLEY ELECTRIC CORP	4	.00	226,337	.12
91	LEAR SIEGLER INC	521	.13	219,616	.12
92	BECHTEL CORPORATION	165	.04	216,016	.12
93	DIGITAL EQUIPMENT CORPORATION	1,928	.46	213,275	.12
94	TRACOR INC	703	.17	208,447	.11
95	E-SYSTEMS INC	450	.11	204,027	.11
96	MONSANTO COMPANY	102	.02	201,427	.11
97	PETROLEOS MEXICANOS	11	.00	195,750	.11
98	EASTMAN KODAK COMPANY	1,210	.29	185,838	.10
99	TODD SHIPYARDS CORPORATION	665	.16	185,611	.10
100	STANFORD LELAND JR UNIVERSITY	216	.05	180,460	.10

Practical Considerations:

Once you decide to compete in the government market, there are two practical aspects to competing for government business which must be considered. Generally, profits from government business will usually not be as high as those you receive from your commercial business. While there are many exceptions to this rule, generally this will be true. Government regulations state that contracting officers should negotiate a price which allows the contractor to earn a "reasonable" profit. The government recognizes that it is not in its long-term interest to establish a contract at a price which will not be profitable for the contractor. However, what is reasonable to you may not necessarily be what is reasonable to the individual contracting officer. This is why implementing proper negotiating techniques and procedures is essential.

The second practical problem related to government contracting is that, although the system is designed to ensure maximum possible competition and is designed to let anyone participate in attempting to win a government contract, the system clearly favors those who are already involved. This is not only because of the inherent complexity of the system, but simply the necessary investment in time and energy which must be made to maximize your company's potential. Learning how to maximize the number of contracts you obtain and the profitability of those contracts requires a thorough understanding of the federal procurement system. Not only must you learn the current system, you must remain current on any changes as they occur. This takes time and effort.

These problems are offset by two factors. The first is that government business is steady and reliable business. You may not make as much profit on any one contract, but you can be assured that in good times and in bad, the government will still be buying goods and services. Despite the recent massive budget cuts, the government still spends approximately $200 billion dollars a year on goods and services. The trick is to work within the parameters of the system so you are not critically affected by unforeseen budget cuts or the loss of any one potential government contract. The second factor is that government business is long-term business and the learning process is a building-block process. The basics of the system are not that difficult to learn. Once you learn the basics, learning the finer points of the system can take place on a learn-as-you-go basis. Additionally, what you learn from one solicitation or contract will prove useful on the next, even if the solicitation is from a different agency. The government is very standardized and repetitive in nature and these characteristics are what make learning the system a manageable endeavor.

The Principle of Competition:

Nowhere is the capitalistic concept of the law of supply and demand more predominant than in government contracting. The entire body of government contract regulations is based on the principles of the free market. The basic assumption is that true competition between sellers will automatically yield fair and reasonable prices for buyers. Accordingly, the entire system has been designed in an attempt to generate true competition. When the system is successful in generating such competition, the job of the contracting officer is easy. Unfortunately, despite this, prior to implementation of the *Competition in Contracting Act,* 50% or more of the total dollars awarded under government contracts were awarded under noncompetitive circumstances. Even after implementation of this act, during the fourth quarter of FY 1986, over 30% of the contract dollars were still being awarded noncompetitively.

The problem is that it is difficult to obtain competition. In order to be considered true competition:

- two or more offers or bids must be received,
- from responsible firms,
- capable of satisfying the requirements of the solicitation,
- at prices within a competitive range.

Each of these restrictions must be met before a contract can be considered to have been awarded competitively. As evidenced by the statistics, this is not always possible.

Federal Acquisition Regulations:

The basic rules of government contracting are published in the *Federal Acquisition Regulations,* Title 48, *Code of Federal Regulations.* These regulations became effective April 1, 1984, and represented an attempt at consolidating all of the various government procurement regulations previously promulgated by the various federal agencies.

Unfortunately, two events taking place since the publication of the original document have resulted in the regulations again becoming complex and confusing. The first was that under the *FAR,* agencies were allowed to issue supplements covering areas specific to that agency which were not addressed in the basic *FAR.* Although these supplements could not contradict the *FAR* and were not supposed to be redundant, over time these supplements have grown tremendously. Not only does DoD have a supplement which is larger than the *FAR* itself, but each service within DoD has its own supplement to the DoD supplement. Therefore, to know all of the rules governing a particular Army contract, you must know the *FAR,* the DoD supplement to the *FAR,* the Army supplement to the DoD supplement, and so on.

The second problem with the *FAR* resulted from politics. The *FAR* went a long way to clarify the rules of government contracting for contracting officers and contractors. Unfortunately, it did not do much for congressional understanding of the system. Relying on media reports and government audits which occasionally misrepresent or misinterpret the facts, Congress has apparently determined it must micro-manage the government procurement system. As a result, legislation is continually being passed specifying detailed procedural requirements which significantly complicate the system as envisioned in the original *FAR.* The *Competition in Contracting Act* and the *Small Business Enhancement Act* are two of the most significant pieces of legislation falling into this category.

As already discussed, certain provisions of these acts were long overdue. For example, the recognition of negotiating as a legitimate competitive method of procurement. However, generally these laws simply complicated the system, placing additional bureaucratic demands on an already overburdened system. If the the time, effort and money which has gone into continually attempting to change the system had been invested in educating contracting officers and contractors on how to use the system as designed, an end to the perceived problems would come much sooner. Congress for some reason has insisted on treating the symptoms of the problem rather than the causes. The reaction to the perceived problems has been to bandage the wound with words, rather than to heal the wound with education and action. Educating government personnel involved in contracting, instructing contractors, and allocating adequate resources to the contracting offices represent the answers to the problems Congress perceives in the system. Similarly, education, combined with appropriate effort, is the answer to the perceived concerns of prospective contractors.

Armed Services Pricing Manual:

After the *FAR*, including its supplements, the second most important document regarding negotiating government contracts is the *Armed Services Pricing Manual (ASPM)*. This manual establishes the DoD policy regarding cost and price analysis and the basic contract price negotiation procedures. For years this document has been the bible of government negotiations for both DoD and civilian agencies. It is the basic tool used by all knowledgeable contracting officers in preparing for complex contract negotiations. The *ASPM* also reflects the basic bias of the government contracting system towards concentrating negotiation efforts on the price aspect of government contracts through the objective approach, rather than the subjective. The document is published by the DoD Office of Acquisition Policy and recently was rewritten. It is available from DoD, Global Engineering Documents, and from government document sources. Excerpts from this manual are also included as an appendix in this book. It is important that contractors obtain the *ASPM* manual as a reference when preparing for negotiations with the government.

Multiple Award Schedule Policy:

Another document of critical importance to negotiating multiple award schedule contracts awarded by the General Services Administration is the *Multiple Award Schedule (MAS) Policy* issued by GSA. This policy statement provides the basic regulations and procedures for negotiating MAS Contracts and is not part of the *FAR*. Since MAS contracting assumes noncompetitive negotiating situations (albeit considered a competitive method of procurement), there are different rules which must be followed. This policy statement is also included as an appendix to this work.

Truth in Negotiations Act:

As we have repeatedly stressed, the government considers itself as a sovereign with certain rights above those of a normal business. One of the ways this is implemented is through the *Truth in Negotiations Act*. This act, passed in 1956, requires that contractors disclose cost and pricing data when negotiating government contracts under certain circumstances. This is to ensure the government is receiving goods and services under noncompetitive circumstances at fair and reasonable prices. One of the major complaints of government contractors is that this act requires companies to disclose confidential data regarding their internal operation to an outside source. There is a great deal of understandable reluctance to release this data, especially since there is a concern that competitors might be able to obtain the data from the government. Cost and pricing data requirements will be discussed in the next chapter. The point to be made here is that if you do not wish to comply with the *Truth in Negotiations Act*, the chances of obtaining a government contract are considerably reduced. You will be limited to only those contracts which are exempt from the disclosure requirements of the act. This approach is taken by many companies. The act does not require that you not make a profit—it does require that you think long and hard about *how* you are going to make a profit and the size it will be.

Regarding the fear that the information will be made available to your competitors—there is some truth and little truth. First, when dealing with government contracts there is certain information that must by law, principally the *Freedom of Information Act,* be made available to the public, including your competitors. For example, the terms and conditions of a contract, including the contractor and the price being paid by the government, must be made available to the public. However, there also is certain information which is prohibited by law from being released to your competitors and others—namely, proprietary financial and operational information such as cost and pricing data.

Many companies understand the restrictions on the legitimate release of certain information, but are concerned that if the information is given to the government it can be obtained by a competitor through illegitimate means or by mistake. Contracting personnel, like Internal Revenue Service personnel, are under a legal obligation not to release proprietary or confidential data. The *Federal Privacy Act* states that a government representative who violates that act by releasing such information can be sued in civil court for the violation. A company cannot stop the IRS from reviewing proprietary financial data and cannot stop a government auditor from reviewing this type of information if a government contract is awarded. Therefore, there is no logic in missing out on a government business opportunity by failing to comply with the requirement to submit cost and pricing data during the proposal stage simply because you are concerned over improper release of the information.

Contracting Officers:

The tendency of contractors new to doing business with the government is to assume that government contracting personnel know what they are talking about—that they are highly-trained professionals, competent in their work. The public, on the other hand, believes that government employees are lazy incompetents and a burden on the taxpayers. The truth, of course, is somewhere between these two perceptions.

There is no question that the better the contracting officer is, the better it is for the taxpayer, the government, and the prospective contractor. A competent contracting officer knows that the rules of the game are fair and that the goal of government procurement is to obtain the required supplies or services at fair and reasonable prices, including a reasonable profit for the contractor. A competent contracting officer will implement the rules using discretion as necessary to ensure that this bottom line objective is met. An incompetent contracting officer will either not know the rules, not understand them, or will fail to implement them for some other reason. It is the incompetent contracting officer whom a contractor must guard against.

The major benefit of the government system is that if you know the rules, you can force even the incompetent contracting officer to follow regulations. Unfortunately, as government operating budget restrictions become even tighter, contractors more and more must ensure that their rights are being protected. When resources are reduced to a point where the workload becomes unmanageable, even a competent contracting officer can fail to follow the rules, either intentionally or unintentionally. The same is true in any profession. Contractors must protect their individual rights by having a thorough understanding of the system.

Chapter 6

Government Negotiating Procedures

This chapter will review the step-by-step formal procedures government contracting officers are directed to follow when receiving proposals in response to a solicitation (RFP) and in conducting contract negotiations.

Pre-negotiation Procedures:

The easiest way to view the proposal evaluation process is to look at it as a weeding-out process with the contracting officer sequentially reducing the number of proposals received until only one offer, or (in more cases than one would expect) no offer is left. The longer an offeror's proposal remains under evaluation, the higher the probability of obtaining the contract.

From the government's point of view, the more offers the better—keep in mind that one of the cornerstones of government contracting is that true competition will automatically yield fair and reasonable prices. However, this desire for maximum competition must be tempered with the fact that only a limited number of proposals can reasonably be expected to be evaluated for any one contract. As a result, the amount of flexibility an offeror has in revising an offer during negotiations, in order to stay under consideration for a longer period of time, will often be directly related to the number of proposals received. Further, what may be an acceptable response to one solicitation under one set of circumstances may not be acceptable under another set of circumstances.

Acceptable vs. Unacceptable Proposals:

After proposals have been received in response to an RFP, the first step a contracting officer will take will be to review the proposals and eliminate those which clearly have no chance of being considered for award. This is done without providing the offerors an opportunity to revise their proposals. Those proposals which are considered unacceptable must in some way fail to comply with the mandatory terms and conditions of the solicitation or otherwise be so deficient that there clearly is no possibility of that offer being considered for award.

One example would be a large business submitting a proposal in response to a solicitation which was set aside for small business participation only. Other examples include an offer to supply a foreign manufactured product when submitted in response to a solicitation which requires a 100% domestic product and an offer which was so deficient from a technical design point of view that it clearly could not be considered for award.

The contracting officer's objective is to waste as a little time as possible, both for government personnel and the contractor, when an offer clearly cannot be considered for award. In making this decision, the contracting officer only considers the offeror's proposal and the terms and conditions of the solicitation. The offer is not considered relative to the other offers received at this stage in the evaluation process.

Some of the guidelines which have been provided to contracting officers regarding this preliminary evaluation of proposals include:

- A proposal should be considered unless it is so technically inferior that there is no possibility that discussions might result in an improvement to the point where the proposal could be selected for award.

- When a criterion is used to reject one proposal, it must be used to evaluate other proposals as well.

- An offeror who fails to comply with the mandatory factors listed in the RFP can be eliminated.

- An initial decision that a proposal is unacceptable is no bar to a later reversal of that decision.

- It is legally permissible to eliminate all offers but one based on technical considerations.

- Offerors should not be excluded solely because the information provided in their proposals is inadequate to allow full evaluation; however, a proposal which is so inadequate as to exhibit an offeror's lack of understanding may be excluded.

When a proposal is due to the government, if you do not have time to prepare a proposal which describes your offer in the best way possible, it is usually best to at least get some kind of basic proposal in on time. As shown above, if you are responsive to the mandatory provisions of the solicitation, there is a chance you will be given an opportunity to revise and refine your proposal later. If your original offer is not submitted on time, with very few exceptions it will not be considered for award no matter how good the proposal. Initial proposals must be adequate to demonstrate an understanding of the requirement and to result in the contracting officer determining that the offer falls within the "competitive range."

During this preliminary decision phase, contracting officers are permitted to clarify proposals with individual offerors. Clarification is defined as:

> "communication with an offeror for the sole purpose of eliminating minor irregularities, informalities, or apparent clerical mistakes in the proposal. It is achieved by explanation or substantiation, either in response to a government inquiry or as initiated by the offeror."

Clarification applies to matters of fact, not discretion. In government terminology, it is not the same as conducting discussions with an offeror. Although this distinction between clarification and discussion may seem trivial, it is of extreme importance to offerors. The term "discussion," when used relative to government contract negotiations, is defined as:

> "any written or oral communication between the government and an offeror (other than communications conducted for the purpose of clarification), whether or not initiated by the government, that (a) involves information essential for determining the acceptability of the proposal, or (b) provides the offeror an opportunity to revise or modify its proposal."

The key distinction between these terms is that in the clarification stage, an offeror is not given the opportunity to revise or modify the proposal. During the discussion stage, an offeror is provided the opportunity to revise the proposal. In addition, a contracting officer can clarify a proposal with only one offeror, and award the contract without clarifying any other proposals and without conducting discussions with any of the offerors. The government always reserves the right to award a contract based on the initial offers received in response to a request for proposal without discussions if it deems such an award appropriate. If a contracting officer conducts discussions with any one offeror, they must, as a minimum, provide all other responsible offerors who submitted proposals within the competitive range an opportunity to revise or modify their proposals.

Competitive Range:

After a contracting officer has weeded out the totally unacceptable offers, the next step is to determine which proposals fall within a "competitive range." The competitive range is based on the evaluation factors stated in the solicitation and is supposed to include all proposals that have a reasonable chance of being selected for award. Contracting officers are encouraged to broadly interpret the solicitation requirements when determining whether an offer is or is not within the competitive range. If there is any doubt whether an offer should be included, it is to be included.

However, as is the case whenever the word "reasonable" appears in a regulation, someone, somewhere along the line, is going to be making a subjective decision. What is reasonable to one person may or may not be reasonable to another. Once the decision is made that a proposal no longer has a reasonable chance of being selected for contract award, the proposal is no longer considered.

Contractors are protected against an unreasonable decision concerning whether their offer is to be considered within the competitive range. This is true generally whenever a subjective decision is permitted to enter into the federal procurement process. Throughout the federal government procurement system, the government endeavors to provide recourse for prospective contractors to ensure that they are treated fairly and reasonably. Unfortunately, a prospective contractor cannot rely on the government personnel to ensure that they are advised of, and take advantage of, the rights available to them. Rather, it is up to the offerors to know what their rights are and to exercise them appropriately.

Responsible Contractors:

During this initial evaluation process, the contracting officer will also be evaluating the offerors to determine if they meet the basic responsibility requirements applicable to all government contracts. The government has strict policy that purchases shall be made from, and contracts awarded to, responsible contractors only. No purchase or award can be made unless the contracting officer makes an affirmative determination that the prospective contractor is a "responsible contractor," regardless of the merit of the offer.

It is the duty of the prospective contractor to affirmatively demonstrate its responsibility, including when required, the responsibility of its subcontractors. In the absence of information clearly demonstrating that the prospective contractor is responsible, the contracting officer must assume that the contractor is nonresponsible.

The general standards of responsibility are provided in *FAR* Subpart 9.104. To be determined responsible, a prospective contractor must:

1. Have adequate financial resources to perform the contract or the ability to obtain them.

2. Be able to comply with the required or proposed delivery or performance schedule, taking into consideration all existing commercial and governmental business commitments.

3. Have a satisfactory record of integrity and business ethics.

4. Have the necessary organization, experience, accounting and operational controls, and technical skills, or the ability to obtain them.

5. Have the necessary production, construction, and technical equipment and facilities, or the ability to obtain them.

6. Be otherwise qualified and eligible to receive an award under applicable laws and regulations.

In addition to these general standards of responsibility, special standards may be developed for a particular acquisition. If applicable, special standards must be set forth in the solicitation and apply to all offerors.

This regulatory policy counters the widely-held belief that all government contracts are awarded to the lowest priced offer. Contracts are awarded to the responsible offeror whose offer is most advantageous to the government, price and other evaluation factors considered.

If a large business has been determined to be nonresponsible, a protest must be filed to overturn the decision. If a small business is found to be nonresponsible, the offeror will be given a second chance at presenting evidence to support its cause. This will be accomplished through the Certificate of Competency (COC) Program of the Small Business Administration (SBA). If a small business is determined nonresponsible and is otherwise in line for award, the contracting officer must request a COC decision from the SBA. The SBA will decide whether to issue a Certificate of Competency to the offeror for the pending contract. The SBA will obtain additional information from the offeror and make a decision. If a COC is issued, the contracting officer must either accept the decision or appeal it to a higher authority within SBA. Generally, contracting officers accept the SBA decision. In the long run, it is easier to award a contract and terminate it for default if the contractor fails, than it is to appeal the original decision. This is an extremely beneficial program for small businesses since one of the principle functions of the SBA is to help them meet minimum responsibility criteria. If a contractor cooperates with the SBA and has a realistic chance at performing the required contract, the odds are highly in favor of that offeror being issued a COC.

The major point to remember regarding acceptable and unacceptable offers is that once a contracting officer goes beyond the clarification stage and begins discussions with any one offeror, it is a whole new ball game. Any responsible offeror within the competitive range must be given the opportunity to revise its proposal in any way it chooses.

Prior to discussions taking place, all an offeror can do besides clarify the proposal is withdraw it from consideration. This may be done any time prior to contract award when an offer has been submitted in response to an RFP. This is different than when submitting a bid in response to a sealed bid solicitation. A bid in response to an IFB is valid for a specific period of time and cannot be withdrawn, with very few exceptions, prior to the end of the acceptance period stated in the bid. The difference between the two processes is based on the basic contract law concepts of "offer and acceptance" and when a binding contract is formed. Contracting officers do not like to publicize this right since in some cases, the ability to withdraw the offer might provide leverage to offerors during the negotiation process.

Notification of Unacceptability:

Under government procurement regulations, contracting officers are required to notify in writing an unsuccessful offeror at the earliest practicable time that its proposal is no longer eligible for award. The notice must at least state in general terms the basis for the determination and that a revision of the proposal will not be accepted. They are also required to provide a formal debriefing to unsuccessful offerors if requested. As are most matters concerning an interpretation of the regulations, when a decision is made that a proposal is unacceptable, such a decision is subject to a formal protest.

Contracting officers are instructed to include a proposal within the competitive range whenever there is any doubt whether it should be included. It is considered better to err on the side of including proposals, rather than eliminating them. Proposals can always be eliminated later if they are found to be truly unacceptable.

After these preliminary decisions have been made, the contracting officer is left with proposals from responsible offerors which are acceptable and fall within the competitive range. These are the offers which will be negotiated—if negotiations are held.

Award Without Negotiations:

Prior to opening discussions with any one offeror, the contracting officer will determine if the award can be made without conducting formal negotiations. Normally, this decision will be made under the following conditions:

- When it can be clearly demonstrated from the existence of full and open competition or accurate prior cost experience with the product or service, that acceptance of the most favorable initial proposal without discussion would result in the lowest overall cost to the government;

- At a fair and reasonable price; and

- As long as the solicitation notified all offerors that an award might be made without discussion, and in fact, no discussions have been held.

It is the exception, not the rule, that a contract is awarded without some form of formal discussions taking place with at least one offeror. If it were anticipated that contracts would be awarded on this basis, the solicitation probably would have been issued as a sealed bid solicitation in the first place. As a result, offerors within the competitive range will usually be given an opportunity to revise their proposal. Sometimes this opportunity may simply consist of receiving a request for a best and final offer. Whether or not the contracting officer has held discussions regarding your offer, once you are permitted to submit a best and final, you can revise the proposal in any way you deem appropriate.

Before the negotiations can begin, the contracting officer has a considerable amount of work which must be completed in preparation for conducting the negotiations.

Cost and Pricing Data:

There are laws and ethics applicable to negotiating in the private sector (Anti-Kickback Status, Uniform Commercial Code, etc.) just as there are in the public sector. Perhaps the biggest difference is the amount of information the government can obtain regarding your position and vice versa. Partially to offset this disadvantage, the government has given itself the right to obtain as much information from offerors as needed to properly establish the government negotiation position.

Cost and pricing data is by far the most critical information which must be provided. The *Federal Acquisition Regulations* define cost and pricing data as meaning:

> "all" of the facts as of the time of the price agreement that prudent buyers and sellers would reasonably expect to affect price negotiations significantly. Cost or pricing data are factual, not judgmental, and are therefore verifiable. While they do not indicate the accuracy of the prospective contractor's judgment about estimated future costs or projections, they do include the data forming the basis for the judgment. Cost or pricing data are more than historical accounting data; they are all the facts that can reasonably be expected to contribute to the soundness of estimates of future costs and as to the validity of determinations of costs already incurred. They also include such factors as:
>
> (a) vendor quotations;
>
> (b) nonrecurring costs;
>
> (c) information on changes in production methods and in production or purchasing volume;
>
> (d) data supporting projections of business prospects and objectives and related operations costs;
>
> (e) unit cost trends such as those associated with labor efficiency;
>
> (f) make-or-buy decisions;
>
> (g) estimated resources to attain business goals; and
>
> (h) information on management decisions that could have a significant bearing on costs."

This definition of cost and pricing data has been reproduced in its entirety for two reasons. First, those of you interested in or currently doing business with the federal government must be aware of the extent of the data the government can request from you. Under the auspices of the *Truth in Negotiations Act,* the government can ask you for data from your accounting records, as well as information regarding all of the assumptions and contingencies you considered when evaluating the factual data in arriving at a final proposed price. This is the way in which the government attempts to get inside the head of the prospective contractor.

Government contracting officers are directed to obtain this cost and pricing data from government prime contractors and subcontractors under specific circumstances. The circumstances requiring this data involve the nature of the procurement, estimated dollar value, and the competition received. Basically, the criteria is that all contract awards or modifications of prime and subcontracts, where the value of the contract or modification is over $100,000, will require that cost and pricing data be submitted unless one of the exceptions to this requirement applies. There are even provisions for the contracting officers to request this data for any contract over $25,000 if necessary to determine the reasonableness of the price. Contracting officers are given significant authority to request this data if they deem it appropriate.

The second reason the complete definition is included is to identify the type of analysis contractors should make in evaluating, the price of a proposal, in attempting to evaluate the government's position, and in establishing the objective position applicable to a specific negotiation.

Cost and Pricing Data Exemptions:

As mentioned above, this data is required for all contracts meeting the established criteria unless specifically exempted from the requirement. The *FAR* exemptions describe specific circumstances which would enable a contracting officer to obtain independently verifiable information of the fairness and reasonableness of the price without cost and pricing data. These exemptions include situations where:

- Adequate price competition was received. If a price can be determined to be reasonable based on the receipt of adequate price competition, cost and pricing data does not have to be obtained. However, the definition of adequate price competition is very restrictive. Adequate price competition is considered to exist if:
  — offers were solicited, and
  — two or more responsible contractors, capable of satisfying the government's requirements, submitted priced offers, which are
  — responsive to the solicitations' expressed requirements, and
  — these offerors competed independently for a contract to be awarded to the responsible offeror submitting the lowest evaluated price.

- Established catalog or market prices. Prices can be evaluated for reasonableness by comparing the prices with established catalog or market prices. Such prices must be for commercial items sold in substantial quantities to the general public, under similar contract terms and conditions as those proposed by the government. Again this is a restrictive definition and if attempting to avoid submitting costs and pricing data based on this exemption, you should review the details regarding this exception contained in *FAR* Subpart 15.804-3(c).

- Prices set by law or regulation. An example of this kind of price would be a utility rate or similar predetermined prices which are non-negotiable.

For a potential contract meeting the regulatory circumstances discussed above, cost and pricing data will be required unless the specific procurement and the offers received fall under one of these three exceptions to the requirement.

Certified Cost and Pricing Data:

When certified cost and pricing data is obligatory, the contracting officer will require that the contractor execute a certificate stating that the cost or pricing data provided is accurate, complete, and current as of the date the contractor and the government agreed on a price. This certificate is an attempt by Congress to hold managers of organizations submitting such data responsible for its accuracy. This also legally positions the government so that it can take appropriate action if the data submitted is later found to be inaccurate.

Defective Cost and Pricing Data:

If, after award, cost and pricing data is found to be inaccurate, incomplete or non-current as of the date of the price agreement, the government is entitled to a price adjustment. This includes an adjustment of the profit or fee of any significant amount by which the price was increased because of the defective data. This means that, after the fact, the contracting officer will review the negotiations and the data previously provided. Then, with the new data, the contracting officer determines what price would have been negotiated if the new data had been known at the time of the original price negotiations. The contracting officers are given a second chance at the negotiations without the contractors having a chance to defend their position. Certainly, every contracting officer is a better Monday morning quarterback than on the day of the game. This is not a desirable position for a contractor. Contractors must be careful that the cost and pricing data submitted are as accurate, complete and current as is reasonably possible.

Cost and Price Analysis:

After the contracting officer receives the cost and pricing data, or determines that the situation meets one of the exceptions to this requirement, price or cost analysis is performed as appropriate to determine the reasonableness of the price. The subject of cost and price analysis is a subject of an entire book in itself. Anyone interested in doing business with the federal government should obtain and read the *Federal Acquisition Regulations* and *ASPM No. 1* for details regarding cost and price analysis. Not only will this serve as an excellent base for evaluating the government's position, but the information can be applied to establishing your position as well. This is particularly useful if you do not already have an adequate cost estimating and pricing system in place.

One of the biggest problems in negotiating price with the government is simply semantics. If your accounting system does not conform to the government's Cost Accounting Standards, your negotiations will be complicated simply by referring to different costs under different names. This is another reason to become familiar with the *FAR* and the *ASPM* regarding cost and price analysis.

Pre-award Audits and Inspections:

When evaluating proposals, the government contracting officer has potentially unlimited resources available to assist in determining the reasonableness of a price. Often a price analyst will have completed a full cost and price analysis, which is forwarded to the contracting officer with appropriate recommendations. Still, determining the reasonableness of the price is the contracting officer's responsibility and, perhaps, is the strongest power they have. The General Accounting Officer, for example, will not consider a protest concerning a determination of price reasonableness. It considers the authority for making this determination to be solely delegated to the contracting officer.

Contracting officers can obtain assistance from agency technical personnel in the technical evaluation of proposals, finance personnel when evaluating the financial capability of prospective contractors, auditors for field pricing support, and inspectors for evaluating a contractor's production and technical capability, and more.

Often, contracting officers are required by regulation to obtain specific assistance. At other times, they are denied the requested assistance due to staffing and funding limitations imposed on the support offices. Each situation, as is usual in contract negotiations, is unique. Prospective government contractors should view each of the government's support offices as another potential ally in the negotiation process. Often prospective contractors respond to requests for information and pre-award audits with skepticism, distrust and annoyance. This in the long run will adversely affect the contractor's negotiating position. Cooperating with contracting officer support personnel is the best way to ensure that your message is passed on through them to the contracting officer, possibly with an endorsement from the support personnel. Pre-award inspections provide an excellent opportunity to prove the reasonableness of your position. A contractor's preparation for a meeting with the government's procurement support personnel should be just as extensive as the preparation required for negotiating with the contracting officer.

Source Selection:

Usually the contracting officer will determine the offer which will be accepted for contract award. This is either done independently or with assistance from appropriate support personnel. Offers are evaluated relative to the solicitation requirements, the reasonableness of the price and the responsibility of the prospective contractor.

For high dollar value, complex acquisitions, a formal source selection group is sometimes established to evaluate offers. Such source selection organizations typically consist of an evaluation board, an advisory council, and a designated source selection official at a management level above that of the contracting officer.

Whether evaluated by the contracting officer alone or by a formal source selection organization, the factors used in the evaluation process and their relative importance must be clearly stated in the solicitation (RFP). Any minimum requirements which must be met in the offer relative to any specific evaluation factor must also be stated. The specific numerical weights which may be employed in the evaluation of proposals, however, do not have to be disclosed.

The evaluation factors usually will be included or referenced in Section M of the solicitation document under the heading "Method of Award" or "Evaluation Factors for Award." It is essential that prospective contractors thoroughly review and understand these factors prior to submitting a proposal. Obviously, this information is critical to the contract negotiation process and cannot be overlooked. The evaluation factors often form the basis for negotiation objectives established by both parties.

Cost Accounting Standards

Public Law 91-379 requires that certain national defense contractors and subcontractors comply with the *Cost Accounting Standards (CAS)* published by the Cost Accounting Standards Board. This includes the requirement to disclose in writing and follow consistently the contractor's actual cost accounting practices. This policy has been extended to certain non-defense contractors as a matter of policy.

The contracting officer is responsible for determining when the cost accounting standards should apply to a particular procurement, and if so, must include the appropriate clauses implementing this requirement in the solicitation. Application of the cost accounting standards, however, is not only dependent on the nature of the acquisition, it is also dependent on the nature of the contractor. For example, small businesses are exempt from the cost accounting standard requirements. When and if these standards apply is totally dependent on the specific procurement and the specific contractor being awarded the contract. *FAR* Part 30 includes the detailed requirements regarding the applicability of these standards and lists the exceptions to these requirements.

If the standards do not apply to your company, they can still prove helpful in negotiating government contracts. Government auditors and price analysts view all costs within the framework of these standards. Thus, when reviewing your offer, they will view your costs from a *CAS* perspective. Recognizing this when preparing your proposal and understanding the basic requirements of the *CAS* will ensure that you do not get caught up in arguing semantics and procedures during negotiations rather than projected costs.

Establishing Negotiation Objectives:

Prior to conducting negotiations, government contracting officers are required to establish negotiation objectives. These objectives can relate to price as well as any other aspect of the solicitation or proposal.

Contracting officers are directed to establish a maximum, a minimum, and a target objective regarding price. The objectives are established using all of the information available to the contracting officer, including:

- The solicitation and the offers received.
- Technical evaluations of the offers.
- Pre-award audit reports.
- Field pricing support reports.
- Cost and price analysis.
- Other information applicable to evaluation of the proposal.

After establishing the objectives, contracting officers must document the objectives and often must have them approved at a higher level in the organization prior to actually commencing negotiations with the offerors. Setting pre-negotiation objectives will be discussed in more detail in the next chapter.

Price Negotiation Memorandum and Approvals:

Contracting officers must document their negotiations in a Price Negotiation Memorandum (PNM). This document explains the negotiation process for the particular acquisition beginning from the point offers are received.

As a minimum the PNM must include the following:

- The purpose of the negotiation.
- A description of the acquisition.

- The name, position, and organization of each person representing the contractor and the government in the negotiation.
- The current status of the contractor's purchasing system when material is a significant cost element.
- If certified cost and pricing data were required, the extent to which the contracting officer:
  — Relied on the cost or pricing data submitted and used in negotiating the price, and
  — Recognized as inaccurate, incomplete or noncurrent any cost or pricing data submitted, the action taken as a result and the affect of the defective data on the price negotiated.
- If cost or pricing data were not required in the case of any price negotiated over $100,000, the exemption or waiver used and the basis for claiming or granting it.
- If cost or pricing data were required in the case of any price negotiated under $100,000, the rationale for such requirement.
- A summary of the contractor's proposal, the field pricing report recommendations, and the reasons for any pertinent variances from the field pricing report recommendations.
- The most significant facts or considerations controlling the establishment of the pre-negotiation objective and the negotiated price including an explanation of any significant differences between the two positions.
- The basis for determining the profit or fee prenegotiation objective and the profit or fee negotiated.

These are the minimum requirements which must be included in the contracting officer's PNM. Contractors negotiating with the government should be aware that the contracting officer must address each of these points. They should be prepared to provide information during the negotiation defending their proposal in a manner which contracting officers can use when writing the PNM.

Documentation and Review Process:

After negotiations are completed and the price negotiation memorandum prepared documenting the negotiations, the contracting officer's recommendation for award usually will be reviewed and approved at a higher level within the organization. Frequently, the proposed contract award will have to pass through several offices for concurrence or approval prior to finalization.

Prospective contractors should be aware that this review process can take considerable time to complete. Also, no matter how final the contracting officer seems at the conclusion of the negotiations, the process may still not be over if one of the review officials adopts a position contrary to that of the contracting officer.

Contracting Officer Prohibitions:

During negotiations contracting officers and other government personnel involved are prohibited from using the following techniques:

- Technical Leveling. Helping an offeror to bring its proposal up to the level of other proposals through successive rounds of discussion, such as pointing out weaknesses resulting from the offeror's lack of diligence, competence, or inventiveness in preparing the proposal.
- Technical Transfusion. They cannot disclose technical information pertaining to a proposal that results in an improvement of a competing proposal.
- Auction Techniques. This restriction prohibits using such techniques such as:
  — Indicating to an offeror a cost or price which it must meet to obtain further consideration.
  — Advising an offeror of its price standing relative to another offeror. It is, however, permissible to advise an offeror that the government considers its cost or price to be too high or unrealistic.
  — Otherwise furnishing information about any other offeror's prices.

A violation of any one of these prohibitions is subject to a formal protest. The best way to prevent these techniques from being used is to subtly make the contracting officer aware that you know they are prohibited from engaging in such techniques. If you do this, be careful not to alienate the contracting officer by making it appear you are threatening. Rather, bring it up in a friendly, indirect way.

Best and Final Offers:

Once discussions have been held with any one offeror, all offerors within the competitive range must be given an opportunity to submit a best and final offer. Each offeror still within the competitive range will be notified that best and final offers will be accepted. A common cutoff date and time will be established allowing a reasonable opportunity for submission of written best and final offers. The date and time established at this stage is just as critical as the date and time established for the receipt of the initial proposals.

Following the evaluation of the best and final offers, the contracting officer or other designated source selection authority will select that source whose best and final offer is most advantageous to the government, considering price and the other evaluation factors included in the solicitation.

Changing Your Offer:

Anytime prior to contract award, you may withdraw a proposal submitted in response to an RFP. After the contracting officer has opened discussions, you may modify your offer in any way you deem appropriate. This includes submitting a revised offer in response to the request for best and final offers.

Reopening Negotiations:

Contracting officers are directed to not reopen negotiations after receipt of the best and final offers unless it is clearly in the government's best interest to do so. If discussions are reopened with any offeror, the contracting officer must issue an additional request for best and final offers to all offerors still within the competitive range.

Contract Award:

The contracting officer will notify the successful offeror by transmitting written confirmation. This confirmation documents the contract award and will reference the original solicitation, the offeror's original proposal, and any changes agreed to during the negotiation process. It will also identify the offeror's best and final offer as the offer accepted by the government.

This chapter concludes the discussion of the federal government's contract negotiation procedures. It is essential that government contractors understand these procedures to maximize their potential for conducting successful negotiations. These procedures also provide an excellent model for establishing proper negotiation procedures in any organization. Using these government procedures as a foundation, the following chapters discuss the recommended approach to negotiating government contracts. The procedures and techniques contained in these chapters are applicable to any complex negotiating situation.

Chapter 7

Pre-Negotiation Planning

If you take anything away from this book, take away a reinforcement of one of the classic recommendations regarding contract negotiations—BE PREPARED.

This most basic of all negotiating fundamentals cannot be overly stressed. In contract negotiations, knowledge is power. In government contracting, the side that prepares the most will be the most knowledgeable. This is because of the extraordinary amount of information available to both sides. In the real world, there will never be enough time to develop all of the information which could be obtained regarding any one negotiation session. The party which uses its time the most judiciously in obtaining and analyzing information will be in the best position to control the process.

The government places primary emphasis on the pre-negotiation planning phase of the negotiating process and, given the contracting officer's potential resources, the contractor must spend additional individual effort simply to stay even.

In the *ASPM*, the principles and techniques of negotiation are classified under the following headings:

- Preparation
- The Team
- Fact-finding
- Objectives
- Pre-negotiation Review
- Conference

Notice that each of these headings covers actions which actually are conducted prior to beginning "negotiations." Actual negotiations begin at the conference. Five of the six major classifications are related to preparation for the negotiations.

This chapter addresses the critical pre-negotiation activities, which prospective contractors should perform. The next chapter will discuss the negotiation conference.

Determining the Purpose of the Negotiations:

The first step in preparing for any negotiation is to determine why you are willing to negotiate with the other party. In the case of government contracting, are you negotiating at the request of the government or at your own instigation? Can you find out why the government is interested in negotiating with you? Is it because of the complexity of the technical requirements or is it because of a lack of competition? You should always try and determine as much as possible about the other party's position prior to entering negotiations.

It is important that a clear goal be defined for the negotiations and that this goal be understood by all of your representatives. There is a substantial difference in approaching negotiations when the goal is to obtain a contract at a specific price or level of profit, versus obtaining a contract at any price because of some intangible benefit to be gained.

Once the overall goal is established, specific objectives must be set which will result in achieving this goal.

Although it may appear that the primary goal should be to obtain the contract at the best price possible, there are many other considerations. One client I worked with was in the process of obtaining major refinancing through its bank. They were also negotiating a million dollar plus contract at the same time. During the contract negotiating, they had one goal in mind: to obtain the contract at almost any price in order to use the contract as collateral with the bank. This was the principal objective of the negotiations. Of course there was a bottom line price where the contract would have no value as collateral, but this point was so low the government would never have expected the contract to be awarded at that price.

Another client was willing to accept a contract at almost any price because it wanted its product to be considered the U.S. government "standard" for that commodity. This was their goal despite the strict restrictions on advertising using government contracts as an implied endorsement. If awarded the contract, the client was going to be the sole government contractor for this particular product. This had enough future benefit, relative to its international market, that they were willing to accept a contract at a price below cost if necessary. Obtaining the contract was the primary objective.

Another client wanted a particular contract simply as fill-in work for his commercial operation and was willing to accept the contract at cost. In his industry, due to a highly fluctuating workload, the government business represented steady business necessary to an economical operation. He too, was willing to settle for a much lower price than would normally be expected. I have had other clients whose only objective was to obtain a contract as long as the end price resulted in meeting strict corporate profit objectives. Unless the end price level projections indicated that the established minimum profit margins would be met, the client was willing to walk away from the contract.

Obviously the list of possible goals for entering into any contract negotiation is almost endless. The process of identifying your own goals and attempting to identify the goals of the other party is essential. In addition, the goals must be identified at the outset of the negotiation process. Once you decide you are going to negotiate a proposal, you must determine why you are willing to negotiate and identify exactly what it is you are willing to negotiate. The "why" is answered in order to determine the purpose of negotiating. The "what" is used to establish specific negotiation objectives.

Selecting the Negotiation Team:

After you have determined the overall goal, you can select the personnel best suited to assist in achieving this goal. This may include representatives from the sales or marketing departments; purchasing or contracting personnel; pricing specialists; production personnel; packaging specialists; or others specializing in accounting, maintenance, quality assurance, contract law, or the various engineering disciplines. One individual should be designated as the negotiation team leader. Once the composition of the team is determined, specific roles should be assigned and objectives established.

The roles depend upon the structure of the organization, the subject of the negotiations, and the skills of the individuals involved. Do not assume that the team leader is always the chief negotiator. Often it is best to appoint someone else as the negotiator, allowing the team leader to manage the overall approach to the negotiation. The amount of effort and extent of participation by the team members will vary depending on the circumstances of the negotiation. In some cases, one person may fill all the roles. A decision must be made concerning the resources needed to perform the negotiations and the resources must be identified as early in the negotiation process as possible.

Negotiation Objectives:

Perhaps the most difficult task I have encountered as a consultant helping others with their contract negotiations is convincing clients that they should establish their negotiation objectives in writing prior to commencing actual negotiations. The common approach by most small businesses is to have "some idea" of what they want to achieve and to be flexible based upon what the government requests. In large businesses, there is a tendency to state that they have formal company policies establishing what is acceptable, ignoring the need to identify the amount of flexibility acceptable given the circumstances specific to the situation. Even large companies have slow periods during which times it may occasionally be wise to deviate from pre-established policies.

Unless the questions are asked, there will be no answers. That is the purpose of the negotiation objective-setting process. The following four sections address setting proper negotiation objectives.

Fact-finding:

Prior to setting objectives, preliminary information gathering should take place. The government does this through obtaining certified cost and pricing data and by conducting pre-award audits and surveys. Prospective contractors should conduct similar information-gathering activities.

The government contracting agency will have purchased the identical products or services previously or, as a minimum, another government agency will have acquired similar products or services at some time in the past. One of the first steps the government takes in preparing for negotiations is to obtain the previous acquisition history for the items or services being purchased. Much of this prior procurement history is public information which should be obtained whenever negotiating with the government. Some of the information can be obtained directly from the contracting officer. Other information must be obtained by filing a request under the provisions of the *Freedom of Information Act*. In addition to information about the previous contract award, you should also determine the level of competition received by the government in response to the previous solicitation for the similar requirement. Before negotiating with the government, you should know what they paid previously for the same or similar products or services, who your competition is likely to be, and what the price is likely to be paid. In the government, this information is developed before commencing negotiations and is documented in the solicitation case file.

In addition to obtaining as much information about the government's situation as you can, you should find out as much about your competitors' positions as well—as long as the methods you employ are legal and ethical. For example, contract collusion clearly is not an acceptable means of obtaining information. Much of the needed information can be obtained simply as a result of competing in your industry on a daily basis. Some is obtained through the grapevine from customers or other competitors. Other sources, such as industry newsletters and publications, newspapers, or professional information services, are all possible legitimate sources of information.

The major problem with this information is that because of the its sensitivity, often the information is not disseminated to those in the organization who need to know. It is up to the negotiation team to investigate potential sources of competitor information, both within and outside of the company.

There is a great potential for abuse in this process. As always, the best advice is to play the game legally and ethically. Personal experience has shown that you can obtain as much information as you need to compete effectively through legitimate means without needing to resort to questionable practices, not to mention the moral and ethical implications involved.

Factfinding not only applies to obtaining information regarding the government's and competitor's positions, but must include obtaining as much information as possible about your own position. This is where the negotiation team is of particular value. You must determine what it is going to cost to perform the contract, and evaluate the accuracy of cost projections. Then evaluate the reasonableness of any contingencies specified in the certified cost and pricing data if submitted, and determine in what areas the negotiating team has available flexibility. Also included in this process is a thorough analysis of the requirements of the solicitation document. Can you perform the contract in accordance with the terms and conditions of the solicitation? If not, you must determine possible alternatives.

After you have obtained information concerning the positions of both parties to the negotiation, you still must ask yourself if there are any other facts relating to this negotiation, either directly or indirectly, which must be considered—facts which are beyond either party's control. Does the current economic forecast influence your negotiating position? Is the contracting officer limited due to agency budget restrictions? Are there intangible benefits associated with the contract, and if push comes to shove, what are you willing to pay for those benefits? These are the kinds of questions you need to ask about the circumstances surrounding the negotiating environment. After you have obtained as much information as time and resources permit, you should establish specific pre-negotiation objectives and a negotiation plan.

Establishing Pre-Negotiation Objectives:

Pre-negotiation objectives are not restricted to price, but include technical and contractual terms and conditions as well. In government contracting, other than public law, anything is negotiable. The regulations provide a great deal of leeway as long as it can be shown that the resulting agreement meets all of the statutory requirements of a government contract. This includes the contract being awarded in accordance with federal procurement procedures, and shown to be in the best interest of the government.

Negotiation objectives fall under one of the following categories:

- **Clarifications.** Although the government will have had an opportunity to clarify your proposal prior to opening discussions, there usually will be additional matters to resolve in the negotiation process. Prior to discussing the major issues, any unresolved questions must be identified and resolved. It is incumbent upon you to ensure you are talking apples and apples, or oranges and oranges, prior to starting the negotiations.

- **Technical.** The specifications or statement of work in a solicitation is always subject to negotiation. However, you should always be careful to ensure your initial proposal satisfies the minimum mandatory technical requirements as identified in the solicitation.

- **Contractual.** Government contracts in particular contain a number of contract terms and conditions which are just as binding on the contractor as the technical requirements. Often there are special reports which must be submitted during contract performance and other clauses require that specific requirements be passed on to your subcontractors. You must review all of the terms and conditions to ensure you understand your obligations under the contract. This includes reviewing all of the clauses and or documents incorporated by reference in the solicitation. The government is notorious for including contractual requirements by reference and not providing prospective offerors with the referenced documents. Government offerors are just as notorious for failing to obtain and read referenced documents prior to submitting an offer.

  Submitting an offer in response to a solicitation without knowing all of the the proposed terms and conditions of the contract is a questionable practice at best. Unless the referenced clauses and documents are reviewed, you do not know all of the terms and conditions applicable to that contract. This is one of the most common mistakes contractors make when negotiating with the government. Although the standard referenced information is essential to a thorough understanding of the proposed contract, it is one of the most frequently ignored aspects of the contract negotiation preparation process. To successfully negotiate, you must obtain, read and evaluate the impact of all referenced documents in any solicitation.

- **Price.** You must determine the maximum price you can justify in the negotiations as well as the lowest price you are willing to accept.

- **Quality.** The quality level can significantly impact the cost of performing a particular contract. The government often requires that high level quality assurance procedures be followed during contract performance under the contract. Prospective contractors must be sure to identify these requirements and consider the costs when establishing their price objectives.

- **Delivery.** Time is money and there is a cost associated with time. You must evaluate the delivery requirements and identify any related costs.

- **Alternatives.** After you have evaluated your position relative to the solicitation terms and conditions, you should identify any alternative terms and conditions which might better suit the needs and interests of your organization. Alternatives should be viewed relative to your competitive position and the potential for achieving the negotiation goals you established.

When evaluating alternatives, always try, if at all possible, to be able to discuss what it would cost to perform the contract exactly as required by the solicitation. No matter how difficult, or how high the price, your negotiating position will improve by offering to perform the contract as specified.

It will preclude your offer from being eliminated as unacceptable due to not responding to the mandatory requirements of the solicitation. It also will point out areas of the contract that might be expensive to perform, informing the contracting officer to ensure that your offer is compared with your competitors on the same basis. Providing a comparison in your proposal registers the difference between the government's requirements and your alternative in the contract file. This forces the contracting officer to document why the alternative was rejected. If the alternative is in the best interest of the government, providing details will make it more difficult to document why the alternative is not acceptable.

Objective Range:

Whenever possible, you should set an objective *range* when setting objectives. There are two types of objectives which can be established. The first is an absolute objective. These are the yes or no, go or no-go types of objectives in the negotiation process. Either you get the other party to agree or you will walk away from the contract. A requirement to supply a product consisting of a specific material which you cannot obtain is an example of this type of objective. Either an alternative material is negotiated as being acceptable or you cannot perform the contract. Yes or no. There is no room to negotiate on these types of objectives.

The other type of objective is the relative objective. These are objectives which do not impact the bottom-line capability to perform the contract, but do affect the desirability of it's performance. These are issues for which there is some relative discretion as to what is acceptable. Price is the easiest example of this type of objective. It is not simply a "yes" or "no" decision, but rather, how much?

When establishing relative objectives you should establish an acceptable range. For example, when setting a price objective you should determine the minimum acceptable price. This is the point at which any lower price would make the contract no longer desirable, regardless of any other factors. It is the bottom line position—the price below which you will not go. You should also set a maximum price. This is the highest price you believe you can demonstrate to the government as being fair and reasonable. The minimum and maximum price objectives represent the boundaries of your negotiation flexibility. This is referred to as the objective range.

When you establish this range, you are saying that you will be satisfied with any price that falls within that price range. The object of the negotiations is to reach agreement on a price which is at the high end of your objective range.

The objective range should be fixed unless new information is learned during the negotiations. Deciding in the middle of negotiations to revise your objectives, without new information, is not recommended. The wisdom of going below this minimum level without some long-term objective in mind should be thoroughly analyzed in this.

After you have established your objective range, you should establish a target objective within that range which represents the most realistic price you anticipate being able to negotiate. You should consider all of the circumstances and remember that your maximum objective represents your parochial point of view. It is important to establish this target objective to provide a realistic appraisal of the outcome of the negotiations.

Once you have established minimum, maximum and target objectives for all of the quantifiable relative objectives, and identified the absolute objectives, you should document them. The *25% Solution* is one approach to establishing and documenting objectives which will ensure that all possible influences applicable to the particular acquisition are considered.

Documenting Objectives:

Documenting the objectives and how they were determined serves a number of purposes. It provides a hardcopy document appropriate for pre-negotiation review and approval by officials in your organization as necessary. It also provides the negotiating team with a complete set of objectives, delineating the team's authority and flexibility. It provides an excellent reference source during negotiations for evaluating the progress of the negotiations and counter proposals. Proper documentation also assists in evaluating the success of the negotiations after completion. This past negotiation analysis can be an invaluable tool when preparing for future negotiation sessions.

Negotiation Conference Agenda:

After the objectives have been established and approved, a negotiation conference agenda should be established. Recognizing that the other party will also have an agenda, often both teams coordinate in advance and agree on a mutually agreeable agenda. This is not always the case. Sometimes the other party is not interested in establishing a mutually agreeable agenda. At other times it simply is not logistically practical. The government will usually establish its own agenda, but will consider the contractor's desires.

Regardless of who prepares the agenda, the important point is that your agenda include all of the issues your party needs to discuss to support your proposal and position regarding the potential contract. The agenda can also be used as a management tool and can be reviewed and approved as appropriate prior to actual negotiations.

Identifying Concessions:

Part of the negotiation process is to establish a common base upon which an agreement can be built. One of the best ways to establish this base is to demonstrate a willingness to concede to the other party's requests, if at all possible. During the pre-negotiation phase, you should identify any issues which may be of value or importance to the other team which do not have the same value or importance to you. These issues can be used during the negotiations as concessions to be agreed to, as necessary, to achieve your overall negotiating goal.

The identification of possible concessions is especially valuable in government negotiations because, frequently, what is important to the government may not be important to you. For example, very often price is not as important to the government as are the technical considerations. Often the extra time for delivery is more valuable to the contractor than it is to the government.

Sometimes these concessions are referred to as "throw-aways." From a successful negotiation point of view, no concession is a throw-away. To throw away something means you receive no value in return. Always in negotiations, you should have a reason for giving something away. You do not necessarily need to receive something in return, however, the concession should only be made with the objective of achieving your overall negotiation goal—not simply thrown away.

As the final step in your preparations for negotiations, you should document your overall negotiation strategy. All appropriate personnel should be in agreement on the approach to be taken prior to commencing negotiations. It is difficult to successfully negotiate an agreement with another party while members of your own team are disagreeing during the negotiation process. This does not mean that team members should not debate among the team and consider alternatives in private during negotiations. They must not, however, disagree in the presence of the other party or approach the negotiations with different strategies in mind.

If you have time to follow through on each of these recommended preparatory steps prior to the negotiation conference, you will be prepared. Unfortunately, usually you will not have enough time. When you do not, you must attempt to do the best you can given the time and resources available. Simply mentally walking through these various steps prior to the commencing negotiations will place you in a far better position than entering the negotiations with a "shoot from the hip," or "let's wait and see what happens" attitude. The single most important step you can take in an effort to maximize your potential for participating in successful negotiations is to: BE PREPARED.

Chapter 8

Conducting Negotiations

Preparing for negotiations is the hard part of the negotiation process. If you are adequately prepared, the actual negotiation are conference can be an enjoyable experience. It may seem like the kind of fun one has playing football. You usually get beat up a little, but if you win, you end up having a good time. Remember that there is always the possibility of a tri-win outcome. Otherwise, you would not have reached the serious negotiation stage. If you have prepared properly and are convincing in your arguments during the negotiations, an agreement acceptable to your organization is more than possible—it is probable.

This is not to say that participating in a negotiation conference is all fun and games. It is serious business and must be addressed as such. The stakes are usually too high to approach the negotiation meeting in a cavalier manner. In addition, even when successful, the celebration will always be tempered with thoughts of what you might have been able to accomplish. How far was the other side willing to bend? How much money did you leave "on the table"? If only you had had more time to prepare. These are all common thoughts that will run through your mind after negotiations have been completed—it's only natural. The better the other party's negotiator, the stronger these feelings will be. Viewing negotiation results in this way is a self-defeating exercise. Eventually you will begin to adopt a losing attitude towards the negotiation process. This is another reason it is important to document your objectives before going into the negotiating meeting. With the objectives documented in advance, no matter how exhilarating the emotional high after the negotiations are completed or how low, you will have an objective means of measuring how well you did relative to your overall negotiating goal. In contract negotiations it is recommended you develop an attitude similar to that of the best of players in any game: enjoy the successes, analyze the mistakes, learn from the mistakes, and apply what you learned to the next game. There will always be another negotiation waiting for you around the corner.

As in any kind of human interaction activity, there is no universal right or wrong approach to conducting the negotiation meeting. The skills and experiences of all of the people involved in the process must be taken into consideration, along with all of the other circumstances of the specific negotiation situation. The *25% Solution,* considering all of the circumstances influencing the specific situation, is one method of preparing for contract negotiations which will help determine the approach to a particular negotiation meeting. The following discussion applies to all negotiation conferences, whether they consist of one-on-one, telephone, written, or full team participation negotiations at another party's location.

Controlling Negotiations:

To maximize your potential for success, your goal is to remain in control of the negotiations to the maximum extent possible. This is not easy since the other party will also be vying for control. The government, for example, directs its contracting officers to always be in control of their contract negotiations. The trick to succeeding at this aspect of negotiations is to be in actual control while making the other party believe that they are in control.

Outside influences may be such that you cannot control the situation. If you identify these influences and evaluate how they affect both parties, you may still be able to control the negotiations. If the outside influences are so strong that you could not be in control of the negotiations in any way, you probably should not be negotiating in the first place. Without exception, the better prepared you are for the negotiations, the the better your chances are of being in control of the negotiation process.

Place:

Where is the best place to physically hold the negotiation conference? Growing up just outside of Detroit taught me one fact of life very early: if you are going to have a confrontation, it is best to have the confrontation on your own turf. Referring once again to the baseball game analogy, you can never underestimate the importance of having the home field advantage. It is always best to have your total support group close at hand. This applies whether they are fans, engineers, administration or production personnel. It is always best to have control of the physical environment and the tools available to the participants. This is true whether it is the type of surface of the playing field or the type of computer system available for your immediate use. Still, for every rule in negotiations, there are times when the exact opposite will be more appropriate. Sometimes, it may be wiser to go to the other party's location. There are a number of strategic decisions which need be made if you are given the opportunity to control the site selection. Usually the government will make you visit their location, but not always. Sometimes the contractor can decide on the meeting location, even when negotiating with the government.

If you are in control of selecting the negotiation site, evaluate the strategic implications and plan ahead for space accordingly. Unless you are intentionally trying to portray a disorganized image—which some people occasionally do—there is no worse start to a meeting than to force the other party to stand around waiting while you try and find some place to meet. Be Prepared. How many times have you had a meeting scheduled, only to arrive and have the person you were to meet swear they had a room reserved for the meeting, but somebody else messed up, and it is not available? How did you feel about that organization? That individual? Don't let this happen to you. Plan ahead and always double-check before the other party arrives to make sure your plans have not been canceled or changed by someone else.

Keeping in mind the long-term view, intentionally playing mind games with the facilities is not a sound idea. Rather, if you are fortunate enough to have the opportunity to arrange the meeting location, there are certain minimum facilities required. You should strive to provide appropriate facilities. If you are not in control of the negotiation site, you should request that, as a minimum, the site meet the following criteria:

- A conference room sufficiently large, well ventilated and maintained at a comfortable temperature.

- A conference table large enough to adequately seat all members of both teams with adequate surface space to handle work papers and support materials.

- A separate room, providing adequate privacy, located near the conference room so that either team can break from the negotiations and meet in private.

- Audio-visual aids which will help in your presentation, and any aids requested by the other party if you are the host.

- Telephones with suitable privacy available to both parties. You will find in team negotiations that a speaker phone is often useful.

This is the way the negotiating setting should be arranged. Unfortunately, it is usually not this organized in the real world. Normally, you will find you are either too cramped or put into a room large enough for a meeting ten times the size. During one negotiating session in which I was involved, we met in a beautiful meeting room with plush comfortable chairs and a large table, only to find that in order to meet alone, we had to frequently stand in the middle of a busy hallway reviewing our negotiating position as the office traffic was bustling by. It was not a desirable situation, but we made do. You too must remain flexible when visiting the other party's location—you must also be persistent. Don't let the lack of private space prevent you from adjourning the negotiations to meet with your team alone. Don't let the lack of a private telephone keep you from checking an important production point with your plant manager if you consider it appropriate. You can always meet alone with your team in a car in the parking lot. There are always pay telephones available. Don't let the facilities affect your negotiation style - that is how to remain in control of the facilities aspect of the negotiation conference.

Agenda:

As discussed in the previous chapter, you should have an agenda of the issues you wish to cover during the negotiation conference. The other party will also have an agenda. Sometimes there will be a mutually agreed upon agenda. Regardless of the form it takes, use the agenda as a reference and tool to ensure that all points needing to be discussed are covered at the meeting. Prior to completing the negotiations all issues should be resolved. At this stage in the process, you can no longer take a "let's take care of that later" attitude.

Time:

Does it matter what time of the day negotiations begin? Of course it does. The time of day can be used as a negotiating tool just like the facilities. In the negotiating process, there is even strategy involved in making this decision. How do you feel first thing in the morning, before your first cup of coffee? How do you feel right after lunch? Is the other party in the habit of having a beer or two at lunch? Are you? How do you feel about staying late to finish a negotiation? How does the other party feel? These are all questions you should ask before agreeing to a specific meeting time.

In some cases you may believe that the shorter the negotiations, the better it is for your organization. If so, schedule a meeting late in the afternoon. The biggest mistake in arranging time is the failure to allocate enough time to the negotiating conference. One can only speculate on the amount of money lost simply because someone had to catch a plane. Always have back-up travel plans. If you do, the other party cannot use time against you and rush you into decisions you might not otherwise make. That one rushed decision, made simply to conclude the negotiations more quickly, could always be the one decision that turns a winning contract into a loser.

Attendance:

Who should attend the actual negotiations? As always, it is dependent upon the situation. The negotiations might be conducted by holding one-on-one telephone discussions. They can be conducted via conference call, with teams on both sides in attendance. The process might consist of bringing your entire team to the other party's location, conducting negotiations in a large conference room with the entire opposing team. Certainly too many participants is not a good idea. On the other hand, it's usually not a good idea to take on six negotiators by yourself. In most negotiations, some balance between these two extremes is achieved.

The government requires that contracting officers have a government attorney present whenever a contractor has an attorney present, as long as a government counterpart is available. Likewise, if you know the government is going to have an attorney attend the conference, you will want to give careful consideration to having your legal counsel attend. Generally, the most important criteria is what the chief negotiator and negotiating team leader feel comfortable with given the specific negotiating situation. In some situations, it is best to have your entire team present throughout the negotiation conference. At other times, it is better to send only one representative with only limited authority. It all depends on the situation. In some cases, it is better to be prepared to make decisions on all aspects of the contract at the time of the negotiation conference. At other times, it is best to simply listen at the negotiation meetings and then regroup, discuss and evaluate where the the other party stands, and meet again. Proper negotiation preparation will help in making the right decision regarding who should attend the negotiation conference given the circumstances specific to the situation.

Method of Communication:

Negotiations can be conducted in person, by telephone, or completely through written correspondence. Once again this decision, if you are given the opportunity to make it, can influence the outcome of the negotiations. The most important factor to consider is the complexity of the negotiations. The more complex, the higher the probability you should attempt to meet in person.

Another major decision is the dollar value of the project. Do the potential rewards, monetary and other, justify the expense of sending an entire team across the country? Is the size of the potential contract worth an extended and expensive long distance telephone call? The potential value to you will help determine the amount of effort and the expense you wish to incur for any one negotiation.

You must also consider your own and your team's personnel strengths and weaknesses. Do you personally do well on the telephone? How well do you perform in one-on-one meetings? Do you negotiate better alone, or with your team present?

These are the types of questions you should ask when given a choice in determining which method of communication will be used to complete the negotiations. In addition to these individual considerations are the practical considerations. The time available to negotiate, logistic matters, the geographic locations of both parties, and so forth, will all have an impact on this decision.

Although a government contracting officer will usually tell you if they want to have a face-to-face meeting, this does not mean you cannot request one if you deem it important to your negotiating position. If you are persistent enough, and discussions have been opened, you will eventually be given the opportunity for a meeting. Likewise, just because the contracting officer asks you to attend a conference at the government site does not mean you have to go. You must evaluate the pros and cons given the circumstances of the negotiating situation when deciding which method of communication you will employ.

In reality, most complex negotiations involve all three mediums in the negotiation process. To be successful, you should master all three forms of communication. You must be able to communicate effectively in writing, on the telephone and in person. In this way, no matter which method of negotiating the other party chooses, your negotiating style will not be affected and you will be able to remain in control.

Understanding the Stages in the Process:

It is important you understand at what stage in the negotiation process you are currently at whenever communicating with the other party. When dealing with the government, it is critical to know whether you are in the clarification stage or the discussion stage. The answer may substantially affect the way in which you phrase a question or a response.

The Phases of a Negotiation Conference

At one time I had the opportunity to assist in conducting a series of intensive workshop-oriented government contracting seminars. One of the more interesting workshops involved mock negotiation training similar to that received by government contracting officers. It was surprising how realistic the actual negotiations became. One of the teams would play the role of a contractor and the other would represent the government. Each team was given a set of specific facts concerning the case study to enable them to establish appropriate negotiating positions. We had a rating system and gave awards to the most effective negotiating team so that a spirit of competition was created. This experience gave me an opportunity to compare a wide variety of negotiation styles and techniques, with all of the negotiations based on the same set of circumstances since the respective government and contractor teams were each given the same facts at each workshop. This experience verified my observations of actual negotiations as viewed from both the contractor and the government sides.

Based on these observations, negotiation conferences appear to progress through a series of common phases:

- Introduction Phase
- Ice Breaking Phase
- Opening Posturing or Gambits
- Establishing Mutual Understandings
- Negotiating Points of Contention

- Sequential Elimination of Issues
- Final Posturing
- Final Resolution
- Review and Summary
- Parting

Each of these phases of the conference is addressed in the following sections of this chapter.

Introduction Phase:

The importance of this seemingly innocuous initial phase of the negotiating process is often underrated and overlooked. The most common mistake I have seen contractors make is simply failing to find out who's who on the other party's team. The government representative will pass around a sign-up sheet asking for the name and title of each contractor representative. The contractor, unless familiar with each individual in attendance, should ask for a copy. This copy should include the names and titles of the government representatives. A good negotiation host will offer a copy to you. You can also pass around your own sign-up sheet. Not only do you want to know the name and title of each representative, you want to determine as best you can their actual authority within the organization. You should attempt to identify the decision makers and power brokers, both within the formal organizational structure and within the informal organization. These individuals may or may not be part of the other party's formal negotiation team. If not, often it will be in your best interest to attempt to bring these people into the actual meeting. Certainly this is true in government negotiations since often you will be negotiating with a contract specialist when you really need to be negotiating with the contracting officer. At other times, you may be stuck negotiating with the contracting officer when you really should be negotiating with the contract specialist. It is important that you know who the players are, their individual roles, and their formal and informal authority within the organization.

Ice-Breaking Phase:

After the formal introductions—or concurrently—there usually is a period of small talk simply killing time waiting for all the team members to arrive before the formal meeting begins. During this time, some preliminary jousting may take place, usually without pressure or commitment. It is the beginning of the formal dance of finding out where the other party is coming from. It represents an attempt at setting the actual tone for the negotiations.

Although both parties are usually aware that the best approach is one of mutual cooperation, the importance of the negotiating conference creates an ever-present, underlying air of tension. The government instructs its contracting officers that "a humorous anecdote often helps" to relieve this tension. You must be careful if you choose to use this approach. The classic warning about avoiding sex, politics, and religion was never more true than when it comes to the opening stages of contract negotiations.

Beginning with the introduction and ice-breaking phases of the negotiation process, you should be as observant as possible throughout the conference. This applies to both what is said and the nonverbal communication of all parties involved. There is usually as much nonverbal communication going on in a negotiation conference as there is verbal communication. This occurs not only between parties, but between the team members on each side. Being alert to all of the nonverbal communication taking place will help you to retain control of the process. You must also be aware that a good negotiator will be observing you in the same way. Take advantage of this particular stage in the negotiation process. You can learn more about who the true decision makers and power brokers are in the first five minutes of introductory chit-chat and preparatory group behavior than in five hours of formal across-the-table discussions.

This is another area where taking the long-term approach to negotiations is important. Over time, you will learn the relative ability of the individual participants to influence the outcome of the final agreement. You also will begin to recognize certain characteristics and traits of the personnel with whom you negotiate. The government warns contracting officers in this regard, advising them to change approaches and tactics with contractors to avoid becoming predictable.

Opening Posturing:

After the initial "My, aren't we all nice people" discussion, usually centering on the weather, sports, food, fashions or the latest news, the negotiation conference will move into another phase. This is the introduction of the "I'm a tough guy, you're all wet, and you better give in or we will never strike a deal" presentations. At this stage, the ice-breaking air of mutual cooperation is turned around into taking the position that "I'm the cooperative, reasonable party, and you're not."

This is the opening posturing or gambit phase of the conference. Picture a peacock in the preliminary stages of a mating dance. The show is the thing, not the substance. This will give you an idea of the flavor of this particular phase of the process. The amount of opening posturing you exhibit and the amount you have to endure will, like all else, vary depending upon the situation. One trend, however, is that this phase tends to last longer and becomes more intense with each successive negotiation meeting related to one specific contract. Each new meeting represents the fact that all of the issues were not resolved at the the last meeting and the tendency is to blame the other party. After all, "we" are the reasonable party at this stage in the negotiations.

Establishing Mutual Understandings:

After all the pawing and snorting associated with the opening posturing phase of the contract negotiation conference, the next step is to identify those areas of the proposed contract where true "agreement" exists and those issues which must be "negotiated." This is also the point where the parties differentiate between irrevocable facts and negotiable issues.

One mistake many prospective contractors make when negotiating with the government is to attempt to negotiate government acquisition policy when negotiating an individual contract. This effort will not result in a change in the policy. First, contracting officers are not in a position to change federal acquisition policy. They are required to operate within the framework of the established procedures. Second, it is unlikely that those in a position to change policy will be in a position to influence this policy in regard to a specific contract. This does not mean that policies over the long run cannot be changed through the proper channels. However, attempting to negotiate a change to established policy after a proposal is submitted in order to improve your chances for award, is not recommended. It would involve considerable effort and the odds for success are extremely low. If you want to change a government acquisition policy, handle the attempt to create the desired change as a separate issue.

Once the solicitation is issued, the policy in effect at the time, coupled with the terms and conditions of the solicitation, establish the rules under which you must negotiate. If you do not agree to abide by these rules, you must attempt to have them changed prior to submitting a proposal. After the proposal has been submitted and you have begun formal discussions, it is usually too late.

The same applies in the private sector. Getting a large corporation or a small company president to change a long-standing policy during negotiations for a specific contract is at the least, a difficult task. These types of changes need to be developed over time.

To retain control of the negotiations you cannot afford to be creating a bad negotiating environment over issues which are generally non-negotiable. Of course, if the issue falls under the category of being considered as one of your absolute objectives. (those which must be resolved or you will walk away from the negotiations), you may be forced to address these issues in the negotiations. It depends on the specifics of the situation.

Negotiating Minor Points of Contention:

This is the phase where you determine whether there really is a conflict between the parties concerning the issues which were not resolved during the previous phase. At this stage in the negotiation process, agreements come relatively easy. The issues are not the subject of intense negotiations, but are resolved through some of the more classic approaches such as give-and-take, compromise, etc. These issues are relatively easy to resolve because they are relatively minor.

There may be a tendency to skip this phase of the process and go right to the biggest problem areas, discussing the major issues first. This approach to negotiations is based on the theory that if the most important issues are irresolvable, there is no need to negotiate anything else. Although such an approach may be appropriate in some circumstances, usually it is more important to establish a mutually cooperative base before negotiating the more difficult issues. The best way to form this base or foundation is through cooperative practice and trial and error. Both parties practice cooperating on the smaller issues, moving up to the larger. Also, the longer you remain in the negotiation process, the higher the probability for success.

Narrowing the areas of disagreements down to those which really need to be negotiated provides the foundation and experience necessary to resolve larger differences. This approach is based on the theory that if either party did not believe the more significant differences were resolvable issues, they would not have reached this stage in the negotiation process.

Sequential Elimination of Most Issues:

After the minor issues have been resolved and the issues to be negotiated identified, the negotiation conference proceeds to the phase during which the parties attempt to resolve the remaining negotiable issues by establishing mutually acceptable positions. At this stage in the negotiation process, agreement with the other party's position is no longer relevant, nor necessary. Reluctant acquiescence is just as meaningful. You and the other party must only truly agree on one issue—the final terms and conditions of the end contract. How you get there, or why you get there, is only as important as far as how it helps you to achieve your overall negotiation goal.

All too frequently, people begin disagreeing over issues which really have no impact on the final outcome. Unless you are intentionally trying to draw attention away from a more meaningful issue, this is a totally nonproductive exercise and should be avoided. A common example is where negotiations break down over semantics. For example, assume the government does not agree to the 15% net profit desired by the contractor, but rather allows a maximum of 10% net profit. Frequently, concentrating on percentages such as these can create unnecessary problems. Further negotiation might reveal that the government is willing to agree to a 10% increase in cost based on the contracting officer's analysis of the certified cost and pricing data you submitted. Thus, the total end price might be at a level the contractor would find acceptable, despite the fact that the "profit" level was not. The government recognizes that this type of situation can frequently occur and discourages contracting officers from negotiating individual cost elements. They are directed to concentrate on the total price to be paid by the government. If you accept the total price, you do not have to agree on the individual elements which go into making up that price.

Many disagreements in negotiations with the government when discussing pricing can be attributed to semantic problems such as described in the example. Unless a company is a major government contractor and their accounting procedures designed in accordance with the requirements of the government's *Cost Accounting Standards*, there may be significant differences in how costs and profit are interpreted. It is important at this point in the negotiation process that you are negotiating real issues and not semantics or other non-issues.

After completing this stage of eliminating the majority of the differences between the two parties, only the most difficult issues should remain unresolved. If there are no more issues unresolved at this stage, the process skips the next two phases moving directly to the review and summary phase. This frequently is what happens when negotiating non-complex agreements involving little in the way of major negotiable conflicts between parties.

Final Posturing:

At this juncture, the negotiation conference ritual takes another turn. Prior to beginning serious discussions regarding the remaining unresolved issues, both parties will usually spend some time going through another posturing phase. Again the objective is to summarize how cooperative you have been and all of the concessions you have made. Each party attempts to explain why their position relative to the remaining issues is, out of necessity, firm. After this last show of force is completed, the next phase is the final resolution of the most serious issues.

Final Resolution:

It is at this stage in the negotiation process where all prospects for achieving a successful outcome to the negotiations seem most doubtful. The remaining issues are usually key issues and there will appear to be no room for movement by either party. Some refer to this as the point of reaching a stalemate or an impasse. Neither party sees an agreement in sight which would be satisfactory. This is the time to review your initial objectives, modifying them as appropriate based on any new verifiable information presented by the other party or obtained from other sources during the negotiations. Once again, remind yourself that the odds are substantially in your favor that there is some overlap between the positions of both parties. Work with the other party in an effort to resolve these remaining issues.

The government's stated objective in the contract negotiation process is to award a contract at a fair and reasonable price. If your objective is also to obtain a contract at a fair and reasonable price and your organization is capable of performing the contract, not reaching an agreement can only mean that one party or the other is being unreasonable. If it is you, then you should either change your position or walk away from the contract. If it is the government representative, enforce your rights in obtaining a fair and reasonable response to your offer. The same holds true in negotiating a commercial contract. If you cannot reach an agreement which is acceptable to you, considering all of the facts and circumstances relating to the negotiation, walk away from the contract. It will do neither party any good in the long run to proceed further.

If you prepare properly for the negotiation conference, approach the negotiations from a reasonable point of view and ensure that both you and the government or other party play according to the rules, you can maximize your potential for reaching an mutually acceptable outcome. This is the best you can expect from any negotiation situation. You can never guarantee that a mutually acceptable agreement will be reached between you and the other party. Competition and other outside influences may play too dominant a role. However, taking these steps will ensure that you maximize the potential *for achieving successful negotiations*.

Review and Summary:

It is important at the end of the negotiating session to summarize what took place and what agreements were reached. This should be done at any time during the negotiation process if you have any questions regarding the other party's current position or regarding their understanding of your position.

It is always essential you complete this phase of the process prior to concluding negotiations. When negotiations are concluded, both parties should clearly understand and accept the terms and conditions to be included in the final agreement. You will have to document the results of the negotiations as part of the end agreement between the two parties. You should also document the results of the negotiations for your internal files as well. This will help you to evaluate the results of the negotiation relative to your pre-negotiation objectives and goals. It will also provide you with an excellent future reference in the on-going process of improving your negotiating skills.

The Parting:

As has been stated repeatedly, government business is long-term business and you never know when you may be negotiating with the same group of people the next time around. The same is true in in the commercial sector. Always try and end the contract negotiation conference on a positive note. You may never know when you may be back.

Chapter 9

Post-Negotiation Actions

After the negotiation conference is over, there is still work to be done. The following tasks must be completed prior to concluding the negotiation process:

- Final Information Gathering,
- Documentation and Review,
- Review and Approval, and
- Confirmation.

These are the post-negotiation actions which finalize the negotiation process. Each step is just as critical as the actions taken during the preparation and the negotiating stages of the process.

Final Information Gathering:

After negotiations are completed, you and your team need to review the negotiations using the notes taken during the negotiation conference and the recollections of the team members attending the conference. The objective is to gather all of the information necessary to summarize what took place during the conference and to document results.

This should be done as soon as possible after the negotiations to ensure that the memories of all parties are as fresh as possible. Generally, the team member responsible for taking notes during the negotiations will go over the notes with the other team members adding information as appropriate.

Documentation and Review:

After the final information regarding the negotiations has been brought together, including the receipt of any information or documents promised by the other party during the negotiation conference, the negotiations need to be formally documented. This consists of taking the completed notes and turning them into a formal file document for future reference.

The government's post-negotiation documentation process is very formal, requiring the preparation of a Price Negotiation Memorandum in a specified format. The documentation process in your organization does not need to be as formal. However, it is imperative that some form of written documentation summarizing the results of the negotiations be part of your organization's internal negotiation process. You never know when you might need supporting documentation regarding your understanding of the negotiations which took place. If there is a dispute at some later date regarding what was said during the negotiation meeting, any documentation of those meetings will be extensively relied upon in resolving such a dispute. If you negotiated with the government, you can be assured that the government representative will have documented the negotiations. The same is true if you are negotiating with any good contract negotiator. You too must adequately document the discussions, if for no other reason than simply self-protection.

This post-negotiation documentation also provides an opportunity to compare the results of the negotiations with your original objectives. If the final agreement is within the objective range you established going into the negotiations, your final agreement should be satisfactory. If your final agreement does not meet the objectives you established going in, you should document the difference and explain why you agreed to terms and conditions which did not meet these objectives. It might be that new information was obtained during the negotiations or that the other party succeeded in changing your mind during the negotiation conference. It could be because of a simple failure on your part to achieve the desired objectives. Whatever the outcome, you need to make this analysis. Only then can you improve your negotiating skills. Always critique your performance and provide recommendations for future negotiations.

The best way to learn how to negotiate is through on-the-job training. The best way to pass on the benefits of your experience to others in the organization is through proper documentation.

Since the negotiations must be documented for evaluation purposes, you should take advantage of the process so that it facilitates completing the other two steps which must be taken at this stage of the negotiation process.

Review and Approval:

The amount of review required prior to finalization of the negotiation process will vary depending upon the type of company, the negotiators involved, and the specific contract being negotiated.

It is usually wise to have at least one independent review of the negotiation results. If you are president of the company as well as the chief negotiator, you may want to have your attorney review the final agreement, or perhaps an assistant. In the government, depending upon the nature of the contract, there are any number of possible reviews one contract could receive prior to being approved. For larger dollar value contracts, for example, the Price Negotiation Memorandum will be prepared and signed by a contracting specialist and submitted for signature and approval to the contracting officer. The negotiation memorandum, along with a copy of the proposed contract, will be submitted for review and approval to one or more of the following:

- Procurement Section Chief
- Procurement Branch Chief
- Procurement Division Director
- Field Attorney

- Competition Advocate Officials
- Operations Chief, Commander, etc.
- Field Audit or Contract Review Officials
- Headquarters Procurement Officials
- Headquarters Audit and Review Officials
- Headquarters Attorney
- Agency Head, Department Secretary, etc.

It is not unusual for a contract to be subjected to this type of review process within the government. Each government official will review the contract to ensure the appropriate regulations and procedures have been followed and to evaluate the negotiation results. Negotiations might be reopened as a result of dissatisfaction with the proposed agreement at any point in the review process. Obviously, part of the problem with such an extensive review process is that it takes time. You must be careful that the review process you establish within your organization does not become overly time-consuming.

In the government, it often appears that there are more people reviewing contracts than there are contracting officers and specialists awarding them. The entire contract review and approval process within some agencies has reached the point of being totally nonproductive. Care must be taken to make sure that this does not happen in your organization. If it takes too many people to review the actions of your contract negotiation personnel, you should probably consider hiring better contract negotiators. Some type of review process, however, is usually appropriate. Care must be taken to ensure that the review process does not begin to take the place of proper negotiations. The credibility of your contract negotiators will be severely damaged if negotiated agreements begin to be frequently overturned during the review process.

You should also be aware of the review process within the other party's organization. Their review process may affect the time it takes to conclude the final agreement. It also will provide an indication of the relative authority of the other party's negotiating team. Often you can prepare your proposal in a way which will facilitate the review process for the other party. Find out what problems the other party has had in the past and how they have been resolved. This will not only help avoid problems with your negotiated end agreements, but it will help foster a mutually cooperative environment during the negotiation process.

Confirmation:

After everyone in your organization has approved the proposed agreement, and everyone necessary in the other party's organization has approved it, the final agreement must be confirmed in writing.

It is strongly recommended you take the initiative in this confirmation process. The government gives you this opportunity by asking offerors for a best and final offer.

This allows the offeror to document the negotiation results according to their understanding of the final agreement. The government will review the best and final offer to make sure it meets their understanding of the negotiated agreement, and will document the changes agreed to in the final contract award. If you do not have control over the format and wording of the negotiation confirmation document, read any proposed confirmation from the other party very carefully. As always, read the fine print in the agreement along with any referenced documents. You should approach this final document just as if it were a totally new document since this new agreement will take precedence over all others. Submit appropriate certifications or other supporting documents when requested by the other party in order to complete the negotiation confirmation process. In a competitive situation, failure to properly take care of these administrative loose ends could lose you the contract.

The last step in the confirmation process is the establishment of a binding contract or, in government terms, a contract award. At this point, the negotiations are completed and contract performance can begin. It does not necessarily mean, however, that you are through with negotiating that particular contract.

Contract Administration:

After a contract is awarded, your organization will still have to administer the contract. There are a number of situations where negotiations related to the administration of the contract may have to be conducted. Changes in technical requirements, the need for accelerated deliveries, failing to comply with all of the contract terms and conditions, and late deliveries are all example of issues which may be negotiated after contract award. The government recognizes that such changes may occur and includes a changes clause in all of its major contracts. This clause allows the contracting officer to change the terms and conditions of the contract as long as the change falls within the general scope of the contract requirements. The adjustment to the contract price caused by any such change is a negotiated matter. If the change costs the contractor money, the contractor is entitled to relief and the contract price is increased. If the change saves the contractor money, the government considers itself entitled to consideration and the contract price is reduced. Whether the change costs money or saves money, and how much, are negotiable issues.

Although such changes on the surface are new negotiations, they actually are extensions of the original negotiating process. This is one of the reasons documenting the original negotiations is so important. These documents will prove extremely valuable in preparing for negotiating changes to a contract. This is particularly true if different individuals handle the contract negotiations during the contract administration phase than those who handled the original negotiations.

Following through with these post negotiation requirements will ensure that you and your organization are as prepared to the maximum extent possible for the next round of negotiations.

Chapter 10

Negotiation Skills and Techniques

Negotiating Skills:

The importance of viewing each negotiation as a distinct process has been stressed throughout this manual. All of the circumstances affecting the specific negotiation must be considered in order to maximize the potential for successful negotiations. This includes the facts of the situation and the individuals involved. Most books on negotiations will discuss the characteristics of a "good negotiator," providing a list of personality traits describing this individual. Recognizing that the proper approach to negotiations is totally dependent on the situation and whatever is legal, ethical and works, my definition of a good negotiator is rather simple.

> "A good negotiator is one who succeeds in negotiating successful agreements."

To further define this individual would be to restrict the personality types or the approaches to the process. There is no skill which might not come in handy at some time in some negotiation situation. Basket weaving might even be a useful skill if the other party's negotiator likes to weave baskets as a hobby. You never know what might prove useful in a given negotiation setting.

In this book we have discussed the basic theories of negotiation and the need to implement the *25% Solution to Negotiations* or some other scientific approach to the process to ensure that all potential influences on the process are considered. Also, we have examined how the government negotiates contracts and why this process is such an excellent learning tool for studying all complex negotiations. The need for adequate preparation prior to participating in negotiations, the various phases encountered in almost all negotiation conferences, and the post-negotiation actions required to properly conclude the the process have likewise been discussed. The last area of discussion concerns negotiation techniques, strategies and tactics.

Negotiation Strategies:

Strategies define and outline the methods and techniques which will be utilized during the negotiation process to reach the desired objectives. Once again, referring to the baseball game analogy, the strategies comprise the overall game plan. Strategies form the umbrella under which all the subsequent negotiating actions fall. The opposite of developing a well-defined strategy is taking the approach of "We'll play it by ear and see what develops." This shoot-from-the-hip approach usually produces poor dividends and results in a less than satisfactory agreement. The following are some recommended strategies applicable to any negotiation situation.

The Reasonable Approach:

Next to adequate preparation, taking a reasonable approach to the negotiation process is the most critical element to successfully negotiating contracts. Reasonability is second behind preparation because, if the circumstances are right and you adequately prepare, you sometimes can successfully negotiate an agreement without acting reasonably. Such negotiation situations are limited in number and short-term in nature.

Reasonable negotiations are based on approaching the negotiations in a rational or logical manner. Information gathering and analysis are essential elements of this type of approach. Some form of scientific approach to the process must also be followed to ensure that you are, in fact, negotiating from a reasonable point of view.

The government summarizes the need for a reasonable approach by stating:

> "There is no substitute for negotiations based on reasonableness, flexibility, mutual trust and a desire to reach a fair and equitable agreement, where possible."

Another aspect to a reasonable negotiating strategy is the belief that the reasonable negotiator can always find another individual in the other party's organization who will act reasonably, even if the other party's negotiator takes an unreasonable approach. An unreasonable negotiator has very little chance of finding another individual in the other party's organization who will listen to an unreasonable approach, especially if the other party's negotiator is approaching the negotiations in a reasonable manner. To maximize your potential for successful negotiations, you must adequately prepare for the negotiations taking a reasonable approach.

Understanding Human Behavior:

The emphasis on preparation, reasonability and the scientific approach to negotiations does not mean that an understanding of human behavior is not necessary to successful negotiations. Whenever interacting with individuals, whether it is in a social setting or in contract negotiations, an understanding of human motives and needs will prove useful. Both your position and the other party's position will be substantially influenced by the individuals involved. It is therefore imperative in any successful negotiation strategy to consider the subjective or human aspect to the process. Science, without an appreciation for art, is nowhere near as creative as science and art combined.

Ethics and Legality:

In any negotiation situation, it is strongly recommended that the approach taken be ethical and legal. To do otherwise is a short-term, foolish policy. In the long term, adopting any other policy serves the interests of neither party and should be avoided at all cost.

Preparation:

When determining your overall negotiation strategy, one strategy to contract negotiations must not be ignored—can you guess what it is?

BE PREPARED!

By now, this should come as no surprise. Any effective negotiation strategy must be built on the foundation of adequate preparation.

Negotiation Tactics:

Tactics are the day-to-day, hour-to-hour, minute-to-minute play and counterplay of the negotiation parties. Tactics are usually planned in advance and revised to meet the needs of the negotiation. In a baseball game, the tactics are the individual plays as opposed to the overall game plan. In contract negotiations, these are often referred to as gambits or ploys, and are the short-term activities taking place during the negotiation process.

In many references regarding contract negotiations, these tactics are frequently given cute or silly names. Even knowing the reasoning behind giving different negotiating tactics cute names—names such as these are supposed to help you remember the concepts—doesn't make them seem any less ridiculous. Some of the tactics recognized by the government include:

- *Blame a Third Party.* This tactic is used as a method by the negotiator to avoid directly responding to questions by citing another party as the source of the decision and stating that the decision cannot be overturned. The chief benefit of this tactic is to ease the tension between the negotiating parties. The bad guy is now another party who is not present. A mutually cooperative effort can sometimes result. This tactic allows the negotiator to avoid answering a direct question by pleading ignorance or lack of authority.

  Blaming a third party must be used with great care as it can certainly be an abused tactic. Also, a good negotiator on the other side will not let you get away with it. They will call your bluff by asking you to bring the third party into the negotiations to discuss the problem, or certainly will force you to document the third party's opposition in writing. In other words, do not make this accusation falsely, you might get caught. If a possible third party objection is a valid parameter in the negotiations, you would be remiss in not using this tactic.

- *The Art of Being Confused.* This tactic takes advantage of the fact people like to talk about what they do and believe that they know more about what they do than anyone else. Simply asking for clarification and listening to the other party may yield a tremendous amount of information.

- *Make the Other Party Appear Unreasonable.* The quickest way to accomplish this is to laugh when the other party proposes a specific price. Incidentally, this will usually irritate the other party, so be prepared. The more subtle approach is to repeatedly concede on points of little value to you. Then, when asking for a concession of higher import from the other party and refused, point to the lack of cooperation and the unreasonability of the other party compared to your responses. Cite your previous concessions as evidence. Remember, the entire concept of successful negotiations is based on the reasonability of both parties.

Demonstrate, in the government's case, areas where the contracting officer appears to be unreasonable and you have a good chance of overturning a particular decision. Government contracting officers are required to act reasonably by regulation.

- *Good Guy/Bad Guy Approach.* When I was a military police officer interrogating suspects, I was continually amazed at how well the good-guy/bad-guy routine would work. If you have ever watched a television cop show, you've seen this technique. This tactic, also called the "Mutt and Jeff routine," consists of one member of the negotiating party being predesignated to be the bad guy. This individual will consistently and staunchly defend the company's point of view, regardless of the flow of negotiations or the facts presented by the other side. The bad guy will leave the impression of not caring whether a contract is established or not. Another individual is designated as the good guy, one who is willing to listen and remain flexible. This individual sincerely wants to negotiate a tri-win agreement. Using the combination of these two types of individuals often brings the good guy and the other party together in a mutual effort to reach a reasonable agreement. Often this is contrary to the desires of the bad guy, whom nobody likes anyway.

- *Place the Other Side on the Defensive.* This tactic consists of asking a series of rapid-fire questions, hoping to uncover inconsistencies or obtain information from the other party which they might not otherwise provide. It is an attempt to throw the other party off balance.

- *Agreement and Rebuttal.* This is the "yes, but" approach to negotiating. You acknowledge the validity of the other party's position in a positive way and then qualify the position according to your own interests. To be successful at this technique, you must make the qualification appear to be a logical extension of the other party's original position.

- *Straw Issues.* This tactic consists of creating a major issue from a minor issue through repeatedly bringing up the minor issue during the negotiations and overemphasizing its importance. Later, you may offer a concession on this minor issue in return for a concession on a major issue. This leaves the other party with the impression that an equitable trade-off occurred, when in fact, it was not equal.

- *Bluffing, Lies and Dirty Tricks.* There are many different tactics falling under these three general categories. Certainly, there are contract negotiators who utilize tactics falling under all three. One government manual even states that: "Bluffing can play a vital role in the negotiation."

In a professional contract negotiation setting, there is no excuse for using any of these. These three tactics, along with illegal or unethical strategies, represent a short-sighted approach to the negotiation process. They are generally used to compensate for inadequate preparation or an unreasonable negotiating position. If not, legitimate negotiating techniques would always work better. The different techniques falling under these categories will not be discussed in this book. They are not worth the time writing about, nor your time reading about. If you want, there are a number of books available which discuss and recommend such tactics. If you use these tactics, remember—most people can be bluffed . . . once.

Proposing Alternatives:

Should you consider proposing alternatives in response to a request for proposal? If it is in your best interest, of course you should. However, you should always include with your proposal, if at all possible, an offer which responds to the other party's terms and conditions as originally described. This maximizes your potential for continuing to be involved in the negotiation process for as long as possible. The longer you are involved, the higher the probability for success. In your proposal and during your negotiations, prove to the other party the reasonableness and the desirability of implementing your alternative by showing how it will result in an end agreement which will better meet the needs and desires of both parties.

Audit Mentality:

When negotiating with the government, remember that all government contract files are potentially subject to an extensive review and audit. The contracting officer must document the file defending the actions taken in establishing that contract. Keeping this in mind when approaching government negotiations will help you to prepare a proposal which will facilitate the contracting officer's documentation of the contract file. This, in the end, is also in your best interest.

Assume the Best, Anticipate the Worst:

In order to implement the various strategies and tactics available to you, you must be prepared to react to the flow of the negotiations. To be adequately prepared, you must ask the proverbial "What if" questions that are ever present in any negotiation situation. By considering the worst-case and best-case scenarios, you will be prepared to respond to varying positions during the negotiation process. These scenarios will also help form the foundation for developing minimum and maximum negotiation objectives.

Multi-Year Contracting:

The government and others are beginning to take more and more advantage of multi-year contracting. Whenever multi-year contracts are involved, there is more flexibility built into the negotiation process. However, there is also considerably more risk. The preparation phase of contract negotiations is even more critical when multi-year contracts are involved. If a bad deal is negotiated, you will be paying the price for a much longer period of time. Extra care must be taken when negotiating these contracts due to the long-term risk involved.

Personality Clashes:

Sometimes there is an unavoidable personality clash between negotiators. If this happens, you must take some kind of corrective action to avoid personalities from interfering with the potential for successful negotiations. Have someone else represent your side, ask to negotiate with the other party's supervisor if need be, or bring in another individual to be the "good guy." After all, once there is a discernible personality clash, you have already been identified as a bad guy for all intents and purposes. The important point is that you cannot afford to let a personality clash interfere with the successful completion of the negotiation process. In order to ensure that this does not happen, you cannot ignore the problem. Rather, you must take some positive action to offset its potential negative influence on the negotiation outcome.

One of the ways to overcome personality clashes in a team negotiating setting is to take advantage of breaks. When teaching seminars on the subject of contract negotiations, I frequently ask the question, "Where are the most difficult negotiation conflicts resolved?" Usually the answer is "at the negotiating table." When I tell them that usually they are resolved in the restroom, it invariably results in laughter. Yet, there is a great deal of validity to this statement. When two teams reach a significant impasse point in the process, particularly at the final posturing stage of the conference, one of the best ways to resolve the impasse is for two opposing team members who have a mutual respect for each other to meet informally and unofficially during a break in the negotiations. This can happen in the hallway, in the coffee line, in the restroom, or in any location away from the other negotiation participants. After these two individuals resolve the basic impasse and the teams reconvene, the negotiations move on to the final resolution stage. To maximize your potential for successful negotiations, take advantage of the breaks to promote your party's position and to minimize the impact of any personality clashes which might occur.

The Truth Above All:

In all aspects of negotiations, the truth should be paramount. As long as you state the truth, you cannot be caught in a lie. Always adequately prepare for the negotiations, considering all of the circumstances involved, including: your position, the other party's position, the objective position, and the uncontrollable parameters. Take a reasonable approach to the negotiations and there will be no need to lie. Sticking to the truth will always serve you best in the long run.

Additional References:

The appendices following this chapter contain various documents and references pertaining to negotiating government contracts. These references will also prove useful as a resource in any contract negotiation situation.

Potential for Successful Negotiations:

If you implement all of the principles described in this manual, will you conduct successful negotiations? The answer is—sometimes. The objective of this book has been to provide you a basic introduction to the tools of successful negotiations. The skill with which you use these tools, the circumstances, and the individuals involved with the specific negotiation, will determine if you are successful. Each negotiation session is unique.

When I first became involved in government contracting, I was involved in a series of negotiations with the representative of a very large corporation, dominant in their industry. The government had a recurring need for one of their products. At that time, no one else was able to produce this product. Therefore, those particular negotiations concerned a sole source acquisition. Not only was the company in the controlling position due to the circumstances, the corporation representative had the reputation of being a skilled and tough negotiator. It proved to be true and she usually controlled the negotiations.

Several years later I was speaking at a seminar where my former boss was also speaking. She heard my story regarding tough negotiations often being settled in the restrooms. My boss asked afterwards, "When did you ever meet Ms. 'Smith' in the restroom?" My response was that I never considered *those* negotiations closed—I just ran out of time.

After gaining considerably more experience, I would like another chance at negotiating each of those contracts. I often think that this time around I would be able to negotiate a far better agreement for the government despite the unfavorable circumstances surrounding the negotiations. Of course, there is always the possibility that the company's representative has also become a better negotiator as well.

The point is that you will never be able to be completely successful in all of your negotiations. There are too many variables beyond your control. Remember, your position only represents 25% of the total possibilities for influencing the negotiation outcome. That is why you must take a methodological approach to the contract negotiation process. It is also why the subjective approach or human behavior approach alone is not adequate. Even if you completely understand yourself and the other party from a human behavior perspective, you will only be able to control 50% of the components possibly influencing the negotiation outcome—your position and their position. This ignores the objective position and the uncontrollable parameters.

To participate in successful negotiations, you must analyze all sides of the negotiation situation and prepare your negotiation plan based on this evaluation. To do this properly, it is essential that the science of negotiations be considered as well as the art.

APPENDIX I

CFR, TITLE 48, CHAPTER 1, FEDERAL ACQUISITION REGULATIONS, SUBCHAPTER C, PART 15, CONTRACTING BY NEGOTIATION.

Federal Acquisition Regulation

final time fixed by the contracting officer establishes that the proposal is acceptable, it shall be so categorized. Otherwise, it shall be categorized as unacceptable.

(g) When a technical proposal is found unacceptable (either initially or after clarification), the contracting officer shall promptly notify the offeror of the basis of the determination and that a revision of the proposal will not be considered. Upon written request and as soon as possible after award, the contracting officer shall debrief unsuccessful offerors (see 15.1002).

(h) Late technical proposals are governed by 15.412.

(i) If it is necessary to discontinue two-step sealed bidding, the contracting officer shall include a statement of the facts and circumstances in the contract file. Each offeror shall be notified in writing. When step one results in no acceptable technical proposal or only one acceptable technical proposal, the acquisition may be continued by negotiation.

[48 FR 42171, Sept. 19, 1983, as amended at 50 FR 1739, Jan. 11, 1985; 50 FR 52429, Dec. 23, 1985; 51 FR 2649, Jan. 17, 1986]

14.503-2 Step two.

(a) Sealed bidding procedures shall be followed except that invitations for bids shall—

(1) Be issued only to those offerors submitting acceptable technical proposals in step one;

(2) Include the provision prescribed in 14.201-6(t);

(3) Prominently state that the bidder shall comply with the specifications and the bidder's technical proposal; and

(4) Not be synopsized in the Commerce Business Daily as an acquisition opportunity nor publicly posted (see 5.101(a)).

(b) The names of firms that submitted acceptable proposals in step one will be listed in the Commerce Business Daily for the benefit of prospective subcontractors (see 5.206(a)(2)).

[48 FR 42171, Sept. 19, 1983, as amended at 50 FR 1739, Jan. 11, 1985; 50 FR 52429, Dec. 23, 1985]

PART 15—CONTRACTING BY NEGOTIATION

Sec.
15.000 Scope of part.

Subpart 15.1—General Requirements for Negotiation

15.100 Scope of subpart.
15.101 Definition.
15.102 General.
15.103 Converting from sealed bidding to negotiation procedures.
15.104—15.105 [Reserved]
15.106 Contract clauses.
15.106-1 Examination of Records clause.
15.106-2 Audit—Negotiation clause.

Subparts 15.2—15.3 [Reserved]

Subpart 15.4—Solicitation and Receipt of Proposals and Quotations

15.400 Scope of subpart.
15.401 Applicability.
15.402 General.
15.403 Solicitation mailing lists.
15.404 Presolicitation notices and conferences.
15.405 Solicitations for information or planning purposes.
15.405-1 General.
15.405-2 Solicitation provision.
15.406 Preparing requests for proposals (RFP's) and requests for quotations (RFQ's).
15.406-1 Uniform contract format.
15.406-2 Part I—The Schedule.
15.406-3 Part II—Contract clauses.
15.406-4 Part III—List of documents, exhibits, and other attachments.
15.406-5 Part IV—Representations and instructions.
15.407 Solicitation provisions.
15.408 Issuing solicitations.
15.409 Pre-proposal conferences.
15.410 Amendment of solicitations before closing date.
15.411 Receipt of proposals and quotations.
15.412 Late proposals and modifications.
15.413 Disclosure and use of information before award.
15.413-1 Alternate I.
15.413-2 Alternate II.
15.414 Forms.
15.415 Economic purchase quantities (supplies).

Subpart 15.5—Unsolicited Proposals

15.500 Scope of subpart.
15.501 Definitions.

15.000

Sec.
15.502 Policy.
15.503 General.
15.504 Advance guidance.
15.505 Content of unsolicited proposals.
15.506 Agency procedures.
15.506-1 Receipt and initial review.
15.506-2 Evaluation.
15.507 Contracting methods.
15.508 Prohibitions.
15.509 Limited use of data.

Subpart 15.6—Source Selection

15.600 Scope of subpart.
15.601 Definitions.
15.602 Applicability.
15.603 Purpose.
15.604 Responsibilities.
15.605 Evaluation factors.
15.606 Changes in Government requirements.
15.607 Disclosure of mistakes before award.
15.608 Proposal evaluation.
15.609 Competitive range.
15.610 Written or oral discussion.
15.611 Best and final offers.
15.612 Formal source selection.
15.613 Alternative source selection procedures.

Subpart 15.7—Make-or-Buy Programs

15.700 Scope of subpart.
15.701 Definitions.
15.702 General.
15.703 Acquisitions requiring make-or-buy programs.
15.704 Items and work included.
15.705 Solicitation requirements.
15.706 Evaluation, negotiation, and agreement.
15.707 Incorporating make-or-buy programs in contracts.
15.708 Contract clause.

Subpart 15.8—Price Negotiation

15.800 Scope of subpart.
15.801 Definitions.
15.802 Policy.
15.803 General.
15.804 Cost or pricing data.
15.804-1 General.
15.804-2 Requiring certified cost or pricing data.
15.804-3 Exemptions from or waiver of submission of certified cost or pricing data.
15.804-4 Certificate of Current Cost or Pricing Data.
15.804-5 [Reserved]
15.804-6 Procedural requirements.
15.804-7 Defective cost or pricing data.
15.804-8 Contract clauses.
15.805 Proposal analysis.
15.805-1 General.

Sec.
15.805-2 Price analysis.
15.805-3 Cost analysis.
15.805-4 Technical analysis.
15.805-5 Field pricing support.
15.806 Subcontract pricing considerations.
15.807 Prenegotiation objectives.
15.808 Price negotiation memorandum.
15.809 Forward pricing rate agreements.
15.810 Should-cost analysis.
15.811 Estimating systems.
15.812 Unit prices.
15.812-1 General.
15.812-2 Contract clause.
15.813 Commercial pricing certificates.
15.813-1 Policy.
15.813-2 Applicability.
15.813-3 Exemptions from commercial pricing certificates.
15.813-4 Procedures.
15.813-5 Contract clause.

Subpart 15.9—Profit

15.900 Scope of subpart.
15.901 General.
15.902 Policy.
15.903 Contracting officer responsibilities.
15.904 Solicitation provision and contract clause.
15.905 Profit-analysis factors.
15.905-1 Common factors.
15.905-2 Additional factors.

Subpart 15.10—Preaward, Award, and Postaward Notifications, Protests, and Mistakes

15.1001 Notifications to unsuccessful offerors.
15.1002 Notification to successful offeror.
15.1003 Debriefing of unsuccessful offerors.
15.1004 Protests against award.
15.1005 Discovery of mistakes.

AUTHORITY: 40 U.S.C. 486(c); Chapter 137, 10 U.S.C.; and 42 U.S.C. 2453(c).

SOURCE: 48 FR 42187, Sept. 19, 1983, unless otherwise noted.

15.000 Scope of part.

This part prescribes policies and procedures governing contracting for supplies and services by negotiation.

Subpart 15.1—General Requirements for Negotiation

15.100 Scope of subpart.

This subpart covers general requirements regarding negotiated contracts. Detailed and specific requirements appear throughout this regulation.

Federal Acquisition Regulation

15.101 Definition.

"Negotiation" means contracting through the use of either competitive or other-than-competitive proposals and discussions. Any contract awarded without using sealed bidding procedures is a negotiated contract (see 14.101).

[50 FR 1739, Jan. 11, 1985, and 50 FR 52429, Dec. 23, 1985]

15.102 General.

Negotiation is a procedure that includes the receipt of proposals from offerors, permits bargaining, and usually affords an opportunity to revise their offers before award of a contract. Bargaining—in the sense of discussion, persuasion, alteration of initial assumptions and positions, and give-and-take—may apply to price, schedule, technical requirements, type of contract, or other terms of a proposed contract.

[48 FR 42187, Sept. 19, 1983, as amended at 50 FR 1739, Jan. 11, 1985; 50 FR 52429, Dec. 23, 1985]

15.103 Converting from sealed bidding to negotiation procedures.

When the agency head has determined, in accordance with 14.404-1(e)(1), that an invitation for bids is to be cancelled and that use of negotiation is appropriate to complete the acquisition, the contracting officer may negotiate without issuing a new solicitation subject to the following conditions—

(a) Prior notice of intention to negotiate and a reasonable opportunity to negotiate have been given by the contracting officer to each responsible bidder that submitted a bid in response to the invitation for bids;

(b) The negotiated price is the lowest negotiated price offered by any responsible bidder; and

(c) The negotiated price is lower than the lowest rejected bid price of a responsible bidder that submitted a bid in response to the invitation for bids.

[50 FR 1739, Jan. 11, 1985, and 50 FR 52429, Dec. 23, 1985]

15.104—15.105 [Reserved]

15.106 Contract clauses.

15.106-1 Examination of Records clause.

(a) This subsection implements 10 U.S.C. 2313(b) and (c) and 41 U.S.C. 254(c).

(b) When contracting by negotiation, the contracting officer shall insert the clause at 52.215-1, Examination of Records by Comptroller General, in solicitations and contracts, except when—

(1) Making small purchases (see Part 13);

(2) Contracting for utility services at rates not exceeding those established to apply uniformly to the public, plus any applicable reasonable connection charge; or

(3) Making contracts with foreign contractors for which the agency head authorizes omission under Subpart 25.9.

(c) In connection with administration of the clause in research and development contracts with nonprofit institutions, including subcontracts under these contracts, the Comptroller General does not require original documentation of transportation costs (exclusive of travel).

[48 FR 42187, Sept. 19, 1983, as amended at 50 FR 1739, Jan. 11, 1985; 50 FR 52429, Dec. 23, 1985]

15.106-2 Audit—Negotiation clause.

(a) This subsection implements 10 U.S.C. 2313(a), 41 U.S.C. 254(b), and 10 U.S.C. 2306(f).

(b) The contracting officer shall, when contracting by negotiation, insert the clause at 52.215-2, Audit—Negotiation, in solicitations and contracts, unless the acquisition is a small purchase under Part 13. In facilities contracts, the contracting officer shall use the clause with its Alternate I.

Subparts 15.2—15.3 [Reserved]

Subpart 15.4—Solicitation and Receipt of Proposals and Quotations

15.400 Scope of subpart.

This subpart prescribes policies and procedures for (a) preparing and issuing requests for proposals (RFP's) and requests for quotations (RFQ's) and (b) receiving proposals and quotations.

15.401 Applicability.

This subpart applies to solicitations issued when contracting by negotiation, except—

(a) Small purchases (see Part 13); and

(b) Two-step sealed bidding (see Subpart 14.5).

[48 FR 42187, Sept. 19, 1983, as amended at 50 FR 1739, Jan. 11, 1985; 50 FR 52429, Dec. 23, 1985]

15.402 General.

(a) Requests for proposals (RFP's) or requests for quotations (RFQ's) are used in negotiated acquisitions to communicate Government requirements to prospective contractors and to solicit proposals or quotations from them. Except as permitted by paragraph (f) below, contracting officers shall issue written solicitations. Solicitations shall contain the information necessary to enable prospective contractors to prepare proposals or quotations properly. Solicitation provisions and contract clauses may be incorporated into solicitations and contracts by reference, when authorized by Subpart 52.1.

(b) Contracting officers shall furnish identical information concerning a proposed acquisition to all prospective contractors. Government personnel shall not provide the advantage of advance knowledge concerning a future solicitation to any prospective contractor (but see 5.404, 15.404, and 15.405).

(c) Except for solicitations for information or planning purposes (see subparagraph (e)(1) below and 15.405), contracting officers shall solicit proposals or quotations only when there is a definite intention to award a contract. Subpart 7.3 provides additional instructions for solicitations involving cost comparisons between Government and contractor performance.

(d) A proposal received in response to an RFP is an offer that can be accepted by the Government to create a binding contract, either following negotiations or, when authorized by 15.610, without discussion. Contracting officers should normally issue RFP's when they consider it reasonable to expect prospective contractors to respond with offers, even though they anticipate negotiations after receipt of offers. An RFP shall not be used for a solicitation for information or planning purposes. Solicitations involving cost comparisons between Government and contractor performance (see 7.302(b)) are not for information or planning purposes.

(e) A quotation received in response to an RFQ is not an offer and cannot be accepted by the Government to create a binding contract. It is informational in character. An RFQ may be used when the Government does not intend to award a contract on the basis of the solicitation but wishes to obtain price, delivery, or other market information for planning purposes (see 15.405).

(f) Oral solicitations are authorized for perishable subsistence. An oral solicitation may also be used when processing a written solicitation would delay the acquisition of supplies or services to the detriment of the Government. Use of an oral solicitation does not relieve the contracting officer from complying with other requirements of this regulation. In addition to other applicable documentation requirements (see Subpart 4.1), documentation of oral solicitations shall include—

(1) A justification for use of an oral solicitation;

(2) Item description, quantity, and delivery schedule;

(3) Sources solicited, including the date, time, name of individual contacted, and prices quoted; and

(4) The solicitation number provided to the prospective contractors.

(g) If, after considering any responses to a proper notice of proposed sole source contract action (see 5.207(d)(3)), the contracting officer determines that more than one source can meet the Government's needs, the contracting officer shall solicit offers using competitive procedures. The contracting officer shall proceed in accordance with 5.203 for publicizing and response times.

Federal Acquisition Regulation

[48 FR 42187, Sept. 19, 1983, as amended at 50 FR 1739, Jan. 11, 1985; 50 FR 52429, Dec. 23, 1985]

15.403 Solicitation mailing lists.

Contracting offices shall establish, maintain, and use lists of potential sources in accordance with 14.205.

15.404 Presolicitation notices and conferences.

(a) *General.* Presolicitation notices and conferences may be used as preliminary steps in negotiated acquisitions in order to—

(1) Develop or identify interested sources;

(2) Request preliminary information based on a general description of the supplies or services involved;

(3) Explain complicated specifications and requirements to interested sources; and

(4) Aid prospective contractors in later submitting proposals without undue expenditure of effort, time, and money.

(b) *Presolicitation notices.* (1) When presolicitation notices are used, the contracting officer shall prepare and issue the notice to potential sources and shall synopsize the notice in accordance with Subpart 5.2.

(2) Each presolicitation notice shall—

(i) Define as explicitly as possible the information to be furnished in the response;

(ii) Indicate whether it is contemplated that the presolicitation notice will be followed by a conference and a formal solicitation; and

(iii) Request an expression of interest in the contemplated acquisition by a specified date.

(3) In complex acquisitions, the presolicitation notice may also request information pertaining to management, engineering, and production capabilities. Detailed drawings, specifications, or plans will not normally be included with a presolicitation notice.

(4) The contracting officer shall furnish copies of the solicitation to (i) all those responding affirmatively to the presolicitation notice and (ii) other prospective contractors upon their request (but see Subpart 9.4, Debarment, Suspension, and Ineligibility).

(c) *Presolicitation conferences.* (1) The presolicitation conference may be used only when approved at a level higher than the contracting officer. It shall not be used as a method for prequalification of offerors.

(2) The contracting officer shall—

(i) Advise all organizations responding to the presolicitation notice of the details of any pending presolicitation conference;

(ii) Conduct the conference and arrange for technical and legal personnel to attend, as appropriate; and

(iii) Furnish copies of the solicitation to all organizations attending the conference, unless they decline to participate in the acquisition.

15.405 Solicitations for information or planning purposes.

15.405-1 General.

When information necessary for planning purposes cannot be obtained from potential sources by more economical and less formal means, the contracting officer may determine in writing that a solicitation for information or planning purposes is justified. If this determination is approved, in accordance with agency procedures, at a level higher than that of the contracting officer, the contracting officer shall then issue the solicitation.

15.405-2 Solicitation provision.

The contracting officer shall insert on the face of each solicitation (other than those excluded by 15.401) issued for information or planning purposes the provision at 52.215-3, Solicitation for Information or Planning Purposes.

15.406 Preparing requests for proposals (RFP's) and requests for quotations (RFQ's).

15.406-1 Uniform contract format.

(a) Contracting officers shall prepare solicitations and resulting contracts using the uniform contract format outlined in Table 15-1. The format facilitates preparation of the solicitation and contract, as well as reference to and use of those documents by offerors and contractors. The uniform contract format is optional for acquisitions outside the

United States, its possessions, its territories, and Puerto Rico. It does not apply to the following:

(1) Basic agreements (see 16.702).

(2) Construction and architect-engineer contracts (see Part 36).

(3) Shipbuilding (including design, construction, and conversion), ship overhauls, and ship repairs.

(4) Subsistence.

(5) Contracts requiring special contract forms prescribed elsewhere in this regulation that are inconsistent with the uniform contract format.

(6) Contracts exempted by the agency head or a designee.

(b) Solicitations to which the uniform contract format applies shall include Parts I, II, III, and IV (see 15.406-2 through 15.406-5). Upon award, contracting officers shall not physically include Part IV in the resulting contract, but shall retain in their contract file Section K, Representations, certifications, and other statements of offerors, as completed by the contractor. Award by acceptance of a proposal on the award portion of SF 33 or SF 26 incorporates Section K by reference in the resultant contract. Contracts requiring a bilateral document shall incorporate Section K by reference in the signed contract.

TABLE 15-1

Uniform Contract Format

Section	Title
Part I—The Schedule	
A	Solicitation/contract form
B	Supplies or services and prices/costs
C	Description/specifications/ work statement
D	Packaging and marking
E	Inspection and acceptance
F	Deliveries or performance
G	Contract administration data
H	Special contract requirements
Part II—Contract Clauses	
I	Contract clauses
Part III—List of Documents, Exhibits, and Other Attachments	
J	List of attachments
Part IV—Representations and Instructions	
K	Representations, certifications, and other statements of offerors or quoters
L	Instructions, conditions, and notices to offerors or quoters
M	Evaluation factors for award

[48 FR 42187, Sept. 19, 1983, as amended at 50 FR 1739, Jan. 11, 1985; 50 FR 52429, Dec. 23, 1985]

15.406-2 Part I—The Schedule.

The contracting officer shall prepare the contract Schedule as follows:

(a) *Section A, Solicitation/contract form.*

(1) Prepare RFP's on Standard Form 33, Solicitation, Offer and Award (53.301-33), unless otherwise permitted by Part 53. The first page of the SF 33 is the first page of the solicitation and includes section A of the uniform contract format.

(2) Prepare RFQ's on Standard Form 18, Request for Quotations (53.301-18). Agencies may overprint the SF 18 to provide for Section A of the uniform contract format.

(3) When neither SF 33 nor SF 18 is used, include the following on the first page of the solicitation:

(i) Name, address, and location of issuing activity, including room and building where proposals or quotations must be submitted.

(ii) Solicitation number.

(iii) Date of issuance.

(iv) Closing date and time.

(v) Number of pages.

(vi) Requisition or other purchase authority.

(vii) Brief description of item or service.

(viii) Requirement for the offeror or quoter to provide its name and complete address, including street, city, county, State, Zip code, and the Data Universal Numbering System (DUNS) Number applicable to that name and address.

(ix) A statement that offerors or quoters should include in the offer or quotation the address to which payment should be mailed, if that address is different from that shown for the offeror or quoter.

(b) *Section B, Supplies or services and prices/costs.* Include on the second page of the solicitation brief descriptions of the supplies or services; e.g., item number, national stock number/part number if applicable, nouns, and quantities. (This includes incidental deliverables such as manuals and reports.) The second page may be supplemented as necessary by Op-

Federal Acquisition Regulation 15.406-5

tional Form 336, Continuation Sheet (53.302-336).

(c) *Section C, Description/specifications/work statement.* Include any description or specifications needed in addition to Section B (see Part 10, Specifications, Standards, and Other Product Descriptions).

(d) *Section D, Packaging and marking.* Provide packaging, packing, preservation, and marking requirements, if any (see 10.004(e)).

(e) *Section E, Inspection and acceptance.* Include inspection, acceptance, quality assurance, and reliability requirements (see Part 46, Quality Assurance).

(f) *Section F, Deliveries or performance.* Specify the requirements for time, place, and method of delivery or performance (see Part 12, Contract Delivery or Performance, and 47.301-1).

(g) *Section G, Contract administration data.* Include any required accounting and appropriation data and any required contract administration information or instructions other than those on the solicitation form.

(h) *Section H, Special contract requirements.* Include a clear statement of any special contract requirements that are not included in Section I, Contract clauses, or in other sections of the uniform contract format.

[48 FR 42187, Sept. 19, 1983, as amended at 51 FR 27119, July 29, 1986]

15.406-3 Part II—Contract clauses.

(a) *Section I, Contract clauses.* The contracting officer shall include in this section the clauses required by law or by this regulation and any additional clauses expected to be included in any resulting contract, if these clauses are not required in any other section of the uniform contract format.

(b) When contracting by negotiation, the contracting officer shall insert the clause at 52.215-33, Order of Precedence, in solicitations and contracts to which the uniform contract format applies.

(c) Any alteration pertaining to the contract shall be included in this section as part of the clause at 52.252-4, Alterations in Contract. See Part 52, Solicitation Provisions and Contract Clauses. Clauses that are incorporated by reference shall be included in this section (see 52.102-1(c)).

[51 FR 2649, Jan. 17, 1986]

15.406-4 Part III—List of Documents, exhibits, and other attachments.

Section J, List of attachments. The contracting officer shall list the title, date, and number of pages for each attached document, exhibit, and other attachment.

15.406-5 Part IV—Representations and instructions.

The contracting officer shall prepare the representations and instructions as follows:

(a) *Section K, Representations, certifications, and other statements of offerors or quoters.* Include in this section those solicitation provisions that require representations, certifications, or the submission of other information by offerors or quoters.

(b) *Section L, Instructions, conditions, and notices to offerors or quoters.* Insert in this section solicitation provisions and other information and instructions not required elsewhere to guide offerors or quoters in preparing proposals or quotations. Any alteration pertaining to the solicitation shall be included in this section as part of the provision at 52.252-3, Alterations in Solicitation. Provisions that are incorporated by reference shall be included in this section. Prospective offerors or quoters may be instructed to submit technical proposals in severable parts to meet agency requirements. The severable parts should provide for separation of technical and cost or pricing data. The instructions may specify further organization of proposal or quotation parts, such as (1) administrative, (2) management, (3) technical, and (4) cost or pricing data.

(c) *Section M, Evaluation factors for award.* Identify all factors, including price or cost, and any significant subfactors that will be considered in awarding the contract (see 15.605(e) and (f) and the multiple award provision at 52.215-34) and state the relative importance the Government places on those evaluation factors and subfactors.

[48 FR 42187, Sept. 19, 1983, as amended at 50 FR 1740, Jan. 11, 1985; 50 FR 52429, Dec. 23, 1985; 51 FR 19715, May 30, 1986]

15.407 Solicitation provisions.

(a) "Solicitations," as used in this section, means requests for proposals (RFP's) and requests for quotations (RFQ's) other than those excluded by 15.401 and those for information or planning purposes. See 15.405-2 for the solicitation provision used with solicitations for information or planning purposes.

(b) The contracting officer may, upon the approval of the chief of the contracting office, insert the provision at 52.215-4, Notice of Possible Standardization, in solicitations for supplies that subsequently might be standardized. See 14.201-6(n) regarding use of the provision in invitations for bids.

(c) The contracting officer shall insert in solicitations the provisions at—

(1) 52.215-5, Solicitation Definitions;

(2) 52.215-6, Type of Business Organization;

(3) 52.215-7, Unnecessarily Elaborate Proposals or Quotations;

(4) 52.215-8, Acknowledgment of Amendments to Solicitations;

(5) 52.215-9, Submission of Offers;

(6) 52.215-10, Late Submissions, Modifications, and Withdrawals of Proposals;

(7) 52.215-11, Authorized Negotiators; and

(8) 52.215-12, Restriction on Disclosure and Use of Data.

(d) The contracting officer shall insert in RFP's the provisions at—

(1) 52.215-13, Preparation of Offers;

(2) 52.215-14, Explanation to Prospective Offerors;

(3) 52.215-15, Failure to Submit Offer; and

(4) 52.215-16, Contract Award.

(e) The contracting officer shall insert the provision at 52.215-17, Telegraphic Proposals, in solicitations that authorize telegraphic proposals or quotations.

(f) The contracting officer shall insert the provision at 52.215-19, Period for Acceptance of Offer, in RFP's that are not issued on SF 33 except those (1) for construction work or (2) in which the Government specifies a minimum acceptance period.

(g) The contracting officer shall insert the provision at 52.215-20, Place of Performance, in solicitations except those in which the place of performance is specified by the Government.

(h) The contracting officer shall insert the provision at 52.215-34, Evaluation of Offers for Multiple Awards, in requests for proposals if the contracting officer determines that multiple awards might be made if doing so is economically advantageous to the Government.

[48 FR 42187, Sept. 19, 1983, as amended at 50 FR 1740, Jan. 11, 1985; 50 FR 52429, Dec. 23, 1985; 51 FR 2650, Jan. 17, 1986; 51 FR 19715, May 30, 1986]

15.408 Issuing solicitations.

(a) The contracting officer shall issue unclassified solicitations to potential sources in conformance with the policy and procedures in Parts 5 and 6.

(b) Solicitations involving classified information shall be handled as prescribed by agency regulations.

(c) If the contracting office is located in the United States and the security classification permits, any solicitation or related correspondence sent to a foreign address shall be sent by international air mail. Similarly, if the security classification permits, contracting offices located outside the United States shall use international air mail in appropriate circumstances.

[48 FR 42187, Sept. 19, 1983, as amended at 50 FR 1740, Jan. 11, 1985; 50 FR 52429, Dec. 23, 1985]

15.409 Pre-proposal conferences.

(a) A pre-proposal conference may be held to brief prospective offerors after a solicitation has been issued but before offers are submitted. Generally, the Government uses these conferences in complex negotiated acquisitions to explain or clarify complicated specifications and requirements.

(b) The contracting officer shall decide if a pre-proposal conference is required and make the necessary arrangements, including the following:

Federal Acquisition Regulation 15.412

(1) If notice was not in the solicitation, give all prospective offerors who received the solicitation adequate notice of the time, place, nature, and scope of the conference.

(2) If time allows, request prospective offerors to submit written questions in advance. Prepared answers can then be delivered during the conference.

(3) Arrange for technical and legal personnel to attend the conference, if appropriate.

(c) The contracting officer or a designated representative shall conduct the pre-proposal conference, furnish all prospective offerors identical information concerning the proposed acquisition, make a complete record of the conference, and promptly furnish a copy of that record to all prospective offerors. Conferees shall be advised that—

(1) Remarks and explanations at the conference shall not qualify the terms of the solicitation; and

(2) Terms of the solicitation and specifications remain unchanged unless the solicitation is amended in writing.

15.410 Amendment of solicitations before closing date.

(a) After issuance of a solicitation, but before the date set for receipt of proposals, it may be necessary to (1) make changes to the solicitation, including, but not limited to, significant changes in quantity, specifications, or delivery schedules, (2) correct defects or ambiguities, or (3) change the closing date for receipt of proposals. Standard Form 30, Amendment of Solicitation/Modification of Contract (53.301-30), shall be used for amending a request for proposals (RFP).

(b) The contracting officer shall determine if the closing date needs to be changed when amending a solicitation. If the time available before closing is insufficient, prospective offerors or quoters shall be notified by telegram or telephone of an extension of the closing date, and the notification shall be confirmed in the written amendment to the solicitation. The contracting officer shall not award a contract unless any amendments made to an RFP have been issued in sufficient time to be considered by prospective offerors.

(c) Any information given to a prospective offeror or quoter shall be furnished promptly to all other prospective offerors or quoters as a solicitation amendment if (1) the information is necessary in submitting proposals or quotations or (2) the lack of such information would be prejudicial to a prospective offeror or quoter.

15.411 Receipt of proposals and quotations.

(a) The procedures for receipt and handling of proposals and quotations in negotiated acquisitions should be similar to the receipt and safeguarding of bids in sealed bidding (see 14.401). Proposals and quotations shall be marked with the date and time of receipt.

(b) After receipt, proposals and quotations shall be safeguarded from unauthorized disclosure. Classified proposals and quotations shall be handled in accordance with agency regulations. Also see OMB Circular No. A-76, the supplemental Handbook, and Subpart 7.3, Contractor Versus Government Performance, for safeguarding cost-comparison information.

[48 FR 42187, Sept. 19, 1983, as amended at 50 FR 1740, Jan. 11, 1985; 50 FR 52429, Dec. 23, 1985]

15.412 Late proposals and modifications.

(a) "Modification," as used in this section, means a modification of a proposal, including a final modification in response to the contracting officer's request for "best and final" offers. The term does not include normal revisions of offers made during the conduct of negotiations by offerors selected for discussion.

(b) Offerors are responsible for submitting offers, and any modifications to them, so as to reach the Government office designated in the solicitation on time. Unless the solicitation states a specific time, the time for receipt is 4:30 p.m., local time for the designated Government office on the date that proposals are due.

(c) Proposals, and modifications to them, that are received in the designated Government office after the

15.413

exact time specified are "late" and shall be considered only if (1) they are received before award is made, and (2) the circumstances, including acceptable evidence of date of mailing or receipt at the Government installation, meet the specific requirements of the provision at 52.215-10, Late Submissions, Modifications, and Withdrawals of Proposals.

(d) When a late proposal or modification is received and it is clear from available information that it cannot be considered for award, the contracting officer shall promptly notify the offeror that it was received late and will not be considered. The notice need not be given when the proposed contract is to be awarded within a few days and the notice prescribed in 15.1001(c)(1) would suffice.

(e) When a late proposal or modification is transmitted by registered or certified mail and is received before award, but it is not clear from available information whether it can be considered, the offeror shall be promptly notified substantially in accordance with the notice in 14.304-2, appropriately modified to relate to proposals.

(f) Late proposals and modifications that are not considered shall be held unopened, unless opened for identification, until after award and then retained with other unsuccessful proposals.

(g) The following shall, if available, be included in the contracting office files for each late proposal, quotation, or modification:

(1) The date of mailing, filing, or delivery.

(2) The date and hour of receipt.

(3) Whether or not considered for award.

(4) The envelope, wrapper, or other evidence of date of submission.

[48 FR 42187, Sept. 19, 1983, as amended at 50 FR 23606, June 4, 1985]

15.413 Disclosure and use of information before award.

15.413-1 Alternate I.

(a) After receipt of proposals, none of the information contained in them or concerning the number or identity of offerors shall be made available to the public or to anyone in the Government not having a legitimate interest.

(b) During the preaward or preacceptance period of a negotiated acquisition, only the contracting officer, the contracting officer's superiors having contractual authority, and others specifically authorized shall transmit technical or other information and conduct discussions with prospective contractors. Information shall not be furnished to a prospective contractor if, alone or together with other information, it may afford the prospective contractor an advantage over others (see 15.610, Written and oral discussion). However, general information that is not prejudicial to others may be furnished upon request.

(c) Prospective contractors and subcontractors may place restrictions on the disclosure and use of data in proposals and quotations (see 15.407(c)(8) and the provision at 52.215-12, Restriction on Disclosure and Use of Data). Contracting officers shall not exclude proposals from consideration merely because they restrict disclosure and use of data, nor shall they be prejudiced by that restriction. The portions of the proposal that are so restricted (except for information that is also obtained from another source without restriction) shall be used only for evaluation and shall not be disclosed outside the Government without permission of the prospective contractor (but see Subpart 24.2, Freedom of Information Act).

15.413-2 Alternate II.

Agency regulations may provide that the following alternate procedures may be used instead of those specified in 15.413-1.

(a) Proposals furnished to the Government are to be used for evaluation purposes only. Disclosure outside the Government for evaluation is permitted only to the extent authorized by, and in accordance with the procedures in, 15.413-2(f).

(b) While the Government's limited use of proposals does not require that the proposal bear a restrictive notice, proposers should, if they desire to maximize protection of their trade secrets or confidential or privileged com-

Federal Acquisition Regulation

mercial and financial information contained in them, apply the restrictive notice prescribed in the provision at 52.215-12, Restriction on Disclosure and Use of Data, to such information (also see 15.407(c)(8)). In any event, information contained in proposals will be protected to the extent permitted by law, but the Government assumes no liability for the use or disclosure of information (data) not made subject to such notice in accordance with the provision at 52.215-12.

(c) If proposals are received with more restrictive conditions than those in the provision at 52.215-12, the contracting officer or coordinating officer shall inquire whether the submitter is willing to accept the conditions of the provision of 52.215-12. If the submitter does not, the contracting officer or coordinating officer shall, after consultation with counsel, either return the proposal or accept it as marked. Contracting officers shall not exclude from consideration any proposals merely because they contain an authorized or agreed-to notice, nor shall they be prejudiced by such notice.

(d) Release of proposal information (data) before decision as to the award of a contract, or the transfer of valuable and sensitive information between competing offerors during the competitive phase of the acquisition process, would seriously disrupt the Government's decision-making process and undermine the integrity of the competitive acquisition process, thus adversely affecting the Government's ability to solicit competitive proposals and award a contract which would best meet the Government's needs and serve the public interest. Therefore, to the extent permitted by law, none of the information (data) contained in proposals (except as authorized in agency regulations) is to be disclosed outside the Government before the Government's decision as to the award of a contract. In the event an outside evaluation is to be obtained, it shall be only to the extent authorized by, and in accordance with the procedures of, 15.413-2(f).

(e) In order to assure that solicited proposals (whether bearing a restrictive notice or not) are properly handled, agency implementing regulations may require the following Government notice to be placed on the cover sheet upon their receipt. (This notice is required for all unsolicited proposals, see 15.508.) This is a Government notice for internal handling purposes and does not affect any obligations or rights the Government may have with regard to the use or disclosure of any information (data) contained in the proposal or quotation.

GOVERNMENT NOTICE FOR
HANDLING PROPOSALS

This proposal shall be used and disclosed for evaluation purposes only, and a copy of this Government notice shall be applied to any reproduction or abstract thereof. Any authorized restrictive notices which the submitter places on this proposal shall also be strictly complied with. Disclosure of this proposal outside the Government for evaluation purposes shall be made only to the extent authorized by, and in accordance with, the procedures in (cite agency regulations implementing 15.413-2(f)).

If agency implementing regulations do not authorize release of proposals outside the Government for evaluation purposes, the last sentence of the foregoing Government notice is to be deleted.

(f) If authorized in agency implementing regulations, agencies may release proposals outside the Government for evaluation, consistent with the following:

(1) Decisions to release proposals outside the Government for evaluation purposes shall be made by the agency head or designee;

(2) Written agreement must be obtained from the evaluator that the information (data) contained in the proposal will be used only for evaluation purposes and will not be further disclosed;

(3) Any authorized restrictive legends placed on the proposal by the prospective contractor or subcontractor or by the Government shall be applied to any reproduction or abstracted information made by the evaluator;

(4) Upon completing the evaluation, all copies of the proposal, as well as any abstracts thereof, shall be re-

turned to the Government office which initially furnished them for evaluation; and

(5) All determinations to release the proposal outside the Government take into consideration requirements for avoiding organizational conflicts of interest and the competitive relationship, if any, between the prospective contractor or subcontractor and the prospective outside evaluator.

(g) The submitter of any proposal shall be provided notice adequate to afford an opportunity to take appropriate action before release of any information (data) contained therein pursuant to a request under the Freedom of Information Act (5 U.S.C. 552); and, time permitting, the submitter should be consulted to obtain assistance in determining the eligibility of the information (data) in question as an exemption under the Act. (See also Subpart 24.2, Freedom of Information Act.)

15.414 Forms.

(a) Standard Form 33 (SF 33), Solicitation, Offer and Award (see 53.301-33), shall be used in connection with negotiated acquisitions when it appears advantageous to begin negotiations by soliciting written offers whose written acceptance by the Government will create a binding contract without further action. Award may be made using the Award portion of SF 33.

(b) Standard Form 26 (SF 26), Award/Contract (see 53.301-26), shall be used when entering into negotiated contracts when the signature of both parties on a single document is appropriate, unless—

(1) The contract is entered into by means of Standard Form 33;

(2) The contract is for the construction, alteration, or repair of buildings, bridges, roads, or other real property;

(3) The acquisition is one for which the FAR prescribes special contract forms; or

(4) Use of a purchase order is appropriate.

15.415 Economic purchase quantities (supplies).

Contracting officers shall comply with the economic purchase quantity planning requirements for supplies in Subpart 7.2. See 7.203 for instructions regarding use of the provision at 52.207-4, Economic Purchase Quantity—Supplies, and 7.204 for guidance on handling responses to that provision.

[50 FR 35479, Aug. 30, 1985]

Subpart 15.5—Unsolicited Proposals

15.500 Scope of subpart.

This subpart prescribes policies and procedures for submission, receipt, evaluation, and acceptance of unsolicited proposals. It does not govern the competitive selection of basic research proposals (see 6.102(d)(2)).

[50 FR 52433, Dec. 23, 1985]

15.501 Definitions.

"Advertising material," as used in this subpart, means material designed to acquaint the Government with a prospective contractor's present products or potential capabilities, or to determine the Government's interest in buying these products.

"Commercial product offer" means an offer of a commercial product that is usually sold to the general public and that the vendor wishes to see introduced in the Government's supply system as an alternate or replacement for an existing supply item.

"Contribution," as used in this subpart, means a concept, suggestion, or idea presented to the Government for its use with no indication that the source intends to devote any further effort to it on the Government's behalf.

"Coordinating office," as used in this subpart, means a point of contact established within the agency to coordinate the receipt, evaluation, and disposition of unsolicited proposals.

"Technical correspondence," as used in this subpart, means written requests for information regarding Government interest in research areas, submissions of research descriptions, preproposal explorations, and other written technical inquiries.

"Unsolicited proposal" means a written proposal that is submitted to an agency on the initative of the submit-

Federal Acquisition Regulation

ter for the purpose of obtaining a contract with the Government and which is not in response to a formal or informal request (other than an agency request constituting a publicized general statement of needs).

[48 FR 42187, Sept. 19, 1983, as amended at 50 FR 1740, Jan. 11, 1985; 50 FR 52429, Dec. 23, 1985]

15.502 Policy.

Agencies may accept unsolicited proposals in accordance with 15.507. To award a contract based on an unsolicited proposal without providing for full and open competition requires that appropriate authority exists in subpart 6.3. In this connection, 6.302-1(a)(2)(i) provides special authority for unsolicited research proposals.

[50 FR 52433, Dec. 23, 1985]

15.503 General.

(a) Unsolicited proposals are a valuable means for Government agencies to obtain innovative or unique methods or approaches to accomplishing their missions from sources outside the Government.

(b) Advertising material, commercial product offers, contributions, or technical correspondence as defined in 15.501 are not unsolicited proposals.

(c) A valid unsolicited proposal must—

(1) Be innovative and unique;

(2) Be independently originated and developed by the offeror;

(3) Be prepared without Government supervision;

(4) Include sufficient detail to permit a determination that Government support could be worthwhile and the proposed work could benefit the agency's research and development or other mission responsibilities; and

(5) Not be an advance proposal for a known agency requirement that can be acquired by competitive methods.

(d) Unsolicited proposals in response to a publicized general statement of agency needs are considered to be independently originated.

(e) Agencies that receive unique and innovative unsolicited proposals not related to their missions may identify for the offeror other agencies whose missions bear a reasonable relationship to the proposal's subject matter.

[48 FR 42187, Sept. 19, 1983, as amended at 50 FR 1740, Jan. 11, 1985; 51 FR 52433, Dec. 23, 1985]

15.504 Advance guidance.

(a) Agencies shall encourage potential offerors to make preliminary contacts with appropriate agency personnel before expending extensive effort on a detailed unsolicited proposal or submitting proprietary data to the Government. These preliminary contacts should include—

(1) Inquiries as to the general need for the type of effort contemplated; and

(2) Contacts with agency technical personnel for the limited purpose of obtaining an understanding of the agency mission and responsibilities relative to the type of effort contemplated.

(b) Agencies shall make available to potential offerors of unsolicited proposals at least the following free written information:

(1) Definition (see 15.501), and content (see 15.505), of an unsolicited proposal acceptable for formal evaluation.

(2) Requirements concerning responsible prospective contractors (see Subpart 9.1), and organizational conflicts of interest (see Subpart 9.5).

(3) Role of technical correspondence before proposal preparation.

(4) Agency contact points for information regarding advertising, contributions, solicitation mailing lists, and other types of transactions frequently mistaken for unsolicited proposals.

(5) Procedures for submission and evaluation of unsolicited proposals.

(6) Information sources on agency objectives and areas of potential interest.

(7) Instructions for identifying and marking proprietary information so that restrictive legends conform to 15.509.

(c) Agency personnel shall conduct personal contacts without making any agency commitments concerning the acceptance of unsolicited proposals.

15.505 Content of unsolicited proposals.

Unsolicited proposals should contain the following information to permit consideration in an objective and timely manner:

(a) Basic information including—

(1) Offeror's name and address and type of organization; e.g., profit, nonprofit, educational, small business;

(2) Names and telephone numbers of technical and business personnel to be contacted for evaluation or negotiation purposes;

(3) Identity of proprietary data to be used only for evaluation purposes;

(4) Names of other Federal, State, local agencies, or parties receiving the proposal or funding the proposed effort;

(5) Date of submission; and

(6) Signature of a person authorized to represent and contractually obligate the offeror.

(b) Technical information including—

(1) Concise title and abstract (approximately 200 words) of the proposed effort;

(2) A reasonably complete discussion stating the objectives of the effort or activity, the method of approach and extent of effort to be employed, the nature and extent of the anticipated results, and the manner in which the work will help to support accomplishment of the agency's mission;

(3) Names and biographical information on the offeror's key personnel who would be involved, including alternates; and

(4) Type of support needed from the agency; e.g., facilities, equipment, materials, or personnel resources.

(c) Supporting information including—

(1) Proposed price or total estimated cost for the effort in sufficient detail for meaningful evaluation;

(2) Period of time for which the proposal is valid (a six month minimum is suggested);

(3) Type of contract preferred;

(4) Proposed duration of effort;

(5) Brief description of the organization, previous experience in the field, and facilities to be used; and

(6) Required statements, if applicable, about organizational conflicts of interest, security clearances, and environmental impacts.

15.506 Agency procedures.

(a) Agencies shall establish procedures, including assurance of accountability, for controlling the receipt, evaluation, and timely disposition of proposals consistent with the requirements of this subpart. The procedures shall include controls on the reproduction and disposition of proposal material, particularly data identified by the offeror as subject to duplication, use, or disclosure restrictions.

(b) Agencies shall establish contact points (see 15.501) to coordinate the receipt and handling of unsolicited proposals. Contact points outside agency contracting offices shall coordinate with qualified contracting personnel.

15.506-1 Receipt and initial review.

(a) Before initiating a comprehensive evaluation, the agency contact point shall determine if the unsolicited proposal—

(1) Contains sufficient technical and cost information;

(2) Has been approved by a responsible official or other representative authorized to contractually obligate the offeror; and

(3) Complies with the marking requirements of 15.509.

(b) If the proposal meets these requirements, the contact point shall promptly acknowledge and process the proposal. If it does not, the contact point shall provide the offeror an opportunity to submit the required data.

(c) Agencies are not required to perform comprehensive evaluations of unsolicited proposals not related to their missions. If such proposals are received, the agency contact point shall promptly reply to the offeror, state how the agency interprets the proposal, and why it is not being evaluated.

15.506-2 Evaluation.

(a) Comprehensive evaluations shall be coordinated by the agency contact point, who shall attach or imprint on each unsolicited proposal circulated for evaluation the legend required by 15.509(d). When performing a compre-

Federal Acquisition Regulation

hensive evaluation of an unsolicited proposal, evaluators shall consider the following factors, in addition to any others appropriate for the particular proposal:

(1) Unique and innovative methods, approaches, or concepts demonstrated by the proposal.

(2) Overall scientific, technical, or socio-economic merits of the proposal.

(3) Potential contribution of the effort to the agency's specific mission.

(4) The offeror's capabilities, related experience, facilities, techniques, or unique combinations of these which are integral factors for achieving the proposal objectives.

(5) The qualifications, capabilities, and experience of the proposed principal investigator, team leader, or key personnel who are critical in achieving the proposal objectives.

(b) The evaluators shall notify the coordinating office of their conclusions and recommendations when the evaluation is completed.

[48 FR 42187, Sept. 19, 1983, as amended at 50 FR 1740, Jan. 11, 1985; 50 FR 52429, Dec. 23, 1985]

15.507 Contracting methods.

(a) A favorable comprehensive evaluation of an unsolicited proposal does not, in itself, justify awarding a contract without providing for full and open competition. Agency contact points shall return an unsolicited proposal to the offeror, citing reasons, when its substance—

(1) Is available to the Government without restriction from another source;

(2) Closely resembles a pending competitive acquisition requirement; or

(3) Does not demonstrate an innovative and unique method, approach, or concept.

(b) The contracting officer may commence negotiation only when—

(1) The unsolicited proposal has received a favorable comprehensive evaluation;

(2) The unsolicited proposal is not of the character described in 15.507(a);

(3) The agency technical office sponsoring the contract supports its recommendation with facts and circumstances that preclude competition, including consideration of the evaluation factors in 15.506-2(a), furnishes the necessary funds, and provides the certification required by 6.303-2(b);

(4) The contracting officer has complied with the synopsis requirements of Subpart 5.2; and

(5) The contracting officer has executed any justification and obtained any approval or determination and findings that is required by Subpart 6.3. (For unsolicited research proposals, see 6.302-1(a)(2)(i). A valid unsolicited proposal for other than research may be accepted only if otherwise permissible under other provisions of Subpart 6.3.)

(c) If the unsolicited proposal is acceptable for award without competition, the agency and offeror shall use the proposal as the basis for negotiation.

[48 FR 42187, Sept. 19, 1983, as amended at 50 FR 1740, Jan. 11, 1985; 50 FR 52433, Dec. 23, 1985]

15.508 Prohibitions.

(a) Government personnel shall not use any data, concept, idea, or other part of an unsolicited proposal as the basis, or part of the basis, for a solicitation or in negotiations with any other firm unless the offeror is notified of and agrees to the intended use. However, this prohibition does not preclude using any data, concept, or idea available to the Government from other sources without restriction.

(b) Government personnel shall not disclose restrictively marked information (see 15.509) included in an unsolicited proposal. The disclosure of such information concerning trade secrets, processes, operations, style of work, apparatus, and other matters, except as authorized by law, may result in criminal penalties under 18 U.S.C. 1905.

15.509 Limited use of data.

(a) An unsolicited proposal may include data that the offeror does not want disclosed for any purpose other than evaluation. If the offeror wishes to restrict the proposal, the title page must be marked with the following legend:

USE AND DISCLOSURE OF DATA

The data in this proposal shall not be disclosed outside the Government and shall not be duplicated, used, or disclosed in whole or in part for any purpose other than to evaluate the proposal; *provided*, that if a contract is awarded to this offeror as a result of or in connection with the submission of these data, the Government shall have the right to duplicate, use, or disclose the data to the extent provided in the contract. This restriction does not limit the Government's right to use information contained in the data if it is obtainable from another source without restriction. The data subject to this restriction are contained in Sheets ——————————.

(b) The offeror shall also mark each restricted sheet with the following legend:

Use or disclosure of proposal data is subject to the restriction on the title page of this Proposal.

(c) The coordinating office shall return to the offeror any unsolicited proposal marked with a legend different from that provided in 15.509(a). The return letter will state that the proposal cannot be considered because it is impracticable for the Government to comply with the legend and that the agency will consider the proposal if it is resubmitted with the proper legend.

(d) The coordinating office shall place a cover sheet on the proposal or clearly mark it as follows, unless the offeror clearly states in writing that no restrictions are imposed on the disclosure or use of the data contained in the proposal:

UNSOLICITED PROPOSAL
USE OF DATA LIMITED

All Government personnel must exercise EXTREME CARE to ensure that the information in this proposal is not disclosed outside the Government and is NOT DUPLICATED, USED, OR DISCLOSED in whole or in part for any purpose other than evaluation of the proposal, without the written permission of the offeror. If a contract is awarded on the basis of this proposal, the terms of the contract shall control disclosure and use.

This notice does not limit the Government's right to use information contained in the proposal if it is obtainable from another source without restriction.

This is a Government notice, and shall not by itself be construed to impose any liability upon the Government or Government personnel for disclosure or use of data contained in this proposal.

(e) The above notice is used solely as a manner of handling unsolicited proposals that will be compatible with this subpart. However, the use of this notice shall not be used to justify the withholding of a record nor to improperly deny the public access to a record where an obligation is imposed on an agency by the Freedom of Information Act, 5 U.S.C. 552, as amended. A prospective offeror should identify trade secrets, commercial or financial information, and privileged or confidential information to the Government (see 15.509(a)).

(f) When an agency receives an unsolicited proposal without any restrictive legend from an educational or nonprofit organization or institution, and an evaluation outside the Government is necessary, the coordinating office shall—

(1) Attach a cover sheet clearly marked with the legend in 15.509(d);

(2) Change the beginning of this legend to read "*All Government and non-Government personnel....*";

(3) Delete the words "*is not disclosed outside the Government and*"; and

(4) Require any non-Government evaluator to give a written agreement stating that data in the proposal will not be disclosed to others outside the Government.

(g) If the proposal is received with the restrictive legend (15.509(a)), the modified cover sheet shall also be used and permission shall be obtained from the offeror before release of the proposal for outside evaluation.

(h) When an agency receives an unsolicited proposal with or without a restrictive legend from other than an educational or nonprofit organization or institution, and evaluation by Government personnel outside the agency or by experts outside of the Government is necessary, written permission must be obtained from the offeror before release of the proposal for evaluation. The coordinating office shall (1) clearly mark the cover sheet with the legend in 15.509(d) or as modified in 15.509(f) and (2) obtain a written agreement from any non-Government

Federal Acquisition Regulation

evaluator stating that data in the proposal will not be disclosed to persons outside the Government.

Subpart 15.6—Source Selection

15.600 Scope of subpart.

This subpart prescribes policies and procedures for selection of a source or sources in competitive negotiated acquisitions. Formal source selection procedures, involving boards, councils, or other groups for proposal evaluation, are in 15.612. Alternative procedures that limit discussions with offerors during the competition are discussed in 15.613.

15.601 Definitions.

"Clarification," as used in this subpart, means communication with an offeror for the sole purpose of eliminating minor irregularities, informalities, or apparent clerical mistakes in the proposal. It is achieved by explanation or substantiation, either in response to Government inquiry or as initiated by the offeror. Unlike discussion (see definition below), clarification does not give the offeror an opportunity to revise or modify its proposal, except to the extent that correction of apparent clerical mistakes results in a revision.

"Deficiency," as used in this subpart, means any part of a proposal that fails to satisfy the Government's requirements.

"Discussion," as used in this subpart, means any oral or written communication between the Government and an offeror (other than communications conducted for the purpose of minor clarification), whether or not initiated by the Government, that (a) involves information essential for determining the acceptability of a proposal, or (b) provides the offeror an opportunity to revise or modify its proposal.

"Source selection authority" means the Government official in charge of selecting the source. This title is most often used when the selection process is formal and the official is someone other than the contracting officer.

[48 FR 42187, Sept. 19, 1983, as amended at 50 FR 1740, Jan. 11, 1985; 50 FR 52429, Dec. 23, 1985]

15.602 Applicability.

(a) This subpart applies to negotiated contracting when source selection is based on—

(1) Cost or price competition between proposals that meet the Government's minimum requirements stated in the solicitation; or

(2) Competition involving an evaluation and comparison of cost or price and other factors.

(b) This subpart does not apply to small purchases under Part 13.

[48 FR 42187, Sept. 19, 1983, as amended at 50 FR 1740, Jan. 11, 1985; 50 FR 52429, Dec. 23, 1985]

15.603 Purpose.

Source selection procedures are designed to—

(a) Maximize competition;

(b) Minimize the complexity of the solicitation, evaluation, and the selection decision;

(c) Ensure impartial and comprehensive evaluation of offerors' proposals; and

(d) Ensure selection of the source whose proposal has the highest degree of realism and whose performance is expected to best meet stated Government requirements.

15.604 Responsibilities.

(a) Agency heads or their designees are responsible for source selection.

(b) The cognizant technical official is responsible for the technical requirements related to the source selection process.

(c) The contracting officer is responsible for contractual actions related to the source selection process, including—

(1) Issuing solicitations to which this subpart applies in accordance with Subpart 15.4 and this subpart;

(2) Conducting or coordinating cost or price analyses as prescribed in Subpart 15.8;

(3) Conducting or controlling all negotiations concerning cost or price, technical requirements, and other terms and conditions; and

(4) Selecting the source for contract award, unless another official is designated as the source selection authority.

15.605 Evaluation factors.

(a) The factors that will be considered in evaluating proposals should be tailored to each acquisition and include only those factors that will have an impact on the source selection decision.

(b) The evaluation factors that apply to an acquisition and the relative importance of those factors are within the broad discretion of agency acquisition officials. However, price or cost to the Government shall be included as an evaluation factor in every source selection. Other evaluation factors that may apply to a particular acquisition are cost realism, technical excellence, management capability, personnel qualifications, experience, past performance, schedule, and any other relevant factors.

(c) While the lowest price or lowest total cost to the Government is properly the deciding factor in many source selections, in certain acquisitions the Government may select the source whose proposal offers the greatest value to the Government in terms of performance and other factors. This may be the case, for example, in the acquisition of research and development or professional services, or when cost-reimbursement contracting is anticipated.

(d) In awarding a cost-reimbursement contract, the cost proposal should not be controlling, since advance estimates of cost may not be valid indicators of final actual costs. There is no requirement that cost-reimbursement contracts be awarded on the basis of lowest proposed cost, lowest proposed fee, or the lowest total proposed cost plus fee. The award of cost-reimbursement contracts primarily on the basis of estimated costs may encourage the submission of unrealistically low estimates and increase the likelihood of cost overruns. The primary consideration should be which offeror can perform the contract in a manner most advantageous to the Government, as determined by evaluation of proposals according to the established evaluation criteria.

(e) The solicitation shall clearly state the evaluation factors, including price or cost and any significant subfactors, that will be considered in making the source selection and their relative importance (see 15.406-5(c)). Numerical weights, which may be employed in the evaluation of proposals, need not be disclosed in solicitations. The solicitation shall inform offerors of minimum requirements that apply to particular evaluation factors and significant subfactors.

(f) In addition to other factors, offers will be evaluated on the basis of advantages and disadvantages to the Government that might result from making more than one award (see 15.407(h)). The contracting officer shall assume for the purpose of making multiple awards that $250 would be the administrative cost to the Government for issuing and administering each contract awarded under a solicitation. Individual awards shall be for the items or combination of items that result in the lowest aggregate cost to the Government, including the assumed administrative costs.

[48 FR 42187, Sept. 19, 1983, as amended at 50 FR 1740, Jan. 11, 1985; 50 FR 52429, Dec. 23, 1985; 51 FR 19715, May 30, 1986]

15.606 Changes in Government requirements.

(a) When, either before or after receipt of proposals, the Government changes, relaxes, increases, or otherwise modifies its requirements, the contracting officer shall issue a written amendment to the solicitation. When time is of the essence, oral advice of changes may be given if the changes involved are not complex and all firms to be notified (see paragraph (b) below) are notified as near to the same time as possible. The contracting officer shall make a record of the oral advice and promptly confirm that advice in writing (see 15.410).

(b) In deciding which firms to notify of a change, the contracting officer shall consider the stage in the acquisition cycle at which the change occurs and the magnitude of the change, as follows:

(1) If proposals are not yet due, the amendment shall be sent to all firms that have received a solicitation.

(2) If the time for receipt of proposals has passed but proposals have not

Federal Acquisition Regulation 15.608

yet been evaluated, the amendment should normally be sent only to the responding offerors.

(3) If the competitive range (see 15.609(a)) has been established, only those offerors within the competitive range shall be sent the amendment.

(4) If a change is so substantial that it warrants complete revision of a solicitation, the contracting officer shall cancel the original solicitation and issue a new one, regardless of the stage of the acquisition. The new solicitation shall be issued to all firms originally solicited and to any firms added to the original list.

(c) If the proposal considered to be most advantageous to the Government (as determined according to the established evaluation criteria) involves a departure from the stated requirements, the contracting officer shall provide all offerors an opportunity to submit new or amended proposals on the basis of the revised requirements; *provided*, that this can be done without revealing to the other offerors the solution proposed in the original departure or any other information that is entitled to protection (see 15.407(c)(8) and 15.610(d)).

[48 FR 42187, Sept. 19, 1983, as amended at 50 FR 1740, Jan. 11, 1985; 50 FR 52429, Dec. 23, 1985]

15.607 Disclosure of mistakes before award.

(a) Contracting officers shall examine all proposals for minor informalities or irregularities and apparent clerical mistakes (see 14.405 and 14.406). Communication with offerors to resolve these matters is clarification, not discussion within the meaning of 15.610. However, if the resulting communication prejudices the interest of other offerors, the contracting officer shall not make award without discussions with all offerors within the competitive range.

(b) Except as indicated in paragraph (c) below, mistakes not covered in paragraph (a) above are usually resolved during discussion (see 15.610).

(c) When award without discussion is contemplated, the contracting officer shall comply with the following procedure:

(1) If a mistake in a proposal is suspected, the contracting officer shall advise the offeror (pointing out the suspected mistake or otherwise identifying the area of the proposal where the suspected mistake is) and request verification. If the offeror verifies its proposal, award may be made.

(2) If an offeror alleges a mistake in its proposal, the contracting officer shall advise the offeror that it may withdraw the proposal or seek correction in accordance with subparagraph (3) below.

(3) If an offeror requests permission to correct a mistake in its proposal, the agency head (or a designee not below the level of chief of the contracting office) may make a written determination permitting the correction; *provided*, that (i) both the existence of the mistake and the proposal actually intended are established by clear and convincing evidence from the solicitation and the proposal and (ii) legal review is obtained before making the determination.

(4) If the determination under subparagraph (3) above cannot be made, and the contracting officer still contemplates award without discussion, the offeror shall be given a final opportunity to withdraw or to verify its proposal.

(5) Verification, withdrawal, or correction under subparagraphs (c)(1) through (4) above is not considered discussion within the meaning of 15.610. If, however, correction of a mistake requires reference to documents, worksheets, or other data outside the solicitation and proposal in order to establish the existence of the mistake, the proposal intended, or both, the mistake may be corrected only through discussions under 15.610.

15.608 Proposal evaluation.

(a) Proposal evaluation is an assessment of both the proposal and the offeror's ability (as conveyed by the proposal) to successfully accomplish the prospective contract. An agency shall evaluate competitive proposals solely on the factors specified in the solicitation.

(1) *Cost or price evaluation.* The contracting officer shall use cost or

price analysis (see Subpart 15.8) to evaluate the cost estimate or price, not only to determine whether it is reasonable, but also to determine the offeror's understanding of the work and ability to perform the contract. The contracting officer shall document the cost or price evaluation.

(2) *Technical evaluation.* If any technical evaluation is necessary beyond ensuring that the proposal meets the minimum requirements in the solicitation, the cognizant technical official, in documenting the technical evaluation, shall include—

(i) The basis for evaluation;

(ii) An analysis of the technically acceptable and unacceptable proposals, including an assessment of each offeror's ability to accomplish the technical requirements;

(iii) A summary, matrix, or quantitative ranking of each technical proposal in relation to the best rating possible; and

(iv) A summary of findings.

(b) All proposals received in response to a solicitation may be rejected if the agency head determines in writing that—

(1) All otherwise acceptable proposals received are at unreasonably prices;

(2) The proposals were not independently arrived at in open competition, were collusive, or were submitted in bad faith (see Subpart 3.3 for reports to be made to the Department of Justice);

(3) A cost comparison as prescribed in OMB Circular A-76 and Subpart 7.3 shows that performance by the Government is more economical; or

(4) For other reasons, cancellation is clearly in the Government's interest.

(c) The requirements of 14.407-3, Prompt payment discounts, are applicable to negotiated acquisitions.

[48 FR 42187, Sept. 19, 1983, as amended at 50 FR 1740, Jan. 11, 1985; 50 FR 26903, June 28, 1985; 50 FR 52429, Dec. 23, 1985]

15.609 Competitive range.

(a) The contracting officer shall determine which proposals are in the competitive range for the purpose of conducting written or oral discussion (see 15.610(b)). The competitive range shall be determined on the basis of cost or price and other factors that were stated in the solicitation and shall include all proposals that have a reasonable chance of being selected for award. When there is doubt as to whether a proposal is in the competitive range, the proposal should be included.

(b) If the contracting officer, after complying with 15.610(b), determines that a proposal no longer has a reasonable chance of being selected for contract award, it may no longer be considered for selection.

(c) The contracting officer shall notify in writing an unsuccessful offeror at the earliest practicable time that its proposal is no longer eligible for award (see 15.1001(b)).

(d) If the contracting officer initially solicits unpriced technical proposals, they shall be evaluated to determine which are acceptable to the Government or could, after discussion, be made acceptable. After necessary discussion of these technical proposals is completed, the contracting officer shall (1) solicit price proposals for all the acceptable technical proposals which offer the greatest value to the Government in terms of performance and other factors and (2) make award to the low responsible offeror, either without or following discussion, as appropriate. Except in acquisition of architect-engineer services (see Subpart 36.6), a competitive range determination must include cost or price proposals.

[48 FR 42187, Sept. 19, 1983, as amended at 50 FR 1741, Jan. 11, 1985; 50 FR 52429, Dec. 23, 1985]

15.610 Written or oral discussion.

(a) The requirement in paragraph (b) below for written or oral discussion need not be applied in acquisitions—

(1) In which prices are fixed by law or regulation;

(2) Of the set-aside portion of a partial set-aside; or

(3) In which it can be clearly demonstrated from the existence of full and open competition or accurate prior cost experience with the product or service that acceptance of the most favorable initial proposal without discussion would result in the lowest overall

Federal Acquisition Regulation   15.611

cost to the Government at a fair and reasonable price; *provided*, That—

(i) The solicitation notified all offerors of the possibility that award might be made without discussion; and

(ii) The award is in fact made without any written or oral discussion with any offeror.

(b) Except as provided in paragraph (a) above, the contracting officer shall conduct written or oral discussion with all responsible offerors who submit proposals within the competitive range. The content and extent of the discussions is a matter of the contracting officer's judgment, based on the particular facts of each acquisition (but see paragraphs (c) and (d) below).

(c) The contracting officer shall—

(1) Control all discussions;

(2) Advise the offeror of deficiencies in its proposal so that the offeror is given an opportunity to satisfy the Government's requirements;

(3) Attempt to resolve any uncertainties concerning the technical proposal and other terms and conditions of the proposal;

(4) Resolve any suspected mistakes by calling them to the offeror's attention as specifically as possible without disclosing information concerning other offerors' proposals or the evaluation process (see 15.607 and Part 24); and

(5) Provide the offeror a reasonable opportunity to submit any cost or price, technical, or other revisions to its proposal that may result from the discussions.

(d) The contracting officer and other Government personnel involved shall not engage in—

(1) Technical leveling (i.e., helping an offeror to bring its proposal up to the level of other proposals through successive rounds of discussion, such as by pointing out weaknesses resulting from the offeror's lack of diligence, competence, or inventiveness in preparing the proposal);

(2) Technical transfusion (i.e., Government disclosure of technical information pertaining to a proposal that results in improvement of a competing proposal); or

(3) Auction techniques, such as—

(i) Indicating to an offeror a cost or price that it must meet to obtain further consideration;

(ii) Advising an offeror of its price standing relative to another offeror (however, it is permissible to inform an offeror that its cost or price is considered by the Government to be too high or unrealistic); and

(iii) Otherwise furnishing information about other offerors' prices.

[48 FR 42187, Sept. 19, 1983, as amended at 50 FR 1741, Jan. 11, 1985; 50 FR 52429, Dec. 23, 1985]

15.611 Best and final offers.

(a) Upon completion of discussions, the contracting officer shall issue to all offerors still within the competitive range a request for best and final offers. Oral requests for best and final offers shall be confirmed in writing.

(b) The request shall include—

(1) Notice that discussions are concluded;

(2) Notice that this is the opportunity to submit a best and final offer;

(3) A common cutoff date and time that allows a reasonable opportunity for submission of written best and final offers; and

(4) Notice that if any modification is submitted, it must be received by the date and time specified and is subject to the Late Submissions, Modifications, and Withdrawals of Proposals or Quotations provision of the solicitation (see 15.412).

(c) After receipt of best and final offers, the contracting officer should not reopen discussions unless it is clearly in the Government's interest to do so (e.g., it is clear that information available at that time is inadequate to reasonably justify contractor selection and award based on the best and final offers received). If discussions are reopened, the contracting officer shall issue an additional request for best and final offers to all offerors still within the competitive range.

(d) Following evaluation of the best and final offers, the contracting officer (or other designated source selection authority) shall select that source whose best and final offer is most advantageous to the Government, considering price and the other factors included in the solicitation (but see 15.608(b)).

[48 FR 42187, Sept. 19, 1983, as amended at 50 FR 1741, Jan. 11, 1985; 50 FR 52429, Dec. 23, 1985; 51 FR 19715, May 30, 1986]

15.612 Formal source selection.

(a) *General.* A source selection process is considered "formal" when a specific evaluation group structure is established to evaluate proposals and select the source for contract award. This approach is generally used in high-dollar-value acquisitions and may be used in other acquisitions as prescribed in agency regulations. The source selection organization typically consists of an evaluation board, advisory council, and designated source selection authority at a management level above that of the contracting officer.

(b) *Responsibilities.* When using formal source selection, the agency head or a designee shall ensure that—

(1) The official to be responsible for the source selection is formally designated as the source selection authority;

(2) The source selection authority formally establishes an evaluation group structure appropriate to the requirements of the particular solicitation; and

(3) Before conducting any presolicitation conferences (see 15.404) or issuing the solicitation, the source selection authority approves a source selection plan.

(c) *Source Selection Plan.* As a minimum, the plan shall include—

(1) A description of the organization structure;

(2) Proposed presolicitation activities;

(3) A summary of the acquisition strategy;

(4) A statement of the proposed evaluation factors and their relative importance;

(5) A description of the evaluation process, methodology, and techniques to be used; and

(6) A schedule of significant milestones.

(d) *Source Selection Decision.* The source selection authority shall use the factors established in the solicitation (see 15.605) to make the source selection decision.

(1) The source selection authority shall consider any rankings and ratings, and, if requested, any recommendations prepared by evaluation and advisory groups.

(2) The supporting documentation prepared for the selection decision shall show the relative differences among proposals and their strengths, weaknesses, and risks in terms of the evaluation factors. The supporting documentation shall include the basis and reasons for the decision.

(e) *Safeguarding information.* Consistent with Part 24, agencies shall exercise particular care to protect source selection information on a strict need-to-know basis.

(1) During the selection process, approval by the source selection authority shall be obtained before any release of source selection data. After the source selection, releasing authority shall be as prescribed in agency procedures. In all cases, agency procedures should prescribe the releasing authority.

(2) Government personnel shall not contact or visit a contractor regarding a proposal under source selection evaluation, without the prior approval of the source selection authority.

(f) *Postaward notices and debriefings.* See 15.1001(c) and 15.1003.

[48 FR 42187, Sept. 19, 1983, as amended at 50 FR 1741, Jan. 11, 1985; 50 FR 52429, Dec. 23, 1985]

15.613 Alternative source selection procedures.

(a) The National Aeronautics and Space Administration (NASA) and the Department of Defense (DoD) have developed, and use in appropriate situations, source selection procedures that limit discussions with offerors during the competition, and that differ from other procedures prescribed in Subpart 15.6. The procedures are the NASA Source Evaluation Board procedures and the DoD "Four-Step" Source Selection Procedures. Detailed coverage of these procedures is in the respective agency acquisition regulations.

Federal Acquisition Regulation 15.705

(b) Other agencies may use either the NASA or DoD procedure as a model in developing their own procedures, including applicability criteria, consistent with mission needs.

Subpart 15.7—Make-or-Buy Programs

15.700 Scope of subpart.

This subpart prescribes policies and procedures for obtaining, evaluating, negotiating, and agreeing to prime contractors' proposed make-or-buy programs and for incorporating make-or-buy programs into contracts. Consent to subcontracts and review of contractors' purchasing systems are separate actions covered in Part 44, Subcontracting Policies and Procedures.

15.701 Definitions.

"Buy item" means an item or work effort to be produced or performed by a subcontractor.

"Make item" means an item or work effort to be produced or performed by the prime contractor or its affiliates, subsidiaries, or divisions.

"Make-or-buy program" means that part of a contractor's written plan for a contract identifying (a) those major items to be produced or work efforts to be performed in the prime contractor's facilities and (b) those to be subcontracted.

15.702 General.

The prime contractor is responsible for managing contract performance, including planning, placing, and administering subcontracts as necessary to ensure the lowest overall cost and technical risk to the Government. Although the Government does not expect to participate in every management decision, it may reserve the right to review and agree on the contractor's make-or-buy program when necessary to ensure (a) negotiation of reasonable contract prices, (b) satisfactory performance, or (c) implementation of socioeconomic policies.

15.703 Acquisitions requiring make-or-buy programs.

(a) Contracting officers shall require prospective contractors to submit make-or-buy programs for all negotiated acquisitions whose estimated value is $2 million or more, except when the proposed contract—

(1) Is for research or development and—if prototypes or hardware are involved—no significant follow-on production under the same contract is anticipated;

(2) Is priced on the basis of (i) adequate price competition or (ii) established catalog or market prices of commercial items sold in substantial quantities to the general public, or has only prices set by law or regulation (see 15.804-3); or

(3) Involves only work that the contracting officer determines is not complex.

(b) Contracting officers may require prospective contractors to submit make-or-buy programs for negotiated acquisitions whose estimated value is under $2 million only if the contracting officer (1) determines that the information is necessary and (2) documents the reasons in the contract file.

15.704 Items and work included.

The information required from a prospective contractor in a make-or-buy program shall be confined to those major items or work efforts that would normally require company management review of the make-or-buy decision because they are complex, costly, needed in large quantities, or require additional facilities to produce. Raw materials, commercial products (see 11.001), and off-the-shelf items (see 46.101) shall not be included, unless their potential impact on contract cost or schedule is critical. As a rule, make-or-buy programs should not include items or work efforts estimated to cost less than (a) 1 percent of the total estimated contract price or (b) any minimum dollar set by the agency, whichever is less.

[48 FR 42187, Sept. 19, 1983, as amended at 51 FR 27119, July 29, 1986]

15.705 Solicitation requirements.

When prospective contractors are required to submit proposed make-or-buy programs (see 15.703), the solicitation shall include—

(a) A statement that the program and required supporting information must accompany the offer;

(b) A description of factors to be used in evaluating the proposed program, such as capability, capacity, availability of small business and labor surplus area concerns for subcontracting, establishment of new facilities in or near labor surplus areas, delivery or performance schedules, control of technical and schedule interfaces, proprietary processes, technical superiority or exclusiveness, and technical risks involved; and

(c) A requirement that the offeror's program include or be supported by the following information:

(1) A description of each major item or work effort (see 15.704).

(2) Categorization of each major item or work effort as "must make," "must buy," or "can either make or buy."

(3) For each item or work effort categorized as "can either make or buy," a proposal either to "make" or to "buy."

(4) Reasons for (i) categorizing items and work efforts as "must make" or "must buy" and (ii) proposing to "make" or to "buy" those categorized as "can either make or buy." The reasons must include the consideration given to the evaluation factors described in the solicitation and be in sufficient detail to permit the contracting officer to evaluate the categorization or proposal.

(5) Designation of the plant or division proposed to make each item or perform each work effort and a statement as to whether the existing or proposed new facility is in or near a labor surplus area.

(6) Identification of proposed subcontractors, if known, and their location and size status (see also Subpart 19.7 for subcontracting plan requirements).

(7) Any recommendations to defer make-or-buy decisions when categorization of some items or work efforts is impracticable at the time of submission.

(8) Any other information the contracting officer requires in order to evaluate the program.

15.706 Evaluation, negotiation, and agreement.

(a) Contracting officers shall evaluate and negotiate proposed make-or-buy programs as soon as practicable after their receipt and before contract award. When the program is to be incorporated in the contract (see 15.707) and the design status of the product being acquired does not permit accurate precontract identification of major items or work efforts, the contracting officer shall notify the prospective contractor in writing that these items or efforts, when identifiable, shall be added under the clause at 52.215–21, Changes or Additions to Make-or-Buy Program.

(b) In preparing to evaluate and negotiate prospective contractors' make-or-buy programs, the contracting officer shall request the recommendations of appropriate personnel, including technical and program management personnel, and the activity small and disadvantaged business utilization specialist. The proposed program shall also be made available to the Small Business Administration representative, if any, for review and recommendation. The contracting officer shall request these recommendations early enough to consider them fully before (1) agreeing to a make-or-buy program or (2) consenting to a change in a make-or-buy program already incorporated in a contract.

(c) The contractor has the basic responsibility for make-or-buy decisions. Therefore, its recommendations should be accepted unless they are inconsistent with Government interests or policy.

(d) Contracting officers shall give primary consideration to the effect of the proposed make-or-buy program on price, quality, delivery, and performance, including technical or financial risk involved. The evaluation of "must make" and "must buy" items should normally be confined to ensuring that they are properly categorized. The effect of the following factors on the Government's interests shall also be considered:

(1) Whether the contractor has justified performing work in plant that

Federal Acquisition Regulation 15.800

differs significantly from its normal operations.

(2) Whether the contractor's recommended program requires Government investment in new or other facilities in order for the contractor to perform the work in plant. (This additional cost to the Government would not be reflected in the contract price.)

(3) The impact of the contractor's projected plant work loading on indirect costs.

(4) The contractor's consideration of the competence, ability, experience, and capacity available in other firms, especially small business, small disadvantaged business, or labor surplus area concerns.

(5) The projected location of any required additional facilities in or near labor surplus areas.

(6) The contractor's make-or-buy history regarding the type of item concerned.

(7) The scope of proposed subcontracts, including the type and level of technical effort involved.

(8) Other factors such as future requirements, engineering, tooling, starting load costs, market conditions, technical superiority, and the availability of personnel and materials.

(e) Contracting officers shall not normally agree to proposed "make items" when the products or services are (1) not regularly manufactured or provided by the contractor and are available—quality, quantity, delivery, and other essential factors considered—from another firm at equal or lower prices or when they are (2) regularly manufactured or provided by the contractor, but available—quality, quantity, delivery, and other essential factors considered— from another firm at lower prices. However, the contracting officer may agree to these as "make items" if their categorization as "buy items" would increase the Government's overall cost for the contract or acquisition program.

15.707 Incorporating make-or-buy programs in contracts.

(a) After agreement is reached, the contracting officer may incorporate the make-or-buy program in negotiated contracts for—

(1) Major systems (see Part 34) or their subsystems or components, regardless of contract type; or

(2) Other supplies and services if (i) the contract is a cost-reimbursable contract, or a cost-sharing contract in which the contractor's share of the cost is less than 25 percent, and (ii) the contracting officer determines that technical or cost risks justify Government review and approval of changes or additions to the make-or-buy program.

(b) It may be necessary to incorporate some items of significant value in the make-or-buy program as "make" or, alternatively, as "buy" even though the opposite categorization would result in greater economy for the Government. If this situation occurs in any fixed-price incentive or cost-plus-incentive-fee contract, the contracting officer shall specify these items in the contract and state that they are subject to paragraph (d) of the clause at 52.215-21, Changes or Additions to Make-or-Buy Program (see 15.708 below). If the contractor proposes to reverse the categorization of such items during contract performance, the contract price shall be subject to equitable reduction.

15.708 Contract clause.

The contracting officer shall insert the clause at 52.215-21, Changes or Additions to Make-or-Buy Program, in solicitations and contracts when it is contemplated that a make-or-buy program will be incorporated in the contract. If a less economical "make" or "buy" categorization is selected for one or more items of significant value, the contracting officer shall use the clause with (a) its Alternate I, if a fixed-price incentive contract is contemplated, or (b) its Alternate II, if a cost-plus-incentive-fee contract is contemplated.

Subpart 15.8—Price Negotiation

15.800 Scope of subpart.

This subpart prescribes the cost and price negotiation policies and procedures applicable to initial and revised pricing of (a) negotiated prime contracts (including subcontract pricing under them when required) and (b) contract modifications (including modifications to contracts awarded by sealed bidding).

[48 FR 42187, Sept. 19, 1983, as amended at 50 FR 1741, Jan. 11, 1985; 50 FR 52429, Dec. 23, 1985]

15.801 Definitions.

"Cost analysis" means the review and evaluation of the separate cost elements and proposed profit of (a) an offeror's or contractor's cost or pricing data and (b) the judgmental factors applied in projecting from the data to the estimated costs, in order to form an opinion on the degree to which the proposed costs represent what the contract should cost, assuming reasonable economy and efficiency.

"Cost or pricing data" means all facts as of the time of price agreement that prudent buyers and sellers would reasonably expect to affect price negotiations significantly. Cost or pricing data are factual, not judgmental, and are therefore verifiable. While they do not indicate the accuracy of the prospective contractor's judgment about estimated future costs or projections, they do include the data forming the basis for that judgment. Cost or pricing data are more than historical accounting data; they are all the facts that can be reasonably expected to contribute to the soundness of estimates of future costs and to the validity of determinations of costs already incurred. They also include such factors as (a) vendor quotations; (b) nonrecurring costs; (c) information on changes in production methods and in production or purchasing volume; (d) data supporting projections of business prospects and objectives and related operations costs; (e) unit-cost trends such as those associated with labor efficiency; (f) make-or-buy decisions; (g) estimated resources to attain business goals; and (h) information on management decisions that could have a significant bearing on costs.

"Field pricing support" means a review and evaluation of the contractor's or subcontractor's proposal by any or all field pricing support personnel (see 15.805-5(a)(2)).

"Forward pricing rate agreement" means a written agreement negotiated between a contractor and the Government to make certain rates available during a specified period for use in pricing contracts or modifications. Such rates represent reasonable projections of specific costs that are not easily estimated for, identified with, or generated by a specific contract, contract end item, or task. These projections may include rates for labor, indirect costs, material obsolescence and usage, spare parts provisioning, and material handling.

"Price," as used in this subpart, means cost plus any fee or profit applicable to the contract type.

"Price analysis" means the process of examining and evaluating a proposed price without evaluating its separate cost elements and proposed profit.

"Technical analysis," as used in this subpart, means the examination and evaluation by personnel having specialized knowledge, skills, experience, or capability in engineering, science, or management of proposed quantities and kinds of materials, labor, processes, special tooling, facilities, and associated factors set forth in a proposal in order to determine and report on the need for and reasonableness of the proposed resources assuming reasonable economy and efficiency.

15.802 Policy.

(a) 10 U.S.C. 2306(f) and 41 U.S.C. 254(d) provide that all executive agencies shall require a prime contractor or any subcontractor to submit and certify cost or pricing data under certain circumstances. The Acts also require inclusion of contract clauses that provide for reduction of the contract price by any significant amounts that such price was increased because of submission of contractor or subcontractor defective cost or pricing data.

(b) Contracting officers shall—

(1) Purchase supplies and services from responsible sources at fair and reasonable prices;

(2) Price each contract separately and independently and not (i) use proposed price reductions under other contracts as an evaluation factor or (ii) consider losses or profits realized or anticipated under other contracts; and

Federal Acquisition Regulation

(3) Not include in a contract price any amount for a specified contingency to the extent that the contract provides for price adjustment based upon the occurrence of that contingency.

[48 FR 42187, Sept. 19, 1983, as amended at 50 FR 1741, Jan. 11, 1985; 50 FR 52429, Dec. 23, 1985]

15.803 General.

(a) Since information from sources other than an offeror's or contractor's records may significantly affect the Government's negotiating position, Government personnel shall not disclose to an offeror or contractor any conclusions, recommendations, or portions of administrative contracting officer or auditor reports regarding the offeror's or contractor's proposal without the concurrence of the contracting officer responsible for negotiation. This prohibition does not preclude disclosing discrepancies or mistakes of fact (such as duplications, omissions, and errors in computation) contained in the cost or pricing data supporting the proposal.

(b) Before issuing a solicitation, the contracting officer shall (when it is feasible to do so) develop an estimate of the proper price level or value of the supplies or services to be purchased. Estimates can range from simple budgetary estimates to complex estimates based on inspection of the product itself and review of such items as drawings, specifications, and prior data.

(c) Price negotiation is intended to permit the contracting officer and the offeror to agree on a fair and reasonable price. Price negotiation does not require that agreement be reached on every element of cost. Reasonable compromises may be necessary, and it may not be possible to negotiate a price that is in accord with all the contributing specialists' opinions or with the contracting officer's prenegotiation objective. The contracting officer is responsible for exercising the requisite judgment and is solely responsible for the final pricing decision. The recommendations and counsel of contributing specialists, including auditors, are advisory only. However, the contracting officer should include comments in the price negotiation memorandum when significant audit or other specialist recommendations are not adopted.

(d) The contracting officer's primary concern is the price the Government actually pays; the contractor's eventual cost and profit or fee should be a secondary concern. The contracting officer's objective is to negotiate a contract of a type and with a price providing the contractor the greatest incentive for efficient and economical performance. The negotiation of a contract type and a price are related and should be considered together with the issues of risk and uncertainty to the contractor and the Government. Therefore the contracting officer should not become preoccupied with any single element and should balance the contract type, cost, and profit or fee negotiated to achieve a total result and price fair and reasonable to both the Government and the contractor. If, however, the contractor insists on a price or demands a profit or fee that the contracting officer considers unreasonable and the contracting officer has taken all authorized actions (including determining the feasibility of developing an alternative source) without success, the contracting officer shall then refer the contract action to higher authority. Disposition of the action by higher authority should be documented.

15.804 Cost or pricing data.

15.804-1 General.

(a) Cost or pricing data submitted by an offeror or contractor enable the Government to perform cost or price analysis and ultimately enable the Government and the contractor to negotiate fair and reasonable prices. Cost or pricing data may be submitted actually or by specific identification in writing.

(b) The Armed Services Procurement Manual for Contract Pricing (ASPM No. 1) was issued by the Department of Defense to guide pricing and negotiating personnel. It provides detailed discussions and examples applying pricing policies to pricing problems. ASPM No. 1 is available for use for instruction and professional guidance. However, it is not directive, and

15.804-2

its references to Department of Defense forms and regulations should be considered informational only. Copies of ASPM No. 1 (Stock No. 008-000-00221-5) may be purchased from the Superintendent of Documents, Attn: Mail List Section, U.S. Government Printing Office, Washington, DC 20402.

[48 FR 42187, Sept. 19, 1983, as amended at 50 FR 1741, Jan. 11, 1985; 50 FR 52429, Dec. 23, 1985]

15.804-2 Requiring certified cost or pricing data.

(a) (1) Except as provided in 15.804-3, certified cost or pricing data are required before accomplishing any of the following actions:

(i) The award of any negotiated contract (except for unpriced actions such as letter contracts) expected to exceed $100,000.

(ii) The modification of any sealed bid or negotiated contract (whether or not cost or pricing data were initially required) when the modification involves a price adjustment expected to exceed $100,000. (For example, a $30,000 modification resulting from a reduction of $70,000 and an increase of $40,000 is a pricing adjustment exceeding $100,000.) This requirement does not apply when unrelated and separately priced changes for which cost or pricing data would not otherwise be required are included for adminstrative convenience in the same modification.

(iii) The award of a subcontract at any tier, if the contractor and each higher tier subcontractor have been required to furnish certified cost or pricing data, when the subcontract is expected to exceed $100,000.

(iv) The modification of any subcontract covered by subdivision (iii) above, when the price adjustment (see subdivision (ii) above) is expected to exceed $100,000.

(2) If cost or pricing data are needed for pricing actions over $25,000 and not in excess of $100,000, certified cost or pricing data may be obtained. There should be relatively few instances where certified cost or pricing data and inclusion of defective pricing clauses would be justified in awards between $25,000 and $100,000. The amount of data required to be submitted should be limited to that data necessary to allow the contracting officer to determine the reasonableness of the price. Whenever certified cost or pricing data are required for pricing actions of $100,000 or less, the contracting officer shall document the file to justify the requirement. When awarding a contract of $25,000 or less, the contracting officer shall not require certified cost or pricing data.

(b) When certified cost or pricing data are required, the contracting officer shall require the contractor or prospective contractor to submit to the contracting officer (and to have any subcontractor or prospective subcontractor submit to the prime contractor or appropriate subcontractor tier) the following in support of any proposal:

(1) The cost or pricing data.

(2) A certificate of current cost or pricing data, in the format specified in 15.804-4, certifying that to the best of its knowledge and belief, the cost or pricing data were accurate, complete, and current as of the date of final agreement on price.

[48 FR 42187, Sept. 19, 1983, as amended at 50 FR 1741, Jan. 11, 1985; 50 FR 52429, Dec. 23, 1985]

15.804-3 Exemptions from or waiver of submission of certified cost or pricing data.

(a) *General.* Except as provided in paragraphs (b) and (c) below, the contracting officer shall not require submission or certification of cost or pricing data when the contracting officer determines that prices are—

(1) Based on adequate price competition (see paragraph (b) below);

(2) Based on established catalog or market prices of commercial items sold in substantial quantities to the general public (see paragraph (c) below); or

(3) Set by law or regulation (see paragraph (d) below).

(b) *Adequate price competition.* (1) Price competition exists if—

(i) Offers are solicited;

(ii) Two or more responsible offerors that can satisfy the Government's requirements submit priced offers re-

Federal Acquisition Regulation 15.804-3

sponsive to the solicitation's expressed requirements; and

(iii) These offerors compete independently for a contract to be awarded to the responsible offeror submitting the lowest evaluated price.

(2) If price competition exists, the contracting officer shall presume that it is adequate unless—

(i) The solicitation is made under conditions that unreasonably deny to one or more known and qualified offerors an opportunity to compete;

(ii) The low offeror has such a decided advantage that it is practically immune from competition; or

(iii) There is a finding, supported by a statement of the facts and approved at a level above the contracting officer, that the lowest price is unreasonable.

(3) A price is "based on" adequate price competition if it results directly from price competition or if price analysis alone clearly demonstrates that the proposed price is reasonable in comparison with current or recent prices for the same or substantially the same items purchased in comparable quantities, terms, and conditions under contracts that resulted from adequate price competition.

(c) *Established catalog or market prices.* A proposal is exempt from the requirement for submission of certified cost or pricing data if the prices are, or are based on, established catalog or established market prices of commercial items sold in substantial quantities to the general public. In order to qualify for this exemption, the terms of the proposed purchase, such as quantity and delivery requirements, should be sufficiently similar to those of the commercial sales that the catalog or market price will be fair and reasonable.

(1) "Established catalog prices" must be recorded in a form regularly maintained by the manufacturer or vendor. This form may be a catalog, price list, schedule, or other verifiable and established record. The record must (i) be published or otherwise available for customer inspection and (ii) state current or last sales price to a significant number of buyers constituting the general public (see subparagraph (5) below).

(2) "Established market prices" are current prices that (i) are established in the course of ordinary and usual trade between buyers and sellers free to bargain and (ii) can be substantiated by data from sources independent of the manufacturer or vendor.

(3) "Commercial items" are supplies or services regularly used for other than Government purposes and sold or traded to the general public in the course of normal business operations.

(4) An item is "sold in substantial quantities" only when the quantities regularly sold are sufficient to constitute a real commercial market. Nominal quantities, such as models, samples, prototypes, or experimental units, do not meet this requirement. For services to be sold in substantial quantities, they must be customarily provided by the offeror, using personnel regularly employed and equipment (if any is necessary) regularly maintained solely or principally to provide the services.

(5) The "general public" is a significant number of buyers other than the Government or affiliates of the offeror; the item involved must not be for Government end use. For the purpose of this subsection 15.804-3, items acquired for "Government end use" include items acquired for foreign military sales.

(6) A price is "based on" a catalog or market price only if the item being purchased is sufficiently similar to the catalog- or market-priced commercial item to ensure that any difference in prices can be identified and justified without resort to cost analysis.

(7) If an item is substantially similar to a commercial item for which there is an established catalog or market price at which substantial quantities are sold to the general public, but the price proposed is not *based on* this catalog or market price (see subparagraph (6) above), the contracting officer may, if doing so will result in a fair and reasonable price, limit any requirement for cost or pricing data to those data that pertain to the differences between the items. When the difference between the catalog or market price of an item or items and the proposed total contract price is $100,000 or more, the contracting offi-

cer shall require submission of certified cost or pricing data to identify and justify that difference unless an exemption or waiver is granted.

(8) Even though there is an established catalog or market price of commercial items sold in substantial quantities to the general public, the contracting officer may require cost or pricing data if (i) the contracting officer makes a written finding that the price is not reasonable, including the facts upon which the finding is based, and (ii) the finding is approved at a level above the contracting officer.

(d) *Prices set by law or regulation.* A price set by law or regulation is exempt from the requirement for submission of certified cost or pricing data. Pronouncements in the form of periodic rulings, reviews, or similar actions of a governmental body, or embodied in the laws, are sufficient to establish the price.

(e) *Claiming and granting exemption.* To receive an exemption under paragraph (c) or (d) above, the offeror must ordinarily claim it on Standard Form 1412, Claim for Exemption from Submission of Certified Cost or Pricing Data, when the total proposed amount exceeds $100,000 and more than one catalog item for which an exemption is claimed exceeds $25,000. When an exemption is claimed for more than one item in a proposal, a separate SF 1412 is required for each such item exceeding $25,000 except as otherwise provided in the solicitation. The contracting officer may grant an exemption and need not require the submission of SF 1412 when—

(1) The Government has acted favorably on an exemption claim for the same item or similar items within the past year. In that case, except as otherwise directed by the contracting officer, the offeror may furnish a copy of the prior claim and related Government action. The offeror must also submit a statement to the effect that to its knowledge since the prior submission, except as expressly set forth in the statement, there have been no changes in the catalog price or discounts, volume of actual sales, or the ratio of sales for Government end use to sales in other categories which would cause a cumulative change in price exceeding $25,000;

(2) Special arrangements for the submission of exemption claims have been made in anticipation of repetitive acquisitions of catalog items; or

(3) There is evidence, before solicitation, that the item has an acceptable established catalog or market price or a price set by law or regulation. Evidence may include (i) recent submissions by offerors or (ii) the contracting officer's knowledge of market conditions, prevailing prices, or sources.

(f) *Verification.* (1) When a prospective contractor requests exemption from submission of certified cost or pricing data, the contracting officer shall ensure that applicable criteria in either paragraph (c) or (d) above, as appropriate, are satisfied before issuing the exemption.

(2) SF 1412 lists three categories of sales related to the established catalog price of a commercial item sold in substantial quantities to the general public: A, Sales to the U.S. Government or to contractors for U.S. Government use; B, Sales at catalog price to the general public; and C, Sales to the general public at other than catalog price. Although "substantial quantities" cannot be precisely defined (see subparagraph (c)(4) above), the following guidelines are provided for determining whether exemption claims submitted under the catalog price provision of SF 1412 meet the "substantial quantities" criterion:

(i) Sales to the general public are normally regarded as substantial if (A) Category B and C sales are not negligible in themselves and comprise at least 55 percent of total sales of the item and (B) Category B sales comprise at least 75 percent of the total of Category B and C sales.

(ii) Sales to the general public are rarely considered substantial enough to grant an exemption if (A) Category B and C sales comprise less than 35 percent of total sales of the item or (B) Category B sales comprise less than 55 percent of the total of Category B and C sales.

(iii) When percentages fall between those above, the contracting officer should analyze the individual situation

Federal Acquisition Regulation

in order to determine whether or not an exemption is justified.

(3) The contracting officer may verify or obtain verification (including audit or contract administration assistance) of the submitted data pertaining to catalog or market prices or prices set by law or regulation. Access to the prospective contractor's records is limited to access to the facts bearing directly on the exemption claimed. It does not extend to cost, profit, or other data relevant solely to the reasonableness of the catalog or proposed price.

(g) *Individual or class exemptions.* The chief of the contracting office may authorize individual or class exemptions for exceptional cases when the contracting officer recommends that an exemption should be made, even though the case does not strictly meet all the criteria for catalog- or market-price exemption. The quantity and prices of actual commercial sales compared with prices offered to the Government, and price relationships as influenced by prevailing trade practices, are the important factors for consideration. The Government's need and the prospective contractor's resistance are not appropriate considerations.

(h) *Price analysis.* Even though an item qualifies for exemption from the requirement for submission of certified cost or pricing data, the contracting officer shall make a price analysis to determine the reasonableness of the price and any need for further negotiation. Unless information is available from Government sources, it may be necessary to obtain from the prospective contractor information such as that regarding—

(1) The supplier's marketing system (e.g., use of jobbers, brokers, sales agencies, or distributors);

(2) The services normally provided commercial purchasers (e.g., engineering, financing, or advertising or promotion);

(3) Normal quantity per order; and

(4) Annual volume of sales to largest customers.

(i) *Waiver for exceptional cases.* The agency head (or, if the contract is with a foreign government or agency, the head of the contracting activity) may, in exceptional cases, waive the requirement for submission of certified cost or pricing data. The authorization for the waiver and the reasons for granting it shall be in writing. The agency head may delegate this authority.

[48 FR 42187, Sept. 19, 1983, as amended at 50 FR 1741, Jan. 11, 1985; 50 FR 52429, Dec. 23, 1985; 51 FR 2650, Jan. 17, 1986]

15.804-4 Certificate of Current Cost or Pricing Data.

(a) When certified cost or pricing data are required under 15.804-2, the contracting officer shall require the contractor to execute a Certificate of Current Cost or Pricing Data, shown below, and shall include the executed certificate in the contract file. The certificate states that the cost or pricing data are accurate, complete, and current as of the date the contractor and the Government agreed on a price. Only one certificate shall be required; the contractor shall submit it as soon as practicable after price agreement is reached.

CERTIFICATE OF CURRENT COST OR PRICING DATA

This is to certify that, to the best of my knowledge and belief, the cost or pricing data (as defined in section 15.801 of the Federal Acquisition Regulation (FAR) and required under FAR subsection 15.804-2) submitted, either actually or by specific identification in writing, to the contracting officer or to the contracting officer's representative in support of ———————* are accurate, complete, and current as of ———————**. This certification includes the cost or pricing data supporting any advance agreements and forward pricing rate agreements between the offeror and the Government that are part of the proposal.

Firm ———————
Name ———————
Title ———————
Date of execution*** ———————

*Identify the proposal, quotation, request for price adjustment, or other submission involved, giving the appropriate identifying number (e.g., RFP No.).

**Insert the day, month, and year when price negotiations were concluded and price agreement was reached.

***Insert the day, month, and year of signing, which should be as close as practicable to the date when the price negotiations were concluded and the contract price was agreed to.

(End of certificate)

(b) The certificate does not constitute a representation as to the accuracy of the contractor's judgment on the estimate of future costs or projections. It does apply to the data upon which the judgment or estimate was based. This distinction between fact and judgment should be clearly understood. If the contractor had information reasonably available at the time of agreement showing that the negotiated price was not based on accurate, complete, and current data, the contractor's responsibility is not limited by any lack of personal knowledge of the information on the part of its negotiators.

(c) Closing or cutoff dates should be included as part of the data submitted with the proposal. Certain data may not be reasonably available before normal periodic closing dates (e.g., actual indirect costs). Before agreement on price, the contractor shall update all data as of the latest dates for which information is reasonably available. Data within the contractor's or a subcontractor's organization on matters significant to contractor management and to the Government will be treated as reasonably available. What is significant depends upon the circumstances of each acquisition.

(d) Possession of a Certificate of Current Cost or Pricing Data is not a substitute for examining and analyzing the contractor's proposal.

(e) Even though the solicitation may have requested cost or pricing data, the contracting officer shall not require a Certificate of Current Cost or Pricing Data when the resulting award is based on adequate price competition, established catalog or market prices of commercial items sold in substantial quantities to the general public, or prices set by law or regulation (see 15.804-3(a) through (d)).

(f) The exercise of an option at the price established in the initial negotiation in which certified cost or pricing data were used does not require recertification.

(g) Contracting officers shall not require certification at the time of agreement for data supplied in support of forward pricing rate agreements (see 15.809) or other advance agreements. When a forward pricing rate agreement or other advance agreement is used in partial support of a later contractual action that requires a certificate, the price proposal certificate shall cover (1) the data originally supplied to support the forward pricing rate agreement or other advance agreement and (2) all data required to update the price proposal to the time of agreement on contract price.

(h) Negotiated final pricing actions (such as termination settlements and total final price agreements for fixed-price incentive and redeterminable contracts) are contract modifications requiring certified cost or pricing data if (1) the total final price agreement for such settlements or agreements exceeds $100,000 or (2) the partial termination settlement plus the estimate to complete the continued portion of the contract exceeds $100,000 (see 49.105(c)(15)).

[48 FR 42187, Sept. 19, 1983, as amended at 50 FR 1741, Jan. 11, 1985; 50 FR 52429, Dec. 23, 1985]

15.804-5 [Reserved]

15.804-6 Procedural requirements.

(a) The contracting officer shall specify (1) whether or not cost or pricing data are required, (2) whether or not certification will be required, (3) the extent of cost or pricing data required if complete data are not necessary, and (4) the form (see paragraph (b) below) in which the cost or pricing data shall be submitted. Even if the solicitation does not so specify, however, the contracting officer is not precluded from requesting such data if they are later found necessary.

(b) (1) Cost or pricing data shall be submitted on Standard Form 1411 (SF 1411), Contract Pricing Proposal Cover Sheet, unless required to be submitted on one of the termination forms specified in Subpart 49.6. Data supporting forward pricing rate agreements or final indirect cost proposals shall be submitted in a format acceptable to the contracting officer.

(2) Contract pricing proposals submitted on SF 1411 with supporting attachments shall be prepared to satisfy

Federal Acquisition Regulation 15.804-6

the instructions and appropriate format of Table 15-2.

TABLE 15-2 INSTRUCTIONS FOR SUBMISSION OF A CONTRACT PRICING PROPOSAL

1. SF 1411 provides a vehicle for the offeror to submit to the Government a pricing proposal of estimated and/or incurred costs by contract line item with supporting information, adequately cross-referenced, suitable for detailed analysis. A cost-element breakdown, using the applicable format prescribed in 7A, B, or C below, shall be attached for each proposed line item and must reflect any specific requirements established by the contracting officer. Supporting breakdowns must be furnished for each cost element, consistent with offeror's cost accounting system. When more than one contract line item is proposed, summary total amounts covering all line items must be furnished for each cost element. If agreement has been reached with Government representatives on use of forward pricing rates/factors, identify the agreement, include a copy, and describe its nature. Depending on offeror's system, breakdowns shall be provided for the following basic elements of cost, as applicable:

Materials—Provide a consolidated priced summary of individual material quantities included in the various tasks, orders, or contract line items being proposed and the basis for pricing (vendor quotes, invoice prices, etc.).

    Subcontracted Items—Include parts, components, assemblies, and services that are to be produced or performed by others in accordance with offeror's design, specifications, or direction and that are applicable only to the prime contract. For each subcontract over $100,000, the support should provide a listing by source, item, quantity, price, type of subcontract, degree of competition, and basis for establishing source and reasonableness of price, as well as the results of review and evaluation of subcontract proposals when required by FAR 15.806.

    Standard Commercial Items—Consists of items that offeror normally fabricates, in whole or in part, and that are generally stocked in inventory. Provide an appropriate explanation of the basis for pricing. If price is based on cost, provide a cost breakdown; if priced at other than cost, provide justification for exemption from submission of cost or pricing data, as required by FAR 15.804-3(e).

    Interorganizational Transfer (at other than cost)—Explain pricing method used. (See FAR 31.205-26).

    Raw Material—Consists of material in a form or state that requires further processing. Provide priced quantities of items required for the proposal.

    Purchased Parts—Includes material items not covered above. Provide priced quantities of items required for the proposal.

    Interorganizational Transfer (at cost)—Include separate breakdown of cost by element.

Direct Labor—Provide a time-phased (e.g., monthly, quarterly, etc.) breakdown of labor hours, rates, and cost by appropriate category, and furnish bases for estimates.

Indirect Costs—Indicate how offeror has computed and applied offeror's indirect costs, including cost breakdowns, and showing trends and budgetary data, to provide a basis for evaluating the reasonableness of proposed rates. Indicate the rates used and provide an appropriate explanation.

Other Costs—List all other costs not otherwise included in the categories described above (e.g., special tooling, travel, computer and consultant services, preservation, packaging and packing, spoilage and rework, and Federal excise tax on finished articles) and provide bases for pricing.

Royalties—If more than $250, provide the following information on a separate page for each separate royalty or license fee: name and address of licensor; date of license agreement; patent numbers, patent application serial numbers, or other basis on which the royalty is payable; brief description (including any part or model numbers of each contract item or component on which the royalty is payable); percentage or dollar rate of royalty per unit; unit price of contract item; number of units; and total dollar amount of royalties. In addition, if specifically requested by the contracting officer, provide a copy of the current license agreement and identification of applicable claims of specific patents. (See FAR 27.204 and 31.205-37).

Facilities Capital Cost of Money—When the offeror elects to claim facilities capital cost of money as an allowable cost, the offeror must submit Form CASB-CMF and show the calculation of the proposed amount (see FAR 31.205-10).

2. As part of the specific information required, the offeror must submit with offeror's proposal, and clearly identify as such, cost or pricing data (that is, data that are verifiable and factual and otherwise as defined at FAR 15.801). In addition, submit with offeror's proposal any information reasonably required to explain offeror's estimating process, including—

   a. The judgmental factors applied and the mathematical or other methods used in the estimate, including those used in projecting from known data; and

   b. The nature and amount of any contingencies included in the proposed price.

3. There is a clear distinction between submitting cost or pricing data and merely making available books, records, and other documents without identification. The requirement for submission of cost or pricing data is met when all accurate cost or pricing data reasonably available to the offeror have been submitted, either actually or by specific identification, to the contracting officer or an authorized representative. As later information comes into the offeror's possession, it should be promptly submitted to the contracting officer. The requirement for submission of cost or pricing data continues up to the time of final agreement on price.

4. In submitting offeror's proposal, offeror must include an index, appropriately referenced, of all the cost or pricing data and information accompanying or identified in the proposal. In addition, any future additions and/or revisions, up to the date of agreement on price, must be annotated on a supplemental index.

5. By submitting offeror's proposal, the offeror, if selected for negotiation, grants the contracting officer or an authorized representative the right to examine those books, records, documents, and other supporting data that will permit adequate evaluation of the proposed price. This right may be exercised at any time before award.

6. As soon as practicable after final agreement on price, but before the award resulting from the proposal, the offeror shall, under the conditions stated in FAR 15.804-4, submit a Certificate of Current Cost or Pricing Data.

7. HEADINGS FOR SUBMISSION OF LINE-ITEM SUMMARIES:

   A. New Contracts (including Letter contracts).

COST ELEMENTS	PROPOSED CONTRACT ESTIMATE—TOTAL COST	PROPOSED CONTRACT ESTIMATE—UNIT COST	REFERENCE
(1)	(2)	(3)	(4)

Under Column (1)—Enter appropriate cost elements.
Under Column (2)—Enter those necessary and reasonable costs that in offeror's judgment will properly be incurred in efficient contract performance. When any of the costs in this column have already been incurred (e.g., under a letter contract or unpriced order), describe them on an attached supporting schedule. When preproduction or startup costs are significant, or when specifically requested to do so by the contracting officer, provide a full identification and explanation of them.
Under Column (3)—Optional, unless required by the contracting officer.
Under Column (4)—Identify the attachment in which the information supporting the specific cost element may be found. Attach separate pages as necessary.

   B. Change Orders (modifications).

COST ELEMENTS	ESTIMATED COST OF ALL WORK DELETED	COST OF DELETED WORK ALREADY PERFORMED	NET COST TO BE DELETED	COST OF WORK ADDED	NET COST OF CHANGE	REFERENCE
(1)	(2)	(3)	(4)	(5)	(6)	(7)

Under Column (1)—Enter appropriate cost elements.
Under Column (2)—Include (i) current estimates of what the cost would have been to complete deleted work not yet performed, and (ii) the cost of deleted work already performed.
Under Column (3)—Include the incurred cost of deleted work already performed, actually computed if possible, or estimated in the contractor's accounting records. Attach a detailed inventory of work, materials, parts, components, and hardware already purchased, manufactured, or performed and deleted by the change, indicating the cost and proposed disposition of each line item. Also, if offeror desires to retain these items or any portion of them, indicate the amount offered for them.
Under Column (4)—Enter the net cost to be deleted which is the estimated cost of all deleted work less the cost of deleted work already performed. Column (2) less Column (3) = Column (4).

Federal Acquisition Regulation 15.804-6

Under Column (5)—Enter the offeror's estimate for cost of work added by the change. When nonrecurring costs are significant, or when specifically requested to do so by the contracting officer, provide a full identification and explanation of them.
Under Column (6)—Enter the net cost of change which is the cost of work added, less the net cost to be deleted. When this result is negative, place the amount in parentheses. Column (4) less Column (5) = Column (6).
Under Column (7)—Identify the attachment in which the information supporting the specific cost element may be found. Attach separate pages as necessary.

C. Price Revision/Redetermination.

CUTOFF DATE	NUMBER OF UNITS COMPLETED	NUMBER OF UNITS TO BE COMPLETED	CONTRACT AMOUNT	REDETERMINATION PROPOSAL AMOUNT	DIFFERENCE
(1)	(2)	(3)	(4)	(5)	(6)

COST ELEMENTS	INCURRED COST— PREPRODUCTION	INCURRED COST— COMPLETED UNITS	INCURRED COST— WORK IN PROCESS	TOTAL INCURRED COST	ESTIMATED COST TO COMPLETE	ESTIMATED TOTAL COST	REFERENCE
(7)	(8)	(9)	(10)	(11)	(12)	(13)	(14)

Under Column (1)—Enter the cutoff date required by the contract, if applicable.
Under Column (2)—Enter the number of units completed during the period for which experienced costs of production are being submitted.
Under Column (3)—Enter the number of units remaining to be completed under the contract.
Under Column (4)—Enter the cumulative contract amount.
Under Column (5)—Enter the offeror's redetermination proposal amount.
Under Column (6)—Enter the difference between the contract amount and the redetermination proposal amount. When this result is negative, place the amount in parentheses. Column (4) less Column (5) = Column (6).
Under Column (7)—Enter appropriate cost elements. When residual inventory exists, the final costs established under fixed-price-incentive and fixed-price-redeterminable arrangements should be net of the fair market value of such inventory. In support of subcontract costs, submit a listing of all subcontracts subject to repricing action, annotated as to their status.
Under Column (8)—Enter all costs incurred under the contract before starting production and other nonrecurring costs (usually referred to as startup costs) from offeror's books and records as of the cutoff date. These include such costs as preproduction engineering, special plant rearrangement, training program, and any identifiable nonrecurring costs such as initial rework, spoilage, pilot runs, etc. In the event the amounts are not segregated in or otherwise available from offeror's records, enter in this column offeror's best estimates. Explain the basis for each estimate and how the costs are charged on offeror's accounting records (e.g., included in production costs as direct engineering labor, charged to manufacturing overhead, etc.). Also show how the costs would be allocated to the units at their various stages of contract completion.
Under Columns (9) and (10)—Enter in Column (9) the production costs from offeror's books and records (exclusive of preproduction costs reported in Column (8)) of the units completed as of the cutoff date. Enter in Column (10) the costs of work in process as determined from offeror's records or inventories at the cutoff date. When the amounts for work in process are not available in contractor's records but reliable estimates for them can be made, enter the estimated amounts in Column (10) and enter in Column (9) the differences between the total incurred costs (exclusive of preproduction costs) as of the cutoff date and these estimates. Explain the basis for the estimates, including identification of any provision for experienced or anticipated allowances, such as shrinkage, rework, design changes, etc. Furnish experienced unit or lot costs (or labor hours) from inception of contract to the cutoff date, improvement curves, and any other available production cost history pertaining to the item(s) to which offeror's proposal relates.
Under Column (11)—Enter total incurred costs (Total of Columns (8), (9), and (10)).
Under Column (12)—Enter those necessary and reasonable costs that in contractor's judgment will properly be incurred in completing the remaining work to be performed under the contract with respect to the item(s) to which contractor's proposal relates.
Under Column (13)—Enter total estimated cost (Total of Columns (11) and (12)).
Under Column (14)—Identify the attachment in which the information supporting the specific cost element may be found. Attach separate pages as necessary.

(c) Closing or cutoff dates should be included as part of the data submitted with the proposal. If possible, the contracting officer and offeror should reach a prior understanding on criteria for establishing closing or cutoff dates (see 15.804-4(c)).

(d) The requirement for submission of cost or pricing data is met if all cost or pricing data reasonably available to the offeror are either submitted or identified in writing by the time of agreement on price. However, there is a clear distinction between submitting cost or pricing data and merely making available books, records, and other documents without identification. The latter does not constitute "submission" of cost or pricing data.

(e) If cost or pricing data and information required to explain the estimating process are required and the offeror initially refuses to provide necessary data, or the contracting officer determines that the data provided is so deficient as to preclude adequate analysis and evaluation, the contracting officer shall again attempt to secure the data and/or elicit corrective action. If the offeror still persists in refusing to provide the needed data or to take corrective action, the contracting officer shall withhold the award or price adjustment and refer the contract action to higher authority, including details of the attempts made to resolve the matter and a statement of the practicability of obtaining the supplies or services from another source.

(f) Preproduction and startup costs include costs such as preproduction engineering, special tooling, special plant rearrangement, training programs, and such nonrecurring costs as initial rework, initial spoilage, and pilot runs. When these costs may be a significant cost factor in an acquisition, the contracting officer shall require in the solicitation that the offeror provide (1) an estimate of total preproduction and startup costs, (2) the extent to which these costs are included in the proposed price, and (3) the intent to absorb, or plan for recovery of, any remaining costs. If a successful offeror has indicated an intent to absorb any portion of these costs, the contract shall expressly provide that such portion will not be charged to the Government in any future noncompetitive pricing action.

(g) (1) The requirement for contractors to obtain cost or pricing data from prospective subcontractors is prescribed at 15.806. However, these data do not have to be submitted to the Government unless called for under subparagraph (2) below.

(2) The contracting officer shall require a contractor that is required to submit certified cost or pricing data also to submit to the Government (or cause the submission of) accurate, complete, and current cost or pricing data from prospective subcontractors in support of each subcontract cost estimate that is (i) $1,000,000 or more, (ii) both more than $100,000 and more than 10 percent of the prime contractor's proposed price, or (iii) considered to be necessary for adequately pricing the prime contract.

(3) If the prospective contractor satisfies the contracting officer that a subcontract will be priced on the basis of one of the exemptions in 15.804-3, the contracting officer normally shall not require submission of subcontractor cost or pricing data to the Government in that case. If the subcontract estimate is based upon the cost or pricing data of the prospective subcontractor most likely to be awarded the subcontract, the contracting officer shall not require submission to the Government of data from more than one proposed subcontractor for that subcontract.

(4) The contracting officer shall require the prospective contractor to support subcontractor cost estimates below the threshold in 15.806(b) with any data or information (including other subcontractor quotations) needed to establish a reasonable price.

(h) Subcontractor cost or pricing data shall be accurate, complete, and current as of the date of final price agreement given on the contractor's Certificate of Current Cost or Pricing Data. The prospective contractor shall be responsible for updating a prospective subcontractor's data.

(i) When the prospective contractor has generally complied with subcontract cost or pricing data requirements, the contracting officer may, in exceptional cases, excuse failure to do so for particular subcontracts and award the prime contract. Each such excuse, unless limited to allowing additional time, requires approval by the chief of the contracting office. For each subcontract involved, the contractor remains obligated to obtain prospective subcontractor cost or pricing data before actual award of that subcontract. For each such subcontract, the contracting officer shall—

(1) Allow additional time for submission of data up to the date of agreement upon the prime contract price;

(2) Withdraw the requirement if data submitted are adequate to support the subcontract estimate;

Federal Acquisition Regulation 15.804-7

(3) Reserve the subcontract item for future pricing;

(4) Consider another contract type; or

(5) Make other arrangements to provide an adequate basis for price agreement.

[48 FR 42187, Sept. 19, 1983, as amended at 50 FR 1741, Jan. 11, 1985; 50 FR 52429, Dec. 23, 1985; 51 FR 27119, July 29, 1986]

15.804-7 Defective cost or pricing data.

(a) If, before agreement on price, the contracting officer learns that any cost or pricing data submitted are inaccurate, incomplete, or noncurrent, the contracting officer shall immediately bring the matter to the attention of the prospective contractor, whether the defective data increase or decrease the contract price. The contracting officer shall negotiate, using any new data submitted or making satisfactory allowance for the incorrect data. The price negotiation memorandum shall reflect the revised facts.

(b) If, after award, cost or pricing data are found to be inaccurate, incomplete, or noncurrent as of the date of final agreement on price given on the contractor's or subcontractor's Certificate of Current Cost or Pricing Data, the Government is entitled to a price adjustment, including profit or fee, of any significant amount by which the price was increased because of the defective data. This entitlement is ensured by including in the contract one of the clauses prescribed in 15.804-8 and set forth at 52.215-22, Price Reduction for Defective Cost or Pricing Data, and 52.215-23, Price Reduction for Defective Cost or Pricing Data—Modifications. The clauses give the Government the right to a price adjustment for defects in cost or pricing data submitted by the contractor, a prospective subcontractor, or an actual subcontractor. In arriving at a price adjustment under the clause, the contracting officer shall consider—

(1) The time by which the cost or pricing data became reasonably available to the contractor;

(2) The extent to which the Government relied upon the defective data; and

(3) Any understated cost or pricing data submitted in support of price negotiations, up to the amount of the Government's claim for overstated pricing data arising out of the same pricing action (for example, the initial pricing of the same contract or the pricing of the same change order). Such offsets need not be in the same cost groupings (e.g., material, direct labor, or indirect costs).

(c) If, after award, the contracting officer learns or suspects that the data furnished were not accurate, complete, and current, or were not adequately verified by the contractor as of the time of negotiation, the contracting officer shall request an audit to evaluate the accuracy, completeness, and currency of the data. Only if the audit reveals that the data certified by the contractor were defective may the Government evaluate the profit-cost relationships. The contracting officer shall not reprice the contract solely because the profit was greater than forecast or because some contingency specified in the submission failed to materialize.

(d) For each advisory audit received based on a postaward review which indicates defective pricing, the contracting officer shall make a determination as to whether or not the data submitted were defective and relied upon. Before making such a determination, the contracting officer should give the contractor an opportunity to support the accuracy, completeness, and currency of the data in question. The contracting officer shall prepare a memorandum indicating (1) the contracting officer determination as to whether or not the submitted data were accurate, complete, and current as of the certified date and whether or not the Government relied on the data, and (2) the results of any contractual action taken. The contracting officer shall send one copy of this memorandum to the auditor and, if the contract has been assigned for administration, one copy to the administrative contracting officer (ACO). The contracting officer shall notify the contractor by copy of this memorandum, or otherwise, of the determination.

(e) If (1) both contractor and subcontractor submitted and (2) the contractor certified cost or pricing data, the Government has the right, under

215

A-39

the clauses at 52.215-22, Price Reduction for Defective Cost or Pricing Data, and 52.215-23, Price Reduction for Defective Cost or Pricing Data—Modifications, to reduce the prime contract price if it was significantly increased because a subcontractor submitted defective data. This right applies whether these data supported subcontract cost estimates or supported firm agreements between subcontractor and contractor.

(f) If Government audit discloses defective subcontractor cost or pricing data, the information necesssary to support a reduction in prime contract and subcontract prices may be available only from the Government. To the extent necessary to secure a prime contract price reduction, the contracting officer should make this information available to the prime contractor or appropriate subcontractors upon request. If release of the information would compromise Government security or disclose trade secrets or confidential business information, the contracting officer shall release it only under conditions that will protect it from improper disclosure. Information made available under this paragraph shall be limited to that used as the basis for the prime contract price reduction. In order to afford an opportunity for corrective action, the contracting officer should give the prime contractor reasonable advance notice before determining to reduce the prime contract price.

(1) When a prime contractor includes defective subcontract data in arriving at the price but later awards the subcontract to a lower priced subcontractor (or does not subcontract for the work), any adjustment in the prime contract price due to defective subcontract data is limited to the difference (plus applicable indirect cost and profit markups) between (i) the subcontract price used for pricing the prime contract and (ii) either the actual subcontract price or the actual cost to the contractor, if not subcontracted, provided the data on which the actual subcontract price is based are not themselves defective.

(2) Under cost-reimbursement contracts and under all fixed-price contracts except (i) firm-fixed-price contracts and (ii) contracts with economic price adjustment, payments to subcontractors that are higher than they would be had there been no defective subcontractor cost or pricing data shall be the basis for disallowance or nonrecognition of costs under the clauses prescribed in 15.804-8. The Government has a continuing and direct financial interest in such payments that is unaffected by the initial agreement on prime contract price.

15.804-8 Contract clauses.

(a) *Price Reduction for Defective Cost or Pricing Data*. The contracting officer shall, when contracting by negotiation, insert the clause at 52.215-22, Price Reduction for Defective Cost or Pricing Data, in solicitations and contracts when it is contemplated that cost or pricing data will be required (see 15.804-2).

(b) *Price Reduction for Defective Cost or Pricing Data—Modifications*. The contracting officer shall, when contracting by negotiation, insert the clause at 52.215-23, Price Reduction for Defective Cost or Pricing Data—Modifications, in solicitations and contracts when (1) it is contemplated that cost or pricing data will be required (see 15.804-2) for the pricing of contract modifications, and (2) the clause prescribed in paragraph (a) above has not been included.

(c) *Subcontractor Cost or Pricing Data*. The contracting officer shall insert the clause at 52.215-24, Subcontractor Cost or Pricing Data, in solicitations and contracts when the clause prescribed in paragraph (a) above is included.

(d) *Subcontractor Cost or Pricing Data—Modifications*. The contracting officer shall insert the clause at 52.215-25, Subcontractor Cost or Pricing Data—Modifications, in solicitations and contracts when the clause prescribed in paragraph (b) above is included.

15.805 Proposal analysis.

15.805-1 General.

(a) The contracting officer, exercising sole responsibility for the final pricing decision, shall, as appropriate, coordinate a team of experts and re-

Federal Acquisition Regulation 15.805-3

quest and evaluate the advice of specialists in such fields as contracting, finance, law, contract audit, packaging, quality control, engineering traffic management, and contract pricing. The contracting officer should have appropriate specialists attend the negotiations when complex problems involving significant matters will be addressed. The contracting officer may assign responsibility to a negotiator or price analyst for (1) determining the extent of specialists' advice needed and evaluating that advice, (2) coordinating a team of experts, (3) consolidating pricing data and developing a prenegotiation objective (see 15.807), and (4) conducting negotiations.

(b) When cost or pricing data are required, the contracting officer shall make a cost analysis to evaluate the reasonableness of individual cost elements. In addition, the contracting officer should make a price analysis to ensure that the overall price offered is fair and reasonable. When cost or pricing data are not required, the contracting officer shall make a price analysis to ensure that the overall price offered is fair and reasonable.

(c) The contracting officer shall require prospective contractors to perform (1) price analysis for all significant proposed subcontracts and purchase orders and (2) cost analysis when the prospective subcontractor is required to submit cost or pricing data or the contractor is unable to perform an adequate price analysis (see 15.806(a)).

15.805-2 Price analysis.

The contracting officer is responsible for selecting and using whatever price analysis techniques will ensure a fair and reasonable price. One or more of the following techniques may be used to perform price analysis:

(a) Comparison of proposed prices received in response to the solicitation.

(b) Comparison of prior proposed prices and contract prices with current proposed prices for the same or similar end items.

(c) Application of rough yardsticks (such as dollars per pound or per horsepower, or other units) to highlight significant inconsistencies that warrant additional pricing inquiry.

(d) Comparison with competitive published price lists, published market prices of commodities, similar indexes, and discount or rebate arrangements.

(e) Comparison of proposed prices with independent Government cost estimates (see 15.803(b)).

[48 FR 42187, Sept. 19, 1983, as amended at 50 FR 1741, Jan. 11, 1985; 50 FR 52429, Dec. 23, 1985]

15.805-3 Cost analysis.

The contracting officer shall, as appropriate, use the techniques and procedures outlined in paragraphs (a) through (f) below to perform cost analysis:

(a) Verification of cost or pricing data and evaluation of cost elements, including—

(1) The necessity for and reasonableness of proposed costs, including allowances for contingencies;

(2) Projection of the offeror's cost trends, on the basis of current and historical cost or pricing data;

(3) A technical appraisal of the estimated labor, material, tooling, and facilities requirements and of the reasonableness of scrap and spoilage factors; and

(4) The application of audited or negotiated indirect cost rates (see Subpart 42.7), labor rates, and cost of money or other factors.

(b) Evaluating the effect of the offeror's current practices on future costs. In conducting this evaluation, the contracting officer shall ensure that the effects of inefficient or uneconomical past practices are not projected into the future. In pricing production of recently developed, complex equipment, the contracting officer should make a trend analysis of basic labor and materials even in periods of relative price stability.

(c) Comparison of costs proposed by the offeror for individual cost elements with—

(1) Actual costs previously incurred by the same offeror;

(2) Previous cost estimates from the offeror or from other offerors for the same or similar items;

(3) Other cost estimates received in response to the Government's request;

(4) Independent Government cost estimates by technical personnel; and

(5) Forecasts or planned expenditures.

(d) Verification that the offeror's cost submissions are in accordance with the contract cost principles and procedures in Part 31 and, when applicable, the requirements and procedures in Part 30, Cost Accounting Standards.

(e) Review to determine whether any cost or pricing data necessary to make the contractor's proposal accurate, complete, and current have not been either submitted or identified in writing by the contractor. If there are such data, the contracting officer shall attempt to obtain them and negotiate, using them or making satisfactory allowance for the incomplete data.

(f) Analysis of the results of any make-or-buy program reviews, in evaluating subcontract costs.

15.805-4 Technical analysis.

When cost or pricing data are required, the contracting officer should generally request a technical analysis of proposals, asking that requirements, logistics, or other appropriate qualified personnel review and assess, as a minimum—

(a) The quantities and kinds of material proposed;

(b) The need for the number and kinds of labor hours and the labor mix;

(c) The special tooling and facilities proposed;

(d) The reasonableness of proposed scrap and spoilage factors; and

(e) Any other data that may be pertinent to the cost or price analysis.

15.805-5 Field pricing support.

(a)(1) When cost or pricing data are required, contracting officers shall request a field pricing report (which may include an audit review by the cognizant contract audit activity) before negotiating any contract or modification resulting from a proposal in excess of $500,000, except as otherwise authorized under agency procedures, unless information available to the contracting officer is considered adequate to determine the reasonableness of the proposed cost or price. When available data are considered adequate for a reasonableness determination, the contracting officer shall document the contract file to reflect the basis of the determination.

(2) Field pricing reports are intended to give the contracting officer a detailed analysis of the proposal, for use in contract negotiations. Field pricing support personnel include, but are not limited to, administrative contracting officers, contract auditors, price analysts, quality assurance personnel, engineers, and small business and legal specialists.

(b) Contracting officers should not request field pricing support for proposed contracts or modifications of an amount less than that specified in subparagraph (a)(1) above. An exception may be made when a reasonable pricing result cannot be established, because of (1) lack of knowledge of the particular contractor, (2) sensitive conditions, or (3) an inability to evaluate the price reasonableness through price analysis or cost analysis of existing data.

(c)(1) When initiating field pricing support, the contracting officer shall do so by sending a request to the cognizant administrative contracting officer (ACO). When field pricing support is not available, or is exempted by agency regulations, the contracting officer may initiate an audit by sending the request directly to the cognizant audit office. In both cases, the contracting officer shall, in the request, (i) prescribe the extent of the support needed, (ii) state the specific areas for which input is required, (iii) include the information necessary to perform the review (such as the offeror's proposal and the applicable portions of the solicitation, particularly those describing requirements and delivery schedules), and (iv) assign a realistic deadline for receipt of the report.

(2) Assignment of unrealistically short deadlines may reduce the quality of the audit and field pricing reports and may make it impossible to establish the fairness and reasonableness of the price.

(3) Agency field pricing procedures shall not preclude free and open communication among the contracting officer, ACO, and auditor.

Federal Acquisition Regulation 15.805-5

(d) Only the auditor shall have general access to the offeror's books and financial records. This limitation does not preclude the contracting officer, the ACO, or their representatives from requesting any data from or reviewing offeror records necessary to the discharge of their responsibilities. The duties of auditors and those of other specialists may require both to evaluate the same elements of estimated costs. They shall review the data jointly or concurrently when possible, the auditor rendering services within the audit area of responsibility and the other specialists rendering services within their own areas of responsibility. The ACO or auditor, as appropriate, shall orally notify the contracting officer immediately of data provided that is so deficient as to preclude review and any denial of access to records or to cost or pricing data considered essential to the performance of satisfactory review. The oral notification shall be promptly confirmed in writing to the contracting officer describing the deficient or denied data or records, with copies of the deficient data if requested by the contracting officer, the need for the evidence, and the costs unsupported as a result of the denial. The contracting officer shall review the written notification and shall take immediate action to obtain the data needed. If the offeror persists in refusing to provide the data, and the contracting officer determines that the data is essential for a fair and reasonable price determination, then the contracting officer shall proceed with the action outlined in 15.804-6(e).

(e) The auditor shall begin the audit as soon as possible after receiving the contracting officer's request. The auditor is responsible for the scope and depth of the audit. As a minimum, the audit report shall include the following:

(1) The findings on specific areas listed in the contracting officer's request.

(2) An explanation of the basis and method used by the offeror in proposal preparation.

(3) An identification of the original proposal and of all subsequent written formal and other identifiable submissions by which cost or pricing data were either submitted or identified.

(4) A description of cost or pricing data coming to the attention of the auditor that were not submitted but that may have a significant effect on the proposed cost or price.

(5) A list of any cost or pricing data submitted that are not accurate, complete and current and of any cost representations that are unsupported. When the result of deficiencies is so great that the auditor cannot perform an audit or considers the proposal unacceptable as a basis for negotiation, the contracting officer shall be orally notified so that prompt corrective action may be taken, as provided by 15.805-5(d). The auditor will immediately confirm the notification in writing, explaining the deficiencies and the cost impact on the proposal.

(6) The originals of all technical analyses received by the auditor and a quantification of the dollar effect of the technical analysis findings.

(7) If the auditor believes that the offeror's estimating methods or accounting system are inadequate to support the proposal or to permit satisfactory administration of the contract contemplated, a statement to that effect.

(8) A statement of the extent to which the auditor has discussed discrepancies or mistakes of fact in the proposal with the offeror.

(f) The auditor shall not discuss auditor conclusions or recommendations on the offeror's estimated or projected costs with the offeror unless specifically requested to do so by the contracting officer.

(g) If field pricing support was not requested, the auditor shall send the completed audit report directly to the contracting officer. If field pricing support was requested, the auditor shall send the completed audit report to the ACO for forwarding, without change, with the field pricing report. The ACO shall consolidate the field pricing report inputs and send a field pricing report, accompanied by the original copy of the audit report, to the contracting officer by the assigned date. The ACO shall send the auditor a copy of the field pricing report (without the audit report and technical analysis). Audit and field pricing reports shall be made a part of the official contract file.

(h) If any information is disclosed after submission of a proposal that the contracting officer believes may significantly affect the audit findings, the contracting officer shall require the offeror to provide concurrent copies to the appropriate field pricing office (ACO and audit offices). In that case, the ACO or auditor, as appropriate, will be requested to immediately review the disclosed information and orally report the findings to the contracting officer, followed by a supplemental report when considered necessary by the contracting officer.

(i) The prime contractor or higher tier subcontractor is responsible for conducting appropriate cost analyses before awarding subcontracts. However, the contracting officer may request audit or field pricing support to analyze and evaluate the proposal of a subcontractor at any tier (notwithstanding availability of data or analyses performed by the prime contractor) if the contracting officer believes that such support is necessary to ensure reasonableness of the total proposed price. This step may be appropriate when, for example—

(1) There is a business relationship between the contractor and subcontractor not conducive to independence and objectivity;

(2) The contractor is a sole source and the subcontract costs represent a substantial part of the contract cost;

(3) The contractor has been denied access to the subcontractor's records; or

(4) The contracting officer determines that, because of factors such as the size of the proposed subcontractor price, audit or field pricing support for a subcontract or subcontracts at any tier is critical to a fully detailed analysis of the prime contract proposal.

(j) When the contracting officer requests the cognizant ACO or auditor to review a subcontractor's cost estimates, the request shall include, when available, a copy of any review prepared by the prime contractor or higher tier subcontractor, the subcontractor's proposal, cost or pricing data provided by the subcontractor, and the results of the prime contractor's cost or price analysis.

(k) When the Government performs the subcontract analysis, the Government shall furnish to the prime contractor or higher tier subcontractor, with the consent of the subcontractor reviewed, a summary of the analysis performed in determining any unacceptable costs, by element, included in the subcontract proposal. If the subcontractor withholds consent, the Government shall furnish a range of unacceptable costs for each element in such a way as to prevent giving away subcontractor proprietary data.

[48 FR 42187, Sept. 19, 1983, as amended at 51 FR 27119, July 29, 1986]

15.806 Subcontract pricing considerations.

(a) Subcontractors must submit to the contractor or higher tier subcontractor cost or pricing data or claims for exemption from the requirement to submit them. The contractor and higher tier subcontractor are responsible for (1) conducting price analysis and, when the subcontractor is required to submit cost or pricing data or if the contractor or higher tier subcontractor is unable to perform an adequate price analysis, cost analysis for all subcontracts and (2) including the results of subcontract reviews and evaluations as part of their own cost or pricing data submission (see 15.805-5(i) through (k)).

(b) Except when the subcontract prices are based on adequate price competition or on established catalog or market prices of commercial items sold in substantial quantities to the general public or are set by law or regulation, any contractor required to submit certified cost or pricing data also shall obtain certified cost or pricing data before awarding any subcontract or purchase order expected to exceed $100,000 or issuing any modification involving a price adjustment expected to exceed $100,000 (see example of pricing adjustment at 15.804-2(a)(1)(ii) and see 15.804-6(g) through (i)). To waive subcontractor cost or pricing data, follow the procedures at 15.804-3(i).

(c) The requirements in paragraphs (a) and (b) above, modified to relate to higher tier subcontractors rather than to the prime contractor, shall apply to lower tier subcontracts for which subcontractor cost or pricing data are required.

[48 FR 42187, Sept. 19, 1983, as amended at 50 FR 1741, Jan. 11, 1985; 50 FR 52429, Dec. 23, 1985; 51 FR 27120, July 29, 1986]

15.807 Prenegotiation objectives.

(a) The process of determining prenegotiation objectives helps the contracting officer to judge the overall reasonableness of proposed prices and to negotiate a fair and reasonable price or cost and fee. In setting the prenegotiation objectives, the contracting officer shall analyze the offeror's proposal, taking into account the field pricing report, if any; any audit report and technical analysis whether or not part of a field pricing report; and other pertinent data such as independent Government cost estimates and price histories. This process may include fact-finding sessions with the offeror when the contracting officer deems appropriate.

(b) The contracting officer shall establish prenegotiation objectives before the negotiation of any pricing action. The scope and depth of the analysis supporting the objectives should be directly related to the dollar value, importance, and complexity of the pricing action. When cost analysis is required, the analysis shall address (1) the pertinent issues to be negotiated, (2) the cost objectives, and (3) a profit or fee objective.

(c) The Government's cost objective and proposed pricing arrangement directly affect the profit or fee objective. Because profit or fee is only one of several interrelated variables, the contracting officer shall not agree on profit or fee without concurrent agreement on cost and type of contract. Specific agreement on the exact values or weights assigned to individual profit-analysis factors (see 15.905) is not required during negotiations and should not be attempted.

15.808 Price negotiation memorandum.

(a) At the conclusion of each negotiation of an initial or revised price, the contracting officer shall promptly prepare a memorandum of the principal elements of the price negotiation. The memorandum shall be included in the contract file and shall contain the following minimum information:

(1) The purpose of the negotiation.

(2) A description of the acquisition, including appropriate identifying numbers (e.g., RFP No.).

(3) The name, position, and organization of each person representing the contractor and the Government in the negotiation.

(4) The current status of the contractor's purchasing system when material is a significant cost element.

(5) If certified cost or pricing data were required, the extent to which the contracting officer—

(i) Relied on the cost or pricing data submitted and used them in negotiating the price; and

(ii) Recognized as inaccurate, incomplete, or noncurrent any cost or pricing data submitted; the action taken by the contracting officer and the contractor as a result; and the effect of the defective data on the price negotiated.

(6) If cost or pricing data were not required in the case of any price negotiation over $100,000, the exemption or waiver used and the basis for claiming or granting it.

(7) If certified cost or pricing data were required in the case of any price negotiation under $100,000, the rationale for such requirement.

(8) A summary of the contractor's proposal, the field pricing report recommendations, and the reasons for any pertinent variances from the field pricing report recommendations.

(9) The most significant facts or considerations controlling the establishment of the prenegotiation price objective and the negotiated price including an explanation of any significant differences between the two positions.

(10) The basis for determining the profit or fee prenegotiation objective and the profit or fee negotiated.

(b) Whenever a field pricing report has been submitted, the contracting officer shall forward a copy of the price negotiation memorandum (PNM) to the cognizant audit office and a copy to the cognizant administrative contracting officer. When appropriate,

15.809

information on how the advisory services of the field pricing support team can be made more effective should be provided separately.

[48 FR 42187, Sept. 19, 1983, as amended at 50 FR 1741, Jan. 11, 1985; 50 FR 52429, Dec. 23, 1985]

15.809 Forward pricing rate agreements.

(a) Negotiation of forward pricing rate agreements (FPRA's) may be requested by the contracting officer or the contractor or initiated by the administrative contracting officer (ACO). In determining whether or not to establish such an agreement, the ACO should consider whether the benefits to be derived from the agreement are commensurate with the effort of establishing and monitoring it. Normally, FPRA's should be negotiated only with contractors having a significant volume of Government contract proposals. The cognizant contract administration agency shall determine whether an FPRA will be established.

(b) The ACO shall obtain the contractor's proposal and require that it include cost or pricing data that are accurate, complete, and current as of the date of submission. The ACO shall invite the cognizant contract auditor and contracting offices having a significant interest to participate in developing a Government objective and in the negotiations. Upon completing negotiations, the ACO shall prepare a price negotiation memorandum (PNM) (see 15.808) and forward copies of the PNM and FPRA to the cognizant auditor and to all contracting offices that are known to be affected by the FPRA. A Certificate of Current Cost or Pricing Data shall not be required at this time (see 15.804-4(g)).

(c) The FPRA shall provide specific terms and conditions covering expiration, application, and data requirements for systematic monitoring to assure the validity of the rates. The agreement shall provide for cancellation at the option of either party and shall require the contractor to submit to the ACO and to the cognizant contract auditor any significant change in cost or pricing data.

(d) Offerors are required (see 15.804-4(g)) to describe any FPRA's in each specific pricing proposal to which the rates apply and identify the latest cost or pricing data already submitted in accordance with the agreement. All data submitted in connection with the agreement, updated as necessary, form a part of the total data that the offeror certifies to be accurate, complete, and current at the time of agreement on price for an initial contract or for a contract modification.

(e) Contracting officers will use FPRA rates as bases for pricing all contracts, modifications, and other contractual actions to be performed during the period covered by the agreement, unless the ACO determines that changed conditions have invalidated part or all of the agreement. Conditions that may affect the agreement's validity shall be promptly reported to the ACO.

(1) If the ACO determines that the agreement is still valid, the ACO shall notify the individual or agency that reported the changed conditions.

(2) If the ACO determines that a changed condition has invalidated the agreement, the ACO shall notify all interested parties of the extent of its effect and initiate revision of the agreement.

(f) When an FPRA has been invalidated, the contractor, ACO, and contracting officer shall reflect the changed condition in proposals, cost analyses, and negotiations, pending revision of the agreement.

15.810 Should-cost analysis.

(a) Should-cost analysis is a specialized form of cost analysis employing an integrated team of Government contracting, contract administration, pricing, audit, and engineering representatives. It differs from regular cost analysis in its depth, in the fact that it is conducted at the contractor's plant, and in the extent to which the Government identifies and challenges inefficiencies in the contractor's management and operations rather than merely challenging certain proposed costs. The purpose of should-cost analysis is to (1) identify uneconomical or inefficient practices in the contractor's management and operations, (2) quantify their impact on cost in order to develop a realistic price objective for

Federal Acquisition Regulation 15.812

negotiation, and (3) lead to both short- and long-range improvements in the contractor's economy and efficiency.

(b) A should-cost analysis should be considered, particularly in the case of a major system acquisition (see Part 34), when—

(1) Some initial production has already taken place;

(2) The contract will be awarded on a sole-source basis;

(3) There are future year production requirements for substantial quantities of like items;

(4) The items being acquired have a history of increasing costs;

(5) The work is sufficiently defined to permit an effective analysis and major changes are unlikely;

(6) Sufficient time is available to plan and conduct the should-cost analysis adequately; and

(7) Personnel with the required skills are available or can be assigned for the duration of the should-cost analysis.

(c) When a should-cost analysis is planned, the contracting officer should state this fact (1) in the acquisition plan (see Subpart 7.1) and (2) in the solicitation.

(d) The contracting officer should decide which elements of the contractor's operation have the greatest potential for cost savings and assign the available personnel resources accordingly. While the particular elements to be analyzed are a function of the contract work task, elements such as manufacturing, pricing and accounting, management and organization, and subcontract and vendor management are normally reviewed in a should-cost analysis.

(e) In acquisitions for which a should-cost analysis is conducted, field pricing reports (see 15.805) are required only to the extent that they contribute to the combined team position. The contracting officer shall consider the findings and recommendations of the should-cost analysis when negotiating the contract price. After completing the negotiation, the contracting officer shall provide the administrative contracting officer a report of any identified uneconomical or inefficient practices, together with a report of correction or disposition agreements reached with the contractor.

15.811 Estimating systems.

(a) The consistent preparation of proposals using an acceptable estimating system benefits both the Government and the contractor by increasing the accuracy and reliability of individual proposals. Cognizant audit activities, when it is appropriate to do so, shall establish and manage regular programs for reviewing selected contractors' estimating systems or methods, in order to (1) reduce the scope of reviews to be performed on individual proposals, (2) expedite the negotiation process, and (3) increase the reliability of proposals. The results of estimating system reviews shall be documented in survey reports.

(b) The auditor shall send a copy of the estimating system survey report and a copy of the official notice of corrective action required to each contracting office and contract administration office having substantial business with that contractor. Significant deficiencies not corrected by the contractor shall be a consideration in subsequent proposal analyses and negotiations.

(c) In determining the acceptability of a contractor's estimating system, the auditor should consider—

(1) The source of data for estimates and the procedures for ensuring that the data are accurate, complete, and current;

(2) The documentation developed and maintained in support of the estimate;

(3) The assignment of responsibilities for originating, reviewing, and approving estimates;

(4) The procedures followed for developing estimates for direct and indirect cost elements;

(5) The extent of coordination and communication between organizational elements responsible for the estimate; and

(6) Management support, including estimate approval, establishment of controls, and training programs.

15.812 Unit prices.

[51 FR 27120, July 29, 1986]

15.812-1 General.

(a) Although direct and indirect costs are generally allocated to contracts in accordance with the Cost Accounting Standards of Part 30 (when applicable) and the Contract Cost Principles and Procedures of Part 31, for the purpose of pricing all items of supplies, distribution of those costs within contracts shall be on a basis that ensures that unit prices are in proportion to the item's base cost (e.g., manufacturing or acquisition costs). Any method of distributing costs to line items that distorts the unit prices shall not be used. For example, distributing costs equally among line items is not acceptable except when there is little or no variation in base cost.

(b) When contracting by negotiation, without full and open competition, contracting officers shall require that offerors identify in their proposals those items of supply which they will not manufacture or to which they will not contribute significant value. The contracting officer shall require similar information when contracting by negotiation with full and open competition if adequate price competition is not expected (see 15.804-3(b)). The information need not be requested in connection with the award of contracts under the General Services Administration's competitive Multiple Award Schedule Program. Such information shall be used to determine whether the intrinsic value of an item has been distorted through application of overhead and whether such items should be considered for breakout. The contracting officer may require such information in any other negotiated contracts when appropriate.

[51 FR 27120, July 29, 1986]

15.812-2 Contract clause.

(a) The contracting officer shall insert the clause at 52.215-26, Integrity of Unit Prices, in all solicitations and contracts other than small purchases under Part 13 or involving construction or architect-engineer services under Part 36 or utility services under Subpart 8.3.

(b) The contracting officer shall insert the clause with its *Alternate I* when contracting without full and open competition or when prescribed by agency regulations.

[51 FR 27120, July 29, 1986]

15.813 Commercial pricing certificates.

[50 FR 27561, July 3, 1985]

15.813-1 Policy.

The Government should not purchase items of supply offered for sale to the public at a price that exceeds the lowest price at which such items are sold by the contractor unless the price difference is clearly justified by the seller or unless exempt under 15.813-3. To this end, 10 U.S.C. 2323 and 41 U.S.C. 253e require an offeror to certify that the price offered is not more than its lowest commercial price or to submit a written statement specifying the amount of any difference and providing justification for that difference.

[50 FR 28103, July 10, 1985]

15.813-2 Applicability.

(a) Except as provided in 15.813-3, commercial pricing certificates are required to be submitted with any offer/proposal covering any item or items that are offered for sale to the public which is submitted in connection with any of the following:

(1) Contracts not awarded on the basis of full and open competition.

(2) Contract modifications including contract modifications for additional items but not including contract modifications that are within the scope and under the terms of the contract, such as contract modifications issued pursuant to the Changes clause, or funding and other administrative changes.

(3) Orders under the provisioning line item of a contract or under a Basic Ordering Agreement or under a similar arrangement.

(b) If the contract, modification or order is awarded without a definitive price, such as a letter contract or an unpriced order, the commercial pricing certificate is not required prior to award but rather will be submitted with the offer or proposal furnished to definitize the price.

Federal Acquisition Regulation

(c) Notwithstanding any limitations contained in paragraph (a) of this section, the contracting officer may require a commercial pricing certificate whenever it is necessary to protect the interests of the Government. Examples could be where adequate price competition does not exist despite full and open competition or where a modification issued pursuant to the Changes clause results in a substitution of commercial items for noncommercial items.

[50 FR 27561, July 3, 1985]

15.813-3 Exemptions from commercial pricing certificates.

(a) For civilian agencies, not including NASA, a certificate of commercial pricing is not required in connection with the acquisition of items unless the items being acquired are individual parts, components, subassemblies, assemblies or subsystems integral to a major system, and other property which may be replaced during the service life of the system, including spare parts and replenishment spare parts, but not including packaging or labeling associated with shipment or identification of an item.

(b) The contracting officer shall not ordinarily require a certificate of commercial pricing when—

(1) The simplified small purchase prodedures of Part 13 are being used;

(2) An order is placed under an indefinite delivery-type contract (a certificate is required in connection with the award without full and open competition of an indefinite delivery-type contract);

(3) The contracting officer determines that obtaining the commercial pricing certificate is not appropriate because of (i) national security considerations; or (ii) differences in quantities, quality, delivery, or other terms and conditions of the contract from commercial contract terms; or

(4) The contracting officer determines that no commercial items are included in the contract, modification or order.

[50 FR 27561, July 3, 1985]

15.813-4 Procedures.

(a) When commercial pricing certificates are required in accordance with 15.813-2 above, the contracting officer shall require the contractor to submit the certificate as set forth in the clause at 52.215-32, Certification of Commercial Pricing. The contracting officer should assess market conditions for the items expected to be covered by the certificate to determine whether the standard 60-day time period specified in the certificate is appropriate. If the frequency of price fluctuations or other circumstances persuade the contracting officer that a shorter or longer period is appropriate, the time period should be modified accordingly.

(b) The contracting officer shall request submission of a new certificate when the validity of the certificate originally submitted with an offer/proposal becomes doubtful prior to award due to submission of a new or revised proposal or as a result of discussions.

(c) If, before agreement on price, the contracting officer learns that the certificate is inaccurate, incomplete, or misleading, the contracting officer shall immediately bring the matter to the attention of the offeror/contractor, request a new certificate, and negotiate accordingly.

(d) If, after award, the contracting officer learns or suspects that commercial prices offered were defective, the contracting officer shall request, as appropriate, an audit to evaluate the commercial prices under authority of paragraph (b) of the clause at 52.215-32. If the contracting officer determines that a certificate is inaccurate, incomplete or misleading, the Government is entitled to a price adjustment for the overcharge (see paragraph (c) of the clause at 52.215-32).

(e) Individual or class determinations made under 15.813-3(b)(3) or (b)(4) will be documented in the contract file.

(f) Possession of a contractor's Certificate of Commercial Pricing is not a substitute for examining and analyzing a contractor's proposal.

[50 FR 27562, July 3, 1985]

15.813-5 Contract clause.

The contracting officer shall insert the clause at 52.215-32, Certification of Commercial Pricing, in all solicitations and contracts unless exempted under 15.813-3(a) or (b)(1).

[50 FR 27562, July 3, 1985]

Subpart 15.9—Profit

15.900 Scope of subpart.

This subpart—

(a) Prescribes policies for establishing the profit or fee portion of the Government prenegotiation objective;

(b) Applies to price negotiations based on cost analysis;

(c) Prescribes policies for agencies' development and use of a structured approach for determining the profit or fee prenegotiation objective (see 15.905 for the contents of a structured approach); and

(d) Specifies (1) situations requiring contracting officers to analyze profit and (2) considerations for that analysis.

15.901 General.

(a) Profit or fee prenegotiation objectives do not necessarily represent net income to contractors. Rather, they represent that element of the potential total remuneration that contractors *may* receive for contract performance over and above allowable costs. This potential remuneration element and the Government's estimate of allowable costs to be incurred in contract performance together equal the Government's total prenegotiation objective. Just as actual costs may vary from estimated costs, the contractor's actual realized profit or fee may vary from negotiated profit or fee, because of such factors as efficiency of performance, incurrence of costs the Government does not recognize as allowable, and contract type.

(b) It is in the Government's interest to offer contractors opportunities for financial rewards sufficient to (1) stimulate efficient contract performance, (2) attract the best capabilities of qualified large and small business concerns to Government contracts, and (3) maintain a viable industrial base.

(c) Both the Government and contractors should be concerned with profit as a motivator of efficient and effective contract performance. Negotiations aimed merely at reducing prices by reducing profit, without proper recognition of the function of profit, are not in the Government's interest. Negotiation of extremely low profits, use of historical averages, or automatic application of predetermined percentages to total estimated costs do not provide proper motivation for optimum contract performance. With the exception of statutory ceilings in 15.903(d) on profit and fee, agencies shall not (1) establish administrative ceilings or (2) create administrative procedures that could be represented to contractors as de facto ceilings.

15.902 Policy.

(a) Structured approaches (see 15.905) for determining profit or fee prenegotiation objectives provide a discipline for ensuring that all relevant factors are considered. Subject to the authorities in 1.301(c), agencies making noncompetitive contract awards over $100,000 totaling $50 million or more a year—

(1) Shall use a structured approach for determining the profit or fee objective in those acquisitions that require cost analysis; and

(2) May prescribe specific exemptions for situations in which mandatory use of a structured approach would be clearly inappropriate.

(b) Agencies may use another agency's structured approach.

15.903 Contracting officer responsibilities.

(a) When the price negotiation is not based on cost analysis, contracting officers are not required to analyze profit.

(b) When the price negotiation is based on cost analysis, contracting officers in agencies that have a structured approach shall use it to analyze profit. When not using a structured approach, contracting officers shall comply with 15.905-1 in developing profit or fee prenegotiation objectives.

(c) Contracting officers shall use the Government prenegotiation cost objec-

Federal Acquisition Regulation 15.905-1

tive amounts as the basis for calculating the profit or fee prenegotiation objective. Before the allowability of facilities capital cost of money, this cost was included in profits or fees. Therefore, before applying profit or fee factors, the contracting officer shall exclude any facilities capital cost of money included in the cost objective amounts. If the prospective contractor fails to identify or propose facilities capital cost of money in a proposal for a contract that will be subject to the cost principles for contracts with commercial organizations (see Subpart 31.2), facilities capital cost of money will not be an allowable cost in any resulting contract (see 15.904).

(d) (1) The contracting officer shall not negotiate a price or fee that exceeds the following statutory limitations, imposed by 10 U.S.C. 2306(d) and 41 U.S.C. 254(b):

(i) For experimental, developmental, or research work performed under a cost-plus-fixed-fee contract, the fee shall not exceed 15 percent of the contract's estimated cost, excluding fee.

(ii) For architect-engineer services for public works or utilities, the contract price or the estimated cost and fee for production and delivery of designs, plans, drawings, and specifications shall not exceed 6 percent of the estimated cost of construction of the public work or utility, excluding fees.

(iii) For other cost-plus-fixed-fee contracts, the fee shall not exceed 10 percent of the contract's estimated cost, excluding fee.

(2) The limitations in subdivisions (1)(i) and (iii) above shall apply also to the maximum fees on cost-plus-incentive-fee and cost-plus-award-fee contracts. However, a deviation to the maximum-fee limitation for a specific cost-plus-incentive-fee or cost-plus-award-fee contract may be authorized in accordance with Subpart 1.4.

(e) The contracting officer shall not require any prospective contractor to submit details of its profit or fee objective but shall consider them if they are submitted voluntarily.

(f) If a change or modification (1) calls for essentially the same type and mix of work as the basic contract and (2) is of relatively small dollar value compared to the total contract value, the contracting officer may use the basic contract's profit or fee rate as the prenegotiation objective for that change or modification.

[48 FR 42187, Sept. 19, 1983, as amended at 50 FR 23606, June 4, 1985]

15.904 Solicitation provision and contract clause.

The contracting officer shall insert the clause at 52.215-30, Facilities Capital Cost of Money, and the clause at 52.215-31, Waiver of Facilities Capital Cost of Money, in solicitations and contracts that are subject to the cost principles for contracts with commercial organizations (see Subpart 31.2). If, however, the contractor elects to claim facilities capital cost of money as an allowable cost in the contractor's proposal, the clause at 52.215-31 is inapplicable in the resulting contract.

15.905 Profit-analysis factors.

15.905-1 Common factors.

Unless it is clearly inappropriate or not applicable, each factor outlined in paragraphs (a) through (f) following shall be considered by agencies in developing their structured approaches and by contracting officers in analyzing profit whether or not using a structured approach.

(a) *Contractor effort.* This factor measures the complexity of the work and the resources required of the prospective contractor for contract performance. Greater profit opportunity should be provided under contracts requiring a high degree of professional and managerial skill and to prospective contractors whose skills, facilities, and technical assets can be expected to lead to efficient and economical contract performance. Subfactors (1) through (4) following shall be considered in determining contractor effort, but they may be modified in specific situations to accommodate differences in the categories used by prospective contractors for listing costs:

(1) *Material acquisition.* This subfactor measures the managerial and technical effort needed to obtain the required purchased parts and material, subcontracted items, and special tooling. Considerations include (i) the

complexity of the items required, (ii) the number of purchase orders and subcontracts to be awarded and administered, (iii) whether established sources are available or new or second sources must be developed, and (iv) whether material will be obtained through routine purchase orders or through complex subcontracts requiring detailed specifications. Profit consideration should correspond to the managerial and technical effort involved.

(2) *Conversion direct labor.* This subfactor measures the contribution of direct engineering, manufacturing, and other labor to converting the raw materials, data, and subcontracted items into the contract items. Considerations include the diversity of engineering, scientific, and manufacturing labor skills required and the amount and quality of supervision and coordination needed to perform the contract task.

(3) *Conversion-related indirect costs.* This subfactor measures how much the indirect costs contribute to contract performance. The labor elements in the allocable indirect costs should be given the profit consideration they would receive if treated as direct labor. The other elements of indirect costs should be evaluated to determine whether they (i) merit only limited profit consideration because of their routine nature or (ii) are elements that contribute significantly to the proposed contract.

(4) *General management.* This subfactor measures the prospective contractor's other indirect costs and general and administrative (G&A) expense, their composition, and how much they contribute to contract performance. Considerations include (i) how labor in the overhead pools would be treated if it were direct labor, (ii) whether elements within the pools are routine expenses or instead are elements that contribute significantly to the proposed contract, and (iii) whether the elements require routine as opposed to unusual managerial effort and attention.

(b) *Contract cost risk.* (1) This factor measures the degree of cost responsibility and associated risk that the prospective contractor will assume (i) as a result of the contract type contemplated and (ii) considering the reliability of the cost estimate in relation to the complexity and duration of the contract task. Determination of contract type should be closely related to the risks involved in timely, cost-effective, and efficient performance. This factor should compensate contractors proportionately for assuming greater cost risks.

(2) The contractor assumes the greatest cost risk in a closely priced firm-fixed-price contract under which it agrees to perform a complex undertaking on time and at a predetermined price. Some firm-fixed-price contracts may entail substantially less cost risk than others because, for example, the contract task is less complex or many of the contractor's costs are known at the time of price agreement, in which case the risk factor should be reduced accordingly. The contractor assumes the least cost risk in a cost-plus-fixed-fee level-of-effort contract, under which it is reimbursed those costs determined to be allocable and allowable, plus the fixed fee.

(3) In evaluating assumption of cost risk, contracting officers shall, except in unusual circumstances, treat time-and-materials, labor-hour, and firm-fixed-price, level-of-effort term contracts as cost-plus-fixed-fee contracts.

(c) *Federal socioeconomic programs.* This factor measures the degree of support given by the prospective contractor to Federal socioeconomic programs, such as those involving small business concerns, small business concerns owned and controlled by socially and economically disadvantaged individuals, handicapped sheltered workshops, labor surplus areas, and energy conservation. Greater profit opportunity should be provided contractors who have displayed unusual initiative in these programs.

(d) *Capital investments.* This factor takes into account the contribution of contractor investments to efficient and economical contract performance.

(e) *Cost-control and other past accomplishments.* This factor allows additional profit opportunities to a prospective contractor that has previously demonstrated its ability to perform similar tasks effectively and economi-

Federal Acquisition Regulation 15.1001

cally. In addition, consideration should be given to (1) measures taken by the prospective contractor that result in productivity improvements and (2) other cost-reduction accomplishments that will benefit the Government in follow-on contracts.

(f) *Independent development.* Under this factor, the contractor may be provided additional profit opportunities in recognition of independent development efforts relevant to the contract end item without Government assistance. The contracting officer should consider whether the development cost was recovered directly or indirectly from Government sources.

[48 FR 42187, Sept. 19, 1983, as amended at 50 FR 23606, June 4, 1985]

15.905-2 Additional factors.

In order to foster achievement of program objectives, each agency may include additional factors in its structured approach or take them into account in the profit analysis of individual contract actions.

Subpart 15.10—Preaward, Award and Postaward Notifications, Protests, and Mistakes

15.1001 Notifications to unsuccessful offerors.

(a) *General.* The Contracting officer shall promptly notify each offeror whose proposal is determined to be unacceptable or whose offer is not selected for award, unless disclosure might prejudice the Government's interest.

(b) *Preaward notices.* (1) When the proposal evaluation period for a solicitation estimated to exceed the small purchase limitation in Part 13 is expected to exceed 30 days, or when a limited number of offerors have been selected as being within the competitive range (see 15.609), the contracting officer, upon determining that a proposal is unacceptable, shall promptly notify the offeror. The notice shall at least state (i) in general terms the basis for the determination and (ii) that a revision of the proposal will not be considered.

(2) In a small business set-aside (see Subpart 19.5), upon completion of negotiations and determinations of responsibility, but prior to award, the contracting officer shall inform each unsuccessful offeror in writing of the name and location of the apparent successful offeror. The notice shall also state that (i) the Government will not consider subsequent revisions of the unsuccessful proposal and (ii) no response is required unless a basis exists to challenge the small business size status of the apparently successful offeror. The notice is not required when the contracting officer determines in writing that the urgency of the requirement necessitates award without delay.

(c) *Postaward notices.* (1) Promptly after award of contracts resulting from solicitations exceeding the small purchase limitation in Part 13, the contracting officer shall notify unsuccessful offerors in writing, unless preaward notice was given under paragraph (b) above. The notice shall include—

(i) The number of offerors solicited;

(ii) The number of proposals received;

(iii) The name and address of each offeror receiving an award;

(iv) The items, quantities, and unit prices of each award (if the number of items or other factors makes listing unit prices impracticable, only the total contract price need be furnished); and

(v) In general terms, the reason the offeror's proposal was not accepted, unless the price information in (iv) above readily reveals the reason. In no event shall an offeror's cost breakdown, profit, overhead rates, trade secrets, manufacturing processes and techniques, or other confidential business information be disclosed to any other offeror.

(2) Upon request, the contracting officer shall also furnish the information described in 15.1001(c)(1)(i) through (iv) above to the successful offeror.

(3) Upon request, the contracting officer shall furnish the information described in 15.1001(c)(1)(i) through (v) above to unsuccessful offerors in solicitations not exceeding the small purchase limitation in Part 13.

229

15.1002

[48 FR 42187, Sept. 19, 1983, as amended at 50 FR 1741, Jan. 11, 1985; 50 FR 23606, June 4, 1985; 50 FR 52433, Dec. 23, 1985]

15.1002 Notification to successful offeror.

The contracting officer shall award a contract with reasonable promptness to the successful offeror (selected in accordance with 15.611(d)) by transmitting written notice of the award to that offeror (but see 15.608(b)).

[50 FR 1741, Jan. 11, 1985, and 50 FR 52429, Dec. 23, 1985]

15.1003 Debriefing of unsuccessful offerors.

(a) When a contract is awarded on a basis other than price alone (see Subpart 15.6), unsuccessful offerors, upon their written request, shall be debriefed and furnished the basis for the selection decision and contract award.

(b) Debriefing information shall include the Government's evaluation of the significant weak or deficient factors in the proposal; however, point-by-point comparisons with other offerors' proposals shall not be made. Debriefing shall not reveal the relative merits or technical standing of competitors or the evaluation scoring. Moreover, debriefing shall not reveal any information that is not releasable under the Freedom of Information Act; for example—

(1) Trade secrets;

(2) Privileged or confidential manufacturing processes and techniques; and

(3) Commercial and financial information that is privileged or confidential, including cost breakdowns, profit, indirect cost rates, and similar information.

(c) The contracting officer shall include a summary of the debriefing in the contract file.

[48 FR 42187, Sept. 19, 1983. Redesignated and amended at 50 FR 1741, Jan. 11, 1985; 50 FR 52429, Dec. 23, 1985]

15.1004 Protests against award.

Protests against award in negotiated acquisitions shall be treated substantially the same as in sealed bidding (see Subpart 33.1).

[48 FR 42187, Sept. 19, 1983. Redesignated and amended at 50 FR 1741, Jan. 11, 1985; 50 FR 52429, Dec. 23, 1985; 51 FR 2650, Jan. 17, 1986]

15.1005 Discovery of mistakes.

For treatment of mistakes in an offeror's proposal that are discovered before award, see 15.607. Mistakes in a contractor's proposal that are disclosed after award shall be processed in accordance with 14.406-4.

[48 FR 42187, Sept. 19, 1983. Redesignated at 50 FR 1741, Jan. 11, 1985; 50 FR 52429, Dec. 23, 1985]

PART 16—TYPES OF CONTRACTS

Sec.
16.000 Scope of part.

Subpart 16.1—Selecting Contract Types

16.101 General.
16.102 Policies.
16.103 Negotiating contract type.
16.104 Factors in selecting contract types.
16.105 Solicitation provision.

Subpart 16.2—Fixed-Price Contracts

16.201 General.
16.202 Firm-fixed-price contracts.
16.202-1 Description.
16.202-2 Application.
16.203 Fixed-price contracts with economic price adjustment.
16.203-1 Description.
16.203-2 Application.
16.203-3 Limitations.
16.203-4 Contract clauses.
16.204 Fixed-price incentive contracts.
16.205 Fixed-price contracts with prospective price redetermination.
16.205-1 Description.
16.205-2 Application.
16.205-3 Limitations.
16.205-4 Contract clause.
16.206 Fixed-ceiling-price contracts with retroactive price redetermination.
16.206-1 Description.
16.206-2 Application.
16.206-3 Limitations.
16.206-4 Contract clause.
16.207 Firm-fixed-price, level-of-effort term contracts.
16.207-1 Description.
16.207-2 Application.
16.207-3 Limitations.

Subpart 16.3—Cost-Reimbursement Contracts

16.301 General.
16.301-1 Description.
16.301-2 Application.

APPENDIX II

CFR, TITLE 48, CHAPTER 2, DEPARTMENT OF DEFENSE FEDERAL ACQUISITION REGULATIONS SUPPLEMENT, SUBCHAPTER C, PART 215, CONTRACTING BY NEGOTIATION.

PART 215—CONTRACTING BY NEGOTIATION

Subpart 215.1—General Requirements for Negotiation

Sec.
215.103 Converting from sealed bidding to negotiation procedures.
215.170 Negotiation of initial production contracts for technical or specialized military supplies.
215.171 Abstract of offers.

Subpart 215.4—Solicitation and Receipt of Proposals and Quotations

215.402 General.
215.406 [Reserved]
215.407 Solicitation provisions.
215.410 Amendment of solicitations before closing date.
215.411 Receipt of proposals and quotations.
215.411-70 Maintenance and disposition of proposals and quotations.
215.414 Forms.
215.470 Master solicitation.

Subpart 215.5—Unsolicited Proposals

215.504 Advance guidance.
215.506 Agency procedures.
215.506-1 Receipt and initial review.
215.507 Contracting methods.

Subpart 215.6—Source Selection

215.603 Purpose.
215.607 Disclosure of mistakes before award.
215.608 Proposed evaluation.
215.613 Alternative source selection procedures.

Subpart 215.7—Make-or-Buy Programs

215.704 Items and work included.
215.706 Evaluation, negotiation, and agreement.
215.707 Incorporating make-or-buy programs in contracts.

Subpart 215.8—Price Negotiation

215.802 Policy.
215.803 General.
215.804 Cost or pricing data.
215.804-2 Requiring certified cost or pricing data.
215.804-3 Exemption from or waiver of submission of certified cost or pricing data.
215.804-4 Certificate of current cost or pricing data.
215.804-6 Procedural requirements.

Sec.
215.804-7 Defective cost or pricing data.
215.804-8 Contract clauses.
215.805 Proposal analysis.
215.805-1 General.
215.805-2 Price analysis.
215.805-4 Technical analysis.
215.805-5 Field pricing support.
215.806 Subcontract pricing considerations.
215.807 Prenegotiation objectives.
215.808 Price negotiation memorandum.
215.809 Forward pricing rate agreements.
215.810 Should-cost analysis.
215.811 Estimating systems.
215.870 Procedures for identifying contractors' unallowable costs.
215.871 Estimated data prices (DD Form 1423).
215.872 Capital investment incentives.

Subpart 215.9—Profit

215.901 General.
215.902 Policy.
215.903 Contracting officer responsibilities.
215.905 Profit-analysis factors.
215.905-1 Common factors.
215.905-2 Additional factors.

Subpart 215.10—Preaward, Award, and Postaward Notifications, Protests and Mistakes

215.1001 Notifications to unsuccessful offerors.
215.1003 Debriefing of unsuccessful offerors.
215.1070 Classified information.

AUTHORITY: 5 U.S.C. 301, 10 U.S.C. 2202, DoD Directive 5000.35, DoD FAR Supplement 201.301.

SOURCE: 51 FR 46146, Dec. 23, 1986, unless otherwise noted.

Subpart 215.1—General Requirements for Negotiation

215.103 Converting from sealed bidding to negotiation procedures.

Unless otherwise specified in agency procedures, the contracting officer shall make the written determination.

215.170 Negotiation of initial production contracts for technical or specialized military supplies.

(a) The production of important new technical or specialized military supplies generally involves development, evaluation, and initial production phases. Examples of such supplies are tanks, radar, guided missiles, aircraft, rockets, and equipment of similar complexity; major components of such equipment as the foregoing; and any items of technical or specialized nature necessary for the use, maintenance or operation of such equipment. Contracting officers shall avoid, wherever practicable, awarding initial production contracts for supplies until completion of the development and evaluation phases. At the time of placing the initial production contract, it is essential that the Government be completely free to select the contractor as the best interest of the Government may dictate. In the placement and administration of research or development contracts, no commitments shall be made to contractors with respect to obtaining subsequent production contracts. Acquisition of initial production quantity of an item shall not be initiated until the item has been approved for service use unless prior approval has been obtained. When justified by special circumstances, acquisition of production quantities in advance of approval for service use may be authorized for the Departments of the Army and Air Force by Heads of the Contracting Activity, and for the Department of the Navy by the appropriate authority set forth in SECNAV Instructions 3900.30 and 3960.2.

(b) In connection with the foregoing, when consistent with FAR 6.302-1(b)(2), it may be in the best interest of the Government that the initial production contract for technical and specialized supplies be placed with the contractor responsible for the development of the design for such supplies. Accordingly, it is essential that, in placing such initial production contracts, an analysis be made of the importance to be attached to the following considerations:

(1) Extensive preliminary research and development work which can be put to most effective use in production by the research and development contractor for any of the following reasons:

(i) A need for adaptation of the newly developed equipment for quantity manufacture, and for introduction of advanced production methods, together with a significant interrelationship between the design engineering and production engineering, which will yield best results from the standpoint of performance, reliability, and producibility; or

(ii) The substantial time and money which would be required for another contractor to indoctrinate and train engineering staff in the specialized techniques or novel design concepts which have been employed, thereby adding to production lead time.

(2) Continuing improvement of the equipment, concurrent with production which can be most effectively accomplished by a single contractor because of the advantages of unified responsibility and close coordination of improved design features with production processes and equipment.

(3) Substantial time and effort which have been already expended by the development contractor in developing a prototype.

(4) The advantages to be gained through obtaining production drawings, e.g., detailed manufacturing, process, and assembly drawings, with rights to use for acquisition purposes at the earliest possible date for competitive reprocurement purposes by placing production engineering contracts and the first production contract with the developer (see (d) below).

(c) When it is in the Government's interest to award the initial production contract to the development contractor, price alone should not be allowed to dictate an award elsewhere unless a fair and reasonable price cannot be negotiated with the development contractor, or unless the price advantage in award to another supplier is so substantial as to outweigh the other factors involved. This paragraph 15.170 is not to be construed to require or to prevent competitive pricing. Initial production contracts shall not be awarded to development contractors who do not have fully adequate and available financial, technical and production resources.

(d) The number of items to be acquired under an initial production contract will be established only after considering all pertinent factors, including the practical minimum quantity suitable to permit the development of the production design and a data

Department of Defense

package adequate to establish competitive acquisition of the item at the earliest practicable date.

(e) To the extent practicable, the initial production contract should also provide for the furnishing of an initial supply of special testing equipment, special tools, demonstration sets, and manuals required for operation, maintenance and training.

215.171 Abstract of offers.

The abstract of offers required by FAR 4.803(a)(10) shall be prepared on Abstract of Offers (SF Form 1409) or Abstract of Offers—Construction (SF Form 1419) appropriately modified (see FAR 53.2) to include all the information necessary for evaluation (but see FAR 15.413 and FAR 15.610). These forms need not be used in the case of acquisition from a single source of supply, for research and development, for the chartering of vessels by the Military Sealift Command, for the acquisition of coal and petroleum products by the Defense Fuel Supply Center, or for perishable subsistence items by the Defense Personnel Support Center.

Subpart 215.4—Solicitation and Receipt of Proposals and Quotations

215.402 General.

(f) Examples of circumstances under which an oral solicitation may be used include those listed in 206.302-2. However, oral solicitation is not to be considered justified solely because a high issue Priority Designator has been assigned to the requirement. Should the issuance of a resulting contractual instrument be unduly delayed, following oral solicitation, the contract file should be documented to describe the reasons for the delay and justify award based upon the oral solicitation.

215.406 [Reserved]

Reserved pending determination to what extent guidance may be necessary.

215.407 Solicitation provisions.

(S-70) Pursuant to the policy of FAR 14.407-3, the contracting officer shall insert the provision at 252.214-7000, Discounts, in solicitations where prompt payment discounts may be offered.

215.410 Amendment of solicitations before closing date.

Requests for quotations may be amended by letter.

215.411 Receipt of proposals and quotations.

215.411-70 Maintenance and disposition of proposals and quotations.

Both solicited and unsolicited proposals shall be maintained and disposed of pursuant to FAR 4.803.

215.414 Forms.

(a) Letter RFPs and RFQs may also be used provided they otherwise comply with the requirements of FAR and this regulation.

(b) In the acquisition of subsistence, DPSC Form 300, Order for Subsistence, may be used for award purposes.

215.470 Master solicitation.

A master solicitation for negotiated contracts may be established, maintained, and utilized in accordance with 214.270.

Subpart 215.5—Unsolicited Proposals

215.504 Advance guidance.

(b)(2) Agencies shall, where applicable, in addition to the requirements of FAR 15.504(b)(2), also make available to potential offerors of unsolicited proposals requirements concerning cost sharing (see 235.003(b)).

215.506 Agency procedures.

215.506-1 Receipt and initial review.

(c) In addition to the requirements of FAR 15.506-1(c), agencies shall advise offerors of the disposition or intended disposition of the material submitted as the unsolicited proposal. The agency shall not deny reconsideration of a timely and appropriately revised or supplemented proposal which meets the requirements of FAR 15.506-1(a). When it is determined that a meritorious unsolicited proposal is not related to the mission of the recipient agency or may be of interest to other agencies in addition to the recipient agency, the recipient agency may identify for the offeror other agencies whose missions bear a relationship to the subject matter of the unsolicited proposal.

215.507 Contracting methods.

(b)(S-70) When the requirements of FAR Part 6 and FAR Subpart 15.5 have been met, contracts for studies, analyses, or consulting services (see FAR 37.2) may be entered into on the basis of an unsolicited proposal. However, when so limited by an applicable DoD Appropriation Act, such contracts may be entered into only when the head of the contracting activity or his designee (no lower than the chief of the contracting office) determines that:

(i) As a result of thorough evaluation, only one source is found fully qualified to perform the proposal work; or

(ii) The purpose of the contract is to explore an unsolicited proposal which offers significant scientific or technological promise, represents the product of original thinking, and was submitted in confidence by one source; or

(iii) The purpose of the contract is to take advantage of unique and significant industrial accomplishment by a specific concern, or to insure that a new product or idea of a specific concern is given financial support; except that this limitation shall not apply to contracts in an amount of less than $25,000, contracts related to improvements of equipment that is in development or production, or contracts as to which a civilian official of the Department of Defense who has been confirmed by the Senate, determines that the award of such contract is in the interest of national defense.

Subpart 215.6—Source Selection

215.603 Purpose.

(d) In addition, source selection procedures are designed to ensure selection of the source whose proposal is in the best interests of the Government, price and other factors considered.

215.607 Disclosure of mistakes before award.

(c)(3) Authority to make the determination is delegated to the head of the contracting activity with authority to redelegate to the chief of the contracting office.

215.608 Proposed evaluation.

(b) Unless otherwise specified in agency procedures, the contracting officer shall make the written determination.

215.613 Alternative source selection procedures.

"Four-Step" Source Selection Procedures are as follows:

(a) *General.*

(1) The Four-Step process, briefly described, is the (i) submission and evaluation of the offeror's technical proposal; (ii) submission and evaluation of the offeror's cost proposal; (iii) establishment of the competitive range and selection of the apparent successful offeror; and (iv) negotiation of a definitive contract.

(2) The conventional process differs in that (i) offerors' technical and cost proposals are submitted and evaluated simultaneously; (ii) definitive contracts are negotiated with all offerors in the competitive range; and (iii) the contractor is selected. One additional difference in the two processes involves discussion of proposal deficiencies. In the Four-Step process, deficiencies are not revealed to the individual offerors, while in the conventional process protracted discussions may evolve around proposal deficiencies.

(3) These procedures are designed primarily to: focus attention on technical excellence, maintain the integrity of each offeror's proposal, provide visibility of discriminating features between proposals, reduce the opportunity for buy-ins, preclude the opportunity for the use of auctioning techniques and assure a disciplined and orderly process in the selection of sources. To this end, early and open dialogue, e.g., pre-solicitation notices and conferences, pre-proposal conferences, informal solicitations and the tailoring of specifications, is encour-

Department of Defense 215.613

aged to establish a better understanding of the Government's needs.

(4) Following the technical evaluation and discussions, cost/price proposals are obtained from each offeror together with any necessary clarifications of technical proposals. Subsequent to the receipt of the cost/price proposals and any technical clarifications, a competitive range is established. Those proposals outside the competitive range are eliminated at this point and the offerors so notified. Limited discussions are then held with the remaining offerors on their cost/price proposals and any technical clarifications. Following such discussions, a proposal may be eliminated from further consideration and the offeror so notified when it is determined to be no longer in the competitive range.

(5) At the completion of technical and cost/price discussions, a common cut-off date for the receipt of final technical and cost/price proposals based upon those discussions is then established and the remaining offerors so notified. An evaluation is then made of each offeror's total proposal and a single offeror is normally selected for negotiation of a contract (see 215.613(h)(7)). In order to release proposal teams at the earliest practical date, all offerors are notified of the contractor selected.

(6) A definitive contract is then negotiated with the selected offeror and contract award accomplished. These negotiations must be completed in a timely manner and must not involve changes in the Government's requirements or the contractor's proposal which would affect the basis for source selection. In the event a definitive contract cannot be awarded on a timely basis, negotiations may be terminated and a new source selection decision made.

(b) *Applicability.* These procedures may be used at the discretion of the Contracting Officer for competitively negotiated research and development acquisitions with an estimated value of two million dollars or more. They may also be used for any other acquisition when approved in accordance with Departmental procedures subject to the restrictions below. Use of these procedures is most appropriate when Government evaluation of initial proposals, without discussion of proposal deficiencies, will be sufficient to determine the best overall offer to the Government. Acquisitions for which these procedures are not used shall follow the procedures of FAR 15.6.

(c) *Restrictions.* These procedures should not be used for acquisitions in which the necessity to conduct extensive negotiations is anticipated. These procedures shall not be used for any acquisitions which:

(1) Are acquired pursuant to FAR 6.302-2;

(2) Are solely for personal or nonpersonal services;

(3) Are for architect-engineer services; or

(4) Have an estimated value of less than two million dollars.

(d) *Procedures.* Acquisitions subject to this paragraph shall be conducted in accordance with the following procedures:

(1) *Solicitations.* Solicitations shall be developed in accordance with FAR 15.4 and shall include the following special requirements and instructions:

(i) A general statement explaining the concept and procedures to be used in the selection of a contractual source of the proposed acquisition.

(ii) The relative importance of technical/system performance criteria.

(iii) A notification that any proposals which are unrealistic in terms of technical or schedule commitments or unrealistically low in cost or price will be deemed reflective of an inherent lack of technical competence or indicative of failure to comprehend the complexity and risks of the proposed contractual requirements and may be grounds for the rejection of the proposal.

(iv) A schedule of planned source selection events including, but not limited to, specific dates for the submission of both technical and cost/price proposals.

(v) Provisions requiring sequential submission of separate technical and cost/price proposals.

(vi) Requirements for the technical proposal to include, where appropriate, identification of trade-offs among performance, production costs, operating and support costs, schedule and logistic support factors; and requirements for cost estimates which illustrate the impact of these trade-offs. In addition, requirements for the technical proposal to include information necessary to indicate that the design to cost and operating and support cost objectives, when used, would be achieved when the item(s) enters production.

(vii) Requirements for the cost proposal to include the detailed, substantiating cost information pertaining to the performance of the contemplated contract and other detailed data necessary for evaluation of cost factors to be considered in the source selection decision.

(viii) A statement that both technical and cost/price discussions will be limited as set forth in (e) and (f) below.

(ix) A notification that negotiations will be conducted only with the selected offeror, and that offerors should represent their most favorable technical and cost/price proposals initially.

(e) *Step one—evaluation and discussion of technical proposals.* A detailed evaluation shall be accomplished on all technical proposals received based upon the established criteria in the solicitation. Upon completion of the initial evaluation, limited discussions shall be conducted with all offerors for the purpose of achieving maximum understanding and clarification of the contents of the proposal. During such discussions, offerors shall not be advised of deficiencies in their proposals. A deficiency is defined as that part of an offeror's proposal which would not satisfy the Government's requirements. Offerors shall be advised of areas of their proposal in which the intent or meaning is unclear or for which additional substantiating data is required for evaluation. When necessary for complete understanding of proposals, clarifications and/or additional substantiating data may be requested concerning those areas of an offeror's proposal when there is uncertainty that a deficiency exists. In most cases, clarification of proposals and additional substantiating data, if required, will be included by offerors with their cost/price proposals in Step Two. When it is apparent from the proposals received that the Government's requirements have been misinterpreted, clarification shall be provided to all offerors to ensure complete understanding.

(f) *Step two—evaluation and discussion of cost/price proposals.*

(1) Following the technical evaluation and discussions, complete, fully documented cost/price proposals and clarifications, if required, of technical proposals shall be obtained. Each proposal shall be evaluated and those which have no reasonable chance for award may be eliminated from the competition at this point and the offerors notified that they are outside the competitive range and will be given no further consideration.

(2) Limited discussions as indicated herein shall then be conducted with all remaining offerors in connection with their respective cost/price proposals, either on an element-by-element basis or in their entirety. These discussions may include (i) rectification and/or correction of inconsistencies or mathematical errors; (ii) correlation of elements of cost with their respective technical efforts, in order to assess the extent of realism in the cost proposal; and (iii) discussion necessary to ensure a complete understanding of the Government's requirements, what is being offered (including delivery schedules, trade-offs among performance, design to cost, life cycle cost, and logistics support factors) and other contract terms. An offeror shall not be advised during these discussions that its proposal or any of its elements are either too high or too low. When discussions of technical proposals are required they shall be limited as stated in (e) above.

(3) Following such discussions, a proposal may be eliminated from further consideration and the offeror so notified (i) when the proposal was initially included in the competitive range because it might have been susceptible of being made acceptable, or (ii) because there was uncertainty whether it was in the competitive range, and in either case, through discussions relating to ambiguities and omissions it becomes clear that the proposal should

Department of Defense 215.613

not have been included in the competitive range initially.

(g) *Step three—common cut-off.*

(1) A common cut-off date for receipt of technical and cost/price proposal clarifications or substantiations shall be established and all participants so notified in accordance with FAR 15.611.

(2) Offerors shall be informed that any changes incorporated in the final proposal must be fully substantiated. Supporting data must provide traceability to the causative technical, business, or financial conditions that brought about any change. Lump sum reductions in cost/price shall not be accepted without supporting rationale.

(3) After the common cut-off date, requirements shall not be imposed for additional proposals or revisions to submitted technical or cost proposals without the prior approval of an official at a level no lower than that of a Head of a Contracting Activity (HCA). Auctioning through repetitive calls for offers is strictly prohibited.

(4) Final detailed negotiations leading to the bilateral execution of a definitive contract shall be deferred until after the selection of an offeror for final contract negotiations.

(h) *Selection of an offeror for final contract negotiations.*

(1) Complete evaluation of all factors in accordance with the criteria set forth in the solicitation, including cost/fee or price, shall be conducted with careful regard for security procedures and good business practice.

(2) Based upon the offeror's latest total acceptable technical and cost proposals, selection of a single source shall be made for the conduct of final negotiations leading to a definitive contract. (This does not preclude selecting more than one source when multiple sources are desired; e.g., competitive prototypes.) Procedures for waiver of this requirement are at (7) below.

(3) Proposals unrealistic in terms of technical or schedule commitments or unrealistically low in cost or price will be deemed reflective of an inherent lack of technical competence or indicative of failure to comprehend the complexity and risks of the contract requirements and may be grounds for rejection of the proposal.

(4) The selection will be based on an integrated decision, involving consideration of technical approach, capability, management, design to cost, operating and support cost objectives, historical performance, price/cost and other factors.

(5) Following selection of the best offeror, all competitors shall be notified of the source to be awarded the contract, subject to negotiation of a satisfactory definitive contract.

(6) The source selection decision is conditional in that award of a fully negotiated contract to the selected offeror must be accomplished within a period of time prescribed by the source selection authority. In the event a definitive contract cannot be awarded on a timely basis, negotiations may be terminated and a new source selection decision made.

(7) Proposed contracts may be negotiated with two or more offerors within the competitive range, if the HCA makes a written determination that a final selection of a single source should not be made until such proposed contracts have been negotiated. Such determination shall not be made solely for the purpose of maintaining a competitive environment. However, such a determination may be based, for example, on unique situations where there are no significant discriminating technical or cost features between two or more offerors. Notification of such determination shall be provided to OASD(A&L)(P) through Departmental procedures.

(i) *Step four—final negotiations and contract award.* Final negotiations leading to bilateral execution of a single definitive contract will be conducted only with the selected offeror except when multiple negotiations are authorized by the HCA. Final negotiations shall include the disclosure and resolution of all technical deficiencies and all unsubstantiated areas of cost. Negotiations shall not involve changes in the Government's requirements or the contractor's proposal which would affect the basis for source selection. In the event that such changes are necessary, the procedures in FAR 15.606 shall be followed. The final negotiated

215.704

contract must represent a reasonable probability that the Government's requirements will be satisfied at a fair and reasonable cost/fee or price.

(j) *Debriefings.* Formal debriefings shall be conducted after contract award, in accordance with FAR 15.1002 and 215.1002.

Subpart 215.7—Make-or-Buy Programs

215.704 Items and work included.

The minimum dollar threshold within DoD referred to in FAR 15.704(b) is $500,000.

215.706 Evaluation, negotiation, and agreement.

(d) Contracting officers shall also give primary consideration to the effect of the proposed make-or-buy program on the contemplated type of subcontract.

215.707 Incorporating make-or-buy programs in contracts.

(a)(2) The contracting officer may exclude the make-or-buy program from (i) cost-plus-incentive-fee contracts to which FAR 15.707(b) is applicable and (ii) from cost-plus-incentive fee contracts having a cost incentive which provides for a swing from target fee of at least 3 percent and a contractor's overall share of cost of at least 10 percent (authority may be requested (see FAR 1.4) to exclude the make-or-buy program from other cost-plus-incentive-fee contracts having different incentive and cost-sharing patterns, whenever the contracting officer finds that such other contracts provide sufficient incentive for control of costs).

Subpart 215.8—Price Negotiation

215.802 Policy.

(b)(2) (This prohibition neither prevents the negotiation of indirect costs and other rates applicable to several contracts nor prohibits FPRA's applicable to several contracts.)

215.803 General.

(b) When necessary, requirements and technical specialists should be consulted. The primary responsibility for the adequacy of specifications and for the delivery requirements must necessarily rest with requirements and technical groups. However, the contracting officer should be aware of the effect which these factors may have on prices and competition, and should, prior to award, inform requirements and technical groups of any unsatisfactory effect which their decisions have on prices or competition.

(d) When products are sold in the open market, costs are not necessarily the controlling factor in establishing a particular seller's price. Similarly, where competition may be ineffective or lacking, estimated costs plus estimated profit are not the only pricing criteria. In some cases, the price appropriately may represent only a part of the seller's cost and include no estimate for profit or fee, as in research and development projects where the contractor is willing to share part of the costs. In other cases, price may be controlled by competition. The objective of the contracting officer shall be to negotiate fair and reasonable prices in which due weight is given to all relevant factors. When negotiations indicate the need for using other than a firm fixed-price contract, there should be compatibility between the type of contract selected and the contractor's accounting system.

215.804 Cost or pricing data.

215.804-2 Requiring certified cost or pricing data.

(a)(1)(ii) The term "price adjustment" or "pricing adjustment" means the aggregate increases and/or decreases in costs plus applicable profits.

(2) Partial or limited data may be requested when less than complete cost analysis (e.g., analysis of only specific factors) will provide a reasonable pricing result on awards under $100,000 without the submission of complete cost or pricing data. The contracting officer shall request only that data which the contracting officer considers adequate to support the limited extent of the cost analysis required and he will not require certification.

(b)(1) Cost or pricing data shall not be required merely in anticipation of post-award review of the contract.

Department of Defense

(2) If, after cost or pricing data were initially requested and received, it is determined that adequate price competition does exist, the data need not be certified.

215.804-3 Exemption from or waiver of submission of certified cost or pricing data.

(a)(1) When economic price adjustment provisions are included in competitive acquisitions, see FAR 16.203-2(b).

(b)(2)(ii) An example of a determinative advantage is where substantial costs, such as start-up or other nonrecurring expenses, have already been absorbed in connection with previous sales, thus placing the competitor in a preferential position.

(3) Examples of a price "based on" adequate price competition are: (i) Exercise of an option in a contract for which there was adequate price competition if the option price has been determined to be reasonable in accordance with FAR 17.207(d); and (ii) an item normally is acquired competitively but in a particular situation only one offer is solicited or received, and the price clearly is reasonable in comparison with recent purchases of comparable quantities for which there was adequate price competition.

(c)(6) In addition, cost or pricing data may be requested, if necessary, where there is such a disparity between the quantity being acquired and the quantity for which there is such a catalog or market price that pricing cannot reasonably be accomplished by comparing the two.

(7) In determining exemptions, it is the item under consideration that must meet the test. The ultimate objective is to achieve fair and reasonable prices for items bought. Altered terms, minor configuration changes, extra inspection requirements, or quantity differences are adequate reasons for pricing items differently from catalog or market prices.

(e)(3) In anticipation of repetitive acquisitions of a catalog item, the contracting officer or the cognizant ACO may make special arrangements for submission of the exemption claim. The submission need not be on a Standard Form 1412, but shall include any data required by the form and include or incorporate by reference all the applicable definitions, representations and rights included in the form. Government approval of the exemption claim shall set forth the effective period, usually not more than one year, and require the contractor to furnish any later information that might raise a question as to the continuation of the exemption. Such approval may be extended to other Government contracting offices with their concurrence.

NOTE.—A copy of each waiver shall be sent to the Deputy Assistant Secretary for Procurement, Office of Assistant Secretary of Defense, Acquisition and Logistics.

(i) Set forth below is a format for the D&F's to be made by the agency head with respect to waiving the requirement for submission of cost or pricing data and certification thereof, as required by 10 U.S.C. 2306(f), and for waiving the inclusion of the clauses required by FAR 52.214-27 and 52.215-25. The format may be used also for the D&F's for such waiver made by the Head of the Procuring Activity for contracts with foreign governments or agencies thereof.

(MILITARY DEPARTMENT OR AGENCY)

Determination and Findings

Authority to Waive Submission of Cost or Pricing Data and Certificate

Upon the basis of the following findings and determination which I hereby make as agency head, the requirement for submission of cost and pricing data and certificate described below may be waived pursuant to the authority of 10 U.S.C. 2306(f), as implemented by FAR 15.804-3(i).

FINDINGS

1. The (2) proposes to enter into a contract with (3) for the acquisition of (4).

2. Pursuant to FAR 15.804-2, the proposed contractor is required to submit certified cost or pricing data. However, waiver of submission of the certified cost or pricing data described below is justified for the reasons indicated: (5).

DETERMINATION

1. The requirement for submission of cost or pricing data for the proposed contract action may be waived.

Date ———————————

215.804-4

NOTES.—

(1) In the case of a contract with a foreign government or agency thereof, delete the words "agency head" and substitute therefor "head of a procuring activity."

(2) Procuring or contracting activity.

(3) Name of supplier.

(4) Brief description of supplies or services.

(5) Describe the cost or pricing data requirements to be waived. (The waiver may be partial, i.e. limited to particular cost or pricing data.) Set forth the circumstances and conditions which make the proposed contract action an exceptional case and state the reasons which justify the proposed waiver.

215.804-4 Certificate of current cost or pricing data.

(c) The data on numerous minor material items each of which by itself would be insignificant may be reasonably available only as of a cut-off date prior to agreement on price because the volume of transactions would make the use of any later data impracticable. Furthermore, except where a single item is used in substantial quantity, the net effect of any changes to the prices of such minor items would likely be insignificant.

215.804-6 Procedural requirements.

(b)(2) The following may be used with the SF 1411:

(i) When Contract Cost Data Reports are required by the purchase request, the contractor shall be required to submit DD Forms 1921 and/or 1921-1 to support the SF 1411. The DD Forms 1921 shall be prepared in accordance with the Contractor Cost Data Reporting (CCDR) System (Army—AMCP 715-8, Navy—OASN(S&L), CBM-CPR, and Air Force—AFLCP/AFSCP 800-15). The contractor supporting data shall be prepared in such a manner as to support each cost element on the DD Form 1921-1.

(ii) *Contract pricing proposal supporting schedules* may be devised by contracting offices to require such supporting data to the foregoing forms as is considered necessary and reasonable through knowledge of industry, company or commodity practices.

(c) To the extent possible, the understanding should relate to the contractor's formal estimating system. Notwithstanding the foregoing, significant matters important to contractor management and to the Government and any related data within the contractor's organization or the organization of a subcontractor or prospective subcontractor would be expected to be current on the date of agreement on price and, therefore, will be treated as reasonably available as of that date. Although changes in the labor base or in prices of major material items are generally significant matters, no hard and fast rule can be laid down since what is significant can depend upon such circumstances as the size and nature of the acquisition.

(e) The referral to higher authority shall also include a complete statement of the attempts made to resolve the matter, including (1) steps taken to secure essential cost or pricing data, (2) efforts to secure the contractor's cooperation in the establishment of a satisfactory business relationship, and (3) any assurances offered, such as agreements to adequately safeguard information furnished.

(f) Since an offeror may propose a price which does not include all preproduction and startup or other nonrecurring costs for the purpose of obtaining the first production contract and for gaining an advantage over competitors in negotiations for future acquisitions, it is important to know whether the offeror intends to absorb any portion of these costs or whether the offeror plans to recover them in connection with subsequent pricing actions under the proposed or future contracts. This information is needed in evaluating competing proposals to determine which proposal is most likely to result in the lowest overall cost to the Government, particularly where the successful offeror is likely to become, in effect, a sole source for follow on acquisitions (including spare parts or other support items).

(g)(3) In addition to submitting cost or pricing data from the prospective subcontractor most likely to be awarded the subcontract, the contractor shall submit other data pertaining to subcontract costs, including other subcontractor quotations. Failure by the contractor to submit subcontract cost

Department of Defense

or pricing data may be cause for disqualification of the contractor from further consideration for award of the proposed contract.

215.804-7 Defective cost or pricing data.

(b)(2) In the absence of evidence to the contrary, the natural and probable consequence of defective data is an increase in the contract price in the amount of the defect plus related burden and profit or fee; therefore, unless there is a clear indication that the defective data were not used, or were not relied upon, the contract price should be reduced in that amount. In establishing that the defective data caused an increase in the contract price, the contracting officer is not expected to reconstruct the negotiation by speculating as to what would have been the mental attitudes of the negotiating parties if the correct data had been submitted at the time of agreement on price.

(d) An auditor's advisory report of post-award reviews of cost and pricing data may result either from a specific request of a contracting officer or from audit action initiated independent of a contracting officer's request.

(e) In exercising the Government's rights in such cases, the contracting officer will consider the varying circumstances discussed below.

(e)(S-70) In some instances, the prime contractor may have reached agreement on price with a subcontractor before the prime contractor and the Government agree on a definitive price. This might occur, for example, if the prime contractor commenced performance under an unpriced action such as a letter contract. In such cases, the subcontractor's cost or pricing data must be submitted with the prime contractor's submission. If any such subcontractor data are subsequently found to be defective, the prime contract is subject to price adjustment in the same manner as would be the case if any other cost or pricing data submitted by the prime contractor proved to be defective.

(e)(S-71) The Government and the prime contractor will normally agree on the price of a contract prior to final agreement on price between the prime contractor and his subcontractor. In such cases, the prime contract price will be based, in part, on subcontract cost estimates. The prime contractor will be expected to support the subcontract cost estimates with subcontractor cost or pricing data. The prime contract price will be subject to adjustment on the basis of defective subcontractor cost or pricing data submitted prior to agreement on the prime contract price if:

(i) Such subcontractor data were not accurate, complete, or current as of the date certified in the prime contractor's Certificate of Cost or Pricing Data, or in some cases were not accurate as submitted by the subcontractor, and

(ii) The prime contract price was increased by a significant sum because of such defective subcontractor data.

(f) Conditions may be prescribed by: the Office of the Assistant Secretary of the Army (Research, Development and Acquisition), for the Army; Office of the Assistant Secretary of the Navy (Shipbuilding & Logistics), DCBM, for the Navy; the Director of Contracting and Manufacturing Policy, Headquarters, USAF (AF/RDC), for the Air Force; and the Executive Director, Contracting, for the Defense Logistics Agency.

(2) Although the action is taken under those price reduction clauses rather than under Part 31 as a practical matter the result is the same, i.e., the increased costs will be disallowed under cost-type contracts or not considered as actual costs for final pricing of redeterminable or incentive-type contracts. The action is taken under the price reduction clauses because not only will the increased costs be disallowed or not considered as actual costs but also the fixed-fee or target profit included in the initial price may be subject to reduction in accordance with (1) and (2) of 215.804-7(e) above.

215.804-8 Contract clauses.

The requirement for inclusion of the specified clauses in contracts with foreign governments or agencies may be waived in exceptional cases by the Agency head (see FAR 15.804-3(i)). The contracting officer shall also include the clause at FAR 52.215-22 when obtaining partial cost or pricing data in accordance with 215.804-2(a)(2).

(S-70) The clause at 252.215-7000, Aggregate Pricing Adjustment, shall be included in all solicitations and contracts which include a clause at FAR 52.215-23, FAR 52.215-24, or at FAR 52.215-25. The Contracting Officer may insert a lesser dollar amount, if appropriate.

215.805 Proposal analysis.

215.805-1 General.

(a) The contracting officer should also note the following:

(a)(S-70) Each contracting officer is responsible for performing or having performed all administrative actions necessary for effective contracting.

(a)(S-71) For certain acquisitions, it may be necessary to convene a formal "Should Cost" (see FAR 15.810) team of specialists to evaluate the contractor's cost projections, supporting standards, and other in-plant management, operational and performance practices, on which cost projections are based.

(a)(S-72) Contract auditors are professional accountants who, although organizationally independent, are the principal advisors to contracting officers on contractor accounting and contract audit matters. Contract audit services are available in two forms:

(i) Audit reports setting forth the results of auditors' reviews and analyses of cost data submitted by contractors as part of pricing proposals, reviews of contractors' accounting systems, estimating methods, and other related matters; and

(ii) "On-the-spot" personal consultation and advice to contracting and contract administration personnel in connection with analyses of contractors' cost representations and related matters by liaison auditors stationed at contracting and contract administration offices. (DCAA provides procurement liaison auditors (PLAs) at most major contracting and contract administration offices to facilitate the receipt and use of audit service and to provide accounting and audit advice as to whether or not audit review of a price proposal should be waived.)

(b) Some form of price or cost analysis is required in connection with every negotiated contract action. The method and degree of analysis, however, is dependent on the facts surrounding the particular acquisition and pricing situation. The extent of cost analysis should be that necessary to assure reasonableness of the pricing result, taking into consideration the amount and complexity of the proposed contract. Normally, a sound conclusion as to value cannot be made on the basis of cost analysis alone. Depending on the information available, a price arrived at by cost analysis should be corroborated through price analysis techniques.

215.805-2 Price analysis.

(b) To provide a suitable basis for comparison, appropriate allowances must be made for differences in such factors as time of prior acquisitions, specifications, quantities ordered, time for delivery, Government-furnished materials, and experienced trends of improvement in production efficiency. It must also be recognized that such comparison may not detect an unreasonable current quotation unless the reasonableness of the prior prices was established and unless changes in the general level of business and prices have been considered.

215.805-4 Technical analysis.

Technical analyses by the Plant Rep/ACO and the team members shall be based on their knowledge of such factors as production, quality assurance, engineering and manufacturing practices and techniques, and information as to plant capacity, scheduling, engineering and production "know-how," Government property, make-or-buy considerations, and industrial security, particularly as these relate to practices of the specific prospective contractor.

215.805-5 Field pricing support.

(a)(1) Contracting officers shall request field pricing reports for contracts and modifications resulting from a proposal in excess of $100,000 for a firm fixed-price contract, $250,000 for a fixed-price incentive

Department of Defense 215.805-5

contract, and $500,000 for a cost type contract. The requirement for subject reports may be waived, with adequate justification, at one level above the contracting officer. Requests for field pricing support should be tailored to ask for minimum essential information needed to ensure a fair and reasonable price is achieved. Information of the type described in (i) through (vi) below, which is often available to the contracting officer from the Plant Rep/ACO or from the Procurement Liaison Auditor (PLA), should be useful in determining the extent of any field pricing support that is needed.

(i) In-house engineering determination of level of effort required in connection with research and development or study contracts.

(ii) Audited cost information from contract awards in process, or recently negotiated contracts.

(iii) Adequately reviewed data on proposed subcontract items which constitute the major portion of the prime contract price proposal.

(iv) Prices of standard commercial items which constitute the major portion of the prime contract price proposal.

(v) Special forward pricing formulas or rates such as for support items, or forecast overhead rates, prescribed in an existing advance agreement.

(vi) Current labor rates; overhead rates, loading factors, per diem rates, and lot data based upon actual costs and labor hours. It should be borne in mind that no single category of information is necessarily sufficient by itself; for example, information as to rates for labor and overhead would normally require data concerning the base elements—labor hours, material costs, etc.—to which the rates apply.

(2) The Plant Rep/ACO, as well as the contract auditor, will be responsible for providing a complete and accurate field pricing report to the contracting officer. To accomplish this end, the Plant Rep/ACO must:

(i) In concert with the auditor and in consideration of the auditor's workload, establish a deadline for the auditor's input, subject to date adjustments when considered necessary (adjustments will be coordinated by the Plant Rep/ACO with the contracting officer and the contract auditor);

(ii) Identify areas for special consideration (these are areas in addition to those specified by the contracting officer);

(iii) Arrange for exchanges of technical and audit information; and

(iv) Be fully responsive to a request for technical information from the auditor.

(a)(S-70) If an audit review will not be required, either as a separate report or as part of a field pricing report, before negotiating any contract or modification for which a proposal is submitted in excess of $500,000, approval shall be obtained at a level above the contracting officer.

(c)(1)(S-70) When field pricing reviews are required, contracting officers should note the following:

(A) The Plant Rep/ACO is the team manager for all contracting officer requests for field pricing support. Therefore, the contracting officer shall send all requests for field pricing support to the cognizant field contract administration activity; generally, the Plant Representative (Plant Rep) for the Services and the Administrative Contracting Officer (ACO) for DCAS(DLA). A copy of the request will also be sent to the cognizant audit activity.

(B) When the contracting officer knows in advance that field pricing support will be required, the contracting officer shall provide the cognizant Plant Rep/ACO and auditor a copy of the solicitation. In addition, the contracting officer may require the contractor to provide copies of the proposal direct to the Plant Rep/ACO and auditor. In this event the contracting officer shall, as soon as possible after receipt of the contractor's proposal, identify those specific areas for which field pricing support is required.

(C) Where audit reports are received on contracting actions that are subsequently canceled or unsuccessful, the cognizant auditor shall be notified in writing.

(c)(1)(S-71) When field pricing reports are requested for acquisition of parts or support equipment, the request shall as a minimum include, but

A-69

will normally be limited to, the following:

(A) A detailed analysis of each line item where the quoted price exceeds 25 percent or more the lowest price of the Government of the item at any time within the most recent 12-month period. These items will be specified in the request for field pricing support.

(B) The results of a review of the description and the price of each line item in the proposal made to assist in identifying any obvious overpricing. Those items, so identified, will be subjected to further analysis.

(C) An analysis of the significant high-dollar-value items. If there are no obvious high-dollar-value items (i.e., the majority of line items are of approximate equal value), a random sampling technique should be used.

(D) An analysis of a random sample of the remaining low-dollar-value line items. Sample size may be determined by subjective judgment, e.g., experience with the contractor, reliability of contractor's estimating/accounting systems, credibility of proposals, etc.

(d) The efforts of all field pricing support team members are complementary, advisory and also offer an excellent check and balance of the various analyses imperative to the contracting officer's final pricing decision. Therefore, it is essential that there be close understanding, cooperation and communication to ensure the exchange of information of mutual interest during the period of analysis. While they shall review the data concurrently when possible, each shall render services within the individual area of responsibility. For example, on quantitative factors (such as labor hours), the auditor may find it necessary to compare proposed hours with hours actually expended on the same or similar products in the past as reflected on the cost records of the contractor. From this information the auditor can often project trend data. The technical specialist may also analyze the proposed hours on the basis of knowledge of such things as shop practices, industrial engineering, time and motion factors, and the contractor's plant organization and capabilities. The interchange of this information will not only prevent duplication but will assure adequate and complementary analysis.

(e) The terms "audit review" and "audit" refer to examinations by contract auditors of contractors' statements of actual or estimated costs to the extent deemed appropriate by the auditors in the light of their experience with contractors and relying upon their appraisals of the effectiveness of contractors' policies, procedures, controls, and practices. Such audit reviews or audits may consist of desk reviews, test checks of a limited number of transactions, or examinations in depth, at the discretion of the auditor. The contract auditor is responsible for submission of information and advice, based on analysis of the contractor's books and accounting records or other related data, as to the acceptability of the contractor's incurred and estimated costs.

(e)(6) Reports of technical analysis and review should be furnished to the auditor at the earliest possible date and at least five days prior to the due date of the audit report to enable the auditor to include the financial effect of technical findings in the audit report (for example, the necessary computations of dollar amounts arising from changes in proposed kinds and quantities of materials, labor hours, etc.). In the event the technical analyses are not available in time to be reflected in the audit report, the audit report shall so state, and this shall be made known to the Plant Rep/ACO so that comments may be incorporated in the submission to the contracting officer. If technical analyses are received later by the auditor, the auditor shall issue a supplemental report if the status of the negotiation is such that a report would serve a useful purpose. The original of all technical reports received by the auditor shall be made a part of the audit report submitted to the Plant Rep/ACO.

(e)(7) When the contracting officer determines that deficiencies in the contractor's accounting system or estimating methods are such that the proposed contract cannot be adequately priced or administered, the contracting officer shall, with the advice of the contract auditor and the Plant Rep/ACO, assure that necessary corrective action is initiated prior to the award of such contract. The auditor is responsible for performing that part of reviews and cost analyses which requires access to the contractor's books and financial records supporting proposed cost or pricing data, regardless of the dollar amount involved.

(e)(8) During the course of the examination, the Plant Rep/ACO and the auditor shall each confer with the contractor to fully understand the basis for each item in the contractor's proposal and to remove any doubts as to the validity and accuracy of their conclusions and findings.

(g) The Plant Rep/ACO (price analyst or negotiator) shall query the auditor or technical personnel about matters in audit or technical reports which appear to need clarification. When developing the Plant Rep/ACO statement to the contracting officer transmitting audit and technical reports, comments or observations shall be added about pertinent matters whether or not covered in the audit or technical reports. However, it is not contemplated, for example, that the price analyst or negotiator should attempt an examination of the contractor's accounting records for this purpose since the contract auditor has this responsibility.

(i) If in the opinion of the contracting officer, Plant Rep/ACO, or auditor, the review of a prime contractor's proposal requires further review of subcontractors' cost estimates at the subcontractors' plants (after due consideration of reviews performed by the prime contractor), such reviews should be fully coordinated with the Plant Rep/ACO having cognizance of the prime contractor before being initiated. If a review is required of a subcontract proposal, the prime Plant Rep/ACO shall forward the request to the subcontract ACO with an information copy to the subcontract auditor. In the event a lower tier subcontract proposal requires review, the request should be coordinated in sequence with the Plant Rep/ACO's at higher tiers in the subcontract chain. The resulting pricing reports, including any audit reports, shall be forwarded by the subcontract Plant Rep/ACO to the prime Plant Rep/ACO with an information copy to the prime auditor. If the review is of a lower tier subcontract proposal, the report shall be transmitted through the Plant Rep/ACO's in the subcontract chain.

(j) The appropriate contract administration activities will be notified by the HCA when review and evaluation of subcontractors' proposals will require extensive field pricing assistance in connection with the acquisition of a major new weapon system, or require special or expedited action by field pricing personnel and such action is being, or has been, delayed.

215.806 Subcontract pricing considerations.

(S-70) Other subcontract pricing considerations include:

(1) Subcontract costs and pricing arrangements are significant elements to be considered during negotiation of prime contracts and during contract administration.

(2) Basic responsibility rests with the prime contractor for decisions to make or buy, for selection of subcontractors, for subcontract prices, and for subcontract performance. The contracting officer who is responsible for negotiating the contract price with the prime contractor must have adequate knowledge of these elements as they affect prime contract prices.

(3) Contractors' "make-or-buy" programs and proposed subcontracts must be reviewed in accordance with FAR 15.7 and with FAR Part 44. Information from these reviews should be used in evaluating subcontract costs when negotiating prime contract prices. The contracting officer, when appropriate, should secure from the contractor information concerning:

(i) The prime contractor's purchasing practices; and

(ii) The principal components to be subcontracted and the prospective or actual subcontractors, including (A) the extent of competition obtained or to be obtained, (B) the basis for the subcontract costs included in the contract pricing proposal (SF 1411), (C) any contractor cost or price analyses of subcontract proposals, including the cost or pricing data submitted by subcontractors, (D) the pricing arrangement contemplated or negotiated, and (E) the extent of subcontract supervision.

(4) The contracting officer is responsible for the reasonableness of the prime contract price which includes self-satisfaction as to the reasonableness of the subcontract costs included in the prime contract price. Field pricing support from the Plant Rep/ACO cognizant of the prime contractor is generally required in determining reasonableness of the prime contract price. In some instances, it may be necessary to obtain field pricing support of proposed subcontracts. On the basis of a request from the contracting officer and/or advice from members of the field pricing team, the ACO cognizant of the prime contractor may request field pricing support from the ACO cognizant of the prospective subcontractor. These actions will be taken in accordance with 215.805-5.

(5) If the prime contractor's analysis is not considered adequate, the ACO will return the analysis package to the contractor for re-accomplishment indicating areas of inadequacy. In this case, the prime contractor will accomplish or cause the accomplishment of the additional review and resubmit the package to the ACO.

(6) When subcontracts have been placed on a price redetermination or fixed-price incentive basis and the prime contract is to be repriced, it may be appropriate to negotiate a firm prime contract price, even though the contractor has not yet established final subcontract prices. The contracting officer may do this when convinced the amount included for subcontracting is reasonable, e.g., where realistic cost or pricing data on subcontract efforts are available. However, even though the available cost data are highly indefinite and there is a distinct chance that one or more of the subcontracts eventually may be redetermined at prices that are lower than those predicted in redetermining the prime contract price, other circumstances may require the prompt negotiation of the final contract price. In such a case, the contract modification which evidences the revised contract prices should provide for adjustment of the total amount paid or to be paid under the contract on account of subsequent redetermination of the specified subcontracts. This may be done by including in the contract modification a statement substantially as follows:

Promptly upon the establishment of firm prices for each of the subcontracts listed below, the Contractor shall submit, in such form and detail as the Contracting Officer may reasonably require, a statement of costs incurred in the performance of such subcontract and the firm price established therefor. Thereupon, notwithstanding any other provisions of this contract as amended by this modification, the Contractor and the Contracting Officer shall negotiate an equitable adjustment in the total amount paid or to be paid under this contract to reflect such subcontract price revision. The equitable adjustment shall be evidenced by a modification to this contract.

(List Subcontracts)

(7) In considering cost-plus-fee subcontracts, the contracting officer shall make every effort to insure that fees under such subcontracts never exceed the fee limitations identified in 215.903(d).

(8) The prime contractor may submit subcontractor claims for exemption at any time to the contracting officer for an advance review of their acceptability, but otherwise the prime contractor shall submit them with its proposal or request for subcontract consent; or other action by the contracting officer, whichever comes first.

215.807 Prenegotiation objectives.

(b) Prenegotiation objectives will be documented in accordance with Departmental procedures.

(S-70) When contract audit review of the offeror's proposal has been requested, the contracting officer shall keep the auditor informed of planned prenegotiation and negotiation activities, including related fact-finding sessions and/or discussions with the offeror, and invite contract audit participation where the contracting officer and auditor agree that a significant contribution can be made.

215.808 Price negotiation memorandum.

(a)(4) Comments should also be included on the current status of their contractor systems (e.g., estimating, accounting, compensation, etc.) to the extent that they impacted and were considered in the negotiation.

(a)(10) The following applies to documentation of profit or fee negotiated:

(i) Since the profit objective is the contracting officer's prenegotiation evaluation of the total estimated profit under the proposed contract, the amounts set forth for each category of cost will probably change in the course of negotiation. Furthermore, the negotiated profit will probably vary from the profit objective, and from a detailed application of the weighted guidelines method to each element of the Contractor's Input to Total Performance as anticipated prior to negotiation. Since the profit objective is viewed as a whole rather than as its component parts, insignificant variations from the pre-negotiation profit objective, as a result of changes of the Contractor's Input to Total Performance, need not be documented in detail. Conversely, significant deviations from the profit objective necessary to reach a final agreement on profit or fee shall be explained. The profit earned as a result of contract performance will generally vary from that anticipated at the time of negotiation.

(ii) When the weighted guidelines method is not used because of unusual pricing situations (see 215.9), the contract file shall be documented to support the exceptions.

(iii) DD Form 1547 (see 215.9) may be used in the Price Negotiation Memorandum, *Provided* that the rationale used in assigning the various rates is fully documented.

(iv) See also FAR 15.807(c).

215.809 Forward pricing rate agreements.

(e) Indirect costs commonly known as overhead are defined and described in FAR 31.203. Criteria for treatment and application of indirect costs to contracts are also set forth in FAR 31.203. To assure a reasonable approximation and allocation of indirect costs on an equitable basis to individual contracts, negotiators shall utilize audited indirect cost data or negotiated indirect cost rates, when available, in connection with negotiation of contracts and shall not, unless authorized by the head of the contracting activity, seek preferential indirect cost rates. If there is any question with respect to audited indirect cost data or negotiated indirect cost rates, or if such are not available, the negotiator should normally use the advisory services of the cognizant Department of Defense auditor.

(e)(2) In assessing changed conditions, the ACO will consider: (i) The type of contract contemplated; (ii) whether the dollar amount of the proposed contract action would significantly change the rates in the agreement; (iii) whether the performance period of the proposed contract action is significantly different from the period to which the rate agreement applies; and (iv) any new data or other information that may raise a question as to the acceptability of the rates.

(f) When contracting representatives have received notice that changed conditions negate FPRA's, individual contracting actions should not be delayed.

215.810 Should-cost analysis.

(b)(S-70)(i) Should-cost analyses shall be performed prior to award of definitive major systems contracts in excess of $100 million for major systems if each of the following conditions are met:

(A) A production contract for the system is to be awarded on a sole-source basis;

(B) Initial production of the system has already taken place;

(C) The current plans for the Department of Defense include production of substantial quantities of identical or similar items;

(D) The work to be performed under the contract is sufficiently defined to permit an effective analysis of what production of the system by the contractor should cost; and

(E) Major changes in the program are unlikely.

(ii) After an initial should-cost analysis has been performed under (i) above, subsequent should-cost analyses need not be performed annually, but must be accomplished at least every four years on contracts meeting the requirements of (i) above.

(iii) Waiver of a should-cost analysis shall be made in accordance with Service procedures, but in no event at a level lower than a general/flag officer or civilian equivalent.

(e) The content of the should-cost analysis team report shall be prescribed by Service procedure. Team leaders should ensure that activities are coordinated to avoid duplication of effort.

215.811 Estimating systems.

(a)(S-70) The establishment, maintenance, and consistent use of formal cost estimating systems by contractors is to the mutual benefit of the Government and industry, particularly where a large portion of the contractor's business is defense work and there are a number of significant proposals requiring review. Contracting activities and contract administration activities are required to furnish full support to a program of encouraging major defense contractors to formalize and follow good estimating procedures. It is recognized that estimating procedures will vary among contractors, and may vary between plants or divisions of a contractor due to differences in products, size and methods of operations, production vs. research, and other factors. While formal systems do not eliminate the need for judgmental factors to be applied by contractors in developing cost proposals, they do provide a sound foundation for the systematic and orderly application of these judgment factors to specific proposals.

(a)(S-71) Reviews and reports shall be accomplished as a joint contract audit and contract administration office team effort, with the contract auditor designated as its head. Reviews shall be tailored to take full advantage of the day-to-day work done as an integral part of both the contract audit and contract administration activities. The program established by the contract audit activity shall be coordinated with the appropriate contract administration activity to assure that team membership includes qualified technical specialists, and that adequate personnel resources are made available to accomplish the program.

215.870 Procedures for identifying contractors' unallowable costs.

(a) The establishment, maintenance, and consistent use of procedures for identifying and segregating unallowable costs, which will assure compliance with CAS 405 and FAR Part 31 will benefit both the Government and contractors. Such procedures may vary between plants or divisions of a contractor due to size, mix of business and complexity of organization. Some of the advantages of sound procedures are that:

(1) A greater degree of confidence can be placed on the accuracy and reliability of contractors' proposals, billings and claims;

(2) They expedite the negotiation process; and

(3) They may reduce the scope of reviews performed by audit and other technical and contracting personnel.

(b) The responsible Federal Contract Audit organization shall review contractors' procedures and practices in conjunction with other contract audit activities. Deficiencies shall be reported to the cognizant ACO, and, as appropriate, contracting officers having substantial business with the contractor. Among the matters to be considered in determining the adequacy of a contractor's procedures are its policy, practices and techniques for:

(1) Assignment of responsibilities within the contractor's organization for reviewing and approving claims against the Government;

(2) Identification of unallowable costs (expressly unallowable, mutually agreed to be unallowable or specifically designated as unallowable by written decision of the contracting officer) together with the individual employees incurring such costs;

(3) Identification and computation of directly associated costs;

(4) Assurance that unallowable and directly associated costs are not included in estimated costs proposed, or incurred amounts claimed by the contractor;

(5) Coordination and communication between the elements of the contractor's organization that prepare proposals and claims and those responsible

Department of Defense

for identifying unallowable and directly associated costs; and

(6) Assuring the adequacy of the documentation maintained by the contractor identifying the unallowable costs together with directly associated costs.

(c) Documentation in support of the contractor's procedures shall be made available to authorized Government personnel.

215.871 Estimated data prices (DD Form 1423).

(a) The Department of Defense requires estimates of the prices of data in order to evaluate the cost to the Government of data items in terms of their management, product or engineering value.

(b) When data are required to be delivered under a contract, the solicitation will include DD Form 1423, Contract Data Requirements List. The form and the provision included in the solicitation request the offeror to state what portion of the total price is estimated to be attributable to the production or development of the listed data for the Government (not to the sale of rights in the data). However, offerors' estimated prices may not reflect all such costs; and different offerors may reflect these costs in a different manner, for the following reasons:

(1) Differences in business practices in competitive situations;

(2) Differences in accounting systems among offerors;

(3) Use of factors or rates on some portions of the data;

(4) Application of common effort to two or more data items;

(5) Differences in data preparation methods among offerors.

For these and other reasons, data price estimates should not be used for contract pricing purposes without further analysis.

(c) The contracting officer shall assure that the contract does not include a requirement for data which the contractor has delivered or is obligated to deliver to the Government under another contract or subcontract, and that the successful offeror furnishes any certification required by the solicitation. However, where duplicate data are desired, the contract price shall include the costs of duplication, but not of preparation, of such data.

(d) In the case of acquisitions of $100,000 or over, the contracting officer, after agreeing upon a negotiated contract price, will adjust the estimated prices in Blocks 26 of the original DD Form 1423 for the data items listed thereon to equal the amount included in the related priced contract line or subline item(s) for the data item(s). Adjusted DD Form 1423 will be maintained so as to be available at each contracting activity. The detachable portion of the DD Form 1423 (Blocks 17-26) with the estimated or adjusted prices shall not appear in the contract.

(e) When printing is to be acquired as an integral part of a contract for other supplies or services, each requirement in the contract for printing shall be listed as a separate line item on DD Form 1423; and the approval or waiver obtained pursuant to Subpart 208.8 shall be appropriately identified.

215.872 Capital investment incentives.

(a) *General.* Although the DoD profit policy is normally sufficient encouragement to increase contractor investment, it is recognized that situations will arise when additional incentives may be appropriate. In these individual cases, a special Capital Investment Incentive clause may be negotiated and included in contracts for research, development, and/or production of weapon systems or material to provide incentives to contractors to invest in severable plant equipment capital assets. Such clause must be tailored to the requirements of the individual situation, and then only after a careful analysis of the benefits in each case is made, to assure optimum results are obtained for the Government. This clause would become operative in the event that the contract or program is terminated or funds are not provided in subsequent fiscal years for the planned acquisition upon which the investment decision was based. Such clause may permit the Government to acquire specific capital investments at no more than the depreciated value. This value may be determined by considering a combination of investment incentives, income tax credits or incentives, and allowable depreciation costs pursuant to cost principles established in FAR Part 31.

(b) *Scope.*

(1) This technique is designed to transfer to the Government some of the risk associated with acquisition of certain capital assets by contractors. Its purpose is to cover only specifically identified cost-effective capital assets. It is not to be used to override the general policy that all facilities needed for the performance of Government contracts will be provided by the contractor as set forth in FAR Part 45.

(2) Capital assets which may be covered by such an investment clause are subject to the following criteria:

(i) Includes only severable industrial plant equipment, and other types of severable plant equipment with a unit value in excess of $10,000, including associated accessories which would be capitalized in accordance with the contractor's disclosed accounting practices, but excluding real property;

(ii) The capital investment would not otherwise be made by the contractor except to substantially benefit the program(s) involved;

(iii) The overall savings that will accrue to the Government on the program(s) for covered equipment exceed the related investment costs by a margin sufficient to make the acquisition economically viable;

(iv) The savings that will result from use of this equipment, as developed under (c) below, will be reflected in the pricing of the individual contracts.

(c) *Determination.* Prior to implementing this investment clause, the contracting officer shall make a written determination that the contractor will not make the investment without the use of this technique. This determination should be detailed and include the following elements:

(i) Consideration of the alternatives of acquiring such equipment through the manner listed in FAR 45.302;

(ii) An analysis of the costs of the investment and the overall cost savings to the Government, including the payback quantities and/or payback periods;

(iii) An assessment of the degree of competition present for the proposed requirement. If a competitive environment is present, the competition may cause the firms to consider bearing the total risks for the investments. When this technique is to be used, it shall be a factor in the source selection evaluation criteria;

(iv) An assessment stating the rationale why the DoD profit policy is insufficient motivation for the investment;

(v) Other considerations which should be addressed are:

(A) Effect upon the contractor's make or buy plan;

(B) Subcontractor participation in the investment technique;

(C) Consistency of depreciation rates with FAR 31.205.11;

(vi) Any other matter which has a bearing on the investment plan.

(d) *Limitations.*

(1) This investment incentive is designed primarily for DoD programs which are listed in the Five Year Defense Program (FYDP) and designated as Defense System Acquisition Review Council (DSARC) Programs, in accordance with DoD Directive 5000.1, "Acquisition of Major Defense Systems." This incentive may also be extended to other DoD programs provided approval is obtained from the Secretary of the Department. The program must provide for a sufficient buy to allow for amortization of the planned investment.

(2) The fiscal authority who commits funds to the resultant contract must certify that the following actions have been accomplished:

(i) The Approval Authority (see (g)(1) below) has approved by fiscal year the amount of contingent Government liability;

(ii) The Approval Authority has notified the Congress in advance that the technique will be used on contracts for a specific weapon system or material program element. Unless there are unusual circumstances, this notification will be included in the justification material submitted to the Congress in support of authorization and appropriation requests. A copy of the notification shall be retained in the contract file.

Department of Defense

(e) *Negotiation requirements.*

(1) Since this investment incentive is predicated on the written determination specified in paragraph (c) above, the impact on contract cost will be recognized in the price(s) negotiated.

(2) In order for items of plant equipment to be covered, they must be listed (nomenclature and value) in the Capital Investment Incentive clause. The items of equipment can be incorporated in the contract using either or both of the following procedures:

(i) When the exact value and nomenclature of the item of plant equipment is known at the time of negotiations, it shall be listed in the investment clause at the time of the contract award. The contractor's proposal should reflect the impact on cost and other benefit to the Government that will accrue from use of the equipment in order to comply with Pub. L. 87-653;

(ii) If the exact value and nomenclature of each investment is not known at the time of negotiations and it can be mutually agreed that certain categories of plant equipment would benefit the Government, an additional provision to the investment clause should be used. This additional provision shall stipulate the conditions which the individual items of plant equipment must meet to be subsequently incorporated into the investment clause and shall establish the requirement for the contractor to submit financial and other justification necessary for the contracting officer to make the determination specified in (c) above. Such items of equipment will be incorporated into the contract by supplemental agreement and the price revised, as appropriate; *Provided:* (A) They meet the contractual conditions and (B) the equipment value, when added to the value of previously covered equipment, will not exceed the stated dollar ceiling.

(3) The limit of the Government's contingent liability is subject to negotiation. Provision should be made to assume only that liability which is sufficient to motivate the contractor to invest.

(4) Application of the weighted guidelines in 215.9 should reflect the assumption of risk by the parties associated with items covered by this technique.

(f) *Contractual requirements.* In order to incorporate this investment incentive, a special contractual Capital Investment clause shall be developed. Such a clause should include but not be limited to the following:

(1) A listing of the exact nomenclature and value of each item of plant equipment covered.

(2) A provision for additions to the listing after contract award, if appropriate. Such provision shall establish the conditions that must be met, the categories of equipment that will be covered, and the requirement for such additions to be incorporated by contract modification. This provision should allow for removal of an item from coverage at the request of the contractor with the concurrence of the contracting officer.

(3) Criteria for ascertaining when this special provision can be invoked as well as the criteria which will cancel the Government's contingent liability under the clause such as end-item quantity thresholds and performance dates, whichever occurs first.

(4) The dollar ceiling of the value of covered items as well as the Government's contingent liability by fiscal year.

(5) A specific method to establish the price to the Government at which each item would be acquired if this special provision is invoked.

(6) A provision that within 30 days of a Government decision that provides a basis for the contractor to invoke the special provision, the contracting officer shall notify the contractor in writing that the event has occurred and its date of occurrence. Further, the provision shall require that within 90 days after notification by the contracting officer, the contractor must provide to the contracting officer, in writing, a list of the specific investments which he desires to have the Government acquire. This list shall not include any investments which have not been incorporated into the investment clause of the contract prior to the contracting officer's notice to the contractor.

(7) A provision that once the contractor requests the Government to

buy any equipment covered by the investment clause, the Government has the right to buy any and/or all other equipment covered by the clause whether the contractor requests it to do so or not.

(8) A provision for deferral of Government acquisition of those items of equipment needed for contract or program completion.

(9) A provision that the investment clause be carried over to successor contracts until the Government's responsibility to acquire the equipment expires.

(10) A provision that a supplemental agreement shall be executed for any equipment acquired by the Government under this special clause.

(11) A provision that as a condition of Government acquisition, the equipment shall be in good operating condition.

(12) Criteria for providing disposition instructions should the special provision for capital investment be exercised. Identify which party is to bear the cost of restoration, storage, disconnect and removal, packing and transportation upon removal of the equipment. The provisions of FAR Subpart 45.6 shall apply unless the contract provides specific exception thereto.

(13) A provision that in the event this special clause is invoked, the limitation stated in FAR 31.205-39 does not prevent acquisition or any payment for the covered equipment.

(14) A provision that this special clause for capital investment shall not apply in the event of contract termination for default.

(15) Provide that this investment clause can be made applicable to subcontracts, if appropriate benefits, as outlined in paragraph (b) above, are available. Provision must be made for Government approval, as outlined in paragraph (c) above, of all equipment for which the Government may assume contingent liability as well as a provision that the clause can be invoked only as a direct flow down from the prime's ability to invoke the clause.

(16) A provision that establishes the extent to which the contractor may use this equipment for other business.

(g) *Administration.*

(1) Approval for use of this investment incentive for contingent liabilities must be obtained from the Secretary of the Military Department or the Director of DLA. Authority up to $50 million may be delegated no lower than the Commander, AFSC, AFLC, NMC, AMC.

(2) In the event that it becomes apparent that the contingent liability resulting from the use of this technique will become an actual obligation, the approval authority shall be notified and immediate steps shall be taken to obtain sufficient funds to cover the obligation. These funds must be made available at the time the actual obligation materializes, to preclude a violation of the Anti-Deficiency Act.

Subpart 215.9—Profit

215.901 General.

(c) Furthermore, low average profit rates on defense contracts overall are detrimental to the public interest. Effective national defense in a free enterprise economy requires that the best industrial capabilities be attracted to defense contracts. These capabilities will be driven away from the defense market if defense contracts are characterized by low profit opportunities. Consequently, negotiations aimed merely at reducing prices by reducing profits, with no realization of the function of profit, cannot be condoned. For each contract in which profit is negotiated as a separate element of the contract price, the aim of negotiation should be to employ the profit motive so as to impel effective contract performance by which overall costs are economically controlled. To this end, the profit objective must be fitted to the circumstances of the particular acquisition, giving due weight to each of the effort, risk, facilities investment, and special factors set forth in this subpart. This will result in a wider range of profits which, in many cases, will be significantly higher than previous norms.

215.902 Policy.

(a)(1) The weighted guidelines method shall be used as the structured approach for determining profit or fee

Department of Defense 215.902

in accordance with 215.905 and the following:

(i) The weighted guidelines method provides contracting officers with a technique that will insure consideration of the relative value of the appropriate profit factors in the establishment of a profit objective and the conduct of negotiations; and a basis for documentation of this objective, including an explanation of any significant departure from it in reaching a final agreement. The contracting officer's analysis of these profit factors is based on information available prior to negotiations. Such information is furnished in proposals, audit data, performance reports, preaward surveys, and the like. Except as set forth in 215.902(a)(2), the weighted guidelines method shall be used in the negotiation of all contracts where cost analysis is performed for:

(A) The manufacturing of supplies and equipment;

(B) Research and development as described in FAR Part 35, encompassing research, exploratory development, advanced development, engineering development, and operational systems development;

(C) Services as described in FAR Part 37.

(1) The profit objective for manufacturing contracts shall be computed, except as indicated in (5) below, using the manufacturing weighted guidelines method, which provides profit opportunity based on facilities capital investment.

(2) The profit objective for research and development contracts shall be computed using the research and development weighted guidelines method unless, in the judgment of the contracting officer, a significant amount of facilities is required for efficient contract performance, in which case the manufacturing weighted guidelines shall be used.

(3) The profit objective for service contracts shall be computed using the service contract weighted guidelines method unless, in the judgment of the contracting officer, a significant amount of facilities is required for efficient contract performance, in which case the manufacturing weighted guidelines shall be used.

(4) In determining whether a particular contract shall be classified as manufacturing, research and development, or services, primary reliance shall be placed on the nature of the work to be performed, as indicated by the coding for Item B8A of the DD Form 350 (see DoD 4105.61-M, Department of Defense Procurement Coding Manual, Volume 1), notwithstanding the appropriation or negotiation authority used. The following guidelines shall apply:

(i) *Manufacturing Weighted Guidelines.* Contracts coded under Section I, Part C, Supplies and Equipment.

(ii) *Research and Development Weighted Guidelines.* Contracts coded under Section I, Part A, Research, Development, Test and Evaluation, except for contracts coded as AD2-, Defense Services, and A—6, Management and Support.

(iii) *Services Weighted Guidelines.* Contracts coded under Section I, Part B, Other Services and Construction; and under Section I, Part A, as AD2- and as A—. Note, however, that there are blanket exceptions for certain services (see 215.902(a)(2)).

(5) The categories listed above are intended to be used as a point of departure in determining which weighted guidelines method applies. Many contracts for research and development and for services will require a significant amount of facilities for efficient contract performance. When this is the case, the manufacturing weighted guidelines method shall be used. Similarly, certain contracts for the manufacture of small quantities of high technology supplies and equipment may not require a significant amount of facilities. In such cases, the research and development weighted guidelines method shall be used. Contracting officers shall apply sound judgment in determining which weighted guidelines method is most appropriate for a particular contracting situation. The difference in profit objectives that would result from the application of alternative weighted guidelines methods shall not be a consideration in making this determination.

(6) In determining whether a significant amount of facilities is required

for efficient contract performance, the contracting officer should assess the facilities needed, including contractor owned and leased and Government owned. When there is a relatively small amount of facilities capital cost of money allocated to the contract because some facilities are provided through operating leases and by the Government, this does not necessarily mean that an insignificant amount of facilities is required for efficient contract performance.

(7) When a method other than the manufacturing weighted guidelines method is used to establish the prenegotiation profit objective, the profit objective shall be reduced by the amount of facilities capital cost of money allowed in accordance with 231.205-10. On cost-plus-award-fee contracts, the base fee shall be reduced by the amount of facilities capital cost of money or the contract shall contain a provision to disallow the cost.

(ii) The contractor's proposal should include cost information for evaluation and a total profit figure. Contractors shall not be required to submit the details of their profit objectives but they shall not be prohibited from doing so if they desire. Elaborate and voluminous presentations are neither required nor desired and may indicate a low index of cost effectiveness, which fact itself shall be taken into consideration by the contracting officer.

(iii) The negotiation process does not contemplate or require agreement on either estimated cost elements or profit elements, although the details of analysis and evaluation may be discussed in the fact-finding phase of the negotiation. If the difference between the contractor's profit objective and the contracting officer's profit objective is relatively small, no discussion of individual factors may be necessary. If the negotiating parties' objectives are relatively far apart, a disclosure of weightings and rationale by both parties may be made concerning the total assigned to contractor effort, contractor risk, facilities investment, and special factors. By thus developing a mutual understanding of the logic of the respective positions, an orderly progression to final agreement should result. Simultaneous, not sequential, agreement will be reached on cost, any incentive profit-sharing formulas or limitation on profits, and price. The profit objective is a part of an overall negotiation objective which, as a going-in objective, bears a distinct relationship to the target cost objective and any proposed sharing arrangement. Since the profit is merely one of several interrelated variables, the Government negotiator shall not complete the profit negotiation without simultaneously agreeing on the other variables. Specific agreement on the exact weights or values of the individual factors is not required and shall not be attempted.

(iv) The prime contractor may use the weighted guidelines or a structured approach that discriminates among different levels of investment if the acquisition would be subject to the weighted guidelines under a prime contract. (For applicability, see 230.570-1(c).) If the acquisition falls into one of the exceptions to the weighted guidelines (see 215.902(a)(2)), the prime contractor may use another method to establish profit objectives. In the absence of a structured approach that discriminates among different levels of investment, similar to the weighted guidelines, the profit objective will be reduced by the amount of facilities capital cost of money allowed in accordance with FAR 31.205-10.

(v) The following factors shall be considered in all cases in which profit is to be specifically negotiated. The weight ranges listed after each factor shall be used in all instances where the weighted guidelines method is used.

WEIGHT RANGES

	Manufacturing [1] (pct)	R&D (pct)	Services (pct)
A. Contractor Effort: Material Acquisition:			
Subcontract Items.	1 to 5	1 to 5	1 to 5
Purchased Parts	1 to 4	1 to 4	1 to 4
Other Material	1 to 4	1 to 4	1 to 4

Department of Defense 215.902

WEIGHT RANGES—Continued

	Manufacturing [1] (pct)	R&D (pct)	Services (pct)
Engineering: Direct Labor.	9 to 15	9 to 15	N/A
Manufacturing: Direct Labor.	5 to 9	5 to 9	N/A
Services:			
Direct Labor	N/A	N/A	5 to 15
Overhead	N/A	N/A	4 to 8
Other: General Management.	6 to 8	6 to 8	6 to 8
B. Contractor Risk	0 to 8	0 to 7	0 to 4
C. Facilities Investment.	16 to 20	N/A	N/A
D. Special Factors:			
Productivity	([2])	N/A	N/A
Independent Development.	1 to 4	1 to 4	N/A
Other	−5 to +5	−5 to +5	−5 to +5

[1] An adjustment factor of .7 is applied to the results of the Contractor Effort evaluation to arrive at the dollar profit objective for this factor (see DD Form 1547). (Also, see 230.70.)

[2] See 15.905-2(a).

(vi) Under the weighted guidelines method, the contracting officer shall first measure the "Contractor's Effort" by the assignment of a profit percentage, within the designated weight ranges, to each element of contract cost recognized by the contracting officer. Although certain classifications of acceptable cost, including travel, subsistence, facilities, test equipment, special tooling, Federal manufacturers' excise taxes, and royalty expenses, may have been historically excluded from the base upon which profit has been computed, they shall not be excluded when using the weighted guidelines method. Not to be included for the computation of profit as part of the cost base is the amount calculated for the cost of money for facilities capital. How this cost is determined and how it will be applied and administered is fully set forth in 230.70.

(vii) The suggested categories under the Contractor's Effort are similar to those on the Contract Pricing Proposal (SF 1411). Often, individual proposals will be in a different format, but since these categories are broad and basic, they provide sufficient guidance to evaluate all other items of cost.

(viii) After computing a total dollar profit for the Contractor's Effort, the contracting officer then shall add the specific profit dollars assigned for Contractor's risk, facilities investment risk, and special factors. Weighted Guidelines Profit/Fee Objective (DD Form 1547) is to be used, as appropriate, to facilitate the calculation of this profit objective.

(ix) The weighted guidelines method was designed for arriving at profit or fee objectives for other than nonprofit organizations. However, if appropriate adjustments are made to reflect differences between profit and nonprofit organizations, the weighted guidelines method can be used as a basis for arriving at fee objectives for nonprofit organizations. Therefore, the policy of the Department of Defense is to use the weighted guidelines method, as modified in (B) below, to establish fee objectives that will stimulate efficient contract performance and attract the best capabilities of nonprofit organizations to defense-oriented activities. The modifications shall not be applied as deductions against historical fee levels but to the fee objective for such a contract, as calculated under the weighted guidelines method.

(A) For purposes of this subparagraph, nonprofit organizations are defined as those business entities organized and operated exclusively for charitable, scientific, or educational purposes, of which no part of the net earnings inure to the benefit of any private shareholder or individual, of which no substantial part of the activities is carrying on propaganda or otherwise attempting to influence legislation or participating in any political campaign on behalf of any candidate for public office, and which are exempt from Federal income taxation under Section 501 of the Internal Revenue Code.

(B) For contracts with nonprofit organizations where fees are involved, the following adjustments are required in the weighted guidelines method.

(1) An adjustment of −1% of the total effort shall be assigned in all cases where the manufacturing weighted guidelines method is used. An adjustment of −3% of the total effort shall be assigned in all cases where the research and development or services weighted guidelines method is used.

(2) The weight range under "Contractor Cost Risk" shall be −1% to 0% in lieu of 0% to 8% for contracts with those nonprofit organizations, or elements thereof, identified by the Secretary of Defense or the Secretary of a Department (or their respective designees) as receiving sustaining support on a cost-plus-a-fixed-fee basis from a particular Department or Agency of the Department of Defense.

(x) In making a judgment of the value of each factor, the contracting officer should be governed by the definition, description, and purpose of the factors, together with considerations for evaluating them as set forth herein.

(a)(2)(i) Under the following listed circumstances, other methods for establishing profit objectives may be used:

(A) Architect-engineering contracts;

(B) Management contracts for operation and/or maintenance of Government facilities;

(C) Construction contracts;

(D) Contracts primarily requiring delivery of material supplied by subcontractors;

(E) Termination settlements;

(F) Cost-plus-award-fee contracts;

(G) Contracts not expected to exceed $500,000; and

(H) Unusual pricing situations where the weighted guidelines method has been determined to be unsuitable. Such exceptions shall be justified in writing and shall be authorized by the head of the contracting activity.

(ii) If the contracting officer makes a written determination that the pricing situation meets any of the circumstances set forth above and that application of the manufacturing weighted guidelines will result in an inequitable profit objective, other methods for establishing the profit objective may be used. These methods shall be supported in a manner similar to that used in the weighted guidelines (profit factor breakdown and documentation of profit objectives); however, investment or other factors that would not be applicable to the contract shall be excluded from the profit objective determination. It is intended that the methods will result in profit objectives for noncapital intensive contracts that are below those generally developed for capital intensive contracts.

215.903 Contracting officer responsibilities.

(b) In analyzing profit, contracting officers should consider the following:

(1) When cost analysis is performed pursuant to 215.805-3, profit consideration shall be in accordance with the objectives set forth below. The Government should establish a profit objective for contract negotiations, which will—

(i) Motivate contractors to undertake more difficult work requiring higher skills and reward those who do so;

(ii) Allow the contractors an opportunity to earn profits commensurate with the extent of the cost risk they are willing to assume;

(iii) Motivate contractors to provide their own facilities and financing and to establish their competence through development work undertaken at their own risk and reward those who do so; and

(iv) Reward contractors for productivity increases. The weighted guidelines method set forth in 215.902 for establishing profit objectives is designed to provide reasonably precise guidance in applying these principles. This method, properly applied, will tailor profits to the circumstances of each contract in such a way that long-range, cost-reduction objectives will be fostered, and a spread of profits will be achieved that is commensurate with varying circumstances.

(2) Development of a profit objective should not begin until after a thorough—

(i) Review of proposed contract work;

(ii) Review of all available knowledge regarding the contractor, including capability reports, audit data, preaward survey reports and financial statements, as appropriate; and

(iii) Analysis of the contractor's cost estimate and comparison with the Government's estimate or projection of cost.

(3) A profit objective is that part of the estimated contract price objective or value which, in the judgment of the

Department of Defense

contracting officer, is appropriate for the acquisition being considered, covering the profit or fee element of the price objective. This objective should realistically reflect the total overall task to be performed and the requirements placed on the contractor. Prior to the negotiation of a contract, change order, or contract modification where cost analysis is undertaken, the negotiator shall develop a profit objective. The weighted guidelines method, if applicable, shall be used for developing this profit objective.

(f) In cases where the change or modification calls for substantially different work, then the basic contract profit and the contractor's effort may be radically changed and a detailed analysis is necessary. Also, if the dollar amount of the change or contract modification is very significant in comparison to the contract dollar amount, a detailed analysis shall be made.

215.905 Profit-analysis factors.

215.905-1 Common factors.

(a) This factor is a measure of how much the contractor is expected to contribute to the overall effort necessary to meet the contract performance requirements in an efficient manner. This factor, which is apart from the contractor's responsibility for contract performance, takes into account what resources are necessary and what the contractor must do to accomplish a conversion of ideas and materials into the final product called for in the contract. This is a recognition that, within a given performance output or within a given sales dollar figure, necessary efforts on the part of individual contractors can vary widely in both value and quantity, and that the profit objective should reflect the extent and nature of the contractor's contribution to total performance. The evaluation of this factor requires an analysis of the cost content of the proposed contract as follows.

(1) Analysis of these cost items shall include an evaluation of the managerial and technical effort necessary to obtain the required purchased parts, subcontracted items, and other materials, including special tooling. This evaluation shall include consideration of the number of orders and suppliers and whether established sources are available or new sources must be developed. The contracting officer shall also determine whether the contractor will obtain the material and tooling by routine orders from readily available supplies (particularly those of substantial value in relation to the total contract cost) or by detailed subcontracts for which the prime contractor will be required to develop complex specifications involving creative design or close tolerance manufacturing requirements. Consideration shall be given to the managerial and technical efforts necessary for the prime contractor to administer subcontracts and select subcontractors, including efforts to break out subcontracts from sole sources through the introduction of competition. These determinations shall be made for purchases of raw materials or basic commodities, purchases of processed material, including all types of components of standard or near standard characteristics, and purchases of pieces, assemblies, subassemblies, special tooling, and other products special to the end item. In the application of this criterion, it should be recognized that the contribution of the prime contractor to his purchasing program may be substantial. This may apply in the management of subcontracting programs involving many sources, new complex components and instrumentation, incomplete specifications, and close surveillance by the prime contractor's representative. Recognized costs proposed as direct material costs, like scrap charges, shall be treated as material for profit evaluation. If intracompany transfers are accepted at price, they shall be evaluated as material. Other intracompany transfers shall be evaluated by individual components of cost, i.e., material, labor, and overhead. Normally, the lowest unadjusted weight for direct material is 2%. A weighting of less than 2% would be appropriate only in unusual circumstances when there is a minimal contribution by the contractor.

(2) Analysis of the engineering, manufacturing, and service labor items of the cost content of the contract shall

include evaluation of the comparative quality and level of the engineering talents, manufacturing and service skills, and experience to be employed. In evaluating engineering labor for the purpose of assigning profit dollars, consideration shall be given to the amount of notable scientific talent or unusual or scarce engineering talent needed in contrast to journeyman engineering effort or supporting personnel. The diversity, or lack thereof, of scientific and engineering specialties required for contract performance and the corresponding need for engineering supervision and coordination shall be evaluated. Similarly, the variety of manufacturing labor skills required and the contractor's manpower resources for meeting these requirements shall be considered. Service contract labor shall be evaluated in a like manner by assigning higher weights to engineering or professional-type skills and lower weights to semiprofessional or other type skills required for contract performance. A weighting in excess of 10% for service contract labor will be justified normally only when the quality, skill, and experience of the service contract labor warrant a corresponding weighting under a research and development contract.

(3)(i) Analysis of conversion related indirect costs and general management (FAR 15.905-1(a)(4)) includes the evaluation of the makeup of these expenses and how much they contribute to contract performance. This analysis shall include a determination of the amount of labor within these overhead pools and how this labor would be treated if it were considered as direct labor under the contract. The allocable labor elements shall be given the same profit consideration that they would receive if they were treated as direct labor. The other elements of these overhead pools shall be evaluated to determine whether they are routine expenses, like utilities, depreciation, and maintenance, and hence given lesser profit consideration, or whether they are significant contributing elements. The composite of the individual determinations in relation to the elements of the overhead pools will be the profit consideration given the pools as a whole. The procedure for assigning relative values to these overhead expenses differs from the method used in assigning values of the direct labor. The upper and lower limits assignable to the direct labor are absolute. In the case of overhead expenses, individual expenses may be assigned values outside the range as long as the composite ratio is within the range.

(ii) It is not necessary that the contractor's accounting system break down the overhead expenses within the classifications of engineering overhead, manufacturing overhead, and general and administrative expenses, unless dictated by cost accounting standards (CAS). The contractor whose accounting system only reflects one overhead rate on all direct labor need not change the system (if CAS-exempt) to correspond with the above classifications. In evaluating such a contractor's overhead rate, the contracting officer can break out the applicable sections of the composite rate which can be classified as engineering overhead, manufacturing overhead, and general and administrative expenses, and follow the appropriate evaluation technique.

(iii) There is a critical factor to consider in the determination of profit in this area. Management problems surface in various degrees and the management expertise exercised to solve them shall be considered as an element of profit. For example, a new program for an item that is on the cutting edge of the state of the art will cause more problems and require more managerial time and abilities of a higher order than a follow-on contract. If new contracts create more problems and require a higher profit weight, follow-ons shall be adjusted downward as many of the problems shall have been solved. In any event, an evaluation shall be made of the underlying managerial effort involved on a case-by-case basis.

(iv) It may not be necessary for the contracting officer to make a separate profit evaluation of overhead expenses with each acquisition of substantially the same product with the same contractor. Where an analysis of the profit weight to be assigned to the overhead pool has been made, the

Department of Defense 215.905-1

weight assigned may be used for future contracts with the same contractor until there is a change in the cost composition of the overhead pool or the contract circumstances, or until the factors discussed in (iii) above are relevant.

(4) See (a)(3) above.

(b) In evaluating contract cost risk, contracting officers should also consider the following:

(1) This factor reflects the policy of the Department of Defense that contractors bear an equitable share of contract cost risk, and to compensate them for the assumption of that risk. A contractor's risk associated with costs to perform under a Government contract is usually minimal under cost-reimbursement type contracts. However, as acquisitions progress from basic research through follow-on production and supply contracts, the use of increased contractor-risk-assumption type contracts is appropriate for increasing the contractor's responsibility for performance. The generally accepted progression of the acquisition spectrum ranging from basic research through supply acquisitions and from cost to firm fixed-price contracts, is shown below:

Type of effort and type of contract

1. Basic Research—Cost, CPFF
2. Applied Research—Cost, CPFF
3. Exploratory Development—Cost, CPFF
4. Advanced Development—CPFF, CPAF
5. Engineering Development—CPFF, CPAF, CPIF
6. Operational System Development—CPIF, CPAF, FPI
7. First Production—FPI
8. Follow-on Production—FPI, FFP
9. Supply—FFP

(2) In developing the prenegotiation profit objective, the contracting officer will need to consider strongly the type of contract anticipated to be negotiated and the associated contractor risk when selecting the position in the weight range for profit that is appropriate for the risk to be borne by the contractor. This is one of the most important factors in arriving at prenegotiation profit objectives.

(3) Evaluation of this risk requires a determination of (i) the degree of cost responsibility the contractor assumes, (ii) the reliability of the cost estimates in relation to the task assumed, and (iii) the complexity of the task assumed by the contractor. This factor is specifically limited to the risk of contract costs. Thus, such risks on the part of the contractor as reputation, losing a commercial market, losing potential profits in other fields, or any risk on the part of the contracting activity, such as the risk of not acquiring an effective weapon, are not within the scope of this factor.

(4) The first and basic determination of the degree of cost responsibility assumed by the contractor is related to the sharing of total risk by contract cost by the Government and the contractor through the selection of contract type. The extremes are a cost-plus-fixed-fee contract, requiring only that the contractor use his best efforts to perform a task, and firm fixed-price contract for a complex item. A cost-plus-fixed-fee contract reflects a minimum assumption of cost responsibility, whereas a firm fixed-price contract reflects a complete assumption of cost responsibility.

(5) The second determination is that of the reliability of the cost estimates. Sound price negotiation requires well-defined contract objectives and reliable cost estimates. Prior production experience assists the contractor in preparing reliable cost estimates on new contracts for similar equipment. An excessive cost estimate reduces the possibility that the cost of performance will exceed the contract price, thereby reducing the contractor's assumption of contract cost risk.

(6) The third determination is that of the difficulty of the contractor's task. The contractor's task can be difficult or easy, regardless of the type of contract.

(7) Contractors are likely to assume greater cost risk only if contracting officers objectively analyze the risk incident to proposed contracts and are willing to compensate contractors for it. Generally, a cost-plus-fixed-fee contract will not justify a reward for risk in excess of 0.5%, nor will a firm fixed-price contract justify a reward of less than the minimum on the weighted guidelines. Where proper contract-type selection has been made, the reward for risk, by contract type, will

usually fall into the following percentage ranges:

(i) Type of contract and percentage ranges for profit objectives developed by using the manufacturing weighted guidelines method:

    Cost-Plus-Fixed Fee..................0 to 0.5%
Cost-Plus-Incentive Fee
    With Cost Incentives Only........ 1 to 2%
    With Multiple Incentives........ 1.5 to 3%
Fixed-Price-Incentive
    With Cost Incentives Only........ 3 to 5%
    With Multiple Incentives........... 4 to 6%
Prospective Price Redetermination................................ 4 to 6%
Firm Fixed-Price............................ 6 to 8%

(ii) Type of contract and percentage ranges for profit objectives developed by using the research and development weighted guidelines method:

    Cost-Plus-Fixed Fee..................0 to 0.5%
Cost-Plus-Incentive Fee
    With Cost Incentives Only........ 1 to 2%
    With Multiple Incentives........ 1.5 to 3%
Fixed-Price-Incentive
    With Cost Incentives Only........ 2 to 4%
    With Multiple Incentives........... 3 to 5%
Prospective Price Redetermination................................ 3 to 5%
Firm Fixed-Price............................ 5 to 7%

(iii) Type of contract and percentage ranges for profit objectives developed by using the service contract weighted guidelines method:

    Cost-Plus-Fixed Fee..................0 to 0.5%
    Cost-Plus-Incentive Fee.............. 1 to 2%
    Fixed-Price-Incentive................. 2 to 3%
    Firm Fixed-Price........................ 3 to 4%

(A) These ranges may not be appropriate for all acquisitions. For instance, a fixed-price-incentive contract that is closely priced with a low ceiling price and high incentive share may be tantamount to a firm fixed-price contract. In this situation, the contracting officer may determine that a basis exists for high confidence in the reasonableness of the estimate and that little opportunity exists for cost reduction without extraordinary efforts. On the other hand, a contract with a high ceiling and low incentive formula can be considered to contain cost-plus-incentive-fee contract features. In this situation, the contracting officer may determine that the Government is retaining much of the contract cost responsibility and that the risk assumed by the contractor is minimal. Similarly, if a cost-plus-incentive-fee contract includes an unlimited downward (negative) fee adjustment on cost control, it could be comparable to a fixed-price-incentive contract. In such a pricing environment, the contracting officer may determine that the Government has transferred a greater amount of cost responsibility to the contractor than is typical under a normal cost-plus-incentive-fee contract.

(B) The contractor's subcontracting program may have a significant impact on the contractor's acceptance of risk under a contract form. It can cause risk to increase or decrease in terms of both cost and performance. This consideration shall be a part of the contracting officer's overall evaluation in selecting a factor to apply for cost risk. It may be determined, for instance, that the prime contractor has effectively transferred real cost risk to a subcontractor and the contract cost risk evaluation, as a result, may be below the range that would otherwise apply for the contract type being proposed. This situation will be found to exist only in a few extraordinary situations under circumstances of (i) a follow-on production contract, in which a substantial portion of the total contract costs represents a single subcontract or a few subcontracts, (ii) the fullest incentive reward and penalty feature on cost performance having been passed by the prime contractor to the subcontractor. In an acquisition in which all of these circumstances are found to exist, a lower than usual profit weight may be applied to the aggregate of all recognized costs including the subcontract portion. The contract cost risk evaluation shall not be lowered, however, merely on the basis that a substantial portion of the contract costs represents subcontracts without any substantial transfer of contractor's risk, since this can result eventually in a lessening of the amount of work let on subcontracts.

(C) In making a contract cost risk evaluation in an acquisition that involves definitization of a letter contract, unpriced change orders, and unpriced orders, under BOAs, consider the effect on total contract cost risk as a result of having partial performance before definitization. Under some circumstances it may be reasoned that the total amount of cost risk has been effectively reduced. Under other circumstances it may be apparent that the contractor's cost risk remained substantially unchanged. To be equitable, the determination of a profit weight for application to the total of all recognized costs, both those incurred and those yet to be expended, must be made with consideration to all attendant circumstances and not be just the portion of costs incurred, or percentage of work completed, prior to definitization.

(D) Time and material, labor hour, overhaul contracts priced on a time and material basis, and firm-fixed-price, level-of-effort term contracts shall be considered to be cost-plus-fixed-fee contracts for the purpose of establishing a profit weight in the evaluation of the contractor's assumption of contract cost risk.

(E) In determining the contract cost risk percentage under CONTRACTOR RISK in profit factors of the weighted guidelines provided in 215.902(a)(1), it is appropriate to consider additional risks associated with foreign military sales (FMS). To be recognized, an additional cost risk factor shall be demonstrated by the contractor to be significant and over and above that normally present in DoD contracts for similar items. If an additional cost risk factor associated with FMS is recognized, the total profit under the CONTRACTOR RISK Section shall not exceed the limits set forth in FAR 15.903(d) for different types of contracts. For example, when the manufacturing weighted guidelines method is used, the limitation will be 0.5% for CPFF contracts, 3% for CPIF contracts, 6% for FPI contracts, and 8% for FFP contracts. The additional cost risk factor shall not apply to FMS made from inventories or stocks nor to acquisitions made under DoD cooperative logistics support arrangements.

(c) See 215.905-2.

(d) This element relates to the consideration to be given in the profit objective in recognition of the investment risk associated with the facilities employed by the contractor. Sixteen to 20% of the net book value of facilities capital allocated to the contract is the normal range of weight for this profit factor. The key factors that the contracting officer shall consider in evaluating this risk are:

(1) The overall cost effectiveness of the facilities employed;

(2) Whether the facilities are general purpose or special purpose items;

(3) The age of the facilities;

(4) The undepreciated value of the facilities;

(5) The relationship of the remaining writeoff life of the investment and the length of the program(s) or contract(s) on which the facilities are employed; and

(6) Special contract provisions that reduce the contractor's risk of recovery of facilities capital investment (termination protection clauses, multiyear cancellation ceilings, etc.). To assist in evaluating new investment, the contracting officer should request the contractor to submit reasonable evidence that the new facilities are part of an approved investment plan and that achievable benefits to the Government will result from the investment. New industrial facilities and equipment shall receive maximum weight when they—

(i) Are to be acquired by the contractor primarily for defense business;

(ii) Have a long service life;

(iii) Have a limited economic life due to limited alternative uses; and

(iv) Reduce the total life cycle cost of the products produced for the Department of Defense.

To the extent that the new investment represents routine replacement of existing assets, a lesser weight shall be assigned.

(e) See 215.905-2.

(f) See 215.905-2.

215.905-2 Additional factors.

(a) *Productivity.*

(1) *General.* A key objective of the DoD profit policy is to reduce the cost of defense preparedness by incentivizing defense contractors' investment in modern cost-reducing facilities and other improvements in efficiency. To the extent that costs serve as the basis for pricing (both cost and profit), success in reducing costs can serve, in turn, to reduce profit dollars opportunity. For example, a fixed-price incen-

tive-type contract is typically used for the first production contract of a major weapon system program. The incentive to increase productivity and reduce cost within one contract works against a contractor on follow-on production contracts because the reduced level of cost becomes a part of the basis for pricing subsequent contracts. In order to mitigate the loss of profit dollars opportunity that occurs when costs are reduced due to productivity gains, a special "Productivity Reward" may be included in the prenegotiation profit objective of a pending acquisition under certain circumstances.

(2) *Applicability criteria.* The "Productivity Reward" may be applied when the following criteria are met:

(i) The pending acquisition involves a follow-on production contract.

(ii) Reliable actual cost data is available to establish a fair and reasonable cost baseline.

(iii) Changes made in the configuration of the item being acquired are not of sufficient magnitude to invalidate price comparability.

(3) *Implementation procedures.* The amount of productivity reward for a given contract is based on the estimated cost reduction that can be attributed to productivity gains. Set forth below are principles and procedures that apply to estimating cost reductions and calculating the productivity reward:

(i) The contractor shall prepare and support the cost reduction estimate.

(ii) The overall contract cost decrease shall be based on estimated decreases measured at the unit cost level.

(iii) The lowest average unit cost (exclusive of profit) for a preceding production run shall serve as the unit cost baseline.

(iv) A technique shall be employed to determine that portion of the cost decrease attributable to productivity gains as opposed to the effects of quantity differences between the base contract and the pending acquisition.

(v) When the parties agree that the estimated overall contract cost decrease is materially affected by price level differences between the base period and the current point in time, an economic price adjustment may be applied to the estimate.

(vi) The productivity reward shall be calculated by multiplying the contract cost decrease due to productivity gains by the base profit objective rate.

(vii) The degree of review and validation of the data supporting the productivity reward calculation shall be commensurate with the materiality of this profit element in relation to the overall price objective.

There may be several methods advanced, by both contracting officers and contractors, to quantify productivity gains. Any technique may be acceptable; *Provided* it takes into account equitably the principles and procedures listed above.

(b) *Independent development.* Contractors who develop items that have potential military application without Government assistance are entitled to special profit consideration on those items as a special profit factor to be considered within the weighted guidelines in arriving at a profit objective. One to 4% of recognized cost is established as the normal range of value for this profit factor. The criteria for selection of the specific percentage shall be the importance of the development in advancing defense purposes, the demonstrable initiative in determining the need and application of the development, the extent of the contractor's cost risk, and whether the development cost was recovered directly or indirectly from Government sources.

(c) *Other factors.* A composite percentage weight within the range of −5% to +5% of the basic profit objective may be assigned to other profit factors in arriving at the total profit objective. These other profit factors, which may apply to special circumstances or particular acquisitions, relate to contractor participation in the Government's Small Business, Small Disadvantaged Business, and Labor Surplus Programs, and to special situations not specifically set forth elsewhere in these guidelines. Participation that is rated as merely satisfactory shall be assigned a weight of zero, generally. Evidence of energetic support may justify a plus weight, and poor support a negative weight.

Department of Defense

Special situations may be assigned either a plus or minus weight, depending on the particular circumstances of the acquisition.

(1) *Small business and small disadvantaged business participation.* The contractor's policies and procedures that energetically support Government small business and small disadvantaged business subcontracting programs, pursuant to FAR Part 19, shall be given favorable consideration. Any unusual effort that the contractor displays in subcontracting with small business or small disadvantaged business concerns, particularly for development-type work likely to result in later production opportunities, and the overall effectiveness of the contractor in subcontracting with and furnishing assistance to such concerns shall be considered. Conversely, failure or unwillingness on the part of the contractor to support Government small business or small disadvantaged business policies shall be viewed as evidence of poor performance for the purpose of establishing a profit objective.

(2) *Labor surplus area participation.* A similar review and evaluation (as required in (1) above) shall be given to the contractor's policies and procedures supporting the Government's Labor Surplus Area Program, pursuant to FAR Part 20. In particular, favorable consideration shall be given to a contractor who (i) makes a significant effort to help find jobs and provide training for the hardcore unemployed, or (ii) promotes maximum subcontractor utilization of certified eligible concerns, as defined in FAR 20.101.

(3) *Energy conservation.* Favorable consideration shall be given to the contractor's initiatives and accomplishments in the conservation of energy.

(4) *Special situations.* Particular situations may justify use of a profit factor other than those specifically identified in these guidelines. These situations shall be identified and the reason(s) for their use documented in the records of price negotiation. Examples of such situations include contractor effort to exploit additional production cost-reduction opportunities or to improve or develop new product/manufacturing technologies to reduce production cost.

Subpart 215.10—Preaward, Award, and Postaward Notifications, Protests and Mistakes

215.1001 Notifications to unsuccessful offerors.

(b)(1) Within DoD, the threshold for notification is $25,000 in accordance with 10 U.S.C. 2304(g).

(b)(2) Acquisitions processed under small purchase procedures are exempt from the requirements of FAR 15.1001(b)(2).

(c) Within DoD, the threshold for notification is $25,000 in accordance with 10 U.S.C. 2304(g).

215.1003 Debriefing of unsuccessful offerors.

(a) Debriefings shall be provided at the earliest feasible time after contract award. They shall be conducted by purchasing office officials familiar with the rationale for the selection decision and contract award.

215.1070 Classified information.

Classified information shall be furnished only in accordance with regulations governing classified information.

PART 216—TYPES OF CONTRACTS

Subpart 216.1—Selecting Contract Types

Sec.
216.101 General.
216.102 Policies.
216.104 Factors in selecting contract types.

Subpart 216.2—Fixed-Price Contracts

216.203-4 Contract clauses.
216.203-70 Fixed-price contracts with economic price adjustment.
216.206 Fixed-ceiling price contracts with retroactive price redetermination.
216.206-1 Description.
216.207 Firm-fixed-price, level-of-effort term contracts.
216.207-1 Description.

Subpart 216.3—Cost-Reimbursement Contracts

216.301 General.
216.301-2 Application.
216.303 Cost-sharing contracts.
216.306 Cost-plus-fixed-fee contracts.

Sec.

Subpart 216.4—Incentive Contracts

216.402 Application of predetermined, formula-type incentives.
216.402-2 Technical performance incentives.
216.403 Fixed-price incentive contracts.
216.403-2 Fixed price incentive (successive targets).
216.404 Cost-reimbursement incentive contracts.
216.404-1 Cost-plus incentive fee contracts.
216.404-2 Cost-plus-award-fee contracts.

Subpart 216.5—Indefinite-Delivery Contracts

216.501 General.
216.502 Definite quantity contracts.
216.503 Requirement contracts.

Subpart 216.6—Time-and-Materials, Labor-Hour, and Letter Contracts

216.601 Time-and-materials contracts.
216.603 Letter contracts.
216.603-2 Application.

Subpart 216.7—Agreements

216.702 Basic agreements.
216.703 Basic ordering agreements.

AUTHORITY: 5 U.S.C. 301, 10 U.S.C. 2202, DoD Directive 5000.35, DoD FAR Supplement 201.301.

SOURCE: 51 FR 46164, Dec. 23, 1986, unless otherwise noted.

Subpart 216.1—Selecting Contract Types

216.101 General.

(a) In addition, the role of profit in selecting contract type includes the following:

(1) Profit, generally, is the basic motive of business enterprise. Both the Government and its defense contractors should be concerned with harnessing this motive to work for the effective and economical contract performance required in the interest of national defense. To this end, the parties should seek to negotiate and use the contract type best calculated to stimulate outstanding performance. The objective should be to insure that outstandingly effective and economical performance is met by high profits, mediocre performance by mediocre profits, and poor performance by low profits or losses. The proper application of these objectives on a contract by contract basis should normally result in a range of profit rates.

(2) Success in harnessing the profit motive begins with the negotiation of sound performance goals and standards. This objective is met if the contractor either benefits or loses in relation to achieving or failing to achieve realistic targets. When award is based on effective price competition, there is reasonable assurance that the contract price represents a realistic pricing standard, including a profit factor which reflects an appropriate return to the contractor for the financial risk assumed in undertaking performance at the competitive price. In the absence of competitive forces, however, the contract type selected should provide for a profit factor that will tie profits to the contractor's efficiency in controlling costs and meeting desired standards of performance, reliability, quality, and delivery. Therefore, in noncompetitive situations, the degree to which available cost estimates are realistic, and the degree of uncertainty affecting the work to be performed, should be carefully considered in determining which type of contract should be selected and how it should be used.

(3) The policies in (1) and (2) above require that the contractor assume a reasonable degree of cost responsibility as early in contract performance as is possible. This can be achieved only through vigorous contract administration and effort on the part of both parties to assure timely pricing. Particularly in fixed-price type contracts providing the price revisions, delays in pricing actions by either party may distort the type of contract which has been agreed upon and such delays must be avoided.

(4) When a contract type providing for a reasonable degree of contractor cost responsibility cannot be negotiated on a timely basis, due to the contractor's unwillingness to assume reasonable risk, profits should be negotiated so as to reflect this fact.

(5) Notwithstanding the validity of profit as a motivating factor in general, there are situations, particularly in the early stages of research and development, in which the profit motive may be secondary. Harnessing the

APPENDIX III

CFR, TITLE 48, CHAPTER 5, GENERAL SERVICES ADMINISTRATION
FEDERAL ACQUISITION REGULATIONS SUPPLEMENT, PART 515,
CONTRACTING BY NEGOTIATION.

General Services Administration

514.470 Advance notice of contract award.

Advance notices of award shall be in writing over the signature of the contracting officer except as otherwise authorized. When an advance notice of award is issued, it shall be followed as soon as possible by the formal contract document.

514.470-1 Circumstances which warrant advance notice.

Advance notices of contract award may be issued by contracting officers under any of the circumstances listed below:

(a) A bid or offer is about to expire and it is necessary to issue an award notice promptly.

(b) Prompt action is necessary to afford the contractor an opportunity to secure necessary materials.

(c) Delivery or performance is urgent and cannot await release of formal contract documents.

(d) The contract involves work of an urgent nature and it is essential that the contractor rush all preliminaries before actual starting of work.

(e) Prompt action is necessary to secure advance predelivery samples on contracts.

(f) A prospective contractor requests advice, orally or in writing, as to whether he is to receive the award, and gives sufficient reasons, to the satisfaction of the contracting officer, why advance notice is desirable.

(g) Other compelling circumstances exist and advance notice is concurred in by the head of the contracting activity.

[49 FR 10820, Mar. 22, 1984, as amended at 50 FR 10053, Mar. 13, 1985]

514.470-2 Telegraphic notices.

When justified by the circumstances described in 514.470-1, telegraphic notice may be used. The notice shall contain, in addition to the requirements set forth in 514.470-4 a statement that written confirmation will follow. Such confirmation shall be issued without delay.

514.470-3 Oral notices.

Oral notices shall not be used.

514.470-4 Content of notices.

Advance notices of award shall include all of the essential elements to identify the award, such as identification of invitation, description of the acquisition, and the contract number. No language shall be used which might, in any way, vary from the terms of the bid.

[50 FR 10053, Mar. 13, 1985]

514.471 Multiple bidding.

(a) If more than one bid is received from a person or firm, or its affiliates in response to an invitation for bids, such bids shall be considered for award if responsive and otherwise acceptable.

(b) If a bidder submits bids on two or more products in response to the same item in an invitation and one of those bids is the lowest received which meets the requirements of the invitation, it may be accepted regardless of whether it is designated by the bidder as an "alternate."

PART 515—CONTRACTING BY NEGOTIATION

Subpart 515.1—General Requirement for Negotiation

Sec.
515.106 Contract clauses.
515.106-1 Examination of records clause.
515.170 Authorization and approval.

Subpart 515.4—Solicitation and Receipt of Proposals and Quotations

515.402 General.
515.403 Solicitation mailing lists.
515.405 Solicitations for information or planning purposes.
515.405-1 General.
515.406 Preparing requests for proposals (RFPs) and requests for quotations (RFQs).
515.406-1 Uniform contract format.
515.406-2 Part I—The Schedule.
515.407 Solicitation provisions.
515.411 Receipt of proposals and quotations.
515.411-70 Recording of offers.

Subpart 512.5—Unsolicited Proposals

515.500 Scope of subpart.
515.501 Definition.

515.106

Sec.
515.504 Advance guidance.
515.505 Content of unsolicited proposals.
515.506 Agency procedures.
515.506-1 Receipt and initial review.
515.506-2 Evaluation.
515.507 Contracting methods.

Subpart 515.6—Source Selection

515.608 Proposal evaluation.
515.608-70 Rejection of all proposals.
515.608-71 Discounts for prompt payment.

Subpart 515.8—Price Negotiation

515.803 General.
515.803-70 Cost-reimbursement contracts (construction contracts).
515.804 Cost or pricing data.
515.804-2 Requiring certified cost or pricing data.
515.804-3 Exemptions from or waiver of submission of certified cost or pricing data.
515.804-6 Procedural requirements.
515.805 Proposal analysis.
515.805-5 Field pricing support.

Subpart 515.9—Profit

515.902 Policy.
515.905 Profit analysis factors.
515.905-1 Common factors.
515.905-70 Non-profit organizations.

Subpart 515.10—Preaward, Award, and Postaward Notifications, Protests and Mistakes

515.1001 Notifications to offerors.
515.1070 Release of information concerning unsuccessful offerors.

AUTHORITY: 40 U.S.C. 486(c).

SOURCE: 49 FR 10829, Mar. 22, 1984, unless otherwise noted.

Subpart 515.1—General Requirements for Negotiation

515.106 Contract clauses.

515.106-1 Examination of records clause.

(a) The contracting officer shall insert the clause at GSAR 552.215-70, Examination of Records by GSA, in solicitations and contracts that do not include the Audit-Negotiation clause prescribed in FAR 15.106-2 and are subject to audit as indicated in GSAR 501.671-3.

(b) In some of the contracts listed in GSAR 501.671-3, it may be appropriate to define the specific area of audit such as (1) the use or disposition of Government-furnished property, or (2) variable or other special features of the contract; e.g., price escalation and compliance with the price warranty or price reductions clauses. In these cases, the contract clause in GSAR 552.215-70 may be appropriately modified with the concurrence of the Office of General Counsel or Regional Counsel, and the Assistant Inspector General-Auditing, or the Regional Inspector General-Auditing, as appropriate.

(c) Insertion of the contract clause in 552.215-70 (modified or not) in contracts does not affect the requirements for use of the Examination of Records clause permitting review of contractor books and records by the Comptroller General or the clauses on audit and records pertaining to verifying cost or pricing data.

[49 FR 10829, Mar. 22, 1984, as amended at 50 FR 2286, Jan. 16, 1985; 50 FR 10053, Mar. 13, 1985]

515.170 Authorization and approval.

Requirements of pre-award and post-award review and approval of contracts are prescribed in the GSA Order, Contract Clearance (APD 2800.1B).

[50 FR 10054, Mar. 13, 1985]

Subpart 515.4—Solicitation and Receipt of Proposals and Quotations

515.402 General.

(a) An oral solicitation is not justified solely because the acquisition is being made under the authority of FAR 6.302-2, Unusual and Compelling Urgency.

(b) Oral solicitations, other than those authorized for small purchases (see GSAR 513.106(c) and 513.106-70), shall only be used under the conditions prescribed in FAR 15.402(f), with prior approval at a level higher than the contracting officer.

[50 FR 10054, Mar. 13, 1985]

515.403 Solicitation mailing lists.

Source lists for negotiated acquisitions shall be established, maintained,

General Services Administration 515.504

and used in accordance with FAR 14.205 and GSAR 514.205.

[50 FR 10054, Mar. 13, 1985]

515.405 Solicitations for information or planning purposes.

515.405-1 General.

Solicitations for information or planning purposes shall be approved by the contracting director.

[50 FR 10054, Mar. 13, 1985]

515.406 Preparing requests for proposals (RFP's) and requests for quotations (RFQ's).

515.406-1 Uniform contract format.

(a) Contracts for utility services and leases of real property are exempted from the requirement for use of the uniform contract format.

(b) All contracts, including leases of real property, shall include the following notice:

The information collection requirements contained in this solicitation/contract, that are not required by regulation, have been approved by the Office of Management and Budget pursuant to the Paperwork Reduction Act and assigned OMB Control No. 3090-0163.

[49 FR 10829, Mar. 22, 1984, as amended at 50 FR 10054, Mar. 13, 1985]

515.406-2 Part I—The Schedule.

The contracting officer shall insert the provision at GSAR 552.215-75, Data Universal Numbering System (DUNS), in solicitations for supplies and services when the contract amount is expected to exceed the small purchase limitation.

[50 FR 10054, Mar. 13, 1985]

515.407 Solicitation provisions.

(a) The contracting officer shall insert the provision at 552.215-71, Telecopier Submissions, Modifications, or Withdrawal of Proposals, in solicitations for supplies and services (including construction) when the contract amount is expected to exceed the small purchase limitation. The provision may be included in small purchase solicitations when firm offers are solicited.

(b) The contracting officer shall insert the provision at 552.215-72, Telegraphic Submissions, Modifications, or Withdrawals of Proposals Received at the GSA Communication Center, in solicitations for supplies and services (including construction) when the contract amount is expected to exceed the small purchase limitation. The provision may be included in small purchase solicitations when firm offers are solicited.

(c) The contracting officer shall insert the provision at 552.215-73, Preparation of Offers-Construction, in solicitations for construction in lieu of the provision at FAR 52.215-13.

(d) The contracting officer shall insert the provision at 552.215-74, Contract Award-Negotiated-Construction, in solicitations for construction in lieu of the provision at FAR 52.215-16.

515.411 Receipt of proposals and quotations.

Classified proposals and quotations shall be handled under FAR 15.411 and the requirements of GSA Order, Freedom of Information Act procedures (ADM 1035.11).

515.411-70 Recording of offers.

Offers shall be abstracted under FAR 14.403 and 514.403.

Subpart 515.5—Unsolicited Proposals

515.500 Scope of subpart.

This subpart implements and supplements the policies and procedures prescribed in FAR Subpart 15.5 for submission, receipt, evaluation, and acceptance or rejection of unsolicited proposals.

515.501 Definition.

"Minimum requirements" refers only to those features that are essential to meeting the Government's need.

[50 FR 10054, Mar. 13, 1985]

515.504 Advanced guidance.

Potential offerors shall be encouraged to make preliminary contacts, as provided in FAR 15.504, with regional

515.505

contracting offices and/or the Office of GSA Acquisition Policy and Regulations before to submitting a detailed unsolicited proposal or proprietary data.

[50 FR 10054, Mar. 13, 1985]

515.505 Content of unsolicited proposals.

Potential offerors shall be provided with the description of requirements for unsolicited proposals in FAR 15.505.

515.506 Agency procedures.

(a) The Office of GSA Acquisition Policy and Regulations (VP) is designated as the GSA contact point for unsolicited proposals. The address is:

General Services Administration (VP)
Washington, DC 20405

(b) Regional contracting activities shall be the local contact points for review and acknowledgment of unsolicited proposals.

515.506-1 Receipt and initial review.

(a) Unsolicited proposals shall be reviewed for the information in FAR 15.506-1, and acknowledged as soon after receipt as possible by the local point of contact as follows:

(1) When an unsolicited proposal is received first by the Region, Service, or Staff Office where the evaluation will be performed under FAR 15.506-2, that organization shall inform the offeror, by letter, that the proposal has been received. The letter should indicate the name, business address, and telephone number of the individual who will evaluate the proposal.

(2) A copy of the letter to the offeror shall be sent to the Office of GSA Acquisition Policy and Regulations (VP).

(b) When an unsolicited proposal is received first by a Region, Service, or Staff Office that is not in a position to evaluate it, the organization shall forward it to VP as soon as possible. VP will review the proposal for the information in FAR 15.506-1, and determine which organization will be responsible for evaluating the proposal.

(1) Then the proposal will be sent to the Region, Service or Staff Office that VP has determined will be responsible for the evaluation.

(2) The Region, Service, or Staff Office responsible for evaluating the proposal shall inform the offeror by letter that the proposal has been received. The letter should indicate the name, business address and the telephone number of the individual who will evaluate the proposal.

(3) If the evaluating office forwards the unsolicited proposal to another region, or office, the evaluating office shall notify VP of the location, name, and phone number of the assigned evaluator.

[49 FR 10829, Mar. 22, 1984, as amended at 50 FR 10054, Mar. 13, 1985]

515.506-2 Evaluation.

The evaluation shall be completed under FAR 15.506-2, as soon as practicable (normally within 45 calendar days). The evaluator shall send the evaluation results plus recommended action to VP. If the proposal is rejected the evaluator shall prepare the response to the offeror for the signature of the head of the organization responsible for the evaluation. A copy shall be sent to VP.

[50 FR 10054, Mar. 13, 1985]

515.507 Contracting methods.

Negotiations may not commence under an unsolicited proposal unless all of the requirements of FAR 15.507(b) are complied with.

[50 FR 10054, Mar. 13, 1985]

Subpart 515.6—Source Selection

515.608 Proposal evaluation.

[51 FR 23061, June 25, 1986]

515.608-70 Rejection of all proposals.

The head of the contracting activity is authorized to reject all proposals received in response to a solicitation pursuant to FAR 15.608(b). This authority may be redelegated. When exercising this authority, the required determination documenting the reasons for rejecting all proposals will be included in the contract file.

[51 FR 23061, June 25, 1986]

General Services Administration

515.608-71 Discounts for prompt payment.

(a) Paragraph (c) of FAR 15.608 provides that the requirements of FAR 14.407-3 are applicable to negotiated acquisitions. The policy of not considering discounts in the evaluation of offers applies to situations where there is direct competition between two or more offerors for a single award. The policy does not apply to sole source procurements or procurements where the evaluation process involves a comparison of the offeror's price to the Government with the offeror's price to its other customers. Accordingly, the policy in FAR 14.407-3 does not apply to Multiple Award Schedule solicitations except in those instances where offers are received on identical products. The clause at 552.232-8, Discounts for Prompt Payment, specifies the extent to which discounts for prompt payment will be considered in the evaluation for Multiple Award Schedules.

(b) The formula for computing the annualized rate of return addressed in the clause at GSAR 552.232-8 is as follows:

$$\text{Discount (\%)} \times \frac{\text{Number of days in a year}}{\text{Total days to due date for payment} - \text{Days to discount due date}} = \text{Rate of return}$$

[51 FR 23061, June 25, 1986]

Subpart 515.8—Price Negotiation

515.803 General.

Access to information concerning the Government cost estimate must be limited to Government personnel whose official duties require knowledge of the estimate. An exception to this rule may be made during contract negotiations to allow the contracting officer to identify a specialized task and disclose the associated cost breakdown figures in the Government estimate, but only to the extent necessary to arrive at a fair and reasonable price. After award, the total amount of the independent Government estimate may be revealed, upon written request, to those firms or individuals who submitted proposals.

[51 FR 16692, May 6, 1986]

515.803-70 Cost-reimbursement contracts (construction contracts).

The consideration and discussions during negotiations of construction contracts shall include, to the extent necessary to resolve uncertainties, such matters as—

(a) The location, size, and character of the work and the estimated cost;

(b) The general conditions for the cost-plus-a-fixed-fee contract and the procedures to be followed;

(c) The organization the contractor will use at the site and proposed salaries for those employees;

(d) The types and amount of contractor's own equipment available for the project;

(e) The amount and nature of work to be performed by the contractor's own forces and by subcontract;

(f) The time for completion, liquidated damages (if specified), insurance, and bonds; and

(g) The fixed fee and the basis upon which its amount was predicated. Factors (a) through (f) affect the amount of the fee.

[49 FR 10829, Mar. 22, 1984, as amended at 50 FR 28579, July 15, 1985]

515.804 Cost or pricing data.

515.804-2 Requiring certified cost or pricing data.

When determining the contract amount for purposes of applying the threshold at FAR 15.804-2 for requesting certified cost and pricing data, the value of the contract plus any priced

515.804-6

the head of the contracting activity. Before submitting a waiver request, action will be taken at levels above the contracting officer to negotiate for the submission of the required cost or pricing data, or a formal determination made by the contracting director documenting the contract file with the reasons for not undertaking such higher level negotiations.

(c) The request for waiver will include a draft determination and finding that addresses: (1) Pertinent circumstances of the procurement necessitating the waiver of the requirement for certified cost or pricing data, (2) the price analysis techniques to be used if the award cannot be foregone, (3) the steps taken by higher authority to obtain the essential cost or pricing data, and (4) the practicability of obtaining the Government's requirements from other sources.

[50 FR 28579, July 15, 1985]

515.804-6 Procedural requirements.

Whenever an offeror refuses to provide the required cost or pricing data, the contracting officer shall refer the matter to the contracting director for resolution (see FAR 15.804-6(e)). Upon referral by the contracting officer, action will be taken by the contracting director to negotiate for the submission of the required cost or pricing data, unless the head of the contracting activity determines, in writing, not to undertake such higher level negotiations and the determination is documented in the contract file.

[50 FR 28579, July 15, 1985]

515.805 Proposal analysis.

515.805-5 Field pricing support.

(a) Within GSA, "field pricing support" is provided by the Assistant Inspector General-Auditing, or the Regional Inspector General-Auditing, as appropriate.

(b) When applying the threshold at FAR 15.805-5 for requesting field pricing support, the value of the proposal (including any priced options) must be used.

[51 FR 16692, May 6, 1986]

Subpart 515.9—Profit

515.902 Policy.

(a) Structured approach for determining profit fee objectives.

(1) The contracting officer's analysis of these profit factors is based on information available to the Government before negotiations. Such information is furnished in proposals, audit data, performance reports, preaward surveys and the like. The structured approach also provides a basis for documentation of a profit objective, including an explanation of any significant departure from this objective in reaching a final agreement. The extent of documentation should be directly related to the dollar value and complexity of the proposed procurement.

(2) The negotiation process does not require agreement on individual estimated cost elements or profit elements. The profit objective is a part of an overall negotiation objective. Specific agreement on the exact weights or values of the individual factors is not required and should not be attempted.

(b) Exemptions from requirement to use the structured approach.

(1) Under exempted procurements, other methods for establishing profit objectives may be used. Generally, such methods will be supported in a manner similar to that used in the structured approach (profit factor breakdown and documentation of profit objective). However, factors within the structured approach considered inapplicable to the procurement shall be excluded from the profit objectives. The following types of procurements are exempt from the structured approach:

(i) Management contracts for operation and/or maintenance of Government facilities;

(ii) Contracts primarily requiring delivery of material supplied by subcontractors;

(iii) Termination settlements;

(iv) Cost-plus-award-fee contracts;

(v) Contracts where only price analysis is required (FAR 15.805);

(vi) Contracts and contract modifications of $100,000 or less in value; and

General Services Administration

(vii) Architect-engineer and construction contracts.

(2) Other exemptions may be made in the negotiation of contracts having unusual pricing situations where the structured approach is determined to be unsuitable. Such exemptions shall be justified in writing and approved by the head of the contracting activity.

515.905 Profit analysis factors.

(a) The following factors shall be considered in all situations in which profit is to be specifically negotiated. The weight ranges listed after each factor shall be used when the structured approach is used.

Profit factors	Weight ranges in percent
Contractor effort:	
Material acquisition	1 to 4.
Conversion direct labor	4 to 12.
Conversion related indirect cost	3 to 8.
Other costs	1 to 3.
General management	4 to 8.
Other factors:	
Contract cost risk	0 to 7.
Capital investment	−2 to +2.
Cost-control and other past accomplishments.	−2 to +2.
Federal socio-economic programs	−.5 to +.5.
Special situations and independent development.	−2 to +2.

(b) GSA Form 1766, Structured Approach Profit/Fee Objective, shall be used to facilitate the profit objective computation. The contracting officer shall measure the Contractor Effort by the assignment of a profit percentage within the designated weight ranges to each element of cost recognized. The amount calculated for facilities capital cost of money shall not be included in the cost base for the computation of the profit objective.

(c) *Facilities capital cost of money.* When facilities capital cost of money is included as an item of cost in the contractor's proposal a reduction in the profit objective shall be made in an amount equal to the amount of facilities capital cost of money allowed.

515.905-1 Common factors.

(a) The categories listed under Contractor Effort are for reference purposes only. Individual proposals may be in different formats; but since these categories are broad and basic they provide sufficient guidance to evaluate all items of cost.

(b) After computing a total dollar profit for Contractor Effort, the contracting officer shall calculate the specific profit dollars for contract cost risk, capital investment, cost-control and other past accomplishments, Federal social-economic programs and special situations. This is done by multiplying the total Government cost objective, exclusive of any cost of money for facilities capital, by the specific weights assigned to the elements within the Other Factors category.

(c) In determining the value of each factor, the contracting officer should be governed by the definition, description, and purpose of the factors together with considerations for evaluating them as prescribed in FAR 15.905-1 and the following:

(1) *General management.* Management problems surface in various degrees and the management expertise exercised to solve them should be considered as an element of profit. For example, a new program for an item that involves advanced state of the art techniques may casue more problems and require more managerial time and abilities of a higher order, than one that is a follow-on contract. If new contracts create more problems and require a higher profit weight, follow-ons should be adjusted downward as many of the problems should have been solved. An evaluation should be made of the underlying managerial effort involved on a case-by-case basis.

(2) *Other costs.* Include all other direct costs associated with contractor performance under this item (e.g., travel and relocation, direct support, and consultants). Analysis of these items of costs for the purpose of assigning profit weights shall include: (i) The significance of the costs, (ii) the nature of the costs, and (iii) how much they contribute to contract performance.

(3) *Contract cost risk.* Where proper contract type selection has been made, the reward for risk by contract type would usaully fall into the following percentage ranges:

	Percent
Cost-reimbursement type contracts	0–3
Fixed-price type contracts	3–7

(i) Within the above ranges, cost-plus-a-fixed-fee contract normally would not justify a reward for risk in excess of 0 percent, unless the contract contains cost risk features such as ceilings on overheads. In such cases, up to 1 percent may be justified. Cost-plus-incentive-fee contracts fill the remaining portion of the 0 to 3 percent range with weightings directly related to such factors as confidence in target cost, share ratio of fee(s), etc. The weight range for fixed-price contracts in wide enough to accommodate the many types of fixed-price arrangements. These include fixed-price incentive, firm fixed-price with economic price adjustment, fixed-price with prospective or retroactive price determination, and firm fixed-price contracts. Weighting should indicate the cost risk assumed, with only firm fixed-price contracts reaching the top end of the range.

(ii) The contractor's subcontracting program may have significant impact on the contractor's acceptance of risk under a contract form. It could cause risk to increase or decrease in terms of both cost and perfomance. This consideration should be a part of the contracting officer's overall eavaluation in selecting a factor to apply for cost risk. It may be determined, for instance that the prime contractor has effectively transferred real cost risk to a subcontractor and the contract cost risk evaluation may, as a result, be below the range which would otherwise apply for the contract type being proposed. The contract cost risk evaluation should not be lowered, however, merely on the basis that a substantial portion of the contract cost represents subcontracts without any substantial transfer of contractor's risk.

(iii) In making a contract cost risk evaluation in the definitization of letter contracts, unpriced change orders, and unpriced orders under basic ordering agreements; consideration should be given to the effect on total contract cost risk as a result of having partial performance before definitization. Under some circumstances the total amount of cost risk may have effectively reduced. Under other circumstances, the contractor's cost risk may have remained substantially unchanged. To be equitable, the determination of a profit weight for application to the total of all recognized costs, both those incurred and those yet to be expended, must be made with consideration to all attendant circumstances; not just to the portion of costs incurred or percentage of work completed prior to definitization.

(iv) Service contracts, such as janitorial, guard servcie, etc., shall have a weight range for cost risk of 0 to 4 percent. There may be instances where a firm fixed-price contract, which is not priced on a labor-hour method, warrants additional consideration for contractor cost risk. In those circumstances, a weight of up to 4 percent is authorized. Conversely, a cost-plus-a-fixed-fee service contract normally should be priced using a zero cost risk factor.

(4) *Capital investment.* GSA contractors are normally encouraged to perform their contracts with the minimum of financial, facilities, or other assistance from the Government. It is the purpose of this factor to encourage the contractor to acquire and use its own resources to the maximum extent possible. The evaluation of this factor for profit weights should include an analysis of the following:

(i) *Facilities.* To evaluate how this factor contributes to the profit objective requies knowledge of the level of facilities use needed for contract performance, the source of financing of the required facilities, and the overall cost effectiveness of the facilities offered. Contractors who furnish their own facilities which significantly contribute to lower total contract costs should be provided with additional profit. Contractors who rely on the Government to provide or finance needed facilities should receive a corresponding reduction in profit. Situations between the above examples should be evaluated on their merits with either a positive or negative profit weight adjustment, as appropriate, being made. However, when a contractor who owns a large quantity of facilities is to perform a contract

General Services Administration 515.905-70

which does not benefit from these facilities, or where a contractor's use of its facilities has a minimum cost impact on the contract, profit need not be adjusted.

(ii) *Payments.* In analyzing this factor, consideration should be given to the frequency of payments by the Government to the contractor. The key to this weighting is to give proper consideration to the impact the contract will have on the contractor's cash flow. Generally, for payments more frequent than monthly, negative consideration should be given, with maximum reduction being given as the contractor's working capital approaches zero. Positive consideration should be given for payments less frequent than monthly with additional consideration given for payments less frequent than the contractor's or the industry's normal practice.

(5) *Cost control and other past accomplishments.* A contractor's past and present performance should be evaluated in such areas as quality of product or service, meeting performance schedules, efficiency in cost control (including need for and reasonableness of cost incurred), accuracy and reliability of previous cost estimates, degree of cooperation by the contractor (both business and technical), timely processing of changes and compliance with other contractual provisions, and management of subcontract programs. Where a contractor has consistently achieved excellent results in the foregoing areas as compared with other contractors in similar circumstances, such performance merits a proportionately higher profit weight is appropriate. A poor record in this regard should be reflected by a reduced or negative weight.

(6) *Federal socio-economic programs.* The contractor's policies and procedures which energetically support such Government programs and achieve successful results should be given positive consideration. Failure or unwillingness on the part of the contractor to support these programs should be assigned negative profit weight consideration.

(7) *Special situations and independent development.* (i) *Unusual pricing agreements.* Occasionally, unusual contract pricing arrangements are made with the contractor wherein they agree to participate in the sharing of contract costs. In such circumstances, a positiveprofit weight may be assigned for this factor commensurate with cost savings.

(ii) *Spin-off benefits.* A negative weight may be appropriate when the contractor is expected to obtain spin-off benefits as a direct result of the contract (e.g., products with commercial application).

515.905-70 Nonprofit organizations.

(a) The structured approach was designed for arriving at profit or fee objectives for other than nonprofit organizations. However, if appropriate adjustments are made to reflect differences between profit and nonprofit organizations, the structured approach can be used as a basis for arriving at fee objectives for nonprofit organizations. Therefore, the structured approach, as modified in paragraph (b) below, shall be used to establish fee objectives for non-profit organizations. The modifications should not be applied as deductions against historical fee levels, but rather, to the fee objectives for such a contract as calculated under the structured approach.

(b) For purposes of this subparagraph, nonprofit organizations are defined as those entities organized and operated exclusively for charitable, scientific, or educational purposes, no part of the net earnings of which inure to the benefit of any private shareholder or individual, and which are exempt from Federal income taxation under section 501 of the Internal Revenue Code.

(c) For contracts with nonprofit organizations where fees are involved, an adjustment of up to 3 percent will be subtracted from the total profit-fee objective. In developing this adjustment, it will be necessary to consider the following factors:

(1) Tax position benefits;

(2) Granting of financing through letters of credit;

(3) Facility requirements of the nonprofit organization; and

(4) Other factors which may work to the advantage or disadvantage of the

515.1001

contractor in its position as a nonprofit organization.

Subpart 515.10—Preaward and Postaward Notifications, Protests, and Mistakes

515.1001 Notifications to offerors.

(a) The provisions of FAR 15.1001 and 515.407 regarding the issuance of advance notices of award shall be followed for negotiated contracts.

515.1070 Release of information concerning unsuccessful offerors.

Information concerning unsuccessful offerors, including identity and pricing data, ordinarily will not be released before award. GSA Order, GSA Freedom of Information Act (FOI) procedure (see ADM 1035.11) should be consulted to determine what information may be disclosed after award. When small purchase procedures are used, the names and dollar amounts of unsuccessful offers may be released upon request without processing through the formal FOI procedures.

PART 516—TYPES OF CONTRACTS

Subpart 516.2—Fixed-Price Contracts

Sec.
516.203 Fixed-price contracts with economic price adjustment.
516.203-4 Contract clauses.
516.203-70 EPA in FSS multiple award schedules.

Subpart 516.3—Cost-Reimbursement Contracts

516.301 General.
516.301-3 Limitations.
516.306 Cost-plus-fixed-fee contracts.
516.307 Contract clause.

Subpart 516.4—Incentive Contracts

516.403 Fixed-price incentive contracts.
516.405 Contract clauses.

Subpart 516.6—Time-and-Materials, Labor-Hour, and Letter Contracts

516.603 Letter contracts.
516.603-3 Limitations.

AUTHORITY: 40 U.S.C. 486(c).

Subpart 516.2—Fixed-Price Contracts

SOURCE: 50 FR 43714, Oct. 29, 1985, unless otherwise noted.

516.203 Fixed-price contracts with economic price adjustment.

516.203-4 Contract clauses.

(a) When the contracting officer makes a determination, in accordance with FAR 16.203-4(d), to use a clause which provides for adjustments based on cost indexes of labor or material, the clause shall be prepared with the advice and assistance of counsel and be approved by the contracting director. The contracting officer shall describe in the contract clause—

(1) The type of labor and/or material subject to adjustment;

(2) The labor rates, including fringe benefits (if any) and/or unit prices of materials that may be increased or decreased;

(3) The index(es) that will be used to measure changes in price levels and the base period or reference point from which changes will be measured; and

(4) The period during which the price(s) will be subject to adjustment.

(b) In Federal Supply Service (FSS) multiple award schedule (MAS) procurements the contracting director will make a determination, in accordance with FAR 16.203-2, to use an Economic Price Adjustment (EPA) clause. In making that determination, the term of the resulting MAS contract will be considered. An EPA clause will generally be included in multiyear contracts but normally will not be used in 1-year contracts. In 1-year contracts, when the contracting director has made a determination to use an EPA clause and the prices are to be negotiated on the basis of discounts from established catalog prices of products sold in substantial quantities to the general public, the contracting officer shall include the basic clause at GSAR 552.216-71 in MAS solicitations and contracts. In multiyear contracts, the alternate clause will be used under these conditions. These clauses are to be used instead of the FAR clauses at 52.216-2, 3, and 4.

APPENDIX IV

CFR, TITLE 48, CHAPTER 5, GENERAL SERVICES ADMINISTRATION
MULTIPLE AWARD SCHEDULE PROCUREMENT ACQUISTION POLICY.

CURRENT GSA MAS NEGOTIATING POLICY

GENERAL SERVICES ADMINISTRATION

41 CFR Ch. 5

Multiple Award Schedule Procurement

AGENCY: Office of Acquisition Policy, GSA.

ACTION: Notice of procurement policies.

SUMMARY: This notice sets forth certain policies and procedures that GSA will follow when contracting for products or services under the multiple award schedule (MAS) program. This issuance also contains guidance to GSA contracting personnel to be used in the MAS negotiation process. Additionally, this issuance contains the schedule of sales and marketing data reflecting the type of information to be obtained from firms in the solicitation phase of the negotiation process.

GSA is issuing this notice to inform all parties interested in and doing business with GSA under the MAS program of the positions taken on certain issues concerning MAS contracting. In addition to identifying changes to and clarifying its position on the draft MAS policies issued for comment on May 24, 1982, GSA believes that the positions adopted will result in a less costly Government procedure; reduce the paperwork burden on industry and Government; permit the timely award of MAS contracts; and continue the protection of the

continued on the following pages.........

Source: FEDERAL REGISTER, November 5, 1982

Government's interests when contracting under this procurement program.

The implementation of the MAS policies set forth in this document will begin with solicitations issued on or after October 1, 1982.

EFFECTIVE DATE: This statement of policies is effective with solicitations issued on or after October 1, 1982.

ADDRESS: Mr. Allan W. Beres, Acting Assistant Administrator for Acquisition Policy, General Services Administration, 18th and F Sts., NW., Washington, D.C. 20405.

FOR FURTHER INFORMATION CONTACT: Mr. Edward J. McAndrew, Office of Policy Formulation, Office of Acquisition Policy, General Services Administration, 18th and F Sts., N.W., Washington, DC 20405 (202-566-1224).

SUPPLEMENTARY INFORMATION:

Background

On May 24, 1982, GSA presented a draft set of MAS policies to industry associations and other interested parties. At that presentation, GSA requested comments on the proposed policies.

The draft policies issued for comment were based on the comments and concerns expressed by the Congress in previous hearings, in reports by the General Accounting Office, by firms and associations doing business under the MAS program, and by customer agencies that order from MAS contracts. In its request for comments, GSA asked interested parties when analyzing the draft policies to keep in mind the comments and concerns that had been expressed.

Comments and Significant Changes in the Policies Set Forth in the Issuance

In response to its May 24, 1982, request for comments, GSA received more than 60 responses. These responses came principally from firms and industry associations that represent firms doing business with GSA under the MAS program. Other responses were received from internal GSA organizations, such as the Inspector General and regional and central office operating procurement elements and from other Government agencies.

With the close of the comment period, June 25, 1982, GSA began an exhaustive analysis of the comments received. Representatives from GSA's Office of Acquisition Policy, the Office of Information Resources Management, the Office of Personal Property, the Office of Inspector General, and the Office of General Counsel participated in developing the revisions adopted in the statement of policies that GSA has issued. In adopting the positions set forth in this issuance, GSA gave serious consideration to the comments expressed by the various, and often competing, interests associated with the MAS program. Because the MAS program primarily involves the purchase of commercial products and services, GSA has aligned the policies with commercial practice to the extent practical given the need for such policies to be consistent with Federal procurement regulations. GSA has tried to make the revised policies cost effective and fair to all parties.

The comments that were received by GSA, for the most part, addressed certain aspects of the draft MAS policies. These issues and the GSA position contained in the revised policies are:

a. *Most Favored Customer.* The most favored customer concept was defined in the draft as including original equipment manufacturer (OEM) and dealer/distributor prices/discounts as the Government's negotiation objective. Comments received from business and industry opposed this concept. In the revised policies, GSA excludes consideration of the OEM and dealer/distributor discount in setting its negotiation objective where an offeror substantiates claims that dealers perform the normal dealer functions for the contractor under the MAS contract or where an offeror claims that the item sold to OEM's is different in physical and performance characteristics and is not the same or similar to the item offered the Government under the MAS contract.

b. *Sales and Marketing Data.* Comments received indicated that the amount of paperwork needed to respond to the data requests is exorbitant. In the revised polices, offerors will be able to certify to those products or services offered that meet the specified tests of commerciality. Sales data will not be required on every model or product offered that is certified as meeting the tests of commerciality. On a sampling basis, the Government will ask for sales data on a selected number of products certified as commercial. For items not certified as meeting the tests of commerciality, sales data is required. The procurement rules for requiring cost and pricing data are unchanged.

c. *Price Reductions Clause.* While some comments received suggested changes to the language in the revised clause and others indicated that the revised clause may still be subject to interpretation, for the most part, there was no opposition to the principal change in the revised clause from the clause presently used in MAS contracts. The revised clause is no longer activated any time that an MAS contractor reduces prices to any customer. Under the revised clause, the clause is activated when prices are changed so as to change the relationship between the Government and the customer or category of customer upon which the award was predicated. Along with narrowing the application of the price reductions clause, the exclusions for certain sales from the application of the revised clause are also changed. The clause in the revised policies is the same as the one contained in the May 24, 1982, draft except for deleting the exclusion for sales to State and local governments. The decision to delete the esclusion for sales to State and local governments was based on a careful analysis of the changes made to the clause. Considering the changes made, operation of the revised price reductions clause should not adversely affect State and local government procurement programs.

d. *Aggregate Discount.* The revised policies include seeking aggregate discounts on MAS contracts. Notwithstanding the position taken by most commentors that the Government should not seek such discounts because of the manner in which orders are placed against MAS contracts, the Government will strive to achieve as part of its negotiation objective an aggregate discount which recognizes not only the manner in which the Government orders but also the aggregate volume of sales expected under the MAS contract. The revised policies reflects latitude in whether such discounts are given when the order in placed or at the conclusion of the contract term.

e. *Maximum Order Limitation.* The revised policies contain the use of the maximum order limitation. This is a change from the draft, which stated that the Federal Supply Service (FSS) will terminate its regular practice of establishing a maximum order limitation in its schedules. Comments received supported the continued use of a maximum order limitation.

f. *Economic Price Adjustments.* The draft policies proposed to terminate the use of an economic price adjustment clause in FSS schedule contracts. The revised policies makes the use of such a clause in FSS schedule contracts optional. The contracting officer will determine whether such a clause should be included in the schedule contracts.

Other Information

Staff members of the appropriate congressional committees were briefed on the revised policies set forth in the issuance.

The revised policies have been given to the Office of Information Resource Management, the Office of Personal Property, and GSA regions for implementation. All GSA contracting people in the Central Office and regions involved with the MAS program were informed of the revised policies and provided a copy of the policy document at a joint meeting held on September 28 1982. In addition, the Office of Information Resources Management and the Office of Personal Property will hold other sessions, as needed, with their contracting personnel on the implementation of the policies. Similarly, audit personnel in the Office of Inspector General have been briefed on the revised policies. The purpose of these sessions is to have the revised policies implemented throughout GSA in a consistent manner. The policies were issued in accordance with 41 CFR 5–1.105(a)(5) and will be incorporated into GSA's formal regulations as soon as is practical.

While GSA is taking steps to implement these policies in the MAS procurement process, GSA's management is committed to continuing its efforts to improve the MAS program. In this regard, the implementation of these policies will be monitored to identify problem areas that may arise. Similarly, GSA is interested in receiving ideas or suggestions from interested parties on further improving the MAS process. After the revised policies have been implemented over a complete procurement cycle for the various products, GSA plans to take another look at the policies and to analyze any difficulties that were encountered in implementation and the suggestions received during the implementation phase which would lead to further improvements.

The complete text of the revised policies follows.

Dated: October 25, 1982.

Ray Kline,
Deputy Administrator of General Services.

Index—Contract Pricing Arrangements
  I. Introduction
  II. MAS Contract Pricing Arrangements
  III. Discount Schedule and Marketing Data
  IV. OEMs and Dealer/Distributor Discounts and Marketing Data
  V. Quantity and Aggregate Discounts
  VI. Maximum Order Limitation (MOL)
  VII. Price Reductions
  VIII. Economic Price Adjustments

Attachment—Multiple Award Schedule (MAS) Pricing Guide
  I. Discount Schedule and Marketing Data
  II. Prenegotiations
  III. Catalog Item Verification
  IV. Price Analysis
  V. Negotiations

Contract Pricing Arrangements

I. Introduction

This policy statement addresses issues concerning the establishment and maintenance of pricing arrangements on multiple award schedule (MAS) contracts for supplies and services. These issues are the most complex of all the issues associated with the MAS program. Continued interest by Congress, General Accounting Office, this Agency's management, and business and industry, made it apparent that a number of problems exist with respect to negotiating pricing arrangements in MAS contracts. Except where otherwise stated, this policy statement applies to the ADTS and FSS MAS contracts.

The contract pricing policies in this document are those which appear to us to require special attention. None of these policies contravene existing Federal Procurement Regulations nor do they obviate the requirements of existing regulations that are not covered in this document.

In providing supply support to our customer agencies, GSA is responsible for determining the method of support. GSA will continue to emphasize the reduction of the number of items on MAS contracts and to increase the use of competitive procurement methods in providing supply support for items currently in the MAS program. While striving toward this goal, we will continue to use the MAS program, where appropriate, to support our customer agencies.

When GSA provides supply support through the MAS program, it acts as the contracting agent for all Government organizations authorized to use the MAS contracts. Our customer agencies, when they purchase items from the schedules, should be able to buy those items at prices that are better than they could obtain from any other source under similar circumstances. In its role as the contracting agent, GSA will attempt to obtain the best pricing arrangement, i.e., discount(s) from commercial price lists, giving full consideration to the Government's large volume of purchases, in the negotiation process.

II. MAS Contract Pricing Arrangements

The Government's goal when negotiating MAS contract pricing arrangements is to obtain a discount from a firm's established catalog or commercial price list which is equal to or greater than the discount given to that firm's most favored customer. The most favored customer (MFC) discount is equal to the best discount given by a firm to any entity with which that firm conducts business, other than the original equipment manufacturers (OEM), or participating dealers, and distributor's discount.

Consideration may be given to awarding an MAS contract where the Government's discount is not equal to or greater than a firm's MFC discount. This recognizes that there are situations where the Government's terms and conditions may be different from those given the firm's most favored customer. Offerors may cite factors that they claim make the Government different from other customers with which they do business. In these situations, it is the offeror who must provide information identifying such factors, the valuation of the factors identified and the method used for developing the valuation. Contracting officers shall obtain information necessary to judge whether these factors and their valuation are reasonable.

Offerors and contracting officers should understand that there is no guarantee that every offeror who submits an offer will receive a contract. In the event that the Government's negotiation objective cannot be met, the contracting officer must exercise judgment in deciding whether to reject an offer. In exercising this judgment, the contracting officer must weigh the effect that the rejection of the offer will have on meeting the Government's needs.

GSA will not award an MAS contract to a firm that does not give the Government a price equal to the best price given or available to its large volume end user customers with comparable terms and conditions except where the Government's overall volume of purchases does not warrant the best price given to end user customers.

In all MAS contracts, the contracting officer is required to make an affirmative determination that the prices offered to the Government are fair and reasonable (FPR 1–3.807–2).

III. Discount Schedule and Marketing Data

All MAS solicitations will require offerors to submit information on sales, discounts and marketing practices. The required information will be used to determine whether products or services offered meet the tests of commerciality and will be used by the Government in the evaluation of the offeror's proposal and the price reasonableness determination. The offeror will certify to the completeness, accuracy and currency of the data at the conclusion of negotiations. Failure to submit the required sales, discount and marketing data will result in no award. If the data is not found to be complete, current and accurate subsequent to award, the defective pricing clause will be activated and consideration will be given to cancelling the MAS contract if still in effect.

Before a catalog price exemption to the need for submission of cost or pricing data can be granted for products or service offered on MAS solicitations, the tests of commerciality must be met. (FPR 1-3.807-1). FPR 1-3.807-2(d) references ASPM No. 1 which contains the quantified criteria (located in ASPM No. 1, Chapter 8) for these tests and shall be used as the basis for the catalog price exemption.

Offerors will be able to certify to those products or services meeting these tests of commerciality in the discount schedule and marketing data sheets. Information will only be required on a representative sample of the best selling items. Data will be required on all other items offered under the solicitation that are not certified as commercial in accordance with the aforementioned criteria. Cost or pricing data shall be required where sales of a product or service to the general public do not exceed 35 precent of total sales of that product or service; or, where the price cannot be considered "based on" established catalog or market prices of commercial items sold in substantial quantities to the general public in accordance with FPR 1-3.807-1(b)(2)(iii).

Even though an item qualifies for an exemption from the submission of cost or pricing data, price analysis must be performed to determine the reasonableness of price and the need for further negotiations (FPR1-3.807-1(b)(2)(iv)).

IV. OEMs and Dealer/Distributor Discounts and Marketing Data

Information on OEM and dealer/distributor discount or pricing arrangememts will be obtained where the same or similar product or service is offered to the Government under the MAS contract.

Where an offeror markets through dealers or distributors, the contracting officer shall require the offeror to provide sufficient information on the functions or services performed and whether these functions or services will be performed under the MAS contract.

Where an offeror sells to OEMs and claims that there is considerable difference in physical or performance characteristics of the products or services sold to OEMs and the products or services offered to the Government, the offeror must provide sufficient information to substantiate such a claim in lieu of OEM discount or pricing data. Where the contracting officer determines that the offeror's claim is not substantiated, the offeror is required to furnish OEM discount or pricing information.

The contracting officer will use the OEM and dealer/distributor data in the price analysis that result in the Government's negotiation position.

V. Quantity and Aggregate Discounts

In establishing negotiation objectives and in the negotiation process, emphasis will be placed on obtaining discounts based on the aggregate volume of sales for an MAS contract. Negotiation objectives will be established to obtain volume discounts in line with the discounts available to the offeror's other customers. In developing negotiation objectives based on the aggregate volume of sales, consideration may be given to taking discounts on aggregate volume of sales at the conclusion of the contract period, although it is preferred that discounts be obtained when orders are placed.

VI. Maximum Order Limitation (MOL)

All MAS contracts will contain an MOL. The level at which the MOL is established will depend upon the Government's discount arrangement under the schedule and the estimate of sales volume above which suppliers are likely to quote lower prices in other types of contracts. The contracting officer will establish the MOL level for the contract at the conclusion of negotiations.

VII. Price Reductions

All MAS contracts will contain the price reductions clause contained in this document. The price reductions clause is intended to maintain the relationship that was established at the time of award between the Government and the offeror's customer or category of customer upon which the MAS contract was predicated. Any changes in pricing practices by the contractor resulting in a less advantageous relationship between the Government and the customer or category of customer upon which the MAS contracts was predicated shall result in a price reduction to the Government to the extent necessary to retain the original relationship.

The following price reductions clause will be used in all MAS contracts:

Price Reduction Clause [1]

a. *General.* This price reductions clause is intended to ensure that throughout the term of the contract, the Government shall maintain its relative price/discount [and /or term and condition] advantage in relation to the Contractor's commercial customer(s) price/discount upon which this contract award was predicated. The customer or category of customers upon which the contract award is predicated will be identified at the conclusion of negotiations.

b. *Pricing Reductions to Customers Other than the Federal Agencies.* (1) Prior to the award of contract, the contracting officer and the offeror shall reach an agreement as to the price relationship between the Government and the offeror's identified customer or category of customers upon which the contract award is predicated. This relationship shall be maintained throughout the contract period. Any change in the contractor's commercial pricing arrangements for the identified customer or category of customers which disturbs this relationship will constitute a price reduction.

(2) The contractor shall report all price reductions made during the contract period to the contracting officer along with an explanation of the conditions under which the reductions were made. Those reductions which do not disturb the Government's price position relative to the contractor's identified customer or category of customers will not be subject to the provisions of this clause. However, the information will be used in conjunction with the negotiations for the following contract period.

(3) If, after the date of the conclusion of negotiations, the contractor (i) reduces the prices contained in the commercial catalog, pricelist, schedule, or other documents (or grants any more favorable terms and conditions) offered by the contractor and used by the Government to establish the prices with the contract; or (ii) reduces the prices through special discounts to the identified customer or category of customers upon which the award was predicated so as to disturb the relationship of the Government to that identified customer or category of customers, a price reduction shall apply to this contract for the remainder of the contract period, or until further reduced, or, in the case of temporary price

---

[1] Note:—Language in brackets apply to ADP/Communications/Teleprocessing Solicitations/Contracts Only.

reductions, for the duration of any temporary price reduction period.

(4) This clause will not apply to contractor's firm fixed price Definite Quantity contracts with specified delivery in excess of the Maximum Order Limitation specified in the contract.

(5) The contracting officer may exempt from the application of this clause any sale at a price below the contract price if caused by an error in quotation or billing, provided adequate documentation is furnished by the contractor immediately following the discovery of the error.

c. *Price Reductions to Federal Agencies.* (This paragraph does not apply to Non-Schedule ADP/Communications/Teleprocessing Services contracts entered into with Federal Agencies.)

Except for temporary "Government-only" price reductions described below, if, after the effective date of this contract, the contractor reduces the price of any contract item to any Federal agency and the sale falls within the contract maximum order limitation, an equivalent price reduction shall apply to all subsequent sales of the contract item to Federal agencies for the duration of the contract period or until the price is further reduced. The contractor may offer to the contracting officer a temporary "Government-only" price reduction which has a duration of 30 calendar days or more, except during the last month of the contract period when any such offer must be for the remainder of the contract period.

d. *Effective Dates and Notifications.* (This paragraph does not apply to Non-Schedule ADP/Communications/Teleprocessing Contracts entered into with Federal Agencies.)

(1) Any price reduction pursuant to b. above, shall be effective for the Government at the same time as the price reduction to the other customer. Any price reduction pursuant to c. above, shall be effective at the time of initial purchase in the Federal Agency (Government) at the reduced price, except in the case of a temporary "Government-only" price reduction which shall be effective at the time of acceptance by the contracting officer. The contractor shall invoice at such reduced price and indicate thereon that the price reduction is pursuant to this Price Reduction Clause until such time as this contract is modified.

(2) The contractor shall notify the contracting officer in writing of any price reduction as soon as possible but not later than 10 calendar days after the effective date. Failure to give timely notice shall require that such price reduction (including temporary price reductions) apply to the contract for the duration of the contract period, or until the price is further reduced, and may constitute a basis for termination of the contract as provided in the Default Clause of the contract.

e. *Contractor's Statement of Price Reduction.* (This paragraph does not apply to Non-Schedule ADP/Communications/Teleprocessing Contracts entered into with Federal Agencies.)

The contractor shall furnish within 10 calendar days after the end of the contract period a statement certifying either (1) that there was no applicable reduction; or (2) that any price reduction was reported to the contracting officer. For each reported price reduction, the contractor shall show the date when the contracting officer was so notified.

VIII. Economic Price Adjustments

An economic price adjustment (EPA) clause will be used in FSS MAS contracts where uncertainty exists as to the stability of market prices during the term of the contract. The contracting officer will determine whether items under the MAS contract are subject to unforeseen price fluctuations, thus warranting the use of an EPA clause. The contracting officer's determination on the use of an EPA clause will be made in the negotiation process.

Multiple Award Schedule (MAS) Pricing Guide

I. Discount Schedule and Marketing Data

A. *Requirement for Offeror To Submit Pricing Data.* FPR 1-3.101(c) provides that proposals shall be supported by statements and analyses or other evidence of reasonable prices and by such information concerning other vital matters as is deemed necessary by the contracting officer. Each MAS solicitation will include Discount Schedule and Marketing Data sheets to be completed for each Special Item Number (SIN) and submitted as a part of the offerors proposal. When this form is completed in its entirety, along with pricing data from current or prior contracts and preaward audits, it should provide the necessary data, in most cases, to enable the contracting officer to complete the price analysis and develop the negotiation objective.

B. *Initial Review of Offerors Proposal.* As soon as possible after receipt of proposals, the contracting officer should review in detail the offeror's submission in response to the Discount Schedule and Market Data Sheets. If the offer has failed to respond to specific data elements or if the response is not adequate, the contracting officer should immediately request that the offeror correct any deficiencies in the data submission. In this regard, a specific date for the receipt of the required data should be established with the offeror. Also, it is important that the data be received well in advance of schedule negotiations to permit adequate time for a price analysis by the contracting officer.

C. *Timeliness of the Procurement Action.* The process, to the extent practical, should begin early enough to allow for award of MAS contracts by the beginning of the proposed schedule period.

II. Prenegotiations

A. *Establishing the Negotiation Objective.* In preparing for negotiations, the contracting officer will establish specific negotiation objectives based upon a properly prepared price analysis. This price analysis will serve as the basis for the negotiation objectives including the rationale for the objectives established. The elements of the price analysis are listed in Section IV of this pricing guide.

B. *Negotiation Objective.* In establishing negotiation objectives, contracting officers must remain cognizant of the Government's goal in negotiating MAS contracts, namely, to obtain discounts equal to or better than an offeror's discounts to its favored customer. The most favored customer discount is defined as the largest discount, other than the OEM or dealer/distributor discount given to any entity with which the offeror does business. There are factors, such as, terms and conditions, warranties and FOB point, that may make the Government different from a firm's other customers. Through proper analysis and documentation, the contracting officer may recognize such differences. However, in recognizing these differences, the contracting officer must also consider the volume purchased by the Government under the MAS contract.

C. *Documentation of the Price Analysis and Negotiation Objective.* The contract file will contain the written price analysis report in support of the Government's negotiation position.

The supporting documentation will necessarily vary depending upon the complexity and estimated dollar volume of the contract. The price analysis and negotiation objective will be a part of the price negotiation memorandum (See section V of this pricing guide). The supporting documentation required at this point in the procurement process will normally include:

1. General description of the procurement.
2. Adequacy of data submitted by the offeror.
3. The elements of pricing analyzed preparatory to establishing the negotiation objective. (See section IV of this pricing guide).
4. The negotiation objectives and the supporting rationale.
5. Major differences between the offeror's proposal and the negotiation objectives.
6. The offeror's documentation and rationale if less than the MFC discount is offered. This will also include the contracting officer's evaluation of that data.

D. *Approval of Negotiation Objectives.* The negotiation objectives should be approved by the chief of the purchasing office or designee.

III. Catalog Item Verification

A. *Definition of Established Catalog Price.* FPR 1-3.807-1(b)(2) states that for an item to qualify as a catalog price, the price must be, or be based on, (A) an established catalog price, (B) of commercial items, (C) sold in substantial quantities, (D) to the general public. The criteria contained in the following paragraphs should be applied in determining whether an item falls within the scope of this definition.

B. *Established Catalog Price (FPR 1-3.807-1(b)(2)(ii)(A)).* This is a price that is included in a catalog, price list, schedule or other form that is regularly maintained by the manufacturer or vendor, is either published or otherwise available for inspection by customers and states prices at which sales are currently or were last made to a significant number of buyers who constitute the general public. The following questions will help you determine if there is an established catalog price.

1. Is there a printed catalog, price list, published price or other formal document showing prices and applicable discounts, if any.
2. Can audit validate from seller's records that the price offered is a regular catalog price with appropriate discounts?
3. If the answer to either (1) or (2) above is not "yes" the proposal does not meet the test of a catalog priced item.

C. *Commercial Item (FPR 1-3.807-1(b)(2)(ii)(B)).* This is an item (the term includes both supplies and services) of a class or kind that is regularly used for other than Government purposes and is sold or traded in the course of normal business operations. The following questions will help you determine if the item is a commercial item.

1. Is the item or service identical to that described in the catalog?
2. Is the item or service so similar it can be priced by reference to catalog prices?
3. Is the item or service so similar that differences can be identified and priced as add-ons or deducts from catalog prices by price analysis or other known prices?
4. If the answer to either (1), (2) or (3) above is not "yes," the proposal does not meet the test of a catalog item.

D. *General Public (FPR 1-3.807-1(b)(2)(ii)(D)).* An item is sold "to the general public" if it is sold to other than affiliates of the seller and to nongovernment entities. Items sold to affiliates of the seller and sales for end use by the government are not sales to the general public. The following questions will help you determine if an item is sold to the general public.

1. Does the seller's data show sales over the appropriate past period as between Government and non-Government entities?
2. Is there general knowledge of large public sales of products regularly stocked by dealers or regularly traded in the marketplace?
3. Can audit validate from the seller's records that sales have been made to non-Government entities?
4. If you did not answer "yes" to any of the preceding checklist items, the proposal does not meet the test of a catalog item.

E. *Substantial Quantities (FPR 1-3.807-1(b)(2)(ii)(C)).* Supplies are sold in substantial quantities when the facts or circumstances are sufficient to support a reasonable conclusion that the quantities regularly sold are sufficient to constitute a real commercial market for the item. This test is usually in terms of total quantities sold, but it also should include the number of times the item has been sold and how many times a given price or price structure has been accepted by buyers free to choose. Nominal quantities, like models, specimens, samples and prototype of experimental units do not meet this requirement. Services sold in substantial quantities are those that are customarily provided by the company, with personnel regularly employed and with equipment regularly maintained solely or principally to provide such services. In order to provide more detailed guidance to contracting officers, and to ensure that the policy is carried out in a more uniform manner among all contractors, GSA has adopted the ASPM No. 1 criteria as set forth in Chapter 8A. Also, the sales data requested in section VII of the Discount Schedule and Marketing Data is set forth in a format to facilitate your analysis of this requirement. The following questions will help you determine if the items have been sold in substantial quantities:

1. Are reported sales to non-Government entities at least 55% of total sales and those at catalog price less applicable discounts at least 75% of this amount? When the answer to this question is "yes" the item meets the "substantial quantity" test.
2. Are reported sales to non-Government entities at least 35% of total sales and those at catalog price less applicable discounts at least 55% of this amount? When the answer to this question is "yes" the test of substantial may be deemed to have been met when (i) the criteria in B, C, and D above are met, (ii) the nature of the item or total quantities sold clearly supports such a conclusion even though the Government is the major user, and (iii) approval of the chief or deputy chief of the Procurement Office is obtained.
3. Can audit verify from the seller's records that commercial sales meet the test of (1) and (2) above?
4. Are reported sales to non-Government entities less than 35% of total sales to all customers (Government and non-Government)? If the answer is "yes," the item does not meet the test of substantial quantities. Therefore, if the item is to be included in the MAS, cost or pricing data must be obtained and evaluated in accordance with FPR 1-3.807.

F. *Catalog Price Exemption.* A catalog price exemption to the need for submission of cost or pricing data can be granted for products or services offered on MAS solicitations when the requirements set forth in paragraphs A through E above have been met.

The Discount Schedule and Marketing Data Sheets provides in section VII for the information to determine commerciality. This section permits offerors to certify to the commerciality of items offered under the solicitation. Along with this certification, offerors are required to submit sales information on a representative sample of the best selling items under the SIN. The contracting officer will establish the representative sample size in the solicitation. For items that the offeror cannot certify as commercial, sales information will be required for each item offered under the solicitation. The information provided will be used in determining whether an item should be exempt from the cost and pricing data requirement.

IV. Price Analysis

A. *Requirement for Price Analysis.* FPR 1-3.807-2(a) states that some form of price or cost analysis should be made in connection with every negotiated procurement action. FPR 1-3.807-1(b)(2)(iv) states that even though an item qualifies for exemption from the requirements for submission of certified cost or pricing data, price analysis must be performed to determine the reasonableness of the price and the need for further negotiation.

B. *Preparation for Negotiations.* Preparation for negotiations after receipt of the offer begins with a properly prepared price analysis report. The price analysis should provide the basis for establishing the specific negotiation objectives and the reasons why these objectives were established.

C. *Price Analysis Techniques.* Most of the data needed to perform the price analysis will be submitted by the offerors as required by the Discount Schedule and Marketing Data Sheets and the historical files on existing or prior contracts. Questions on the proposal that arise during the price analysis effort will be addressed to the offeror. The price analysis may include the following elements, as appropriate:

1. Discount arrangements on the existing or prior year contract. Data from these sources can be accumulated prior to receipt of proposals. Information should include: estimated and actual sales volume; categories of customers and discount arrangements; the MAS discounts negotiated; and, any problems or significant events that were experienced during the negotiations affecting the Government's negotiation position. Price reduction information submitted in accordance with the price reductions clause shall also be included. This information is the data base from which to start the price analysis after proposals are received.

2. Offeror's commercial sales data. The sales data submitted in Part B, VII of the Discount Schedule and Marketing Data Sheets will be used to determine price reasonableness, the commerciality of products or services offered and the discount the Government should receive. As a general rule, the larger the percent of commercial sales to total sales, the more reliance the Government can place on prices being set in the marketplace. Because products or services available under schedules should be for the most part commercial items, it is essential that the commerciality of the products or services be established preparatory to negotiations. Where products or services do not clearly meet the tests of commerciality, contract negotiators are required to analyze whether these products or services are comparable to others which meet the tests of commerciality or there are other circumstances that can be used in judging why such items should be considered commercial. Additional information may be required from the offeror in assessing commerciality. Where products or services are not commercial, cost or pricing data is required.

3. The prices and discounts proposed by the offeror. The offeror's proposal should be reviewed to ascertain an understanding of the prices or discounts offered to the Government as compared with offeror's discounts to other entities and to determine if the sales data required is included in the proposal. The analysis of the proposal should determine the reasons for differences between the offered discounts, and other discount arrangements; whether there are special discount arrangements; or other concessions that the offeror makes which should be included in determining the Government's negotiation position.

4. Net price evaluation. Comparison of net prices may be utilized in the evaluation of offers under MAS contracts. Every effort should be made to include products with the lowest net price on the schedule even though there may be instances where the offeror offering the lowest net price may not offer the most favored customer pricing. In addition, you may compare the net prices offered by one offeror with net prices of similar items offered by other offerors to assist in the price reasonableness determination. This may be done on a sampling basis using the high dollar volume items listed on the Discount Schedule and Marketing Data Sheets.

5. Recommendations contained in preaward audits or from other pricing specialists or from other appropriate sources.

6. Trend analysis of price changes using appropriate indices such as the Producer Price Index, other similar market indicators, and price changes in similar produces offered by other companies.

7. The comparison of offered prices/discounts to local retail and discount house catalog prices.

8. The overall discount policy of the offeror. The Discount Schedule and Marketing Data sheets require that complete disclosure regarding discount policy and price reductions in any other form be made. This would include, but not limited to, such things as quantity discounts, end-of-year discounts, discounts for multiple quantities, free service or installation, training, bonus goods of any kind, trade-in allowances, rebates of any kind, F.O.B. point, payment terms, incentives, guaranteed prices. The price analysis should determine whether any such items are included in the offeror's proposal to the Government and the consideration that they should be given in establishing the Government's negotiation position.

9. That the offeror's price to the Government takes into account the volume of Government business anticipated for a fixed period, such as a fiscal year, rather than the size of the individual purchase order (FPR 1-3.807-12).

D. *OEM and Dealer/Distributor Discounts.* 1. An integral part of the price analysis is the consideration given to OEMs and dealers in the establishment of the Government's negotiation position. While the government's goal in negotiating schedule discounts is to obtain an offeror's most favored customer discount other than the OEM or dealer discount, it is none the less necessary for the Government to assure itself that these entities are performing OEM or dealer functions. Accordingly, appropriate information will be obtained from the offeror where an offeror sells to OEMs or dealers.

2. An offeror will be required to furnish information on its dealer/distributor pricing or discount arrangements regardless of whether these entities will participate under the schedule contract. Information will be obtained on the functions that the dealer/distributor performs and which of these functions will be performed under the schedule contract. Where a dealer performs a significant number of functions for the offeror, the Government's negotiation objective will be other than the offeror's dealer/distributor price or discount.

3. Where an offeror sells the same or similar products or services to an OEM that are offered to the Government under the MAS solicitation, the offeror will be required to furnish information on its OEM pricing or discount arrangements. Where an offeror sells to an OEM and claims that there is considerable difference between the item sold to the OEM and the item sold through the MAS contract, the offeror will be given the opportunity to demonstrate such differences. If the differences can be substantiated, the Government's negotiation position will be other than the offeror's OEM price or discount.

V. Negotiations

1. Negotiations can begin upon completion of a properly prepared price analysis and establishment of the Government's negotiation objectives.

2. During the negotiations, Government negotiators will address the following:

   a. Aggregate discounts based on the estimated volume of sales under the schedule contract giving consideration to the Government's manner of ordering.

   b. In FSS, the use of an economic price adjustment clause considering the uncertainty of prices for the contract term and the resultant improved discounts offered the Government by the offeror for this price protection. The use of the EPA clause is a matter for negotiation.

3. In the event that the Government's negotiation objective cannot be met, the contracting officer must exercise judgment in deciding whether to reject the offer. In exercising this judgment, the contracting officer must weigh the effect that the rejection of the offer will have on meeting the Government's needs. Whenever a decision is made to award an MAS contract where the Government's discount is not equal to or better than the MFC discount, the contracting officer will:

   a. Ensure the analysis and reasons for this decision are fully documented and justified in the contract file.

   b. Obtain approval for such a decision at a supervisory level higher than the contracting officer, regardless of the dollar value.

4. The Government will not award an MAS contract to a firm that does not give us a price equal to the best price given or available to its volume end user customers under similar circumstances except where the Government's overall volume of purchases for the contract period does not warrant the best price given to end user customers.

5. At the conclusion of negotiations, the contracting officer will decide on the level of the MOL in the contract. The level of the MOL depends on the Government's negotiated discount arrangement and the estimate of sales volume above which suppliers are likely to quote lower prices in other types of contracts.

6. In all MAS contract negotiations, the contracting officer is required to make an affirmative determination that the prices negotiated are fair and reasonable (FPR 1-3.807.2).

7. FPR 1-3.811 requires that a price negotiation memorandum (PNM) be prepared at the conclusion of each negotiation. The PNM is the document that brings together all the principal elements of the negotiation leading to the decision the price/discount is fair and reasonable. In support of that decision, the PNM should contain the significant considerations shaping the pricing/discount arrangement. These include:

   a. A summary of the offer received (prices, terms, etc.), the Government's negotiation position (objectives) and the negotiation results. Any revised or adjusted offers and any reversed or adjusted Government negotiation objectives will be explained.

   b. Names and titles (position) of the Government and contractor representatives who participated in the negotiations.

   c. Reference to the price analysis report should be made or, where appropriate, actual incorporation of the price analysis. (Elements of the price analysis report are in Section II, paragraph C of this pricing guide).

   d. Where cost of pricing data is required, the narrative should cover the products or services that require it, the source of the data, the analysis of the data and its use in negotiations. Where the requirement for cost or pricing data is waived, the determination and findings in support of such waiver will be appended to the PNM.

   e. Where preaward audit or other pricing assistance is available, the PNM should identify the recommendations. Where the recommendations are not used, appropriate rationale will be included on why they were not used. Any alternate position will be documented and supported with factual data.

   f. Any exceptions to the Government's terms and conditions will be documented as will any special or non-standard contract provision.

   g. The PNM will document the initial negotiation objectives and actual negotiations including the offers and counter-offers made by the parties with supporting rationale for all Government positions.

   h. The document will include the MOL level established with supporting rationale.

   i. The document must clearly demonstrate and support that the price/discount negotiated is reasonable. It must document any decision to accept less than the best pricing arrangement granted to the most favored customer. The PNM should also identify the offeror's data used in the negotiation process.

   j. The PNM should be signed and dated by the contracting officer as evidence that it is the official record of negotiations and it complies with GSA policies and procedures.

Price Analysis Check Sheet

	Yes	No
1. Did the offeror submit adequate data in response to the solicitation?		
2. If data submitted by offeror was not adequate, did you request that deficiences be corrected?		
3. Did offeror than submit adequate data?		
4. Did you verify that the items meet the test of:		
a. Established catalog price (FPR 1-3.807-1(b)-(2)(ii)(A))?		
b. Commercial item (FPR 1-3.807-1(b)(2)(ii)(B))?		
c. General public (FPR 1-3.807-1 (b)(2)(ii)(D))?		
d. Substantial quantites (FPR 1-3.807-1 (b)(2)(ii)(C) and ASPM No. 1, Chapter 8A)?		
5. Did you prepare a price analysis on the offerors proposal?		
6. Did you compare the offerors prices/discounts to existing or prior contracts' and reconcile differences?		
7. Did you compare proposed price lists to prior lists and evaluate changes?		
8. Did the offeror propose the MFC discount to the Government?		
9. If MFC discount was not offered, did the offeror's proposal provide the required documentation in support thereof?		
10. If MFC discount was not offered, did you evaluate why and use it in developing the Government's negotiation position?		
11. On a sample basis, did you compare "net prices" on high dollar volume items to similar items offered or available from other sources?		
12. Are the prices negotiated at least equal to the best price that the offeror grants to its end user most favored customer?		
13. Does the PNM contain an affirmative determination that the prices negotiated are fair and reasonable and set forth the basis for such determination?		

Solicitation No. ———

Discount Schedule and Marketing Data

Instructions to Offerors

Part A. General Information, applies to each GSA Special Item Number (SIN) for which an offer is submitted. (If all information is the same, SINs may be combined.)

Part B. Separate discount and sales information, *must be completed for each Special Item Number* for which an offer is submitted. (If discount information is the same for all products under each SIN, SINs may be combined. However, separate sales information rerquired under Part B IV must be provided for each SIN.)

Information required by each space *must* be furnished. If not applicable, indicate by "N/A". Information furnished in Part B relating to discounts, allowances and sales information will be treated as "Confidential" by the Government except for final prices and discounts awarded by the Government. *Failure to provide current, accurate and complete information under Parts A and B may subject the offeror to liability for refunds pursuant to the price reductions or Defective Pricing Clauses.*

Part A—General Information

(Applicable to all special item numbers)

I. *Offeror's Marketing Category* (check applicable item)

  (a)——Manufacturer selling direct—has no dealers.

  (b)——Manufacturer selling direct to the Government even though he has dealers.

  (c)——Manufacturer selling to the Government through dealers.

(d)—— Dealer selling direct to the Government. (Dealer must submit manufacturer's price list).
(e)—— Other (specify)——

II. *Identification of a Price List as the Basis for This Offer* (check and attach—copies of the price list)
(a)—— Manufacturer's catalog/pricelist (indicate type)——
(b)—— Dealer's catalog/pricelist
(c)—— Retailer's catalog/pricelist
(d)—— Other (specify)——

III. *Warranty:* (question (b) applies only to FSS solicitations)
(a) Submit your standard commercial warranty or specify where it may be found in your catalog or pricelist included with this offer.
(b) The warranty offered to GSA is more favorable—— less favorable—— or equal to—— the commercial warranty? (check one). Describe and provide the value (expressed as a percentage of the catalog price) if more favorable or less favorable——%.

IV. *Installation and Instruction* (this section only applies to FSS)
(a) Are installation and instruction included in this effort? Yes——, No—— (check one). If *Yes*, give details or indicate where the information may be found in your catalog or pricelist.
(b) Are installation and instruction provisions offered herein to the Government more favorable than those in commercial customers? Yes——, No—— (check one). If *Yes*, describe and provide the value (expressed as a percentage)——%.

V. *Other Data:* (In FSS solicitations, answer "Yes" Or "No" for each question)
(a)—— Do you maintain stock on hand of the items offered?
(b)—— Do you display the Special Item Number(s) offered in showroom?
(c)—— Do you provide any design and layout assistance related to this Special Item Number free of charge?
(d) If you are a dealer, will you arrange to have other dealers participate in the schedule contract should you receive a contract?
(e)—— Will you administer all incoming orders, including requests for expediting and follow-up?

Solicitation No. ——

Part B—Discount and Sales Information
Name of Offeror ——
GSA Special Item Number ——

I. *Identification of Items Offered.* How many Model/type of catalog items do you offer under this GSA special Item Number —— (enter number).

II. *Discounts.* The following concessions are offered to the Government for delivery FOB destination. In ADTS solicitations, list also concessions to the Government for delivery FOB origin.
(a) Discount offered on the above GSA Special Item Number is —— % from pricelist dated ——, *plus* prompt payment discount, as stated on the first page of this solicitation (additional details may be entered below or attached). If discounts vary, show discounts on pricelist.
(b) Aggregate or end of contract additional discounts. An additional discount of —— percent is offered to the Government which will be applied to the actual aggregate sales in excess of the following base figure under this contract:
1. For current MAS contractors, aggregate sales (annualized) to the Government for most recent 12 month period under similar contract(s) is $——, based on sales during the period —— to ——.
2. For other offerors, projected aggregate sales under this contract is $——.
(c) Quantity Discounts. List below any quantity discounts included in this offer. (Question (2) below applies only to FSS).

	Regular discounts (percent)	Quantity discounts (percent)	Aggregate discounts	Commissions to other than employees (percent)	Prompt payment	FOB point	Other
(1) To dealers/retailers							
(2) To distributors/wholesalers							
(3) To educational institutions							
(4) To state, county, city, and local governments							
(5) To original equipment manufacturers (OEM)							
(6) To others (specify); e.g., national accounts, sales agreements, etc.							
(7) If a dealer, indicate discount from manufacturer's price list							

III.c. Do you have in effect, for any customer of any class within the MOL or outside of the MOL, other discounts and/or concessions including but not limited to the following, regardless of price list, which result in lower net prices than those offered the Government in this offer?
Yes—— No—— rebates of any kind, including year-end or end of contract discounts?
Yes—— No—— multiple quantity unit pricing plan?
Yes—— No—— cumulative discounts of any type which cover items being offered?
Yes—— No—— products (models)/services that may be combined for maximum discounts?
Yes—— No—— others (specify).
If answer to any of the above is "Yes", provide detail explanation including the value expressed as a percentage of the list price.

Special Item No. ——

IV. (a) Are any of the models/products offered herein sold by the offeror under a different trade name(s)? Yes ——, No ——. If "Yes," explain and provide applicable pricelists.
(b) To your knowledge, are there identical products offered herein contained in any other GSA Federal Supply Schedule contract? Yes ——, No ——. If "Yes", identify the product, schedule and contract.
(1) Can models/products be combined within special Item Number? Yes —— No ——. If yes, provide details.
(2) Can special Item Numbers be combined? Yes —— No ——. If yes, provide details.
(d) Other beneficial terms, discounts, or concessions included in this offer such as prompt renewal discounts, purchase option credits, etc. (List below and provide detail explanations.) (This section applies only to FSS solicitations).

III a. List below the best discount and/or concessions resulting in the lowest net price (regardless of quantity and terms and conditions) to other than authorized GSA contract users from *price list* for the same or similar products or services offered to the Government under this solicitation. (Show actual percentage and delivery terms)

(c) Summarize any significant changes in concessions offered herein as compared with those set forth in any current GSA contract.

V. *Allowances:* (This section only applies to FSS solicitations). Do you offer any of the following allowances to any customer which are not available to a GSA contract user under this contract? (Enter "yes" or "no" for each. If yes, explain.)
(a) —— Trade-in allowances?
(b) —— Return/Exchange goods policy?
(c) —— Reduced prices on samples, demonstrator models, reconditioned items or floor models?
(d) —— Do you give any allowances not mentioned above?

VI. *Sales Information* (This section only applies to FSS solicitations). Estimate the percentage of your sales made to the U.S. Government under Federal Supply Schedule Blanket Purchase Arrangements (check one of the following):
None ——. 25% or less ——. 25% to 49% ——. 50% to 74% ——. 75% or more ——

List agencies below:
1. ——
2. ——
3. ——
4. —————— etc.

VII

Solicitation No. ――――― Special Item No. ――――― Offeror Name ―――――

A. This section requires (1) that sales information be provided to enable the contracting officer to determine that the items meet the test of commerciality in FPR 1-3.807-1 and ASPM No. 1, Chapter 8A; and, (2) that pricing data is furnished in sufficient detail to enable the contracting officer to perform a price analysis in accordance with FPR 1-3.807-1(b)(2)(iv).

B. The offeror certifies that, except for the individual models/types or catalog numbers cited in paragraph C below, all other models/types or catalog numbers offered in response to this solicitation meet the tests of commerciality in FPR 1-3.807-1 and ASPM No. 1, Chapter 8A. Of the individual models/types or catalog numbers so certified, sales information shall be provided in the table below for each of the ――― models/types or catalog numbers with the largest dollar sales volume. The sales information provided is for the prior 12 months, from ――――― to ――――― for this special item number.

 1. Total annual sales to the Government under this special item number $―――――.
 2. Total annual sales (to all entities) under this special item number $―――――.

1	2	3	4	5	6	7	8
Model/type or catalog No.	Total annual sales to Fed. Govt. $―percent of column 5	Total annual sales to nongovernment customers at catalog price (less published discounts)	Total annual sales to nongovernment customers at other than catalog price $―percent of column 3 if more than 25 percent	Total annual sales: Columns 2, 3, and 4	Provide information below for largest discount granted to any nongovernment customer Quantity—Discount	List the largest discount at which the item was sold for comparable sales/quantities shown in column 2 to any nongovernment customer during the past year Quantity—Discount	Is the discount in block number 6 greater than your current offer under this solicitation? Yes―― No――. If yes, provide complete documentation and rationale of the difference. Merely submitting copies of documents such as terms and conditions of commercial contracts, commercial warranties, etc., will not be adequate to justify the difference

C. Sales information in the table below shall be provided for each individual model/type or catalog number in the above special item number that is not certified commercial when experienced annual government sales are $100,000 or more.

1	2	3	4	5	6	7	8
Model/type or catalog No.	Total annual sales to Fed. Govt. $―percent of column 5	Total annual sales to nongovernment customers at catalog price (less published discounts)	Total annual sales to nongovernment customers at other than catalog price $―percent of column 3 if more than 25%	Total annual sales: Columns 2, 3, and 4	Provide information below for largest discount granted to any nongovernment customer Quantity—Discount	List the largest discount at which the item was sold for comparable sales/quantities shown in column 2 to any nongovernment customer during the past year Quantity—Discount	Is the discount in block number 6 greater than your current offer under this solicitation? Yes―― No――. If yes, provide complete documentation and rationale of the difference. Merely submitting copies of documents such as terms and conditions of commercial contracts, commercial warranties, etc. will not be adequate to justify the difference

NOTES:
 1. Federal Government sales include all sales to U.S. Government and its instrumentalities and for U.S. Government use, sales directly to U.S. Government prime contractors and to their subcontractors or suppliers at any tier, for use as an end item or as part of an end item, by the U.S. Government.
 2. Nongovernment customer is defined as other than Government or affiliates (include sales to distributors, dealers, OEM, national accounts, educational institutions, state, etc.)
 3. Discounts are reductions to catalog or market prices (published or unpublished) applicable to any customer, including OEMs, dealers, distributors, national accounts, states, etc.; and any other form of price reduction such as concessions, rebates, quantity discounts, allowances, services, warranties, installation, free parts, etc., which are granted to any customer

END

APPENDIX V

ARMED SERVICE PRICING MANUAL DEPARTMENT OF DEFENSE, CHAPTER 8, HOW TO NEGOTIATE AND JUSTIFY A PRICE.

CHAPTER 8

HOW TO NEGOTIATE AND JUSTIFY A PRICE

CONTENTS

8.1	Competition and Price Negotiation	8- 1
8.2	Written or Oral Discussions and Competitive Range	8- 2
8.3	Price Negotiation Defined	8- 4
8.4	Principles and Techniques	8- 5
	Preparation	8- 5
	The team	8- 6
	Factfinding	8- 8
	Objectives	8- 8
	Prenegotiation review	8-11
	Conference	8-12
8.5	Negotiation	8-12
	Price negotiation – a discussion of techniques	8-12
	Negotiation of multi-item contracts	8-14
	Tracking	8-15
	Gamesmanship	8-16
	Principles	8-17
8.6	The Need for Documentation	8-19
8.7	Documenting Price Analysis	8-20
8.8	Documenting Larger Procurements	8-21
	Roles of team members	8-21
	Requests for proposals	8-22
	Requests for information and assistance	8-23
	Recommendations	8-24
	Reporting cost analyses	8-26
	Reports after negotiation	8-27
	Distribution of PNM	8-33

8.1 Competition and Price Negotiation

Contract price negotiation usually is required when competitive proposals have been solicited and always is required when other-than-competitive procedures are used to acquire goods and services. Exceptions to this principle are set out in acquisition regulations, but the message is clear: only when contracting through sealed bidding can you expect not to bargain with offerors before awarding a contract. Price negotiation is not required and in fact has no place in sealed bidding.

Competitive acquisition by sealed bidding works because there are many sellers that can furnish the product or service to be procured (and there are many sellers because there are many buyers for their wares). The presence of many buyers and many sellers creates the marketplace in which competition prevails, and competition sets the price.

Competition can be created, even when there is no marketplace and there may be only one buyer, by describing the required product or service in terms that more than one seller can meet. With expectations of significant present and future sales, many will try to get into the business and there will be head-to-head competition for at least the first quantity.

With several responses, you usually will need to negotiate, to hold written or oral discussions with all in the competitive range. Unlike sealed bidding, selection and award are separate actions. Final negotiations are conducted with the selected offeror or offerors, and award is made after agreement is reached on terms and conditions, including price.

8.2 Written or Oral Discussions and Competitive Range

Contracting officers are required to conduct written or oral discussions with all responsible offerors that submit proposals within a competitive range. The few exceptions to this requirement are enumerated in the acquisition regulations. Written or oral discussions need not be undertaken when the existence of full and open competition or accurate prior cost experience with the product or service assures that acceptance of the most favorable initial proposal without discussion would result in a fair and reasonable price.

If this exception is to be used, the solicitation document has to have notified all offerors of the possibility that award might be made without discussion. An award on this basis must be made without any written or oral discussion with any offeror; if discussions are opened with one offeror, they must be opened with all.

The concepts *written or oral discussions* and *competitive range* have been difficult to define and deal with because their application, in most instances, is based on judgment. Written or oral discussions are said to lead to leveled proposals where price becomes the sole discriminator and auctioning occurs. Leveling is said to occur when discussions lead to a transfusion of the best features of each proposal into all other competing proposals, although leveling can occur without transfusion. The nature and content of discussions with offerors are critical factors, and leveling must be avoided.

Your discussions should not disclose the strengths or weaknesses of competing offers, nor should they disclose any information that would let one offeror improve its proposal at the expense of another.

You must determine which proposals are within a competitive range using price or cost, technical, and other salient factors stated in the solicitation and must include all proposals that have a reasonable chance of being selected for award. You shouldn't determine competitive range by comparing an offeror's score (after its proposal has been evaluated) with a predetermined score that was structured before or during source solicitation.

You should examine the grouping or arrangement of scores for all proposals. Borderline proposals should not be excluded from consideration if they are reasonably susceptible of being made acceptable. Another way of putting it is this: a proposal must be regarded as being within the competitive range unless it is so deficient or out of line in price or technical merit as to preclude further meaningful negotiations. Where an offeror's failure to provide detailed information renders its proposal inferior but not unacceptable, the proposal should be considered within the competitive range for written or oral discussions.

In the case of an RFP that solicits unpriced technical proposals, you evaluate proposals to determine those that are acceptable or that, after discussions, may be made acceptable. After discussions, prices are solicited for all acceptable proposals.

No proposal from a responsible source offering an acceptable technical proposal is to be rejected for failure to fall within a competitive range unless the technical proposal includes a price proposal that, for good and sufficient reason, is found to be so deficient or out of line as to preclude further meaningful negotiations.

All offerors selected to participate in discussions (those whose proposals have been determined to be within the competitive range) are to be advised of deficiencies in their proposals and given a reasonable opportunity to correct or resolve them. A deficiency is defined as that part of an offeror's proposal that fails to satisfy the Government's requirements. Advising an offeror of a deficiency in its proposal does not mean that it will be told how to correct it. That decision and what to do about it is strictly up to the offeror, and the correction or resolution of deficiencies may require an offeror to submit revised cost or pricing data.

In this difficult and demanding environment, offerors must not be played against each other. Auction techniques must not be used. Examples of auctioning include indicating a price that must be met to obtain further consideration, informing an offeror that its price is not low in relation to another, or repeatedly calling for best and final offers.

At the conclusion of discussions with offerors within the competitive range, you set a final, common cutoff date for the submission of written final offers. You notify all remaining eligible offerors of the cutoff date and allow sufficient time to prepare and submit competitive offers. If your notification is oral, you must confirm it in writing. This notification must say, in effect, that discussions have been concluded and offerors now are being given an opportunity to submit best and final offers.

Final contract negotiations differ from written or oral discussions held previously. Generally, written or oral discussions are conducted to obtain information for evaluation and selection purposes. Final contract negotiations use that and later information to establish the contract terms.

Application of the concepts of *written or oral discussions* and *competitive range* may be different for major systems and equipments than for other items and services. But whether it is a large or less-than-large procurement, the fundamentals should not be applied differently.

In summary, there are six steps in the process of reaching final contract negotiations after the receipt of proposals or offers:

    a. Evaluate and rank offers in light of the evaluation criteria specified in the solicitation.

    b. Identify the proposals that are within a competitive range.

    c. Identify and eliminate unacceptable proposals (those containing such deficiencies in price and/or technical merit as to preclude further meaningful negotiations).

    d. Conduct written or oral discussions with the offerors identified in Step 2, and, if necessary, permit revision of individual proposals in order to correct deficiencies.

    e. Notify each offeror with which discussions have been conducted of a final, common cutoff date for submission of written best and final offers.

f. Select the source or sources for final negotiation and award.

8.3 Price Negotiation Defined

Price negotiation puts the cap on the process of negotiation. Negotiation -- the process of bargaining among buyers and sellers -- is the way to prove to the contractor the reasonableness of your findings and conclusions. Bargaining requires communication and implies a willingness to reach a mutually satisfactory agreement on, or settlement of, a matter of common concern. Communication may be in writing, by telephone, or face-to-face. If face-to-face, it may be an informal conversation or a more formal conference.

Price negotiation is a technique used in the absence of effective price competition to reach a sound decision on price. That is its purpose. When you use this technique, your objective obviously is a fair and reasonable price and a contract type that will sustain the price. However, your immediate reason for negotiating is to find a basis for agreement with the offeror.

There are two parties to the negotiation. You represent the Government, and it is in your interest to make a contract that promises to pay the contractor a fair and reasonable price for delivering the needed equipment or service on time. You are trying to create a contract that will encourage this and also encourage the contractor to control and then reduce the costs of contract performance. You balance price and quality and try to get the required quality at the most reasonable price. This may mean the lowest price, or as low as possible under the circumstances.

On the other hand, the offeror has different objectives based on factors of great interest to it. While profit surely will be one of those objectives, its importance can diminish in specific situations. You may or may not learn what these objectives are during negotiations, but this is not critical. The important thing to remember is that the company and its representatives will probably be trying to achieve objectives different from yours.

The negotiation of price, therefore, should establish an area within which you and the company can agree, an area that will allow both you and the company to realize your separate objectives. The sense and soundness of this observation may not be apparent. To clarify it, we'll look at an example.

Garsap proposes to furnish 100 M-2 automatic electrogyros at a firm unit price of $6,000. The Government objective is $5,140 each on an FFP contract. This $5,140 is the figure the negotiator wants to reach after discussions with Garsap. The task seems formidable, and no doubt will be; the 14-percent spread between the objective and the company's asking price is a significant difference of opinion and, seemingly, of objectives. Negotiations will explore known facts with the company's representatives so that the Government negotiator, Tammy Watkins, can test her interpretations of the facts. It will also be Tammy Watkins' purpose to get from the company the latest information about costs incurred (if any) since Garsap prepared its offer. It is likely that the exploration will produce factors that will cause Watkins to revise her objective upward and the company to lower its asking price.

It is also likely that the resulting difference between the two positions will be the range within which agreement can be reached. The price finally agreed to will be one that Watkins thinks is reasonable for the M-2 gyros and one that Garsap will accept as sufficient for its purposes. We must assume, in the absence of certain knowledge to the contrary, that Garsap will be interested in making a profit on the sale and that the company will be satisfied that it can make an adequate profit at whatever price it ultimately agrees to.

8.4 Principles and Techniques

In this section we will talk about the principal steps and techniques of negotiation under the following headings:

a. Preparation.

b. The team.

c. Factfinding.

d. Objectives.

e. Prenegotiation review.

f. Conference.

The central theme of this section may sound naive and quaint, but if you retain only one idea, make it this: be prepared. In other words, make sure the offeror submits the necessary cost or pricing data, and make sure that you do your homework, check your facts, prepare your case, have an objective, anticipate arguments, and develop responses.

Sooner or later, before you make an award, you will have to talk price with a person who will be arguing that the offer is reasonable and probably too low for safety. You may view the price as too high, but even if you are right, you'd better have good reasons handy to sell the offeror on the idea that it won't lose everything but will make an adequate and equitable return at your price.

You will be meeting with a person who has strong feelings of self-interest and the future. No matter how patriotic and public-spirited the individual, the offeror's first interests must be perpetuation of company and job and furtherance of career. The offeror will be prepared to argue for the price and contractual arrangement offered. Your task will not be easy, no matter how well you prepare, but you won't have a chance with a haggling "Your price is too high. Knock 10 percent off and I might be able to buy it."

Haggling and horse-trading suggest pushcart peddlers, oriental bazaars, and sharp practices. They are more elementary forms of negotiation in which the buyer must truly beware. Your negotiations should have little in common with any of these. However, you should remember one thing: the buyer who knows what he wants, knows how to test the quality of offered goods, and has a basis for determining value does not get taken even when buying horses.

Preparation

Preparation includes getting cost or pricing data from the company, analyzing the offer, doing additional factfinding or verifying, developing a Government position regarding the offer (a negotiation objective), and planning, in general terms, the strategy for the impending negotiation conference.

Your strategy should be based on a thorough understanding of the characteristics of the industry and should be tailored to the situation and the company. The depth of preparation and the number and kinds of people you line up for the negotiation team will depend on the importance and difficulty of the proposed procurement, the money involved, and the time available. It may also depend on the degree of price competition obtained.

The team

For significant procurements, the help of specialists will be needed in preparing for and conducting the negotiation. While you will either do the job alone or use only limited outside help for most relatively simple, small-dollar procurements, the pricing of more complex procurements cannot be a one-man show.

You may need help in evaluating kinds and quantities of material and recent purchases and in projecting that price experience into the future. You may need help in determining the need for certain types of labor and the realism of the hours projected and the prices anticipated. You may need help in analyzing risks and determining the present stage of development of the item, the amount of work yet to be done, the likelihood of success in solving state-of-the-art problems, or the similarities and differences between the present requirement and the equipment that preceded it.

If buying repair, modification, or maintenance of existing equipment, you may need help in assessing the probable or actual condition of the equipment to be repaired or modified or evaluating the record of work done earlier on the same or similar equipment. You may be looking for help in evaluating the reasonableness of the present level of an offeror's indirect costs and the projection of indirect costs into the future. You may want help in interpreting engineering drawings of the equipment to be procured so as to visualize the manufacturing processes required or determine whether the offeror can do the job within the hours estimated.

No matter what the problem, specialists in pricing, auditing, production, packaging, maintenance, quality control, contract administration, contract law, and various fields of engineering are available within the organization or within the Government. The real concern is how to use them and how to plan so that they will be available when you need them.

The team is not a formal, identifiable organizational entity. Instead, it is a group created by the person responsible for developing the Government's negotiating objective and plans. It lasts until the contract has been negotiated and awarded, and then it is disbanded.

The PCO, the contracting officer assigned responsibility for making the procurement, is the team chief. The PCO provides overall knowledge of the procurement situation, special contract clauses that may influence prices, past buys of the same or similar equipment, experience with the offeror or offerors, and similar factors.

The PCO may or may not be the principal negotiator. The choice of negotiator will depend on organizational concepts, duty assignments, and obviously, the skills available. The PCO may or may not take charge in the planning, analysis, and factfinding stages. No matter how these duties are handled, the PCO will provide team leadership as the one responsible for the contract.

If the buying organization has contract price analysts, one of them should support the contracting officer. The price analyst should ask for field pricing support and assimilate analyses of costs from the ACO (and others assigned to the contract administration organization), the auditor, the project engineer, and other specialists.

The pricing specialist may be in the best position (from experience and ability) to conduct the price negotiation. If so, the specialist should be named the principal negotiator. The rule is that the best person does the talking for the Government. However, when the best negotiator is not also the team chief, the negotiator must wait for the contracting officer's nod before signing off.

The ACO is the contracting officer assigned the responsibility for administering any resulting contract. The ACO and the field pricing team will furnish assistance to the PCO on request. Using a team of specialists, the ACO reviews the proposal and reports back to the buying organization.

Specialists can evaluate the following: the need for the kinds and amounts of material and labor supporting the proposal; the indirect expense rates, particularly if a forward pricing rate agreement has been negotiated; the need for special tools and test equipment; the requirement for and the cost of particular kinds of preservation packaging; the need, if any, for financial or facilities assistance; and the reasonableness of scrap and spoilage factors.

Equally important is a summary of the total field review effort. These separate cost analyses will be based on knowledge of production, quality control, packaging, engineering, and manufacturing practices and techniques, and on information about plant capacity, scheduling, engineering and production skills and experience, make-or-buy, Government property, and industrial security as these factors relate to the offeror.

When asked, the auditor performs a cost analysis and reports findings to the ACO for transmittal to the PCO. The report covers both incurred (if any) and estimated costs. It includes advice about disclosed accounting practices, about cost or pricing data submitted and identified, and about the appropriateness of accounting methods to the requirements of the contract type contemplated. It also describes any other characteristics of the system that the contracting officer should know about. If the reports of specialists included conclusions about amounts or kinds of material and labor, the significant findings will have been given to the auditor. The auditor also identifies all cost or pricing data that the contractor submitted in writing during the conduct of the analysis.

These analyses reports are bundled up and sent, with the ACO's summary comments, to the PCO. Each specialist reports things as he sees them, interpreting facts and making judgments on the basis of his specialty and in light of his experience. Ultimately, these reports need to be studied and digested and conflicts resolved.

The PCO, or the individual who will negotiate with the company, should be the one to do the digesting. The Government negotiator will have to discuss all relevant points with the company's negotiators and must know and understand any compromises or other resolutions of differences, first among the Government specialists and second, between Government and company positions. If all the differences relate to questions of fact, it might not be necessary for the negotiator to be in on their resolution. But when it is a matter of opinion and judgment, the more he knows about the details, the better.

(There are special requirements and procedures for resolving situations when the contracting officer's proposed disposition of contract audit report recommendations differs significantly from the recommendations themselves. These are covered in DoD Directive No. 7640.2.)

The project engineer should contribute knowledge of design and of the offeror's technical approach as these influence costs and should have opinions on materials and engineering hours, particularly. However, the opinions, as well as those of all other specialists, must not be accepted without evaluation and testing.

The ACO convenes a team when given responsibility for completing certain pricing actions. The team functions in the same manner as described for the PCO. The ACO, or a pricing specialist, should request input from the auditor and other specialists. On certain repetitive jobs, the team usually will follow standard procedures developed locally to handle certain kinds of jobs. Spare parts and support equipment lend themselves to a standard approach.

The pricing team has only one spokesman. This may be the contracting officer, a contract specialist, or a price analyst. One spokesman means one quarterback to call the plays; it does not mean a one-man effort. The specialists are there to help the spokesman.

During factfinding they feed questions as the company's representatives explain their position. One of the specialists may take over at the spokesman's request and handle the inquiry into the factual basis for projections of certain costs. Specialists listen, and during recesses suggest areas for further exploration and recommend conclusions regarding types and amounts of costs.

In the final negotiation session, the roles are much the same; the spokesman is still calling the shots, and the others are standing by to help and counsel. But at this point the spokesman is less likely to let others do much talking, except during caucuses. The principal reason for this change is that it becomes tactically more critical for the team to present a single front and move in a single direction; this is sometimes difficult when there is unrestrained participation. We will return to this point later.

Factfinding

Factfinding closely follows the first analysis of an offer. When cost analysis is required, this first analysis breaks the proposal apart and lays open its details for searching examination. The first cut raises questions and reveals areas to be explored in detail.

As the name says, you look for facts to establish comparability with other products or services so as to be able to analyze the price or prices offered. When cost or pricing data are submitted and cost analysis is required, you go for two kinds of facts. First, you want to establish the actual costs of doing the same kinds of tasks, one benchmark against which you measure the probable future costs under the upcoming contract. Second, you try to isolate the assumptions and judgments the offeror has actually made in getting from indicated current to probable future costs.

Factfinding may be done in several ways. If the problems are defined clearly, you may be able to set down questions to ask and specific facts and analyses to develop and let specialists do the digging. You may have to go over the proposal with the offeror's estimators, engineers, accountants, production people, and others to understand their problems and their approaches and to know where to look in greater depth. Such preliminary negotiations are not intended to end in an agreement on anything, although a factfinding session could end in an understanding or agreement on the factual basis from which the offeror projected the costs of contract performance.

Factfinding may be the first stage of a two-stage negotiation conference, with a short interval between stages to permit the Government negotiator to evaluate the facts, establish a negotiation objective, and get necessary clearances. This might be the procedure on smaller, less complicated procurements where considerable historical data, including prices, exist. For other procurements there may be a very clear break between factfinding and negotiation -- a recess taken to run down leads, make necessary explorations, and digest the acquired information.

Objectives

Factfinding should resolve all questions of fact and all disagreements about cost or pricing data. Hopefully, the remaining areas of disagreement will be staked out and the dollars at issue identified. The differences that exist now are differences of opinion as to value, as to what will happen, and as to the significance of particular facts. Points of view asserted in the final negotiation may still lead to some changes in your ideas about a fair and reasonable price, but the relative positions are fairly well defined.

In addition, you probably are not firmly committed to one set of ideas about costs, profits, and price. For example, you may have defined the possibilities and come up with different prices for different situations. One would be the price if all went well and if certain machining processes worked out as hoped. Another would be the price if all predicted events took place but not as soon as hoped for. A third might be the "worst case" situation. These possibilities and the associated probabilities reflect the relative uncertainties of the procurement and help you measure your confidence in any given estimate.

On the other hand, the issues might not be clearly defined and the achievement of a certain cost level will depend not on any breakthrough or fortuitous combination of circumstances but rather on how well the offeror can do the job and control costs. You know that you are dealing with estimates and probabilities, and that actuals can and probably will vary from what you think is a really tight and good estimate.

You are dealing with a range, therefore, and you are trying to create a contractual climate in which the company will control and then reduce costs at the same time it maintains quality and makes timely delivery. You should express your objective as a number and qualify that number with a range of probable outcomes.

For instance, you may have concluded that the work should be done for $275,000 but you also acknowledge that the final cost might be as low as $230,000 or as high as $300,000. If these expectations are reasonable, you should tailor the proposed contract to them. A further consideration must be the company's offer and what you think the company is likely to accept, but this should influence your strategy, not your objective. If you expect it will be hard to sell your objective to the company, you should have various contract packages ready to offer.

When you acknowledge that you are talking a range of costs or prices rather than a single final cost or a single objective, you open up some interesting areas. Going back to the $275,000 figure, assume that you think an incentive arrangement fits the situation, and assume that you tailor it this way:

Target cost	$275,000
Target profit	35,000
Target price	$310,000
Ceiling	$325,000
Share	60/40

Assume also that the range of your cost expectations is $230,000 to $300,000. (If $275,000 seems too small for an incentive contract, add another set of zeros.) This arrangement is illustrated in Figure 8-1.

Chapter 8 ASPM

FIGURE 8-1. PROPOSED FPI CONTRACT DEMONSTRATING RANGE OF PROBABILITY

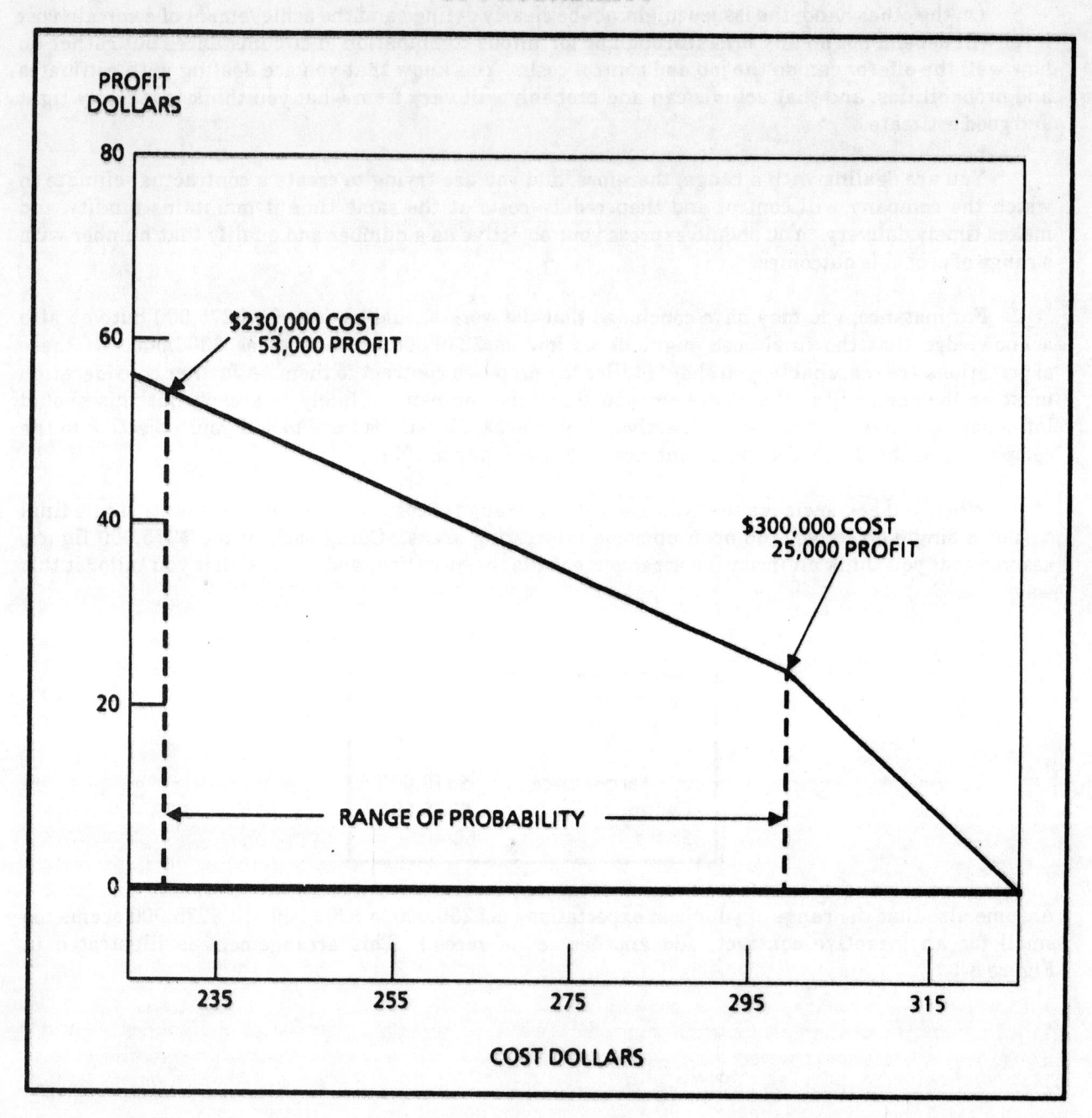

If this is your counteroffer, you are in effect saying that you are willing to write a contract with this arrangement:

Target cost	$230,000
Target profit	53,000
Target price	$283,000
Ceiling	$325,000
Share	60/40

Or this:

Target cost	$300,000
Target profit	25,000
Target price	$325,000
Ceiling	Same
Share	0/100 overrun
	60/40 underrun

Or an arrangement using any other combination of cost and profit read off the chart.

With these factors of plus 9 to minus 16 percent from target of $275,000, an FFP arrangement probably would not be a reasonable alternative. Your objective would be FPI and your negotiation flexibility would come from variations in targets, share, and ceiling. Of course, you may change in the negotiation conference.

For example, assume you recheck all the facts and conclude that a more realistic estimate is $280,000 and that the probable variation is plus or minus 4 percent. In this case, you might propose an FFP arrangement of $310,000 or $315,000. Because you are offering a price well within the range you had when you went into negotiations, it is the narrowing of the range of probable variance from estimate that gives you the confidence needed to talk FFP. The numbers are the same, but your evaluation of the situation has changed significantly.

Prenegotiation review

This talk about the negotiation conference illustrates some characteristics of an objective and some things that might cause you to agree to an arrangement different from the one you went in with. Let's back off for a moment and discuss a vital step that should be taken between the time you come up with a price objective and the time you enter into negotiations with the offeror.

Good sense tells you to touch base with your superior, to tell your boss about your objective, how you developed it, and why a contract within some range of that objective would be a reasonable proposition. However, chances are that the decision to touch base is not yours to make; most procurement organizations require some supervisory review before starting negotiations or consummating an agreement.

The larger the procurement, or the more important and far-reaching it may be in its effect, the higher this review will go in the organization and the more formal will be its requirements and procedures. The principle is the same, however, regardless of level.

The review is conducted so that management (your boss) can be assured you have done your homework and are entering into negotiations with a well-conceived and realistic plan. From your point of view, the advantage of the review is the opportunity to get policy guidance and management support in the handling of particular problems. Don't discount the chance it gives you to show your abilities, either.

The review can be a five-minute rundown of the facts and the objective if it is a small deal and if you're talking to your immediate supervisor. It can be a formal, flip chart/vugraph presentation by the team to an assembly of top procurement managers. It can be a written justification and request for clearance to proceed. From your point of view, departmental regulations will have set up the requirement and you will have no choice.

Your interest is in selling management on your intentions, taking care not to box yourself in on a specific, single objective. You must have room to negotiate, freedom to move up or down from your objective as the facts and circumstances change in negotiation. You might well want to suggest, if no one else does, that you check back before reaching agreement if the arrangement you are prepared to accept is significantly different from any of the alternatives discussed in the prenegotiation review.

Conference

We've said that there may not be a clear break between the factfinding session and the negotiation conference. Before beginning the negotiation conference, you will explore, develop, and confirm your understanding of facts, what conclusions, if any, are conjectures based on your interpretations of the facts, and what the areas of disagreement are, as well as their dollar magnitude. Having done these things, you will have established the basis for agreement because you will know if a reasonable, realistic contract is possible.

8.5 Negotiation

Thus far we have addressed essentials of contract price negotiation. The rest of this chapter is devoted to ideas you may find useful in conducting contract price negotiations.

Price negotiation – a discussion of techniques

Broadly speaking, there are two ways to negotiate agreement on a contract price: (1) cost element by cost element or (2) total price. When analysis of estimated costs is not required, the second way is the only possible way. When cost analysis is performed, both ways are open. Nevertheless, only one, total price negotiation, is the technique to use.

Your task is to establish a price objective by:

    a.   Careful review and evaluation of the estimated costs supporting the offeror's price proposal, element by element and in total.

    b.   Evaluation of current and past prices for the same or similar product or service.

    c.   Value analysis or eyeballing.

    d.   Factfinding. You discuss and question cost elements, profit, design and production problems, delivery schedule, and data requirements; in short, any and all matters likely to influence the cost of performing the contract. You do this with the offeror to understand the factual bases for the proposal, the estimating assumptions, and the factory, engineering, purchasing, and administrative operations represented by the costs.

    e.   Establishing, with the help and agreement of a pricing team and the concurrence of management, a price objective.

With a price objective and management's go-ahead, you can start the negotiation conference. Your efforts are directed toward reaching agreement with the offeror on all contract terms and conditions, saving price and pricing arrangement for last.

Good technique says you will summarize the relative position of each party and review and restate the facts as verified during factfinding. You will point out specific areas of difference as to costs and present the facts and judgments that support your position and your counterproposal. To move from there to agreement, you do not have to get the offeror's separate agreement on an exact value for each element supporting the price.

To put this in perspective, consider that both you and the offeror usually start negotiations with separate understandings of the significance of the cost experience (relevant data showing what it has cost to do work similar to the proposed contract task) and of estimates of the cost of the new work.

Cost experience is factual and serves as the basis for the offeror's cost or pricing data. These data must be accurate, complete, and current and usually are derived from the company's books and accounting records. Auditors can tell you whether the books and records display costs accurately and are therefore not misleading. Because you are dealing with facts, there is no reason for you to disagree on what costs have been or on how these costs should be distributed.

The second factor -- estimates of the cost to do the new work -- is essentially a judgment about the company's future performance and its ability to control and reduce contract costs and how likely some events are to occur. In evaluating estimates, you must reach conclusions about future events, consider probabilities, and weigh the cost impact of divergent actions. This means you must depend on cost projections and trends and assess how risks should be distributed, how much potential there is for cost reduction, and how you can use this potential in negotiating price. These assessments require judgments on matters that cut across individual cost elements and may be unrelated to any specific cost element.

There are obvious reasons why you and the offeror will differ in your views of future events. You are expected to work toward an objective that will require the contractor to exert positive efforts in order to earn a fair profit. In presenting your version of a reasonable price, you tend to minimize the difficulties and the likelihood that unfavorable events will occur.

On the other hand, the company can be expected to work toward achieving a negotiation objective based on the occurrence of what it asserts will be unfavorable events. You rarely will agree with the contractor's estimates, and the contractor will not often agree with yours. However, both estimates should be founded on the same factual basis. Further, both parties should bargain in the understanding that the total of an estimate is a sum of possibilities, not certainties, and they should recognize that a compromise of extremes may be necessary to a fair settlement.

Viewed in this perspective, it becomes clear that you may severely hamper negotiations if you attempt to reach a separate agreement on each cost element. Separate agreements are uneconomical and tend to lead to higher prices for the following reasons:

   a.   Separate agreements generally are consecutive rather than concurrent. This makes it difficult to give proper consideration to pricing possibilities that cut across cost elements. You tend to lose sight of important relationships between cost elements. Further, it is wasteful of time and money to agree on element A only to find in negotiating B, factors that cause you to reopen A and then, having agreed to A and B, to find in negotiating C that you must reopen A and B, and so forth. A worse consequence of this tangle is the frequent failure to see the need to reopen discussions on earlier elements. This failure generally results when you lose the ability to separate the important from the unimportant.

   b.   Separate agreements frequently cause other substantial delays in negotiations, in addition to those just described. Bargaining impasses on a number of separate cost elements can result. Reasonable trade-offs are discouraged, and the offeror insists on contingency allowances for each cost element rather than a reasonable contingency factor applicable to all elements. You tend to lose bargaining power in those areas where the offeror is unyielding if you have already agreed on elements where the offeror is relatively acquiescent.

   c.   Separate agreements on individual cost elements keep you from reaching a proper balance among the other elements of the contract pricing arrangement, all of which are interrelated and each of which is related to the total cost estimate. All these elements (price, contract type, profit sharing arrangement, and any limitations on profit or price) must be balanced if the price is to be a sound one.

   d.   Separate agreements are apt to lead to bad pricing. The end result might be a seductively flawless package of discrete cost elements with the cost experience and cost projection factors, including contingencies, precisely defined for each element. All you need to do is add a profit element and the price is complete. Herein lies the seduction: everything adds up so precisely that there is no apparent need for the powerful negotiating leverage that price analysis and total price negotiation so often provide.

   The fact is that the sum of cost estimates and profit, no matter how carefully drawn and analyzed, may miss being a sound and equitable price by a wide margin. This is shown time after time when competition is introduced into a situation that has been sole-source. An analysis of cost effectiveness and value, either opposing or complementing cost analysis, can lead to substantially lower price objectives than those indicated by a simple addition of the separate cost and contingency elements. The technique of negotiating separate agreement on each cost element, with its forced compartmentalization of contingencies, points in the opposite direction.

   e.   If the cost is controversial, there is nothing to be gained from trying to get the offeror to agree to exclude some or all of it from the estimate. You are better off if you conserve your energies and arguments to sell your counteroffer on the total package. Your counteroffer obviously will be at a price level that excludes the costs you consider unreasonable or unallowable. The offeror doesn't have to agree to those exclusions, even if it can accept the price. An offeror will frequently concede dollars when it will not concede principles; the total-price technique is designed to make it possible to do so.

Negotiation of multi-item contracts

   So far we have talked about a negotiation objective and negotiation of total price in terms of a single, distinct item of work and not total contract price. For instance, in an earlier example in this chapter, we talked about negotiation in terms of the unit and total prices of 100 electrogyros and not 100 gyros plus spare parts, handling equipment, and handbooks. Many negotiations will cover several different items or tasks, each of which will be priced out on the contract schedule. When this is the case, or when you are negotiating the prices of a long list of spare parts, you have to negotiate in such a way that you do not lose sight of the values of the individual items.

To illustrate, assume you are buying end items, spare end items, spare parts, special tools and handling equipment, handbooks and manuals, engineering drawings, and training devices. You get an SF 1411 from the offeror and as many cost breakdowns (contract pricing proposals) as necessary to cover the various items. While you are concerned with what it is going to cost to buy all those items, you must end up with prices for each item identified in the schedule, and each of those prices must be reasonable for the product to which it relates. Costs have meaning in pricing only when they can be related to the effort that causes the costs to be incurred.

This means that unit costs must be the language of analysis, even when other factors make it necessary to negotiate on a total contract rather than an item basis. In this situation, your offers and counteroffers should be the sum of the prices for each of the contract items, and you should insist that the company do it the same way.

Tracking

You write a price negotiation memorandum (PNM) to demonstrate that the negotiated price is fair and reasonable. The PNM takes the reader from the proposal to the negotiation objective and ultimately to the contract price. In doing this, it will show clearly and unmistakably the cost or pricing data used in the process and certified to at the completion of negotiations. This will include both the initial SF 1411 submission and what was submitted later in writing. The transition from one point to the next must be explained; you must show the facts and explain the judgments that moved you from proposal to objective to agreement.

You will have collected a lot of paper by the time you've finished negotiations. You'll have the contract price proposal, supporting schedules, subcontractor cost or pricing data, identification of the source of other data, and revised and supplementary data. The data will have come from the company.

You'll also have reports and work papers from Government personnel who have looked into the company data. Taken together, the two groups of data should tell what data were submitted and which were considered to be factual and a suitable basis for projection.

This won't be the whole story. You also will have to show in the narrative portion of the PNM how you got from facts, to objective, to the price agreed to. This will mean an identification of significant factual data, explanation of how the facts influenced your estimates of future costs, and what factors persuaded you that your number was a good one to use.

You also will have to identify the data you did not use, did not rely on, including any cost or pricing data you found to be inaccurate, incomplete, or noncurrent.

People have said that you can't reconstruct the events of the negotiation to show how the cost or pricing data submitted by the offeror influenced the price negotiated unless you have negotiated on an element-by-element basis, agreeing to specific values for each element of cost.

This is not true if you use the technique of negotiating total price properly and your PNM reports what happened. To illustrate, look at this excerpt from the PNM written by Tammy Watkins, the Government negotiator on the Garsap procurement discussed at the start of this chapter:

	CONTRACTOR'S PROPOSAL	GOVERNMENT OBJECTIVE	NEGOTIATED*
Material	$1,300	$1,200	$1,275
Manufacturing labor	1,125	925	925
Manufacturing overhead	2,025	1,625	1,625
Engineering labor	350	320	350
Engineering overhead	315	270	300
Factory cost	$5,115	$4,340	$4,475
G&A	155	130	135
Total cost	$5,270	$4,470	$4,610
Profit	730	670	690
Unit price	$6,000	$5,140	$5,300*

*Agreement was reached on $5,300 per unit, but not on each element in this column. Derivation of values for the costs will be explained in the narrative portion of this memorandum.

This shows what happened, in summary. The accompanying narrative explains each element in detail, identifying the sources of data for the proposal and showing updated costs that, in the case of material, confirmed the validity of the contractor's estimate except for the $25 by which the estimate exceeded a supplier's firm quote. It shows for labor the actual hours of manufacturing labor expended and indicates the "as of" date for the latest reading of costs. It reports the team's position that a different starting point and steeper slope in the learning curve gave a more realistic estimate of hours and shows how the updated actual hours confirmed the team's original estimate.

Each element of cost was discussed in the negotiations, and Tammy Watkins was able to redefine her real differences with Garsap. As a result, after talking and asserting the merits of her position on each cost element, Watkins concluded she could move from her original ideas, to the extent indicated in the "negotiated" column and explained in the narrative. Accordingly, she made a counteroffer to Garsap and finally reached agreement at a unit price of $5,300.

An orderly negotiation, together with a carefully constructed PNM, will provide a map adequate for anyone seeking to reconstruct the events of the past and to assess the consequences of error, oversight, or willfully misleading actions on the part of the offeror.

Gamesmanship

There are many gambits and ploys available in negotiation. They have names like:

> Making the Other Party Appear Unreasonable
> Putting the Other Party on the Defensive
> Blaming a Third Party
> The Sugar-Vinegar Device
> Straw Issues
> The Walkout
> The Recess
> The Here It Is Friday Afternoon and You've Got to Catch the Plane Squeeze

Perhaps you are familiar with these tools of the bargaining process, having either used them or having had them used on you. These tactics and other strategems of negotiation are employed regularly (and many times unknowingly) in the process of arriving at mutually satisfactory agreements as buyers and sellers shape their respective positions.

Principles

There are also certain principles that should govern your negotiating practices. These will be mentioned briefly.

Relationships with Contractors

Successful negotiation demands that you establish and maintain sound, cooperative, and mutually respectful relationships with contractors. Merchandise can't be sold in an atmosphere of distrust and deception; neither can your ideas, opinions, and objectives. Successful negotiation depends on your ability to sell yourself and your position; because of this you may need to set the tone for the conference. Any indication of distrust, any flat, unsupported statements that the price is too high, any prolonged questioning in areas that are irrelevant are clearly out of order and will weaken your position and lessen your chances of success. In factfinding and negotiations your review and questions must not degenerate into an effort to prove the offeror wrong.

Individuality

How you actually plan and conduct a negotiation is your choice. There is no one way to do it. As with anything else, you must establish your own style, do what is right for you. You may want to use different approaches with different companies. In most cases you should use different approaches with the same company, particularly if you deal regularly and repetitively with the same people. It is usually a mistake to let your approaches and reactions become predictable.

Basically, this refers to how you dress up your objectives when you make a counteroffer. One negotiator may come in with an offer way below the objective. Another deals in ranges, and any counteroffer will be from the low end of the range. A third may come out flat, after discussions, with a counteroffer that is the same as the objective. There is nothing wrong with any one of these, if it fits, but you may get better results if you use one or both of the others, from time to time.

Policy in Negotiations

DoD procurement policies are rules for you to follow, but they are not necessarily policies and rules that the offeror must live by. The parties to a negotiation may never agree on policies and rules, but they can agree on a mutually satisfactory contract at a mutually satisfactory price.

When DoD policy has a bearing on a position you take, you must know that policy and should know why it exists, the circumstances that led to its formulation, and why it applies to the case at hand. You should be prepared, without necessarily identifying it as a policy, to review in detail the reasons why it makes good sense to apply it. This obviously is intended to put the offeror in position to accept your counteroffer even though it might not accept the policy.

Conversely, you should not throw an unexplained policy on the table as an obstacle in the path of the company. If you operate this way, you can expect the company to respond in kind.

Citing Higher Authority

Indiscriminate use of "It looks good to me, but I can't get my boss to buy it" can lead to confusion and weakening of your negotiating position. You have certain review and approval channels through which you must take your negotiated agreement before it comes out as a contract, but companies know that and have every right to expect you to be able to make a decision and sell it up through whatever channels are required. The prenegotiation review procedure is your insurance and the company's assurance that this can be done. If you abuse the higher-authority citation, the contractor quite properly may try to negotiate directly with that authority.

The point is clear: you are negotiating as a representative of the Government and you are supported by all echelons of the Government. As long as you operate within established policies and procedures, you need not quote anyone. Your comments and positions in negotiations must be yours and not those of someone higher up the ladder.

This is not to say you should not clear all questionable items with higher authority; in some instances, that is what recesses are for. If you are to complete the negotiation effectively and in good time, you must be the authority, as far as the company's negotiator is concerned, and the only contact for negotiating contracts. It may help to remember that the company's negotiator probably has to clear certain matters with management, that the negotiator's authority is limited.

Precedent

Precedent can be an enormously restrictive factor in negotiations, because it frequently establishes patterns that outlive their usefulness. You must be guided by what makes sense for the procurement you are negotiating, and not by patterns you and others may have created on earlier deals. This covers the whole range of treatment of particular costs, of use of the particular rates, of taking certain positions, the works.

Look at each negotiation as if it were the first one you had ever had with the company. Obviously, you don't make new rules each time out, and if it's a pricing action on a contract in being, you don't ignore the understandings and conditions of the agreement on the contract package itself. But you should bring new and current thinking to each negotiation and measure these ideas against precedent so you can come up with better contractual arrangements.

Collaboration

The negotiator should hold a prenegotiation conference with team members. The purpose is to discuss and develop a position on all important aspects and to agree generally on the role each will play during negotiations with the company. Also, from time to time during a negotiation, you can expect team members to reach different conclusions because of varying interpretations of matters discussed.

Forewarn team members to avoid public disagreement, but if controversy arises, get the team together, away from the company's representatives, to consult and give each one the chance to talk. You have the right and obligation of the final decision, but you should accept and use the help specialists offer. There cannot always be full agreement among all team members in the conclusions reached and the counteroffers made, but there should be a minimum of disagreement and no misunderstandings.

It also follows that you should always present the company's representatives with at least the appearance of unanimity. There should be no airing of differences among the Government team when it meets with the offeror.

ASPM
Chapter 8

Don't-but-do

The following list repeats some of the ideas already mentioned and provides some helpful hints and reminders:

a. Don't dictate, negotiate. You represent the Government; be a reasonable person.

b. Don't expose anyone to ridicule or insult.

c. Don't try to make anyone look bad.

d. Don't be predictable in your approach.

e. Do be discriminating. Accept a good offer. Don't feel you always have to knock something off the price.

f. Do fight hard on the important points; win the war, not the battles. Don't start fights you have no chance of winning or which, if you do win, would not be worth the fight.

g. Do remember you usually are in at least as good a negotiating position as the company's representatives. The resources of the Government are extensive, and the diversified experience you gain doing business with many companies can give you what you may lack in depth of knowledge of a single company's situation. The company usually needs your business at least as much as you need its product or service.

h. Do be courteous and considerate. Do what you say you will. Have integrity.

i. Do know when to talk and when to listen. Do stop talking when you've made your point, won your case, reached agreement.

j. Do remember that negotiation is a two-way street and that prenegotiation preparation is the most important attribute of successful buying.

8.6 The Need for Documentation

A contract pricing action must be supported by written evidence that the price is fair and reasonable. This evidence must be detailed enough to reflect the most significant considerations shaping the pricing arrangement.

We are concerned here with the pricing records for all procurements other than those placed by sealed bids. We also are primarily concerned with written communications. As standard practice, requests for information and help in contract pricing should be in writing.

Earlier segments of this manual have covered the elements of contract pricing, from contract type through price, cost, and profit analysis techniques to negotiation of the contract arrangement. We now are looking at the various written communications that support the contract pricing effort and report on the results of the preliminary work. We set up guidelines to follow when you ask for pricing help, report the results of price and cost analyses, describe the development of the negotiation objective, and summarize the results of the negotiation conference.

Reports of analysis and other responses to requests for specific information contribute to the factual basis for deciding that the offered price is fair and reasonable or for setting the price objective if a negotiation conference is necessary. The PNM and any supporting reports of analysis are used in the reviews that precede approval of the proposed contract.

For these reasons, and because of the number of procurements, personnel turnover, and use of contract files in succeeding procurements and in historical and investigational research, these reports and memorandums must permit a rapid reconstruction of all major considerations of the particular pricing effort.

To restate this very important principle: the official contract file must include a written document that demonstrates clearly and conclusively that the price is right. In making this demonstration, the document must show all the significant facts that were considered in reaching agreement with the company. It also must indicate the extent to which the data submitted were not considered or, although considered, were not relied on in reaching agreement.

The document, with its attachments, must identify the cost or pricing data submitted or otherwise acquired and used in the process. It must be complete enough in its narrative to show how the facts influenced your judgments about future costs. It must show how you got from contractor-furnished cost or pricing data, to Government objective, to agreed-to price. It must show the updated costs, new facts, and new interpretations of old facts that persuaded you to move from your negotiation objective, if in fact you did, to the price agreed to.

A pricing communication is intended either to get or to give information. A request for information must be clear, precise, and to the point. The same is true for the response. However, because truisms won't get the job done, we will present standard formats for various pricing communications and give you a few basic do's and don'ts.

The amount of documentation needed depends on the type of action. If the contract award is made after price analysis, the documentation need not be as elaborate and detailed as for an award made after both price and cost analysis. We will cover documentation for price analysis actions first and then take up more involved documentation.

8.7 Documenting Price Analysis

You document in order to show that the contract price is fair and reasonable. You do this by showing the price the contractor offered, the data used to evaluate the offer, and the conclusions reached, and by explaining why the conclusions were sound ones.

The person performing a price analysis prepares a report. This person may be a buyer, a contract negotiator, a contracting officer, a price analyst, or some other individual. The price analysis may give a sufficient basis for deciding that the price is fair and reasonable. However, when price analysis is not enough, cost analysis is needed; the price analysis will include any investigations undertaken to corroborate the findings and conclusions of the cost analysis. Reports of these investigations generally will be incorporated into the PNM.

If an abstract of proposals is required and the facts shown in it demonstrate the presence of competition and the basis for award, there is no need to write a separate pricing report. When a PNM is needed, you must set forth the facts and circumstances that caused you to agree to the price. The recital should be short; how short will depend on the facts, how far you had to go before reaching a decision, and how much self-discipline you have. Two examples of acceptable memos are:

a. "Apex, Inc., quoted a unit price of $275 for 12 MA-1 generators to be delivered two months after contract award. Offers were solicited from four companies. Apex was the only responder. Unit price of $275 is $5 less than the price of 20 MA-1 generators on contract -1234 awarded to Apex 10 months ago. Award of -1234 was made to Apex, the lowest offeror, after analysis of competitive proposals received from three other companies: Acme, Epitome, and Excel. Based on favorable comparison with the competitively established firm fixed price of $280, unit price of $275 is considered fair and reasonable."

    b.   "Proposals for 15 coolers were solicited from three firms. The abstract of proposals shows the companies and the quoted prices. Ace Distributors quoted a price of $423, manufacturer's list less 10 percent, that was $80 lower than the next lowest offer. Ace's list price in its current catalog is $470, and 10-percent discount is customary in the trade. Award was made to Ace on this basis."

The principle is this: unless it has been made unnecessary by documentation such as a self-explanatory abstract of proposals, you will put in the contract or purchase order file a memo detailed enough to convince the reader that the price is fair and reasonable. It is not enough for you to say, "The proposal was reviewed in detail and I have concluded that the price is fair and reasonable. Janis Jacklin, Buyer." Another unacceptable memorandum is the kind that says, in its entirety, "The price of $50 is fair and reasonable because it is $5 less than the last procurement. Byron Bliss, Buyer."

If a comparison with past prices is the basis for concluding that the price is fair and reasonable, show prices, quantities, sources, contract type, date, production or delivery schedules (if known), and reasons why the previous prices are good standards for comparison.

If reasonableness of price is established by comparison with a catalog price and discount schedule, state the facts and show the catalog price if it is different from the offer. The same rule applies when an item (brand name or competing products of a similar nature) is available from several sources. State the market price or market price range if it is different from the offer. If reasonableness is established by comparison with a Government estimate, state this fact, list the estimated figure, and tell why the estimate is a valid basis for comparison.

If reasonableness is established, ultimately, by telephone or face-to-face negotiations with the offeror(s), describe the offer(s), your objective, and the negotiated price and summarize the principal reasons for reaching agreement on the price and making the award. If it is necessary to award at the offered price, even though you are not completely satisfied with it, describe the efforts you made to establish another basis for award and the reasons why they didn't work.

8.8 Documenting Larger Procurements

For the rest of this chapter, we will look most closely at situations where the dollars and the nature of the procurement are such that pricing assistance is obtained from outside the procurement activity. We assume that in these situations cost analysis will be necessary and that price analysis input from the field will be limited. We also assume that the decision about who will write a particular kind of report will be based on direction and guidance in standard operating procedures (SOPs) or in other parts of this manual.

Roles of team members

We can summarize the roles this way:

    a.   The contracting officer, in the RFP, asks offerors to use SFs 1411 to submit proposals and supporting cost or pricing data. An offeror is the primary source for its cost or pricing data, and the data are as much a part of the proposal as the price, delivery schedules, and other terms and conditions. These data include both prime and subcontractor data.

    b.   The contracting officer requests technical and field pricing assistance, but a contract price analyst in the procurement organization may make the request in the contracting officer's name. If there is no price analyst, the requestor may be the negotiator or the buyer. Requests for specialized pricing assistance come from the person responsible for the price decision or from someone designated by that person.

c.   The ACO, or a price analyst in contract administration, requests cost analyses from the auditor and other specialists. The requests will be for information that either the PCO or the ACO, when functioning as a PCO, needs. The ACO or the designated price analyst collects and consolidates the several reports, adding comments and analyses as needed, and forwards them to the PCO. If the negotiation will be done by the ACO, the separate reports of analysis will be used to develop a negotiation objective.

d.   The auditor prepares a report after reviewing the facts and evaluating the projections of future costs. This is done by reviewing the contractor's books and records. The auditor reports on any other facts that may have a significant bearing on the proposed price. The auditor is not limited to those data submitted or identified in writing by the offeror. The auditor may comment on cost or pricing data not submitted by the offeror that may have a significant effect on the proposed contract price. Further, if the cost or pricing data submitted are not accurate, current, or complete, the auditor sets the information out in the audit report.

e.   Technical reports are written by specialists working in contract administration, when asked by the contracting officer. They report findings that result from applying their special knowledge to elements of the proposal. The auditor includes any financial effect of these findings in the report. Any differences between technical and audit analyses, such as projections of direct labor hours using learning curves, are presented to the contracting officer.

f.   A PNM is written by the contracting officer, or more likely, by another person named to do it. Again, depending upon the organization, this may be the price analyst, negotiator, or buyer. In any event, it is an individual who actively participated in negotiating the pricing arrangement.

There are two major types of pricing reports: those written before negotiations and those written after. The ensuing discussion of report formats makes specific suggestions about what kind of comments and information to include in what parts of the reports. In this we are not always consistent and complete. For example, the content of a PNM for the final settlement of an incentive contract would be different from the PNM for the initial negotiation of the same contract. We have not always made that distinction in discussing the content; to do so would result in considerable repetition to no real advantage.

We say no real advantage because the principal variable is the amount of actual cost data available in the different pricing situations. The existence of actual costs of the contract being negotiated or from preceding contracts has a distinct bearing on the way the analysis is made and the way negotiations are conducted. The auditor's report tells what was done and how the available cost experience was used. The other cost analysis reports do the same.

The PNM summarizes the actual negotiation proceedings; if actual costs were available, they would have been a factor in analysis and would have helped shape the objective. As a consequence, actual costs will be reported in the PNM. Despite this general disclaimer, we do provide suggestions about the proper place for particularly meaningful comparisons of actual and estimated costs, or of incurred-to-date and total estimated costs.

Requests for proposals (RFPs)

RFPs will specify the kind and extent of pricing information the offeror must submit to support its proposal. To make sure this gets done and done right, a contract price analyst should be in the act early in the planning stage to help with this part of the RFP. The RFP should tell the offeror to use

A-138

the SF 1411 and to return a complete package so that you won't have to ask repeatedly for data or spend a lot of time digging out the necessary factual information.

If you have repeated negotiations with a company, you probably should work out an agreement with the company on the detail it will furnish with its proposals. The level of detail can be tailored even more if Government people are assigned to the plant. The resident people can help by pointing out potential problems and the specific information that should be requested.

Requests for information and assistance

Request pricing assistance as soon as possible in the procurement cycle. If the procurement has been programmed and constitutes an important part of your organization's total workload, you may want to line up the necessary field pricing support for both prime and subcontract proposals before the RFP is prepared. Required data can be anticipated and requested in the RFP so the necessary work can be scheduled on an orderly basis. In other instances, generally on smaller, more routine procurements, requests for field assistance can wait until you have received the proposal and are satisfied that the proposal is complete and requires field review.

Requests for assistance must be specific about the areas to be evaluated, the type of information wanted, and the time available for the analysis. Give the field as much time as you can. If you are particularly concerned with the estimated material cost, you might ask for an analysis limited to the cost of material. For example, your request might read like this:

"Material accounts for about half the total estimate. I need to know how that estimate was developed. Are the quantities realistic? How do scrap and obsolescence factors compare with the company's recent experience? What are the trends? How is material priced? How current are the prices that are used? How are sources selected?"

At the same time, you might ask a different specialist for some other information, and that request might read like this:

"We've asked for an analysis of the quantities and prices of the material estimate. We sent you a copy of that request. In addition, we need your help on yield. What is the ratio of number of units put into production to the number of acceptable finished units coming out? Is this an acceptable yield for this product? Is the company doing anything to get and keep the rate within acceptable limits? Is the estimated yield within this figure? Please include any other specifics dealing with material such as kinds and quantities of material, particular problems in machining and assembling parts and components, and quality and delivery problems with suppliers. Negotiations are tentatively set for the 25th, which is three weeks from this Tuesday. We need your answers by the 19th."

The rule is to be as specific as possible when requesting information and assistance. To do this, you must know something about the product or service being procured and its cost. You also limit the area of review as much as possible to expedite the response. However, you can only tell the specialist what it is that bothers you, what questions you want answered, and when you need it. How he comes up with the answers is his speciality.

You are interested, of course, but only to the extent that the report must convince you that the specialist has done enough to ensure reliable answers, explored all reasonable avenues, and has not overlooked any significant factors. You should never go out with a general "Give me an analysis of this proposal" request unless you know nothing about the company or the problems that you may encounter in analysis and negotiation.

To restate: Be as specific as possible about what you want done; limit the area of analysis whenever possible; set a due date for the reply; and recognize that while you can prescribe what you want, you cannot limit the scope of review. Many proposals do not need complete analysis. Recent negotiations with the same company may have established a basis for negotiation of the current proposal. You may need only the latest, most current information on direct costs, with only limited verification of labor and indirect cost rates.

Requests for analysis of particular cost elements by engineers, packaging technicians, inspectors, and others also must be specific. Conservation of their time is one, but not necessarily the most important, reason. The more specific the request, the more responsive will be the answer. It is not enough to get an answer in the jargon of the specialist; you must be able to understand and use it.

Another basic ground rule is that you buy hardware and services, not costs, and it is the ultimate cost you are concerned with. Your objective in requesting pricing support is to have a factual basis for determining the value of what you're buying. If we lose sight of this objective it is easy to find ourselves caught up in the tangle of parochial quarrels over specific costs.

Recommendations

When you are responsible for reaching an agreement with the company on a pricing arrangement, you go to others (auditor, ACO, engineer) for advice and assistance. You use what you get from them in making your decision about the proposed price and, if a negotiation conference is to follow, in developing the negotiation objective.

For this reason, you will not ask the ACO (and through the ACO, any of the field specialists) or any other persons outside your procurement office to give you a recommendation on the fairness and reasonableness of the contract as a whole or on total costs, proposed prices, or profit weights and rates. In asking for a recommendation you are asking someone else to make your decision for you, something that person may be in no position to do and something you should not delegate.

You go to these people for the facts on which to base your decision and not for the decision itself. Generally, you will know more about the overall situation and be in a better position to make these decisions. You are looking for facts and informed opinions based on facts, and you are asking the specialists for information on matters within their areas of special competence. You should not ask them to give you a negotiation objective, which is what a price recommendation at this point would amount to.

Examples will help explain what we are saying about recommendations. The field pricing package the ACO sends in should have summary conclusions like the following:

a. "A unit learning curve computer program was used to analyze the historical lot average hours. The program performs a least squares, log-log transformed linear regression to the weighted lot data points. (The data points are shown in the attached printout.) The results of the analysis indicate a slope of 83.5 percent, a T^1 of 25,892 hours, and a coefficient of determination (R^2) of .94. Projections for the proposed production units indicate that the average unit hours will be 8500 hours per unit (see attached printout). Because the proposed units are follow-on production at approximately the same rate, this projection appears to be realistic and reasonably attainable."

b. "Considering the foregoing findings about the bill of materials' prices, and correcting for the overstatement of quantity requirements, the material cost of producing this equipment should be within plus or minus 2 percent of $760 per unit."

c. "The rate of 215 percent results from the suggested deletion of $358,250 from the overhead expense pool and the addition of $210,000 to the labor base. It is realistic for the period of contract performance."

ASPM Chapter 8

What you don't want is something like this:

"Based on the foregoing, the price of $9,735 per unit is fair and reasonable and recommended for your use."

There is one other rule. You should evaluate the quality of the pricing assistance you receive. Whether the reports are good or bad, you should give the sender your verdict and support it with specifics. Otherwise, the sender may operate with no sure knowledge of whether he has satisfied your needs and may assume, in the absence of evidence to the contrary, that he is doing a good job.

Unless departmental procedures require written prenegotiation clearance, written records before negotiations generally will be restricted to field pricing reports from the auditor and the ACO. Separate written price analysis reports, as distinguished from cost reports, may be in order when cost analysis is not needed and the reasonableness of the price can be established without negotiation.

Cost analysis reports, together with the offeror's cost or pricing data, are the other records used to form a prenegotiation objective. These are advisory reports, the means by which the person who made the analysis tells you what he found. What you do with this information is your business and your responsibility. The advisory reports should identify what was analyzed, what factual data (not already identified by the offeror in its contract pricing proposal) were used in the analysis, what conclusions were reached, and what reasons support the conclusions.

Ordinarily, conclusions must be expressed in terms of dollars or percentages if they are to be useful. An analyst who concludes that the offeror has overestimated the labor hours needed to do the job can't stop there. The advisory report also must say what estimated hours should be and why.

You may have sensed that we're still skirting the question of whether or not the report should make a recommendation. What makes us so skittish is the people problem. If the PCO, ACO, contract price analyst, and auditor are all qualified, know and talk to each other, respect each other's abilities, and make allowances for any biases or blind spots, we really don't care how they split the job or what they say to each other. However, in the absence of these qualities, we must delineate the tasks as they are normally divided and include the prohibition that the reporter will not, unless specifically requested, make recommendations on subsequent actions or decisions.

Only when the price analyst at the procuring activity is unable to participate in the negotiation and, as a consequence, is unable to write or help write the PNM, will he need to write an analysis report before negotiations take place. If the price analyst cannot participate, the report will help the team develop its objectives and negotiate with the company.

If preliminary analysis leads to the conclusion that the offer is fair and reasonable and there is no need to hold a negotiation conference, a report will be needed. It will summarize the actions taken and give the reasons why it is sound to award without further discussion. These instances occur infrequently. Departmental procedures may require this type of report as a clearance request before authorizing completion of the contract action.

Even though you must develop an objective before entering the negotiation stage with the company, you don't need to write up the objective in a separate report unless this is required by departmental contract clearance procedures. If the negotiation objective was cleared with management using charts or transparencies, copies of the presentation will be adequate documentation. If it was cleared informally, the PNM should indicate the level of clearance.

Reporting cost analyses

The following are minimum standards to be met when reporting the results of a cost analysis. The report will include the indicated information to the extent it is available and relevant to the particular pricing action. The auditor's report always will include a review of the influence of the contractor's actual costs on the estimate/proposal. The cost analysis report also should identify the cost or pricing data reviewed.

Identification is not the chore it seems; the offeror will have completed an SF 1411 and submitted or otherwise identified much of the cost or pricing data required. The cost analysis report will identify only those additional or updated elements of data submitted in writing or otherwise acquired during the process of review.

Obviously, not all analyses will require the same detail or emphasis; length and detail will vary with the situation. The following format will be followed:

a. *What was analyzed.* Identify the company, the purchase request, the RFP or contract number, the product or service involved, the price or prices proposed, and the specific areas analyzed. If the complete proposal was analyzed, make a summary comparison of the proposal with the results of the analysis, broken down by major elements and presented in tabular form.

b. *How it was analyzed.* Show the date that the company prepared the cost estimate. Indicate, by name and title, the Government contributors to the analysis and the company personnel contacted. Describe supplies and services. Indicate delivery schedule and past delivery performance for the same or similar item. State the extent to which Government facilities will be used and whether additional facilities are required or contemplated. (If the analysis covers additional work under an existing contract, or interim or final repricing, indicate the extent of Government facilities actually used.) If a significant amount of leased plant or equipment is involved, discuss the need for the lease and the reasonableness of the terms.

In discussing particular cost elements, show how the costs were estimated. Cite current estimating methods reviews. Any time actual costs are available and relevant, show the relationships between experience and the trend projection. Clearly indicate the *as of* dates of the actuals. Direct costs of materials and labor and the amounts for special tooling and test equipment usually get close scrutiny during analysis.

Put the results in this part of the report and show how these costs were analyzed. Indicate any assumptions made by the company about prices, rates, quantities, manufacturing processes, type of tooling, rate of production, overtime, and other basic factors in the operations. Show nonrecurring and recurring costs separately, if they are relevant and identifiable.

If you used a computer to analyze data, briefly describe the program in your report. If it is well known, the name of the program may be enough; if it is not, a description probably will be necessary. A copy of the printout, including the data used, should be attached to the report. You don't have to repeat the information in the report if it is in the printout. However, between what you put in the report and what is in the printout, the recipient must be able to get the full story of what you did, what you used, and the results.

If subcontracting has been given special attention, state the basis for the estimate, the relationship of estimates to the current orders, and, if a subcontract is placed, the type of contract. If the contract type is an incentive with target and ceiling, indicate which figure was used to price the subcontract amount. Comment on the adequacy of the company's procurement procedures, stating whether the purchase methods have been reviewed and whether acknowledged weaknesses have been corrected.

Include profit in the report as a specific subject only if comments on individual costs and performance factors have not disclosed relevant information useful in assigning weights. However, the determination of weight ranges and profit dollars is the PCO's responsibility. Recommend specific weight ranges and profit dollars only in the most unusual circumstances. Analysis of facts bearing on profit factors should be reported to the PCO as a matter of course; rate recommendations should be included only upon request.

c. *Conclusions.* Conclusions will be supported by the findings of fact already reported. If there are differences in the interpretation of the data, as, for example, between the auditor and the production specialist on the need for certain types of tooling, you may acknowledge this so the PCO can know that controversy exists about the significance of certain facts.

Conclusions are not recommendations, but they may include suggestions for items and assumptions to be discussed further with the company's negotiators. They will show the relative significance of some of the reported facts and why the negotiator might need to pursue these matters in negotiations.

State why some costs are good and how much significance can be attached to the costs, particularly when projecting future events. In other words, do not concentrate on costs questioned or set aside for the contracting officer's consideration, thus blessing by inference, if not fact, the rest of the estimate.

Reports after negotiation

The PNM is the only document required after negotiations have been concluded. Its purpose is obvious. It tells the reader the story of the negotiation. What was the offer and what were the costs in the SF 1411 package? What was the Government's price objective and what were the costs supporting that goal? What cost or pricing data were submitted but not relied on and not used? What were the goals as to delivery and pricing arrangement? What was discussed? What were the compelling arguments? What disposition was made of the principal points raised in preliminary analyses, included in the objective, and discussed in the negotiations? What values, cost and other, support the agreed-to price? If these are different from those supporting the objective, what justifications are there for the difference?

The PNM is, first, a sales document that establishes the reasonableness of the agreement you have reached with the company. Second, it is the permanent record of your decision. It charts the progress from proposal through negotiations and does so in specifics.

The PNM will be the source document if it becomes necessary to reconstruct the events of the procurement. You may not be around to help, so you must leave tracks that strangers can follow. In addition to proving that the price is fair and reasonable, the PNM must identify data not relied on. It must convince the reader that you did all that needed to be and could be done to reach a fair and reasonable price.

The question of length is critical, because it is very easy to go into excessive detail in reporting the events of an extended negotiation. You must guard against this and, perhaps just as importantly, against using the jargon of the specialists involved.

This advice is somewhat fatuous, however, because ultimately you will find yourself writing for the most important of your probable readers: the individual or group that has the final say on whether the contract is approved. This will dictate the detail of your PNM and, to some extent, its style. All we can do here is to ask you and your bosses to be reasonable and strike the balance between too few words and too many.

We will provide the format to follow: subject, introductory summary, particulars, procurement situation, negotiation summary, and miscellaneous. While the format is standard, the content must vary to report the actual events of the analysis and negotiation. What events will be reported depends on whether the negotiation is to agree on the terms of a definitive contract, a definitive contract superseding a letter contract, a firm-up of an FPIS contract, new work to be added or changes to an existing contract, or the final settlement of an incentive arrangement.

The principal cause of differences among PNMs, in addition to the dollars at stake, may be the amount of actual cost and performance data available and relevant to the negotiation. The availability of the data will shape the course of analysis and tell you the kind and amounts of information to include in the PNM.

You might be right if you assumed that the more data there are, the longer the PNM, but we're not sure this relationship exists. In fact, if we were betting, we would go the other way; the existence of meaningful actual costs should make it possible to be quite precise in explaining what was done and why it made good sense to do it.

The PNM format is explained in the following subparagraphs.

a. *Subject.* This is a memorandum for many readers with different purposes, so the subject should be fairly complete. Don't address it to any particular individual or office. The subject, together with the introductory summary (the first segment of the PNM), should give the reader a complete picture of the negotiation. For example, the subject might be:

PRICE NEGOTIATION MEMORANDUM

Garsap Corporation
Dover, Oklahoma
Contract XX XXXXXXXX,
Production of M-2 Electrogyros
FY XX Funds, Case File #3145

b. *Introductory summary.* This will be the first segment of the PNM. Show the type of contract and the type of negotiation action involved, together with a comparison of the company's proposal, the Government's negotiation objective, and the negotiated results. Identify specifically the contract items included in the total figure shown as the negotiated amount. In one case you might note that items 1 through 4 are included in the total figure but are identified separately later in the PNM. In another instance a detailed item breakout might be included in the introductory summary. No matter how you do this, the information should be shown on one page. For example:

"This is the first buy of 100 each M-2 electrogyros. There was no letter contract. Negotiations were completed 16 September 19X2 with Garsap, the designer and sole manufacturer of the M-2 gyro. The Garsap proposal, the Government objective and the negotiated agreement for the total 100 gyros are compared below. Each figure is predicated on the contract being FFP.

	PROPOSED	OBJCTIVE	NEGOTIATED*
Estimated cost	$527,000	$447,000	$477,000
Estimated profit	73,000	67,000	70,000
Total price	$600,000	$514,000	$547,000
Profit rate, percent	14	15	14.7

*Figure of $547,000 was negotiated for an FFP contract. The breakout of cost and profit represents adjustments made by the Government negotiators to their objective and was not agreed to by the company. No attempt was made to get agreement."

A more involved example is:

"Negotiations to definitize subject letter contract as an FPIF arrangement were completed 9 July 19X2. The total incentive package, comparing the proposal, our objective, and the negotiated arrangement, is as follows:

	PROPOSED	OBJCTIVE	NEGOTIATED*
Target cost	$3,122,521	$2,865,000	$2,950,000
Target profit	468,380	272,200	265,500
Target price	$3,590,901	$3,137,200	$3,215,500
Profit, percent	15	9.5	9
Contract type	FPIF	FPIF	FPIF
Share:			
Over	95/5	50/50	60/40
Under	70/30	50/50	80/20
Ceiling	$4,059,277	$3,409,350	$3,422,000

Attachment 1 to this memo shows the negotiated arrangement in graphic form."

If the negotiation is the final settlement of an incentive arrangement, the initial and adjusted targets and the ceiling should be shown here. Reasons for the adjustments will be explained in the segments on the procurement situation and appropriate paragraphs of the negotiation summary.

You must make this first segment into what its title says it is: an introductory summary. The ideas exemplified above must be a part of each PNM. Complete uniformity on the opening page accomplishes many things for many people, including making comparable data from all buying activities readily available. The proposed, objective, and negotiated figures shown must be truly comparable figures representing the same elements of work. If the scope has changed, suitable adjustments should be made. These changes should be explained later in the memorandum.

c. *Particulars.* The purpose of this second segment is to cover the following without duplicating any information that was included in the Subject.

    1. Contract or purchase request number, including supplemental agreement number if appropriate.

    2. Complete name and location of company.

    3. Quantities.

    4. Unit prices quoted and negotiated. If many, attach as a schedule.

    5. Dates and places of factfinding, prenegotiation review, and negotiation.

    6. Names and titles of participants in prenegotiation review.

    7. Names and titles of company and Government personnel in attendance, identifying the principal negotiators.

d. *Procurement situation.* This is the third segment. In describing the procurement situation, include any outside influences and time pressures. Show the delivery schedule or period of performance. If there is a difference between the schedule desired or required and that proposed by the company, discuss the resolution or compromise, if any. If the pricing is prospective, state the type of contract contemplated in the RFP.

List any previous buys of the same or similar items. Include when, how many, schedule, unit or total price, production rate, and other similar features. If the prices of previous buys were adjusted in accordance with redetermination or incentive clauses, show both target and final prices. You need list only the most recent or most relevant of such prior procurements.

Discuss the factors influencing source selection and any facilities furnished the company as a result of this buy, together with an indication of the percentage of the Government's share in the total investment. Reference to facilities furnished in terms of total dollars ordinarily will be enough. Discuss any unique features of the procurement.

If the negotiation is to firm up an FPIS arrangement or to convert a letter contract to a definitive instrument, indicate how much of the contract task is completed. In the final settlement of an incentive arrangement, any changes from the initial contract quantities or schedules will be explained here.

e. *Negotiation summary.* This fourth segment will show the company's contract pricing proposal, the Government's negotiation objective, and the negotiation results tabulated in parallel form and broken down by major elements of cost and profit. Whether these will be summary figures for total contract value, summary for the total price of the major item, unit price for the major item, or some other presentation will depend on how negotiations were conducted. The general rule is to portray the negotiation as it actually took place. Unit cost and profit figures may not give the true picture of the significance of each element; you should show total as well as unit values in the narrative that follows.

If, to price out a multiple line item procurement, you have developed a computer model that provides both unit and total prices, all you have to do is attach the detailed printout of the unit price breakdown.

A parallel tabulation gives a quick comparison of events, but it obviously can mislead and so needs explanation in the narrative portion of the PNM. Besides, we can now hear the cry, "We negotiated price; we didn't agree on separate elements of cost and profit. How can I show what I didn't do and don't know?"

True, you did not agree with the offeror on values for purchased parts, subcontracts, other material, engineering, model shop, tooling, fabrication and assembly labor, and so forth. However, if you used cost analysis, you talked about those costs and others. The offer was supported by estimates of those costs. Government analyses were concerned with them -- your objective gave them values. You had reasons, both factual and judgmental, for the values in your objective, and you tested again the validity of those reasons.

Besides, in the interval between offer and negotiations, both facts and judgments probably changed, because later data were pumped into the system. Because of this, interpretations changed too. As you negotiated, your ideas about some of those values in your objective changed and, with that, your objective also changed. When you finally shake hands, you should know what you think the costs are going to be; these are the numbers you put in the *Negotiated* column.

It is important that you identify, and in so doing, tie the knot on the thread that traces costs, relied on and not, from proposal through analysis, updating, and negotiation to their influence on the price finally reached.

Discuss in succeeding paragraphs the treatment of each of the major elements in the company's proposal. Devote separate paragraphs to the major cost categories of the breakdown. Start the discussion of each cost with a comparison of the amounts in the proposal, the objective, and the estimate supporting the price agreed to. The narrative will consist of a paragraph describing the basis of the contractor's estimate, another paragraph discussing the basis of the Government's negotiation objective, and a paragraph discussing the results of the negotiations.

Make these paragraphs as precise as possible in identifying factual data, their sources, and their currency. Where seemingly significant cost or pricing data submitted by the contractor were not relied on or not used, identify them here. The reasoning supporting the objective and any significant departures from it in moving toward agreement on price should establish, with little room for question, which data were used and which were not relied on.

If the negotiation is to definitize a letter contract, firm up unpriced orders, or otherwise agree to prices that are based in part on work that was authorized and started earlier, show the trends of the data, segregate recurring and nonrecurring costs, indicate percentage of physical completion of the contract, show actual costs incurred from inception to date, and, if significant, show the contractor's current estimate to complete.

If the negotiation is to establish the final price of an incentive arrangement, make two comparisons. First, compare the contractor's statement of actual costs incurred with acceptable actuals. Acceptable actuals are those that are reasonable, allowable, and allocable. Explain differences. Second, compare the initially estimated costs, adjusted where possible for changes, with the final acceptable contract costs. Where differences are significant, identify the causes, if possible.

These separate discussions should establish the reasonableness of the Government negotiation objective and the price negotiated. The PNM will tell how reports of cost analysis and price analysis were used and show how the principal findings in each were reconciled or otherwise taken care of in the agreement finally made.

When there are significant differences between the negotiation objective and the comments and conclusions of these advisory reports, you should supply the answers to the questions you know will be asked. The same goes for significant departures from your prenegotiation position regarding any element of the supporting price proposal.

Contracts that used certified cost or pricing data contain clauses that provide for possible adjustment if the data are later shown to have been defective. The clauses provide that the contracting officer will determine whether the price agreed upon was increased by reason of the defect. While negotiations are conducted to reach agreement on fair and reasonable prices, and every effort must be directed to that end, memorandums must be written to permit that determination, should the facts make one necessary.

For example, assume you relied upon a current overhead rate of 350 percent and negotiated a price with the contractor after resolving many judgmental factors, but, through it all, you believed that the certified current overhead rate was 350 percent. You subsequently discover that the rate does not reflect an increase in the base during the month before the negotiation meeting, and that the increased base is expected to continue for the life of your contract. You relied on inaccurate data, and your future decision to adjust the price, if a significant sum is involved, will be easy if your memorandum clearly spells out the reliance on the 350-percent rate.

On the other hand, suppose you decided in the negotiation that this company's overhead was hopelessly out of line. This conclusion is based on your knowledge of other companies and on advice from the ACO and the auditor. You probably will tell the company about this conclusion and you will undoubtedly get a reaction, either a counterargument or some recognition of the validity of your position, or both.

You may go ahead and ultimately negotiate a price that reflects the company's acceptance of your position, or you may use a rate of 325 percent in developing your objective, without an indication of acceptance by the company, and still get its agreement on a total price that is close to your objective. Your memorandum will show that you did not rely on the submitted cost or pricing data. A defect disclosed later would probably not warrant any adjustment in price.

Remember that the contractor's judgment is not involved, but the facts supporting the judgment are. If your judgment rests on these facts and they are defective, you will consider adjusting the price. If the total price was based on only a part of the data, you must identify the part that you did not rely upon and furnish your rationale for the solution you adopted.

You must delineate the basis for the price negotiated in such a way that the data not relied on can be identified, so future discovery of defective cost or pricing data can be evaluated and the amount of any necessary price adjustment fixed. It is equally important to be able to show that no price adjustment is indicated, if such is the case.

For prospective price negotiations, estimated profit is an integral part of the negotiation objective. The development of the profit objective for those negotiations should be discussed in this part of the PNM.

In most cases the weighted guidelines method will have been used. When it has, you should use DD Form 1547, Weighted Guidelines Profit/Fee Objective, filling in the spaces for the cost objective and profit weights. The form should be appended to the PNM. The rationale supporting assigned weightings should be detailed in the body of the memorandum. Even when weighted guidelines are not used, the PNM should include, in similar detail, the system used to develop the profit objective and the weights used.

After this detail, the narrative must justify and explain the selection of contract type and the specific pricing arrangement agreed to. As to contract type, where the selection is obvious, as with a repeat buy of an item bought in quantity many times, little or nothing need be said.

When incentive arrangements are used, explain fully the incentive parameters and how they were developed. If you negotiate a CPIF (cost incentive only) arrangement, explain the range of incentive effectiveness and how you arrived at the cost-sharing arrangement. You can do this in a short paragraph explaining where and why actual costs may vary from target and assessing the probabilities that there will be significant variances. For FPIF arrangements, explain the considerations involved in establishing sharing arrangements and price ceilings. If costs have already been incurred, explain how they were considered in setting the contractual arrangement.

When multiple incentives are used, you must give particular attention to the interrelationships of the various segments of the incentives. This includes, in addition to the reasons why incentives were placed on particular performance characteristics, a brief discussion of trade-off possibilities between cost, performance, and time.

Cost/profit charts showing the relationships between cost and profit on straight cost incentive arrangements, and between the cost and other incentives on multiple incentive arrangements, should be attached to the PNM. If you used a computer in structuring the incentives, attach copies of trade-off curves and tables.

In the final paragraphs, summarize the reasons the agreed price is fair and reasonable. When, in order to reach agreement, you have made an additional concession in price without changing your ideas about cost, the circumstances must be explained. If the arrangement offers an incentive, and you have traded cost for profit, explain the mathematics of the trade-off.

In the highly unusual case where you consider that the most likely final price will be significantly higher or lower than the negotiated targets or price, discuss this probability openly and document it fully for use in planning, programming, budgeting, and later analysis. In every case remember that the purpose of this summary is to demonstrate the reasonableness of the price negotiated and not to explain negotiated reductions from the company's proposal.

    f. *Miscellaneous.* Reference to and remarks regarding such things as audit reports and ACO analyses should go here.

Distribution of PNM

Whenever cost or pricing data are used, send copies of the PNM to the auditor and to the ACO, even if their services were neither requested nor used.

Suggested Readings

Written or Oral Discussions and Competitive Range

FAR	15.605	Evaluation factors
	15.608	Proposal evaluation
DFARS	15.608	Proposed Evaluation
FAR	15.609	Competitive range
	15.610	Written or oral discussion

Chapter 8 ASPM

Price Negotiation Defined

FAR 15.803 General

Principles and Techniques

FAR 15.805-5 Field pricing support
DFARS 15.805-5 Field Pricing Support
FAR 15.807 Prenegotiation objectives
DFARS 15.807 Prenegotiation Objectives

Negotiation

<u>Give and Take: The Complete Guide to Negotiating Strategies and Tactics</u>. Karrass, Chester L.; New York, Thomas Y. Crowell Company, 1974.

The Need for Documentation

FAR 15.808 Price negotiation memorandum
DFARS 15.808 Price Negotiation Memorandum